The Psychology of Attention

The Psychology of Attention

Harold E. Pashler

A Bradford Book
The MIT Press
Cambridge, Massachusetts
London, England

This book was set in Sabon using Ventura Publisher under Windows 95 by Wellington Graphics and was printed and bound in the United States of America.

Library of Congress Cataloging-in-Publication Data

Pashler, Harold E.
  The psychology of attention / Harold E. Pashler.
    p. cm.
  "A Bradford book."
  Includes bibliographical references (p.) and index.
  ISBN 0-262-16165-6 (hardcover : alk. paper)
  1. Attention. I. Title.
BF321.P37 1997
153.7'33—dc20   96-29300
                                            CIP

To Christine

Contents

Preface

The psychology of attention has become a particularly active and vigorous area of research in cognitive and perceptual psychology. Interest in attention also has been growing among researchers in neighboring fields, including neuroscience, animal learning, social psychology, connectionist modeling, artificial intelligence, and psychophysiology. The past few decades of cognitive research have produced a wealth of information about many different phenomena related to attention. While the results have multiplied, efforts to relate different attentional phenomena to each other seem to have dwindled somewhat. Ambitious attempts at general theory such as those proposed by pioneers in the area, including Broadbent (1958) and Deutsch and Deutsch (1963), have receded into the background, and a small number of experimental tasks and effects have been studied intensively. The best-known examples of these include speeded visual search tasks, effects of spatial cues on rapid detection of spots of light in a blank field, and various sorts of interference effects, such as the psychological refractory effect and what is sometimes called negative priming. Empirical investigation of particular tasks is essential, of course, but to arrive at a meaningful understanding of attention, experimental findings obtained with very different methods and paradigms have to be related to each other. Furthermore, theoretical analysis of attention must ultimately illuminate behaviors and capabilities found outside the laboratory as well as those most readily measured inside it.

This book is offered as a modest attempt to address these needs. The first goal is to organize what has been learned from principal areas of attention research within human experimental psychology. Most of the research described here falls into what is often termed the information-processing tradition. Roughly speaking, this tradition focuses on behavior (and in some cases, physiological responses) of human beings instructed to carry out specific, often quite simple, cognitive and sensorimotor tasks involving controlled stimuli in laboratory environments. This book aims not only to summarize but also to relate the numerous attentional phenomena and effects that tend to be considered in isolation from each other—published side by side in the same journals, generally regarded as different manifestations of attention, but rarely compared or related. For reasons that are described in chapter 1, when attempting to organize empirical observations, an effort is made to keep diffuse or ambiguous theoretical terms (including attention itself) from getting in the way; thus, use of the word "attention" as a theoretical construct will be minimized. The discussion touches on early writings on the subject and research from psychophysics to a greater extent than is usual in the information-processing tradition, although this could certainly have been carried further. An effort, albeit a limited and speculative one, is made to relate attentional phenomena studied by cognitive and perception psychologists to broader psychological issues.

The primary focus, then, is on organizing some major empirical generalizations about attentional phenomena that emerged from the past several decades of work in the information-processing tradition. This should, it is hoped, have value in and of itself. Research in this area has uncovered many interesting and nonobvious facts about the functioning and limitations of the human mind. These facts provide constraints on any theory that would aspire to describe the inner workings of the mind, and some of them undoubtedly have important implications for the functional architecture of the brain as well. Knowledge of the basic limitations in processing multiple stimuli and carrying out multiple tasks also has practical implications for designing systems in which people interact with machines, especially where rapid and accurate responding is vital (e.g., flying airplanes, driving cars).

The book has a second goal: to propose some contributions to attentional theory, drawing and expanding on my own recent research. The modern study of attention began with several very bold and divergent proposals about how attention might work. In retrospect, these proposals seem premature, given the very limited evidence available at the time. Looked at squarely, the evidence is still insufficient to resolve fully the major theoretical questions one might hope to answer. However, significant progress has been made on many fronts. This book examines the most important theoretical ideas about attention in a critical fashion, advancing some necessarily tentative suggestions about how the underlying issues may be resolved. These suggestions do not introduce radically new conceptual tools (the discussion is focused squarely on the much-debated issues of serial and parallel processing, capacity limitations, bottleneck, etc.), but the conclusions are in some cases quite out of step with what appear to be the prevailing beliefs among researchers.

This book presumes no specific background in experimental psychology. I hope it will be useful to researchers interested in attention, whether their primary field is cognition and information processing or a neighboring field, to graduate students entering these various fields, and perhaps to advanced undergraduates with an interest in the subject.

A few topics within the experimental psychology of attention—especially vigilance (sustained attention in monitoring low-frequency events) and the role of attention in animal learning—have spawned sizable literatures but are barely mentioned here. Drawing connections between these phenomena and the topics that are my main focus would have been a worthwhile challenge, and I regret not having the time necessary to attempt it. Readers who want to learn more about vigilance might start with See et al (1995) and Parasuraman (1984); useful discussions of attention in animal learning can be found in Mackintosh (1994) and Hall (1991).

This book is about the psychology of attention, not the neural underpinnings of attention, but the top topics are increasingly and fruitfully intertwined. The book discusses a number of neuropsychological and neurophysiological observations directly relevant to issues of functional architecture (e.g., perceptual selectivity, the structure of short-term memory). The well-known attentional defects associated with unilateral neglect do not have particularly direct implications for cognitive architecture in my opinion, and the literature on these phenomena is not reviewed here (see Kinsbourne, 1987, and Jeannerod, 1987 for insightful discussions of neglect). Chapter 6 builds on and expands a review of dual-task interference in simple tasks that appeared in the *Psychological Bulletin* in 1994 (Pashler, 1994e).

Acknowledgments

I am grateful to many individuals who contributed in various ways to the writing of this book. James E. Hoffman, Gordon Logan, John Palmer, and an anonymous reviewer read the entire volume and offered very useful and detailed comments. Logan also indulged me with lengthy arguments about automaticity and other topics; although he may well disagree with what ultimately emerged, these discussions undoubtedly improved its clarity. Six students or former students—Mark Carrier, Clark Fagot, Dawn Morales, Doug Rohrer, Eric Ruthruff, and Ling-Po Shiu—provided extensive and incisive comments. I consider myself fortunate to have worked with these highly motivated and talented individuals and to have had the benefit of their input.

A number of other experts generously shared their knowledge on particular topics or offered comments on individual chapters or sections; these include Irv Biederman, Nicholas Christenfeld, Rich Ivry, Steve Luck, John Maunsell, Robert McCann, Stephen Monsell, Werner X. Schneider, Roger Schvaneveldt, Christopher Wickens, and Jeremy Wolfe. Early versions of the book were used in graduate seminars at Brown University and Johns Hopkins University, and as a result, I had the benefit of comments from Howard Egeth, Cathleen Moore, Tom Ghirardelli, Tim Grandison, Sharma Hendel, and others. I also benefited from several discussions with Andries Sanders, who extended warm hospitality to me when I visited the Free University, Amsterdam, in Fall, 1995.

Some, although by no means most, of the research described in this book was conducted in my laboratory with support from NASA, the Office of Naval Research, and the National Institutes of Mental Health

(1-R29-MH45584). Alann Lopes, an excellent programmer analyst, made essential technical contributions to most of these projects. In addition, several very capable undergraduate honors students made important contributions to particular projects; these include Quincy Robyn-Whipple, Andrea Alfonso, and Krista MacFarland. I have benefited from numerous stimulating discussions of attention and perception with colleagues and former colleagues at UCSD, especially Jeff Miller, Alan Osman, and V. S. Ramachandran.

Finally, I cannot adequately acknowledge the intellectual debt I owe to Jonathan Baron of the University of Pennsylvania for his generous but bracing supervision when I was a graduate student working in his laboratory, and to James C. Johnston of the NASA Ames Research Center for countless hours of discussion of experimental psychology and much else. I also appreciate the assistance of Fiona Stevens, Amy Pierce, Michael Rutter, and Katherine Arnoldi of The MIT Press in patiently guiding me through the writing and production of this book.

The Psychology of Attention

1

Introduction

What Is the Psychology of Attention About?

One of William James's most famous statements was that "everyone knows what attention is" (James, 1890/1950), echoing an earlier claim by Munsell: "On attention itself, it is needless to discourse at length; its nature and conditions are familiar to every thoughtful student" (Munsell, 1873, p. 11). The present book takes a more empirical and more skeptical tack, assuming instead that no one knows what attention is, and that that there may even not be an "it" there to be known about (although of course there might be). The rationale for rejecting James's dictum will be discussed shortly. First, however, it should be acknowledged that there is certainly something to what James said. The word "attention" is commonly encountered in ordinary language, and people seem to understand each other well enough when they use it. This suggests that they must share some important notions and experiences in common. It is not unusual, of course, for an area of research to have a name that also figures in common parlance; for example, fields of study are devoted to bacteria and sedimentary rocks. However, although people talk about bacteria or about sedimentary rocks, they do not often have articulated theories or strong convictions that were not arrived at, directly or indirectly, from scientists and science teachers. In contrast, people talk about attention with great familiarity and confidence. They speak of it as something whose existence is a brute fact of their daily experience and therefore something about which they know a great deal, with no debt to attention researchers.

It is worth reflecting briefly on what most people think they know about attention as a preliminary to approaching the topic scientifically. Two primary themes or aspects characterize the phenomena people allude to with the term attention: selectivity and capacity limitation. Selectivity is apparent in a number of undeniable facts about human experience and behavior. One is that conscious perception is always selective. Everyone seems to agree that, at any given moment, their awareness encompasses only a tiny proportion of the stimuli impinging on their sensory systems. The second fact is that this selectivity holds not only of conscious states of mind, but also of the impact of stimuli on behavior. Whether we are walking, driving, playing tennis, or choosing what book to pick up, the stream of behavior we produce reflects only a small subset of the sensory stimulation, and typically only a subset of the stimuli that could potentially guide the same types of behaviors (e.g., the page contains other text that we could read; other paths are available for us to walk along). In short, the mind is continually assigning priority to some sensory information over others, and this selection process makes a profound difference for both conscious experience and behavior.

The second phenomenon to which casual usage of "attention" alludes is our limited ability to carry out various mental operations at the same time. Two activities that a person can easily carry out one at a time often pose tremendous problems when attempted simultaneously (e.g., listening to the radio and reading a book), even when these activities are in no way physically incompatible. This applies to many kinds of mental activities, including analyzing new perceptual input (as in listening to the radio and reading a book), thinking, remembering, and planning motor activity.

In the commonsense metaphysics implied by our ordinary talk about mental life (what some philosophers like to call folk psychology), selectivity and processing limitations are both described as attentional because they are really just the flip side of the same coin. The coin, of course, is attention itself. Folk psychology postulates a kind of substance or process (attention) that can be devoted (paid) to stimuli or withheld from them. Whether or not attention is allocated to a stimulus is usually thought to depend on a voluntary act of will; in the metaphysics of folk psychology, this ultimately depends on a choice made by the self. Sometimes, however, attention is directed or grabbed without any voluntary choice having taken place, even against strong wishes to the contrary; this is the phenomenon of distraction. Selectivity arises because awareness of a stimulus, and subsequent memory for it, is usually assumed to occur only when that stimulus is attended, voluntarily or involuntarily. The available quantity of attention is assumed to be finite, and this finiteness is supposed to account for capacity limitations; paying attention to one thing means having less attention available to pay to other things. Attention, according to folk psychology, can be devoted not only to stimuli, but also to activities, tasks, and behaviors (as in "pay attention to your driving"). Allocating more attention to any given task enhances performance, it is thought, although for certain highly automatic activities that do not require attention, such as breathing or tying one's shoes, too much attention may even be harmful.

A variety of other notions play a role in folk psychology talk about attention, and some of these issues go beyond selectivity and limited capacity. One is effort—the sometimes aversive experience of exertion that generally accompanies sustained mental activities; in folk psychology, this is often equated with the attention demanded by the task. Another example is perceptual set: the tendency for our perception of a stimulus to change depending on whatever expectations we may have about various aspects of the stimulus. It is often said that people see or hear what they expect to see or hear, and this selectivity is usually linked with attention.

Thus, our commonsense metaphysics of mental life points out, and in a very loose way might be said to try to explain, a number of phenomena: selectivity of perception, voluntary control over this selectivity, and capacity limits in mental functioning that cannot be attributed to mere limitations in our sensory or motor systems. These are the core phenomena addressed by attention research, and all will be discussed in this book. Unfortunately, the metaphysics of mental life that goes along with the commonsense use of the term attention is so entrenched and so compelling that whenever one uses the word one finds these notions intruding on one's thinking. This has several consequences, some innocuous and others pernicious. For example, many psychologists use "attention" as a theoretical construct in accounting for some range of phenomena, saying, for example, "I will measure the rate at which attention is shifted toward a location in the visual field" with regard to a study of visual cueing. This can be taken as a mere shorthand for "I will postulate a mechanism that can be allocated to certain input channels defined by location, and I assume for the sake of discussion that it probably has something to do with what ordinary people refer to as attention," leaving open exactly how close this linkage may be. Less innocuous are the many cases in which the notion of attention smuggles its way into the description of experimental manipulations (e.g., attention was reduced by having the subject remember seven digits) and observations (spare attentional capacity was measured by response times), obscuring the fact that these manipulations could have many different interpretations that ought to be considered, some of which would satisfy few or none of the assumptions contained in the ordinary conceptions of attention.

The dangers of taking substantive words from ordinary language and assuming a corresponding entity have been noticed for a long time, of course; philosophers at least as far back as Bacon (1620/1960) have warned against assuming that where there is a word there must be a thing (this is often called reification). Closer at hand, one of the pioneers of modern attention research, the late Donald Broadbent (1982), emphasized the dangers in the uncritical use of "attention." However, like all vices, reification is more easily deplored than prevented, and examples such as the ones mentioned in the preceding paragraph can be found throughout the present-day literature on attention (including some articles written by the author).

To try to avoid these pitfalls, the word is used sparingly in this book. When the goal is to uncover generalizations that are fairly close to the data, a special effort will be made to prevent assumptions imported from common sense from obscuring the description of phenomena or findings. Banishing the word totally would require cramped language, however, so an intermediate strategy will be followed. In chapters 2 through 4 that focus on empirical phenomena, the use of "attention" will be restricted to describing the field of study or the instructions given to a subject, as in "In a study of selective attention . . . " or "Subjects were told to attend to the tones played in the left ear . . . " In the same spirit, stimuli will sometimes be described as attended or unattended. "Attention" will not, however, be used to refer to a putative internal process or mechanism (as in "Is attention necessary for memory?" or "The subject's attention was diverted with a secondary task."). In the fifth and sixth chapters the role of attention as a theoretical construct will be considered explicitly and critically, and a framework postulating several distinct attentional mechanisms will emerge in the remaining chapters.

Approaches to the Analysis of Attention

Between 1880 and 1920 a great deal was written about the psychology of attention by some very insightful writers such as Oswald Kulpe, Edward Titchener, and William James.[1] These psychologists inquired about the nature and significance of attention using terms and concepts borrowed directly and unapologetically from commonsense psychology—the self, the will, conscious perceptions and sensations, and attention itself. Their method of attack involved a mixture of introspection and, to a lesser degree, formal experimentation. The questions these writers asked make good sense in the context of this framework. Consider a few examples. How does attention to a stimulus change the conscious perception of the stimulus? Does it make the stimulus more intense? Does it make it more clear? Are clarity and intensity really different things? These four questions probably generated the most vigorous controversies in the early literature (see, e.g., Newhall, 1921; Titchener, 1908; Kulpe, 1902; Munsterberg, 1894). Divided attention was also a topic of interest, starting with the basic question of whether it is possible to attend to several inputs at once (see, e.g., James, 1890/1950, p. 405). Another topic of interest was how the speed of responses to a stimulus depends on whether a person chooses to attend to the stimulus or to the response (e.g., Cattell, 1893/1947).

The fact that many disagreements arose in this literature and that introspective methods were unable to resolve them are quite notorious. This should not obscure the fact that many of these authors succeeded in describing the texture of subjective mental life with great subtlety and clarity, and actually shared many important points of agreement. On the other hand, when it came to uncovering mechanisms and processes—asking about the workings of attention—the writers lacked concepts and terms with which to begin. For example, on the basic phenomenon of attentional selectivity, early writers strove continuously to reduce somehow the inner act of selection to overt acts of selection such as eye movements and postural adjustments (see Smith, 1969 for a review). However, most thinkers of the time, including James and Kulpe (along with Helmholtz), recognized that inner acts of selection simply did not have to be accompanied by any overt signs whatever. Having concluded that, they lacked any concepts with which to press on and ask more about what *was* going on. Consider, for example, James's description of the operations of selection: "[there is an] anticipatory preparation from within of the ideational centres concerned with the object to which the attention is paid." The language is evocative but the content is unsatisfying. Paschal (1941) suggests that early attention theorists developed a certain malaise on account of their difficulties in moving beyond these kinds of conceptualizations.

Before long, behaviorism and learning theory came to dominate American psychology for some decades, relegating the area of attention to some degree of obscurity. Behaviorists were seemingly uncomfortable not only with introspective methods, but also with the existence and demonstrable potency of selective attention itself. Selectivity is a problem for anyone who wishes to predict behavior purely on the basis of the objective stimulation making up the animal's learning history. For all these reasons, the behaviorist period was marked by a decline in psychological work in attention, although as Lovie (1983) points out, the disappearance was less complete than is sometimes claimed.

The Information-Processing Approach

This book discusses attention within the framework of the contemporary, information-processing approach. This framework had its origins in research carried out in England during and after the Second World War. It views the mind as an information-processing system whose function can, it is hoped, be revealed most clearly by making systematic observations of the fine-grained features of human behavior in laboratory situations. The ultimate goal is to work out some account of how the mind processes information, an account that is mechanistic but posed at the functional level. It is sometimes mistakenly supposed that this tradition inherently depends on some likening of the mind to a particular kind of computer, especially the conventional digital computer. In fact, human information-processing research may provide the clearest evidence about how different the mind and the digital computer are in their underlying modes of function. The core idea of the information-processing approach is to analyze the mind in terms of different subsystems that form, retain, and transmit representations of the world. The nature of these subsystems, the kinds of transformations they carry out, and the temporal relationship and relative discreteness (or nondiscreteness) of their activities are all viewed as facts to be discovered, not assumed at the outset. Obviously, one cannot say in advance whether or not the mind can be successfully analyzed in these terms. Many optimistic forecasts have been offered; other writers began pronouncing the demise of this approach at least twenty years ago when it was barely under way (e.g., Newell, 1973; Anderson, 1987).

There is probably no good a priori reason to assume that a system as complex as the brain must allow of a functional description that is illuminating and reasonably accurate. After all, it seems conceivable that the only accurate mechanistic description might be one of neurons and their interactions, with mental activity being too nebulous to be characterized. Even if a true functional analysis is potentially available, we have no guarantee that we can arrive at this analysis by studying the input-output behavior of the system, or, for that matter, by studying its physical components. Trying to decide what can in principle be learned from any particular type of research is probably futile; the success or failure of information-processing psychology can be assessed only on the basis of the insights that do or do not emerge from the research it spawns.

This book will try to convince the reader that behavioral experiments can provide important information about attentional phenomena and many illuminating hints about the basic architecture of the mind. A fuller analysis of this architecture may well require recourse to neural as well as psychological levels of analysis, but in that case it seems unlikely that neural observations devoid of careful functional analysis will reveal much that is interesting about cognition. The reader will have to make his or her own judgments about how convincing and illuminating the functional analysis is proving to be.

What kind of data are to be used in analyzing human information-processing machinery at a functional level? As noted, early attention theorists relied on introspection. Introspection is now widely agreed to be an inadequate basis for arriving at insights into how mental processes work. It should not be dismissed entirely, however. Few writers today would claim that introspection can tell us much about processes operating at very fine time scales—say, a few hundreds milliseconds or less. For example, if you try to recall your telephone number, you probably find that the number pops into your head without your having any way to decompose this experience into finer elements. On the other hand, if you plan a strategy in chess, you probably find that you consider a number of alternative moves and countermoves one after another in a sequence. It seems dogmatic and unreasonable to claim that these latter introspections have no relationship to the events that culminate in the choice of a chess move (cf. Ericsson and Simon, 1980). Then in many intermediate cases people seem to want to claim at least some direct access to their mental activities. An example is the weighing of different factors in choosing which car to buy; people often have opinions about the role of different factors in a decision, but the validity of these reports is debatable (Nisbett and Wilson, 1977; Kraut and Lewis, 1982).

Where does attention lie along this spectrum? Many of the important questions about attention clearly fall into the first category: processes that occur rapidly and seem opaque to the individual. This does not imply that introspections about these phenomena are uninteresting. After all, if different individuals tend to agree about a certain aspect of experience—and the writings of classic attention theorists contain numerous points of agreement—then one could reasonably expect a complete understanding of mental architecture to explain *why* they should agree, even if this understanding does not give any credence to the actual assertions that people agree upon.

Consider a concrete example. Writers in the eighteenth and nineteenth centuries were interested in whether people could divide attention among more than one object, and their introspections on the topic differed tremendously. Some, such as Dugald Stewart (1792/1971), insisted that it was impossible. Others, like James, said it was not possible unless an entire collection of things was apprehended as a single object. Munsell

(1873), by contrast, had no difficulty reaching a completely different answer: "Can a man attend to more than one thing at a time? To this the answer must be decidedly, yes!" (p. 12). Porter (1868) agreed, arguing that our ability to compare implies simultaneous consciousness of two things. The contemporary approach as represented in this book begins with the assumption that in the first place there may or may not be anything called attention to be divided, and that if such an entity does exist, a person's introspections would not necessarily provide accurate information about whether it could be divided. However, to the degree people are consistent in what they report about their experiences when trying to divide their attention, one would hope that a good psychological theory of attention would have something to say about this. For example, in a whole-report task, in which people try to report as many letters or digits as possible from a briefly flashed array (discussed in chapter 3), observers can usually report about four or five items. Almost invariably, though, they report that they "saw" many more (e.g., Sperling, 1960). A good psychology of attention does not have to include "seeing" as a theoretical term and endorse the observers' claims that they see all the letters, but it ought to have something to say about why people so often seem tempted to make that claim.

Theory Testing

Broadly speaking, how are theories about information-processing mechanisms to be tested using behavioral data? What kinds of inferences are to be trusted? One rather idealized approach to theory testing is sometimes termed strong inference (Platt, 1964). The essence of this strategy comes from Bacon (1620/1960), who said, "It is granted only to proceed at first by negatives, and at last to end in affirmatives after exclusion has been exhausted." The strategy consists of trying to test broad classes of models or very general claims about a phenomenon, aiming for critical tests; that is, tests that could potentially rule out the alternatives, ultimately leaving only the correct account standing. In a well-known article published in *Science* in 1964, Platt eloquently described the success of this approach in many areas of biology and physics. Broadbent's seminal book on attention (1958) advocated exactly the same strategy, offering an illuminating analogy between theory testing and the game Twenty

Questions. In this game one player thinks about something, and the other players try to figure out what he or she is thinking about. The other players are allowed to ask the first player only a series of yes-or-no questions. To progress as efficiently as possible in this game, one has to rule out large classes of possibilities at a time, and this is best done by asking very general questions. Posing highly specific questions at the outset (are you thinking about a Zebra?) is inefficient, since there are so many possibilities at that level of specificity. Similarly, both Broadbent and Platt argued that optimum scientific reasoning involves asking progressively more fine-grained questions, making certain to use tests capable of ruling out competing alternatives. Better known than Platt's elimination-oriented strategy is Popper's dictum that a theory is supported to the extent that it successfully predicts the outcome of experiments or observations that could potentially have falsified the theory. According to Popper (1959), it is the hallmark of a sound scientific theory that it should undergo the risk of falsification; the more risks, the more credible is the theory that survives.

As many philosophers and scientists have pointed out, the ideals of critical experiments and falsificationism are reached only rarely. There are various reasons for this. Often one cannot enumerate all the possible hypotheses that might be considered making the idealized strong inference strategy impossible. Furthermore, empirical tests invariably rely on ancillary assumptions of various kinds (Lakatos, 1978). Nonetheless, the Popperian and strong inference strategies offers a useful standard for evaluating experiments and inferences based on experimental results. One should probably expect, however, that in areas as treacherous psychology, critical experiments will be relatively rare. More often, after a series of nearly critical experiments, one theory may account for the data in a fairly straightforward way; competing accounts can survive too, but only by shouldering a large number of unreasonable and ad hoc modifications.[2] In this way, truth may be reached in the limit; from a Bayesian perspective, the posterior probability of the theory may continue to increase.

Another useful concept (perhaps especially in psychological research) is the idea of converging measures (Garner, Hake, and Eriksen, 1956), alternative tests that pose the same questions but rely on different kinds of assumptions. The rationale is simple enough: when one seriously doubts the validity of the assumptions that underlie one test or another, one gains leverage by using tests that make assumptions that are independent of each other. Another intuitively natural observation is that experiments that make predictions for experiments whose outcomes have many degrees of freedom provide stronger support than experiments with only a few relevant outcomes. This notion can be readily justified in a Bayesian framework (Howson and Urbach, 1989; Jefferys and Berger, 1992). Unfortunately, this feature is not present in experimental psychology as often as one might hope. An experiment with three possible outcomes (e.g., A > B, A = B, A < B) supports a theory that correctly predicts the outcome, especially when competing theories make a different prediction. However, it cannot increase its credibility as much as an experiment with 20,000 possible outcomes, where the theory predicts the correct one, or, as sometimes occurs in physical sciences, predictions prove accurate to six decimal places or better.

These generalizations about theory testing may strike the reader as fairly banal and not worth belaboring. Nonetheless, a surprisingly large amount of research in experimental psychology, especially in leading journals of psychological theory, pays little heed to these principles. Instead, detailed and complex formal models are constructed and applied (usually with simulations) to fit the data. Typically, investigators have broad theoretical claims in mind; as a test of these claims, they construct a model that instantiates them, along with enough extra machinery to "predict" specific observations (e.g., a reaction time, a percentage correct). This machinery can be quite extensive. Papers of this kind typically present figures that compare "observations" and "predictions," usually with a stunningly close fit. Apparently this process is taken by many to provide support for the veracity of the model, or at least for a broader theory which the model exemplifies.

Despite the patina of rigor provided by the specificity and formality of the modeling, this should not be mistaken for genuine empirical testing (Roberts & Pashler, submitted). A close fit does not demonstrate that the model excludes any possible outcomes, much less any plausible ones. Even when there are observations the model could not have fit, the credit may belong not to the underlying theory but rather to the machinery added to allow "predictions" to be made (this machinery is not restricted to the so-called free parameters of the model, but often includes many aspects of a model that are not required by the basic theory). Third, even in those rare cases in which the theory really does predict the outcomes obtained, the enterprise is weakened by the failure to consider competing models and their predictions. Unless one has reason to believe that significant competing models do not make identical predictions, the model's victory may be chimeric. In cases where investigators have re-examined complex models backed up by data fitting, they often find that the data can be fit just as well using models that make radically different assumptions (e.g., Coltheart and Coltheart, 1972; J. C. Johnston et al., 1985). Evidently, then, data fitting should not be confused with theory testing.

The fact that the two are so often confused in scientific psychology is peculiar, especially because data fitting has fallen into poor repute in other fields. Unfortunately, it seems that psychologists sometimes mistake formalism and (apparent) precision in a theory for rigor in the empirical testing of that theory. These are two completely different things; whereas precision is a desirable feature in knowledge, it is not obviously a desirable feature in untested speculation. The data-fitting approach criticized here should not be confused with the field of mathematical psychology, which includes a greater number of contributions that derive nonparametric predictions from large classes of models, thereby facilitating genuine theory testing (see Townsend and Ashby, 1983, or Schweickert and Townsend, 1993, for examples relevant to attention).

In this book, the focus is on information-processing approaches to the phenomena associated with attention, undertaken without an assumption that the mind contains a structure or process that corresponds to that term. The emphasis is on experimental work that evaluates competing hypotheses, especially research that attempts to derive and test distinctive predictions of broad classes of models, because this is the most efficient way to home in on the truth. Complex models that have been fitted to data only in a post hoc fashion are not discussed. The aim is to see what functional implications can be drawn from the experimental literature on attention. Proposed architectures for attention that have been presented as purely speculative or have been justified only by data fitting are not addressed.

Background: Modern Theories of Attention

Now this chapter examines two important theories that emerged in the 1950s and 1960s and that framed a great deal of work that has taken place in the intervening years: early selection theories and late selection theories. This modern phase of attention research was inaugurated by post-World War II researchers in Great Britain, notably, Colin Cherry, Donald Broadbent, and Alan Welford. The major findings of these investigators are described in chapters 2 and 6. The transition from the early theorizing about attention to this modern phase was marked by a number of fundamental changes. One change, already described, was methodological: from theories based primarily on introspective observation to theories based on various kinds of behavioral data. A second change reflected the emergence of new concepts that permitted the events that make up human perception to be fractionated. Writers such as James and Titchener spoke of the conscious percepts elicited by stimuli and speculated on how attention might affect different attributes of the percepts, such as clarity or intensity. They did not, however, view perception as a process of achieving successively more elaborated and defined internal descriptions of a stimulus. In particular, they had little to say about the relation between attention and stimulus *identification,* an issue that emerged in the 1950s as central in modern attention theory (at a cost of neglecting other important issues; see Shulman, 1990). In fact, the idea of identification was not unknown in pretwentieth-century psychology; Hoffding (1896), for example, made a clear distinction between having a visual percept of an object and recognizing its identity. However, this distinction played little role in the most influential early analyses of attention.

The early and late selection theories that we are about to discuss dealt primarily with the perceptual aspects of attention, and the findings described in the next three chapters are critical for appraising these theories. In chapter 5 these theories are reexamined in light of that evidence. In addition to describing the contents of these accounts, the rest of this chapter discusses the logical relationship between different components of these theories. Those familiar with the history of attention research may believe that these theories have grown stale over the past few years, which is certainly a reasonable sentiment. It is nonetheless essential for readers to be aware of them in examining the evidence discussed in the first part of the book, for several reasons. One reason is that these theories motivated much of the research on attention, so the thrust of modern studies is hard to grasp without knowing something about them. The second reason is rather puzzling: although these accounts engendered an enormous volume of literature, the logical relationship between them and the broader space of possibilities of which they are a part has rarely been examined, and never to my knowledge in a systematic fashion. When one does examine it systematically, one can arrive at a more inclusive and coherent framework than the commonly recognized dichotomy (or occasionally trichotomy) of attention theories.

Early Selection Theories

The earliest and best known modern theory of attention was Broadbent's (1958) Filter theory, often referred to as early selection theory. Broadbent's basic hypothesis was that all stimuli reaching the sensory system are processed to the point at which certain physical attributes (e.g., location, loudness, and pitch of auditory stimuli) are analyzed and explicitly represented. He suggested that the machinery that identifies stimuli (e.g., recognizing an individual letter or word and comprehending its meaning) is capable of handling only one stimulus at a time. Thus, he postulated a filtering device responsible for determining which stimuli are to be processed further, and thought that it worked on the basis of the preliminary analysis of simple physical attributes. The mechanism responsible for selection he termed the selective filter—the workhorse of attentional selection. The term early selection theory and Broadbent's term filter theory are now commonly used to refer to this entire set of propositions. Early selection conveys the idea that all selection occurs early in the stream of processing. It is critical to note that the word early does not refer to time, but rather to the sequence of processing stages: selection is said to precede stimulus identification. Early selection theories are often represented with a structural diagram like that in figure 1.1 (Kahneman, 1973).

As the figure shows, all stimuli proceed far enough into the system to reach the first box (representing analysis in terms of physical features), whereas only the single selected stimulus proceeds farther, to the point

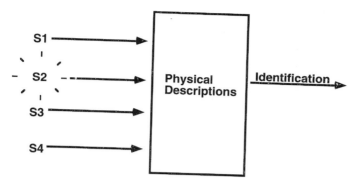

Figure 1.1
Early selection theory. The physical properties of the attended stimulus (S2) and the unattended stimuli (S1, S3, S4) are computed, but only the attended stimulus (S2) is identified.

of recognition. This kind of representation is not particularly apt for considering what early selection theory would imply for the time course of processing when a person attempts to perceive many stimuli. To make these implications more explicit, it is helpful to use a diagram in which time runs along the horizontal axis, as in figure 1.2. In this figure and subsequent ones, various stimuli presented to a person's sensory receptors are referred to with the abbreviations S1, S2, and so on. The physical attributes of the corresponding stimuli are referred to as PA1, PA2, and so on. Once a stimulus has been recognized, the internal representation that corresponds to its recognition may be depicted as an identity code, and the identity codes corresponding to S1, S2, and so on are abbreviated ID1, ID2, and so on. As an additional convention, highlights are placed around any stimuli the subject attempts to select for awareness and further processing.

The top panel in figure 1.2 shows the implications of early selection theory for the time course of processing two stimuli, of which only one, S1, is to be deliberately attended. According to the theory, the system works out the physical attributes of both S1 and S2 immediately, and then the identity of S1 (but not S2) is determined. The bottom panel shows the sequence of processing that must occur when two stimuli S1 and S2 are both attended; that is, the individual attempts to recognize

Attend to One Object:

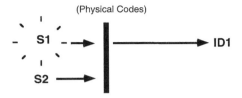

Attend to More than One Object:

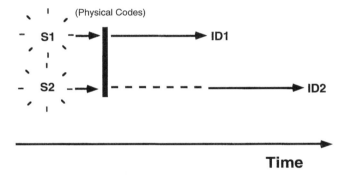

Figure 1.2
Time course of processing, according to early selection theory, when only one stimulus is attended (top panel) or two stimuli are both attended (bottom panel).

both of them. Perceptual processes, through the point of retrieving the physical attributes, operates in parallel; more elaborate processing involved in identifying stimuli occurs serially, with one stimulus analyzed and then the next.

Late Selection Theories
The most extreme alternative to Broadbent's early selection theory is what is usually called late selection theory. Well-known versions of the theory were proposed by Deutsch and Deutsch (1963), Norman (1968), MacKay (1973), and more recently by Duncan (1980b). These formula-

tions differ in interesting ways, but they have one basic idea in common: recognition of familiar objects proceeds unselectively and without any capacity limitations. One cannot voluntarily choose to identify or recognize something, according to these theorists. Whether there is just one sensory input or many does not affect the extent to which stimuli are analyzed or the timing of such analyses. Selective processing, which *is* subject to capacity limitations, is assumed to begin only after analysis is completed. Since by most accounts people seem to be unaware of many stimuli they attempt to ignore, such theories naturally suppose that awareness depends on these subsequent mechanisms. Duncan (1980b), for example, envisioned a transfer process that sends the results of an (unconscious) analysis process to further mechanisms. Enduring memory for what was perceived, and the ability to make a voluntary response are also assumed to depend on this transfer.

Figure 1.3 shows a typical way of depicting late selection theory. It is nothing more than a relabeling of the early selection diagram, with the label "physical descriptions" replaced by "semantic descriptions."

Several points about this theory—which may or may not be obvious—should be noted at the outset. First, it obviously does not claim that all the stimuli transmitting or reflecting energy to a person's sensory

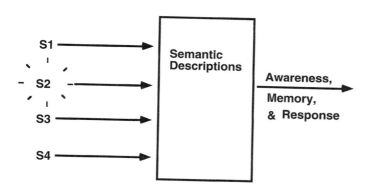

Figure 1.3
Late selection theory. The identity of both the attended stimulus (S2) and the unattended stimuli (S1, S3, S4) are computed alike. However, only the attended stimulus (S2) is selected for access to a system required for awareness, memory and response.

apparatus are identified. Limitations having nothing to do with processing capacity or attention may prevent this from happening. For example, a visual object in the periphery of the visual field may reflect a pattern of light to a part of the retina that contains too few receptors to pick up the information necessary for the object to be recognized, whether or not it is attended. This kind of recognition failure is not an attentional effect, and it does not contradict late selection theories. The same is true of *masking* (roughly, the harmful effects of one stimulus on the perception of another). For example, a visual stimulus that would otherwise be recognizable may fail to be identified because a stimulus follows it in the same part of the visual field (backward visual masking) or adjacent to it (lateral masking). In both cases, masking prevents a target stimulus from being identified even when the observer has every opportunity to attend to the target and tries hard to ignore the masking stimuli. Therefore, the assertion of late selection theory that stimuli are analyzed independent of attention or capacity limits should not be taken to mean that stimuli can always be identified; rather, it claims that voluntary control will have no effect on whether or not they are identified.

What does it mean to say a stimulus is fully analyzed? Modern attention theorists generally understood this to refer to whatever modes of categorizing a stimulus the person has practiced extensively. Categorizing letters, words, and speech into their respective linguistic categories, and categorizing objects such as tables and chairs in their basic-level categories are examples of what these theorists had in mind. It is doubtful that any late selection theorist intended the theory to cover whatever arbitrary descriptions a person *might* apply to a stimulus (the second-from-the-largest square, the only word on the page that contains more vowels than consonants, etc.). This point was implicit in most late selection formulations, however, and made explicit in only a few (e.g., Shiffrin and Schneider, 1977; LaBerge and Samuels, 1974).

Oddly enough, although late selection theorists talked mostly about linguistic descriptions of written and spoken language tokens, most of them had almost nothing to say about understanding language at the level of sentences and propositions. Many students, when they first hear about late selection theory, immediately point out that a person cannot understand two streams of speech at the same time. How then, they ask, could anyone suppose that semantic analysis proceeds unselectively and without capacity limits? Do late selection theorists suppose that the meaning of the unattended sentence is computed unconsciously? The only one to address this issue explicitly was MacKay (1973). He proposed that although comprehending the meaning of individual spoken words was not subject to voluntary control or capacity limitations, under-standing sentences requires storage in long-term memory, which, he suggested, is possible for only one sentence as a time. MacKay's sugges-tions are unique, however; otherwise, late selection theorists seem to have viewed single-word recognition as the paradigmatic case of semantic analysis, a usage that would strike a linguist, for example, as rather peculiar.

Late selection theory, then, amounts to the idea that irrespective of what a person might choose to attend to or ignore, the neural machinery that recognizes stimuli as belonging to familiar categories performs its computation for all incoming stimuli to the degree the sensory input is adequate to permit this. The implications of this theory for the time course of processing for attended and unattended stimuli are shown in figure 1.4. When S1 and S2 are presented at the same time, both are processed to point of being identified in parallel, whether only one is attended, as in the top panel, or both are, as in the bottom panel.

Major Alternatives

Readers who have not encountered these two classic theories of attention and the large literature that has sprung up around them will undoubtedly notice that they make fairly extreme claims. This is widely recognized, but many attention studies were and continue to be interpreted as favor-ing either early or late selection theory, as though it was somehow given that one of them had to be correct. Since the early 1970s a number of alternatives have been suggested, and most investigators seem to suspect that some form of compromise theory will be necessary. What is not widely agreed is how the space of plausible alternatives should be viewed. The goal of this section is to provide a rough taxonomy of the major possibilities. No attempt is made to be exhaustive or detailed; as in Twenty Questions, it is not efficient to spend a great deal of time elabo-rating on possibilities that are shortly to be ruled out by empirical

Attend to One Object:

Attend to More than One Object:

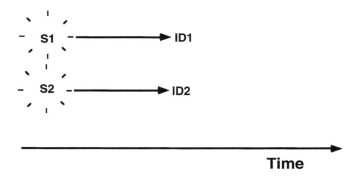

Time

Figure 1.4
Time course of processing according to the late selection theory, when only one stimulus is attended (top panel) or when two stimuli are both attended (bottom panel).

evidence. However, it is worth considering what some of the possibilities would look like. The next section provides a rather breezy tour of the logical space of possible theories. When we return to general issues of attention theory in chapter 5, this space will be reexamined against the backdrop of empirical evidence.

One place to start is by noting a glaringly obvious alternative theory that has received surprisingly little explicit consideration. This possibility, often raised by undergraduates at their first introduction to the field of attention, is called the *controlled parallel* theory, and it is shown in figure

Attend to One Object:

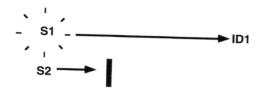

Attend to More than One Object:

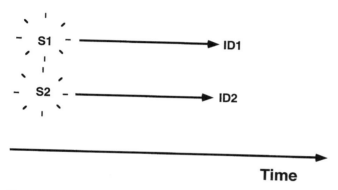

Time

Figure 1.5
Controlled parallel processing, a natural alternative to early and late selection theories proposing parallel or serial identification depending on which is advantageous.

1.5. The basic idea is that when one stimulus is attended and another is rejected, the rejected stimulus is not analyzed beyond the physical level, as in early selection theory. When two stimuli are attended, both are identified in parallel, as in late selection theory. This possibility is an obvious one because it postulates that the system carries out the processing that would be most advantageous.

What is the relationship between the controlled parallel model and the two classic theories? All three can be seen as arrayed on a continuum, but it is not clear what single dimension of difference might be. It seems misleading, therefore, to describe the controlled parallel model as an intermediate theory. A more accurate view is that two separate questions are addressed by all three theories. The first question is, are rejected stimuli analyzed fully? The second is, can multiple *attended* stimuli be processed simultaneously when that is advantageous? Viewed in this way, all three theories are seen to reside within a two-by-two matrix. Figure 1.6 shows this matrix. The columns correspond to answers to the first question, and the rows of the matrix correspond to answers to the second. Late selection theory offers a positive answer to both questions, and early selection theory offers a negative answer to both. The controlled parallel theory offers the answers no and yes, respectively.

Having created a two-by-two matrix with three cells occupied, one naturally wonders why the lower-left hand cell is empty. To fit into this cell, a theory would have to claim that unattended stimuli are invariably identified (lack of selectivity), yet when two stimuli are attended, they must be identified one at a time. This requires the rather odd notion of a sequential process that keeps on marching—identifying stimuli one after another—even when there is no intention to analyze them. Is this account so strange that it can be dismissed? Perhaps not.

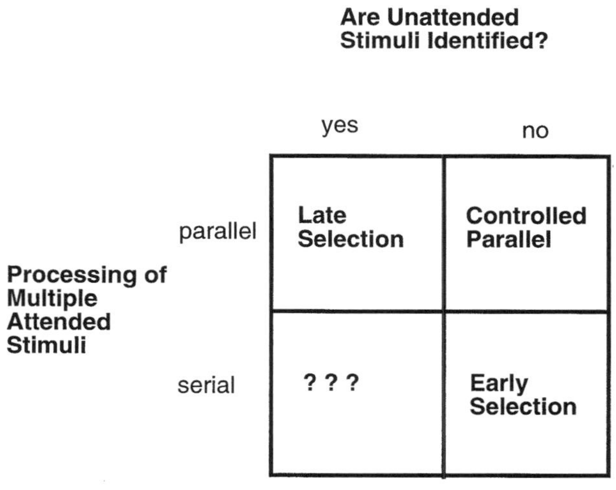

**Are Unattended
Stimuli Identified?**

		yes	no
Processing of Multiple Attended Stimuli	parallel	**Late Selection**	**Controlled Parallel**
	serial	**? ? ?**	**Early Selection**

Figure 1.6
A two-by-two matrix of alternatives represents a simplified version of the space of possibilities.

When someone classifies a single stimulus and makes a rapid response that depends on the result, evidence about this *particular* stimulus is probably collected even after there is enough evidence for a response to be chosen (Rabbitt and Vyas, 1981; Levy and Pashler, 1995). For that reason, subjects are usually aware of the errors they have just made in speeded classification tasks (Rabbitt, 1979). Similarly, Saul Sternberg's well-known analysis of short-term memory scanning proposed that when people must decide whether a probe item matches any elements in a previously heard memory set, the comparison of the probe with items in memory continues even after a match has been found. This idea does not stand up well to empirical test (Monsell, 1978; McElree and Dosher, 1989), but few dismiss it as preposterous. Therefore, the idea that perceptual analysis might operate sequentially but exhaustively surely deserves at least a name. Henceforth, it will be called the uncontrolled serial model. What we are left with, then, is a two-by-two matrix with possible theories in all four cells, rather than the set of two extreme alternatives often envisioned in discussions of attention theory.

Elements of Compromise: Attenuation and Sharing

Of course this two-by-two matrix still sorts theories at a very coarse level, omitting from consideration many obvious intermediate possibilities. We turn now to some other theories that have been considered from time to time and demonstrate that their space cannot be captured fully in any matrix, no matter of how many dimensions.

One natural idea was suggested by Treisman (1960), who proposed that rejected messages are *attenuated* rather than completely blocked (the evidence for this idea is discussed in chapter 2). Treisman's idea had two parts. The first was that rejected stimuli are only filtered out partially, rather than completely. The second was an idea about when and how this partial information might be handled. Treisman suggested that recognition takes place through accumulation of information or activation in detector units. Unattended (and therefore attenuated) stimuli would not produce enough activity to cause the corresponding detector to reach its threshold. However, when the detector represents a concept that is somehow related to concepts that have recently been activated, which Treisman called *priming,* partial activation might suffice for recognition.

The implications of this filter-attenuation theory for *divided* attention were never clear. For example, would attending to more than one stimulus at the same time cause all the stimuli to be attenuated in the same way as an ignored stimulus would be? This question will be discussed further; for the moment, we can represent the idea of attenuation schematically as in figure 1.7.

A second widely recognized idea with elements of compromise between early and late selection theories is *graded capacity sharing*. This refers to the possibility that recognizing stimuli takes mental capacity or resources, and the total amount of this capacity is limited. Capacity might be shared among different perceptual processes, thereby reducing the amount available for any individual stimulus and causing its recognition to take longer. Figure 1.8 shows the theory as it applies to the case of one and two objects, *both attended*. To make it easy to think about capacity sharing (at the price of narrowing the concept further than one ought to), this figure follows McLeod (1977) in assuming that a given task requires a fixed total amount of capacity X time. This simplifying assumption allows one to represent the capacity allocated to a process at a given moment as the width of a channel. With time proceeding from left to right, the area of the channel represents the total capacity X time (i.e., work). If a process demands a fixed allocation of capacity X time before it can be completed, then sharing capacity equally between the two processes will double the time required for each, as shown in the figure. Obviously, this assumption is far too restrictive to be taken seriously, but it makes the general idea quite clear.

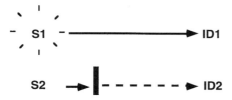

Figure 1.7
Filter-attenuation theory. According to this hypothesis, the information from the unattended stimulus is reduced in quality or intensity, although partial identification may still occur.

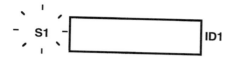

One Stimulus Attended

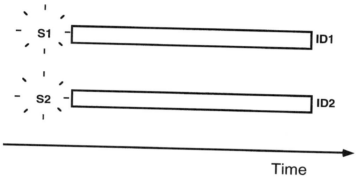

Two Stimuli Attended

Time

Figure 1.8
Capacity sharing. When two stimuli are attended, processing resources (represented by the height of box between stimulus and identity abbreviated ID) are divided, resulting in slower processing.

Various formulations of capacity-sharing accounts have been proposed. Kahneman (1973) suggested that allocation of finite resources might account for a broad range of limitations people have in doing different activities at the same time (in his version, the same resources were shared not only by perceptual activities, but also by cognitive and motor control processes). Accounts specifically focused on perceptual recognition and comparison were proposed by Townsend (1974), who showed that mean response times in visual search tasks could be accounted for in terms of capacity shared among different perceptual analyses. Shaw and Shaw (1977) and van der Heijden (1975) proposed somewhat similar formulations.

Proposals of this type, regarding possible capacity sharing in perceptual recognition, focused almost entirely on divided rather than selective

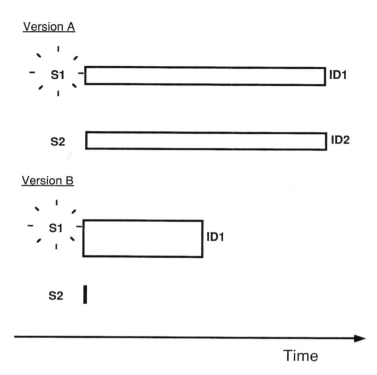

Figure 1.9
Two possible versions of capacity sharing when one input is attended (S1) and another is not (S2). In version A, the unattended item takes capacity; in version B, it does not.

attention. Thus, none of them had much to say about whether or not *rejected* stimuli also grab capacity, although it seems clear from Kahneman's (1973) formulation that he assumed they did not. In figure 1.9, Kahneman's version B depicts capacity divided exclusively among the attended items. The top panel shows the alternative version A, according to which the unattended stimuli also receive full capacity.

How does capacity sharing relate to early and late selection theory? The notion of capacity allocation is sufficiently general that other theories can be subsumed under it if one chooses. Early selection theory claims that processing capacity is allocated on an all-or-none basis to one stimulus at a time, and, one naturally assumes, generally only to the relevant stimulus. Late selection theory maintains that there are enough processing resources for all the stimuli that could ever arise to be processed at maximum efficiency, and these resources are never denied to any stimulus. (Once one supposes that, however, there is not much gain in speaking of resources in the first place.) The general point is simply that capacity sharing is consistent with either early or late selection theory, but also allows intermediate possibilities.

Capacity sharing also points toward a whole class of intermediate theories that differ qualitatively from the classic ideas. Suppose limited resources can be simultaneously shared among different stimuli. The two panels in figure 1.9 represent two versions of such an intermediate theory; they differ only with respect to the locus of selectivity. The top panel is most naturally seen as a version of late selection theory modified to postulate graded capacity sharing, and the bottom panel is most naturally considered a version off the controlled parallel model, subject to the same modification.

At this point it is probably best to call a halt to the proliferation of theoretical alternatives. The possibilities discussed so far illustrate some of the most natural, or most influential, ideas about selection and capacity limits. With a little ingenuity, one could go on without limit, entertaining ever more baroque possibilities from one's armchair. Thus, one might combine capacity sharing with Treisman's hypothesis of attenuation for rejected stimuli by supposing that rejected stimuli tend to grab any spare capacity not already allocated. Or perhaps rejected stimuli grab a fixed amount of resources, leaving the balance to be allocated in a controlled way, and so on. However, it is undoubtedly more efficient to examine the empirical findings of studies of selectivity, capacity, and set, and return to these theories once some empirical constraints have been set out.

This rather breezy tour suggests a few general conclusions. First, it is not easy to provide an exhaustive taxonomy of functional analyses of attentional control and capacity limits in perception. Second, classic theories differ with regard to several key issues, and—most critically— these issues are at least partly orthogonal to each another. It is odd how rarely this orthogonality has been discussed, as it has important implications. Since the theories differ on a number of orthogonal issues, one should never ask whether the findings of a particular study favor late selection or early selection. Rather, one should ask how they bear on more specific hypotheses such as, rejected stimuli are always processed to the point of recognition or, certain types of stimuli cannot be recognized without capacity limitations. Before turning to the empirical findings, an overview is provided of some of the kinds of tasks that have been most commonly used in studies of attention and perception, and some terminology is introduced that is useful in referring to these tasks.

Methods and Terms: Laboratory Measures of Attention

Chapters 2 through 4 examine the basic experimental findings on attention and perception. A perceptual experiment just about always involves instructing the subject to perform some sort of task, even when the instructions do not inform the subject about the real purpose of the experiment. Attention researchers have used many variations on a rather modest number of different tasks, but they have a bewildering number of terms for these tasks. Fortunately, a simple taxonomy of basic tasks will cover most of the research designs. Insofar as possible, we will use the most common names, but since so many terms exist, the ones selected are probably used by a plurality, rather than a majority, of writers.

Filtering Tasks

In the filtering task, subjects are presented with more than one stimulus at the same time. Their job is to report something (the *reported attribute*) about just the subset of the presented stimuli that satisfy a certain *selection criterion*. The selection criterion is a physical attribute such as location, color, or loudness. The reported attribute is usually some category to which the stimulus belongs, one that is dependent on its symbolic identity. Clear-cut examples of instructions that define filtering tasks are "read only the red letter" and "read whichever word is being pointed at by the arrow." Selective shadowing (immediate repetition of spoken material) is also a filtering task. "Shadow the message presented to the left ear" defines a filtering task in which the selection criterion is ear of origin, or, more precisely, location as derived from interaural intensity differences, and the identity of the spoken words is the reported attribute. "Shadow just the man's voice" is another filtering task, with pitch the selection criterion. This oversimplifies the situation, because there is typically spectral overlap between a man's voice and a woman's.

The term "filtering task" obviously should not be taken to prejudice the issue of whether or not filter theory (Broadbent's early selection theory) is accurate. It is a fact that people can readily perform many kinds of filtering tasks. If late selection theory is correct, it would have to postulate mechanisms that allow people to select stimuli based on arbitrary physical attributes. It might even postulate that selection functions best when the selection criterion is physical (Duncan, 1981). The critical claim of late selection theories for filtering tasks is that the rejected stimuli are identified just the same as if they were attended (see figure 1.3). The controlled parallel and early selection theories would deny this claim, whereas Treisman's attenuation hypothesis would modify it.

Several variants of the filtering task have been widely investigated. In one such variant, the selection criterion is not specified well in advance, as in the cases described above. Rather, it may be specified shortly before the stimulus, simultaneous with it, or shortly after. The effects of the timing of precues can help in exploring the time course of the selection process itself (chapter 2), but they do not address either of the questions noted in figure 1.6. Many studies used *postcueing* (selection cues that followed the stimulus) to examine questions about sensory storage (i.e., information that outlasts the stimulus). Sperling (1960) was the first to observe that cues that follow a visual display by a short fraction of a second can be used to select information from a brief sensory memory system capable of holding onto much more information than a person can ever report. Studies of this sort addressed the questions of how much information is available and what kind of information it is. This literature is discussed briefly in chapter 3. These studies have some bearing on issues related to early and late selection, but that relationship is somewhat indirect. Chapter 2 deals with selective attention tasks, and almost all of the studies described in that chapter are filtering tasks.

Monitoring Tasks

The second category of tasks also involves numerous stimuli presented at the same time. However, the question asked of the subject depends on the categorical identity of more than one of the stimuli. In general, the word *monitoring* tends to be used with auditory stimuli or with visual displays that involve multiple frames,[3] and *search* is used more when the task involves a single visual display.

Monitoring and search tasks are commonly referred to as *divided-attention* tasks, reflecting the idea that one has to divide one's attention over several stimuli to carry out such tasks. This label is intuitively appropriate, but in line with the discussion above it will be avoided since it presupposes a claim that has to be tested, namely, that something called attention is divided in these tasks but not in selective-attention tasks.

Something else that has created considerable confusion is the use of the term late selection to describe tasks requiring selection on the basis of the identity of a stimulus. Once one adopts this way of speaking, one has to say that the simple fact that people can satisfactorily perform a monitoring task shows that late selection is possible. But of course this is misleading: the mere fact that people can do these tasks certainly does not support late selection theory, which states that these identities are computed unselectively, in parallel, and without capacity limitations (see figure 1.3). Therefore, the term late selection is reserved for the theory.

What is distinctive in the theory is the claim that selection *in the filtering tasks* involves selective processing that takes place only *after* all stimuli have been identified. The fact that, one way or another, people are capable of selecting a stimulus on the basis of its identity ("name the digit in the display") provides no special support for late-selection theory. Any viable early selection account would also have to account for it, which it could do by supposing that such a task would require sequential processing. According to the late selection or controlled parallel theory, monitoring can be accomplished in parallel without capacity limitations. Capacity-limited processing will obviously predict some reduction in efficiency with increasing numbers of attended items. The converse is not true: impairments with more attended stimuli do not logically imply capacity limits, a less than obvious point that is discussed in chapter 3.

Tasks Involving a Single Stimulus

Whereas many cognitive psychologists tend to regard both filtering and monitoring tasks as fairly austere, from the perspective of psychophysicists they are elaborate compared with the basic detection and discrimination designs. These classic psychophysical tasks do play an important role in attention research (they appear frequently in chapters 2 and 4). Therefore, it is necessary to introduce some standard terminology for them as well.

In these tasks, there is only one stimulus and no selection criterion at all, at least, none that is explicit. In the yes/no detection task, the subject decides in each trial whether or not a stimulus was present. This kind of task is often analyzed with the help of signal-detection theory (Swets, 1964). The basic idea of signal detection theory is that every time a trial occurs and a stimulus is or is not presented, the subject's decision about whether or not to report a signal is based on the output of (certain channels in) the sensory system, which can be represented as a scalar quantity. This quantity is assumed to be subject to some random variability—random from the point of view of the experimenter. Classic signal detection theory furthermore assumes that the noise has a Gaussian distribution.

The subject is assumed to set a threshold and to respond "yes" in case the decision variable lies above this threshold. Variation in the probability that a target is present, or in the payoffs for different outcomes (e.g., correct detection, false alarm) is assumed to result in changes in the threshold. Variation in signal intensity is assumed to alter the strength of the signal (i.e., the difference between the signal-alone distribution and the signal-plus-noise distribution). This analysis has been applied not only to detection of stimuli at threshold, but also to search and monitoring tasks (e.g., Shaw, 1984; Palmer, Ames, and Lindsey, 1993)

Another popular task for exploring detection near threshold is the two-interval forced-choice procedure. Here, a signal is always presented in one of two successive temporal intervals, and the subject is required to indicate in which interval the signal occurred. If one assumes that this decision is made simply by comparing the magnitude of the sensory variable during the two intervals and choosing the interval in which it was higher, one can use percentage-correct accuracy as a measure of detection performance. Detection tasks with at most a single stimulus are discussed extensively in connection with divided attention (chapter 3) and perceptual set (chapter 4). This provides an abbreviated overview of the most basic experimental designs that recur throughout the book. Of course, individual experiments tend to involve variations or refinements of the basic designs.

Organization of the Book

The organization of the next four chapters of this book has already been hinted at. Chapters 2 through 4 deal with three major areas of study involving normal human subjects in the field of attention as it relates to perception. Chapter 2 deals with selective attention, tasks in which subjects are presented with some information to which they try to attend, and other information that they attempt to ignore. The main questions are what determines the effectiveness of selection and how extensively the ignored stimuli are processed. Chapter 3 discusses divided attention, situations in which an individual tries to process multiple stimuli presented at the same time. The primary question is how much perceptual analysis of simultaneous inputs can be achieved when such processing is advantageous. Examples of questions considered in this chapter include the following: if a person hears a different spoken word in each ear, can he or she recognize both at once? Can a person read a word and detect the occurrence of a tone at the same time? Chapter 4 examines the phenomena of perceptual set. The processing of a stimulus can sometimes be affected by a person's expectations about that stimulus. These expectations might concern some property of the stimulus other than the one that is reported. For example, many studies assessed whether a person is better able to identify a brief stimulus if he or she knows in advance where it will be presented in the visual field. These expectations might also pertain to the same attribute as what the observer reports. A question, then, would be whether a person can identify a letter more quickly and efficiently if he or she knows the letter will be drawn from a small set of known alternatives.

Chapter 5 returns to the main theoretical issues of attention as they relate to perception. It reviews the main empirical generalizations that emerged from the studies described in the previous three chapters, and asks how the phenomena of selective attention, divided attention, and set can be understood in a common framework. The role of attention as a theoretical construct or set of constructs reappears in this chapter.

Chapters 6 and 7 address problems of divided attention that go beyond perception and recognition of stimuli, examining the limitations that arise when people try to perform more than one task at the same time (where "task" refers to cognitive judgments and production of motor responses, rather than just recognition of sensory input). Chapter 6 deals with dual-task performance, and Chapter 7 with attention and memory. There are several reasons for discussing perceptual aspects of attention (chapters 2–5) separately from postperceptual (i.e., cognitive, memorial, and motor-related) aspects. While the boundaries between perception and postperceptual processes are not always clear, the neuropsychological evidence shows that brain damage frequently results in impairments confined to one or other of these domains (McCarthy and Warrington, 1990). Perceptual versus postperceptual is therefore an a priori reasonable candidate for a fundamental division in cognitive architecture. More critically, however, the findings of attention studies described here (especially in chapter 6) specifically argue for a distinction between perceptual attentional limitations and more central limitations involved in thought and the planning of action. Nonetheless, the connections between perceptual and postperceptual processing are numerous, and many remain to be carefully mapped out in future research. Chapter 8 addresses three broad issues that have been significant in attentional research, especially in recent years: automaticity, mental effort, and cognitive control, including research on task set.

The overall thrust of this book is bottom-up: experimental findings first, empirical generalizations that go beyond particular paradigms second, and glimmerings of general theory last. However, experiments without questions are mind numbing, and the more empirical sections of the book are focused around questions posed at a medium level of abstraction. The reader familiar with the attention field will find some of the conclusions reached here broadly in line with mainstream views, but others may appear more idiosyncratic and even disagreeable, especially with regard to the concept of processing capacity and automaticity. The hybrid view of attentional selectivity advocated in chapter 5 probably falls in the first category. By contrast, the conclusions of chapter 4, which suggest that noise reduction provides a better account of cueing effects in single-item displays than capacity allocation, challenge many widely held views. Chapter 6 argues that central attentional limitations often reflect a discrete processing bottleneck, harking back to the earliest studies of divided attention in the laboratories of Craik and Welford. Chapter 7 analyzes the role of attention in different memory systems. Recent research in this area has focused on the putative role of attention in distinguishing between implicit and explicit memory storage, but a very different view is presented here, focusing on the relationship between attentional mechanisms and short-term memory. Readers knowledgeable in the field will undoubtedly, therefore, find some points they disagree with; I hope they will also find the argumentation explicit and empirical enough that the disagreements will promote empirical progress rather than confusion.

I

Attention and Perception

2

Selective Attention

We are almost always subjected to a barrage of different sources of sensory information at any instant. You can verify this by pausing and trying to survey the various sensations impinging upon you at this very moment. You will probably find some auditory stimuli (an aircondi- tioner?) and kinesthetic stimuli (the back of the chair?), as well as many visual inputs originating in this text, but also more peripheral visual stimuli. Probably you would agree that you were not aware of more than a few of these stimuli at the moment you began trying to enumerate them. As described in chapter 1, a great deal of dispute surrounds what happens to stimuli that are rejected. The process of selecting from among the many potentially available stimuli is the clearest manifestation of selective attention.

Two questions about selective attention have been the subject of most of the research reviewed here. The first concerns what factors make selective attention more or less easy and efficient. The second is, what are the consequences of selective attention for processing both attended and rejected stimuli? This question leads directly to some of the key issues over which early and late selection theories disagree. The first question, regarding ease and efficiency, is also relevant to that dispute, but less directly so.

Probably the best-known real life example of selective attention is listening to a single voice in a room full of people talking at the same time. For over a decade, most contemporary studies of auditory selective attention examined a laboratory analogue of this everyday phenomenon, beginning with the work of Cherry (1953). Examples of visual selective attention also abound, but the phenomenon of visual selectivity is more elusive. The reason it is elusive is because the casual observer tends to think of visual selective attention as consisting of nothing more than fixations of the eye, and assumes that changes in attention are equivalent to eye movements. As James (1890, p. 437), Helmholtz (1924, p. 455), and presumably many others before them noted, this identification is not valid: we can choose which visual stimulus to attend to without moving our eyes. Consider the case of reading, activity that depends on taking in information from one or at most a few words at a time. For purely sensory reasons, words become less legible as they move toward the periphery, but nonetheless one can easily choose to read the word above or below the fixated word. One can even move one's eyes to scan one line of text while reading the line immediately above or below this line, although doing so feels unnatural and effortful. It is hardly surprising that the distinction between visual selection and eye movements is so easily overlooked, however, because there is rarely any reason to try to fixate one object and attend to another. The relation of eye movements and selective attention has further intricacies that are discussed toward the end of this chapter. The point of this example is to demonstrate that even in the most routine of our activities, visual selection is not exclusively achieved by movements of the eye, but depends on internal selective mechanisms as well.

This chapter describes many laboratory phenomena that illustrate the voluntary control of visual selection without eye movements. For example, an observer may be shown a display of colored letters (too brief to allow an eye movement) and asked to report the identity of the red letter. In other cases, an observer may view a display of several words and try to name which one an arrow points toward. In each case, a well-defined selection criterion determines which stimuli are to be selected and which are to be rejected. The criterion of selection is a simple physical attribute. Logically speaking, whether a stimulus fits this criterion can be determined without identifying it (e.g., as a letter, word, or picture). These tasks satisfy the defining attributes of filtering tasks, as described in chapter 1.

The goal of this chapter is to explore some of the most important empirical results from studies of filtering tasks, and the implications of these results for the mechanisms of selective attention. Limiting the discussion to filtering tasks does not by any means imply that selective attention mechanisms are involved only when a task explicitly requires filtering. In fact, the next two chapters (on divided attention and set) describe some quite different situations in which selective attention mechanisms may also be involved. For example, in chapter 4 we consider what happens when a single visual stimulus is briefly presented for report, and the observer may be cued in advance where the stimulus will be. Logically, this task too might involve some of the same processes as selection from a crowded display. However, it is useful to begin with filtering tasks, in which the requirement for selection is obvious and inescapable.

Auditory Selective Attention

Cherry's Studies: Reports about the Unattended

The researches of E. Colin Cherry (1953) provided a powerful impetus for contemporary work on selective attention, and they continue to be widely cited. Cherry performed ingenious experiments in which two auditory messages were presented simultaneously, one to each ear (*dichotic* presentation). Dichotic presentation generally gives a listener the experience of two streams of sound, each localized roughly at the ear of input. Although it produces strong localization, it is an unnatural stimulus, because localization is normally achieved on the basis of multiple cues, of which intensity differences are only one (Scharf and Houtsma, 1986).

Cherry instructed his subjects to shadow one of the messages (i.e., repeat it back without delay). He observed several things. First, subjects found it fairly easy to carry out the task, which Cherry thought remarkable in itself (although he acknowledged this was presumably well known to people administering hearing tests). His second observation was that when subjects were asked, after they had finished shadowing, to describe the contents of the rejected message, they could say almost nothing about it, except that sounds had been present. When the message on the rejected ear started out in English and then switched to German, subjects rarely noticed this. The same was true when English speech was played backward on the rejected channel. On the other hand, when the speaker switched gender (and pitch), or when speech was replaced with a 400-Hz tone, listeners almost always noticed and remarked on it.

Cherry concluded that "certain statistical properties [of the rejected message are] identified, but that detailed aspects, such as the language, individual words, or semantic content are unnoticed" (1953, p. 978). In a well-known follow-up to his work, Neville Moray (1959) examined this striking lack of memory for the rejected message in more detail. His subjects shadowed the message presented to one ear while a message recorded in the same voice was played to the other ear. In some cases, the same word list was repeated thirty-five times in the rejected message. A recognition test on the words from the list disclosed that subjects were no more likely to recognize these words as having been presented than they were to recognize never-presented words. It is not surprising that words on the attended channel were recognized at a reasonably high level.

These results are not peculiar to processing of linguistic input. Diana Deutsch (1986, pp. 32–20) reported informally obtaining the same kinds of effects with melodies played on the piano. Listeners sang along with the melody presented to one ear. When questioned about the melody presented to the other ear, they were able to say very little about it. As Deutsch pointed out, the phenomenon is even more remarkable with musical stimuli than with speech, since music (but not speech) often involves several perceptual streams proceeding in parallel. It is somewhat hard to see how a person who never processed more than one melodic line at a time could have a very rich appreciation of, say, the music of Bach. This reinforces a point made on purely logical grounds in chapter 1: the need to distinguish between the processing people *can* accomplish when they try to divide their attention, on the one hand, and the processing that is accomplished when they try to focus on a particular stimulus, on the other.

Factors Affecting the Difficulty of Selection

In Cherry's original studies, the ear of arrival (and presumably the subjective localization that resulted) provided the basis for segregating the two messages. He also noted (perhaps no surprise) that the task was much harder when an irrelevant message spoken in the same voice was played in the same ear as the relevant message. This effect is not restricted to irrelevant spoken messages: Egan, Carterette, and Thwing (1954) observed a similar advantage when they played noise to the same or different ear to which speech was played.

As noted earlier, presenting messages to different ears causes them to be subjectively localized in or near the ears themselves, as a result of the unnaturally extreme difference in the intensity of the signals at the two ears. It turns out that even moderate differences in interaural intensity produce enough localization to improve selective shadowing a great deal compared with zero differences (Treisman, 1964a). Intensity is not the only cue that the auditory system uses to localize sound. Another one is the difference in the time at which a sound arrives at the two ears (and closely related to that, the phase of the signals at the two ears). A sound to the extreme right or left of a listener will arrive at the nearer ear up to about 0.7 msec earlier than it arrives at the farther ear. Despite the very brief intervals involved, the auditory system makes effective use of this cue, especially at low frequencies. A variety of psychophysical studies, principally using measures of detection thresholds, shed light on the relationship to selective attention. They found that people are better able to hear a pure tone superimposed on noise when the interaural timing localizes the tone and the mask at different points in space. This is known as the masking level difference (MLD), and it has been studied extensively since it was first discovered by Langmuir and colleagues (see Scharf and Buus, 1986, for a succinct review).

Suppose a tone is presented to one ear (monaurally) against a background of noise presented to both (binaurally). When the noise at the two ears is correlated and in phase, the threshold for detection is typically about 9 db lower than it is when the noise at the two ears is uncorrelated. Subjectively, the correlated in-phase presentation makes it sound as though a single noise source is located in the center of the head, producing subjective distance from the source of the tone to be detected. Interaural time differences seem to help in selectivity among speech signals as well. Broadbent (1954) delayed one of two messages briefly, and listeners found this helpful in focusing on one of the messages.

The early observation that people can selectively shadow the message played to the left or right ear led to the general (mis-)impression that ears constitute natural or basic channels that can always be processed separately without difficulty. As noted above, dichotic presentations are quite unnatural, and hearing typically relies heavily on elaborate decoding of the pattern of input to the two ears to construct a representation of sound sources in the three-dimensional world (see Warren, 1982, for an overview). For this reason, it would be surprising indeed if the two ears constituted fundamental input channels, as these early studies sometimes are taken to imply.

Indeed, later studies provided a more realistic picture. Consider, for example, the findings of Treisman and Riley (1969), who had their subjects shadow the message in one ear while a different message in a different voice was played in the other ear. Unlike in the earlier studies, the authors used digital signal processing to synchronize the individual pairs of words on the two channels in a precise way, shrinking or stretching each word to have a duration of 250 msec. Under these conditions, shadowing one message was very difficult, and many intrusions from the rejected channel were noted. The investigators suggested that subjects may find it difficult to determine which ear a sound is coming to unless some of it (perhaps especially the onset) coincides with silence on the other ear. This suggestion is consistent with work in auditory psychophysics that suggests that auditory localization relies heavily on the initial onsets of acoustic stimuli (Hafter and Buell, 1985; Zurek, 1980).

In summary, filtering tasks show excellent selectivity by spatial location at least under conditions in which localization cues are adequate. This, however, should not lead one to think of the two ears as channels per se. Rather, it appears that various cues leading to the perception of sounds having different locations in the world provide the basis for successful filtering; dichotic presentations may or may not provide such conditions, depending on the temporal relation of the two inputs.

People can also filter effectively on the basis of frequency differences between attended and rejected messages. Treisman (1964b) had listeners monitor one of two messages played binaurally (i.e., each of two messages played at equal intensity in both ears). Under these conditions, she found that differences in voice pitch improved selectivity considerably. A woman's voice was shadowed with 74% accuracy when the irrelevant message was spoken in a man's voice (reading the same type of material), but only 31% accuracy when the irrelevant message was spoken by the same woman. With both messages coming into both ears, such differences may partly reflect frequency-selective masking at peripheral levels in the auditory system, and when the subjects are shadowing there is the complication that they hear their own voice as well. Underwood and Moray (1971) circumvented these problems by having listeners monitor one of two messages to detect digit targets. With both dichotic and monaural presentations, they detected more targets when one voice was male and the other female, compared with when both voices were recorded by speakers of the same gender. Male and female voices overlap in their frequency content and differ in other ways as well. It would be interesting to analyze the critical factors that enhance selection in this situation. It could be studied using synthetic speech, but this does not appear to have been done as yet.

The fact that differences of pitch and location facilitate selective attention was one of the main pieces of evidence cited by Broadbent in support of his filter theory. According to his interpretation, these physical attributes are the only attributes of messages that are extracted, regardless of whether or not the message is attended to. In his view, this preliminary analysis is used to define channels for the purpose of subsequent selection. It is no coincidence that subjects also tend to notice changes occurring in these attributes in rejected messages, as Cherry found also.

The ease of auditory selection also depends on the number of channels on which information is presented. Treisman (1964a) used three different channels to present different messages recorded by the same speaker. Messages on the left and right channels were played to the left and right ears, respectively. A third (middle) channel was created by playing messages at equal volume to the two ears. As noted above, this results in sound that is subjectively localized midway between the ears. When subjects shadowed the message played to the right ear, shadowing was scarcely affected by playing a single additional message on either the middle or left channel, compared with no rejected message at all, confirming Cherry's observations. However, when two irrelevant messages were played, one to the left channel and one to the middle channel, shadowing of the right channel was substantially impaired. This could potentially have happened either because there were two different messages to be rejected, or because two different spatial channels contained information that had to be rejected. Treisman concluded it was the two channels rather than the two messages that created the problem, because when the irrelevant messages were both played on the middle channel (or on the left channel), the problem was largely eliminated.

Does having to reject two distinct channels impair selection when the channels are defined by frequency instead of location? To answer this question, Treisman placed a male and a female voice on the central channel while subjects shadowed the right channel. Performance was impaired here also, arguing that it is rejecting any two separate channels that poses special difficulty. The problem in monitoring one of three channels did not occur when the irrelevant channels contained speech sounds ("bet bet bet" or "a a a"), rather than speech, and Treisman therefore concluded that the problem could not be attributed to peripheral auditory masking (Scharf and Buus, 1986). The difficulty remained when the messages consisted of passages spoken in Czech. The reason for this difference was not clear. Treisman's observations are intriguing, but they have not apparently been followed up.

What conclusions can be drawn from these studies of selective listening? First, differences in subjective sound location between attended and rejected stimuli clearly facilitate selective attention to a spoken message. Merely having messages presented to different ears does not make it trivial to select a message, however; the messages must be at least partly nonoverlapping in time. Differences in pitch also facilitate selectivity. Finally, the difficulty of auditory selection seems to be increased when the number of rejected channels grows beyond one.

What Is Noticed in the Rejected Message?

As described, Cherry was struck by how little subjects spontaneously reported about the rejected channel. Broadbent's early selection account drew support from the fact that what subjects tend to notice pertains to just the attributes that serve as effective cues for selection, such as pitch and location. However, under certain conditions subjects sometimes *do* spontaneously notice something of the linguistic content of the unattended channel.

One example was noted by Cherry in his initial report (1953). He tried playing the same message to the two ears, separated in time by a variable delay. He started with a comparatively long interval (he did not make it clear whether the attended or rejected message was leading or lagging) and gradually reduced it. Subjects noticed the repetition when the lag got down to the range between 2 and 6 seconds. Treisman (1964c) examined spontaneous detection of repetition more carefully. Her subjects either shadowed the message in the right ear or simply listened to it, knowing they would have to describe it later. In either case, they were led to believe that listening to the sounds played in the left ear would cause trouble and should be avoided. The task was performed over and over with 40-second passages, and the lag between the repeated messages was shortened until the subjects spontaneously remarked on the repetition. Once this happened, the experiment ended.

When both channels contained the same sentences, all subjects noticed the repetition of content and whether the passages were spoken in the same voice or a different one. However, the lag had to be much shorter for the repetition to be noticed when the message in the rejected channel led. Here, repetition was noticed at about $1^{1}/_{2}$ seconds, on average, compared with about $4^{1}/_{2}$ seconds when the message in the attended channel led. The results were similar when the messages consisted of speech played backward, showing that understanding the words and sentences was not critical for detecting repetition.

How does spontaneous noticing of repetition bear on the extent to which the to-be-ignored material is processed? Broadbent (1958) assumed the existence of a sensory memory that holds onto 1 or 2 seconds' worth of rejected material, now commonly referred to as echoic memory. Of course, he supposed that this memory included physical, but not semantic, descriptions of the sounds. To account for repetition detection, one must suppose that when new sensory information arrives, it is matched against this memory. The existence of some matching processes can be argued for on other grounds, since listeners detect periodicity in repeated segments of white noise up to about 1 or 2 seconds in duration (Guttman and Julesz, 1963; Warren and Bashford, 1981). In this case, listeners hear the periodicity as a whooshing or "motorboating,"depending on the frequency; obviously, this sort of implicit periodicity detection might not be related to the conscious detection of repetition studied by Cherry and Treisman. In any case, since people can detect repetition even when the rejected message lags, one would have to suppose that sensory memory for the attended message is compared with incoming material on the rejected channel, as well. Since the matching is acoustic rather than lexical or semantic, this does not conflict with an account like Broadbent's; it should also be kept in mind that noticing a repetition in a long segment might reflect merely intermittent or low-fidelity matching, and does not imply continuous high-fidelity matching.

What poses more of a problem for a theory like Broadbent's, however, is Treisman's observation that repetitions of the same sentences are detected even when they are spoken in different voices. Of course, detecting repetition of the same words by a different speaker might not necessarily involve semantic processing of words, but it surely requires more than a direct comparison of elementary acoustic features. Treisman also tried presenting a messages in English to one ear and the French translation to the other ear to listeners fluent in both languages. Relatively few of them detected the "repetition," so perhaps the degree of semantic processing implied by the different-voice same-message results may not be that great.

All of these results can be reconciled with Broadbent's model simply by supposing that subjects occasionally relax their selectivity and sample the rejected channel. When the selected message leads, any word from the rejected channel that was checked would be one that occurred just a little earlier on the selected channel. It is reasonable to suppose that these selected words would be in a postsensory short-term storage, so it is hardly surprising that the repetition would be readily detected in this situation, even when the lag is longer than the life of auditory sensory memory. Things are is a little more complicated when the rejected message leads. Any word sampled on the rejected message would not yet have been spoken on the attended channel, so to explain repetition detection one must suppose that the word that was sampled would itself have to be held onto until its match appeared on the attended channel. It is not hard to see why under these conditions repetition detection would be less effective, with the result that repetition could be detected only at relatively shorter lags. However intriguing, detection of speech repetition does not rule out even such extreme perceptual selectivity as that suggested by Broadbent's account.

The results can also be accounted for in terms of Treisman's attenuation theory (see chapter 1). She supposed that when the attended message led, processing these words primed the detectors for them, and therefore when the same words appeared on the rejected channel, they were recognized and, at least briefly, *selected* themselves. Her account of the rejected-leads condition was less explicit, but it seemed to rely on sensory memory in the manner suggested in the previous paragraph. There is no doubt that the result could be reconciled with late selection theories as well.

Findings regarding detection of repeated speech are therefore not critical for choosing among very different accounts of the fate of unattended stimuli. However, the detection phenomena are intrinsically interesting and deserve further study for this reason alone.

In a well-known study, Moray (1959) verified what many have noticed outside the laboratory: a listener tends to notice his or her own name spontaneously when it happens to appear in a rejected message. As Loftus (1974) pointed out, many textbooks have implied that people usually or even always notice their own names. In fact, the results were less dramatic: when the rejected message contained the word "You may stop now," subjects noticed and reported this only 6% of the time. On the other hand, the message "John Smith [the name of the subject], you may stop now" was noticed and acted upon 33% of the time. This went up to 80% when subjects were clued in advance to be on the lookout for new instructions (it is not clear whether or not they were led to expect new instructions to appear in the rejected channel). Of interest, Oswald, Taylor, and M. Treisman (1960) observed that sleeping subjects are often awakened by their own name.

The fact that people detect their own name was cited as support by late selection theorists such as Deutsch and Deutsch (1963). Treisman (1960) accounted for it by supposing that detectors for certain stimuli were perpetually primed, with the result that detection could occur even on the basis of attenuated stimulus information. Since the effect occurs only intermittently, it can be reconciled with a model such as Broadbent's simply by supposing that filtering lapses from time to time. This possibility illustrates a general difficulty in interpreting selective listening results: effects of rejected stimuli may be due to processing that happens only occasionally, and even voluntarily, when subjects become curious about what they are missing on the other channel.

Subtler Measures of the Fate of Rejected Sounds

The research described showed that listeners consciously trying to attend to a message have little or no enduring memory for the words or the meaning conveyed on a rejected channel, except for their own name or sounds identical to those on the attended channel. These are fascinating observations, but not theoretically decisive with respect to the fate of rejected stimuli. Subsequently, many researchers claimed to find stronger evidence against selective perception. In these studies, the contents of the unattended channel were neither spontaneously reported nor revealed by memory probes. Instead, more indirect and subtle sorts of evidence proved that their contents had been analyzed to the point at which their meaning was registered. Most of these studies were reported after Deutsch and Deutsch proposed their late selection theory in 1963, and the results were often taken to provide strong support for that theory.

If an individual can say nothing about the contents of a rejected channel, how could one infer from the person's behavior that the person had, at some level, analyzed the meaning of the stimuli? Experimenters have shown a high degree of ingenuity in finding ways to demonstrate this. Treisman (1960) created dichotic messages consisting of two passages, one in each ear. The subject was instructed to shadow one channel and ignore the other. At an arbitrary point the two passages switched, with the message formerly on the left channel continuing in the right channel, and vice versa. When the two passages consisted of ordinary prose recorded in the same voice, about 30% of the time the subjects' shadowing switched channels along with the message.[1] When this occurred, subjects generally shadowed only a few words from the "wrong" channel, and promptly jumped back to the channel they were supposed to be shadowing. One intriguing aspect of the results is that when this happened, the subjects rarely noticed that anything funny had happened. Figure 2.1 shows a typical record, with the words the subject shadowed in capital letters. A less well-known but intriguing observation was that

```
"...I SAW THE GIRL    song was WISHING ..."
"...  me that bird    JUMPING in the street..."


"...SITTING AT A MAHOGONY    three POSSIBILITIES..."
"...let us look at these     TABLE with her head..."
```

Figure 2.1
Examples of the intrusions observed by Treisman (1960). In each selection, the capitalized words are the ones spoken by the subject, whose instructions were to shadow only one line (the one written on top). Reprinted with permission.

when one prose passage was recorded in a man's voice and the other in a woman's, the subjects often noticed the switch but rarely followed it.

Treisman accounted for the channel-jumping phenomenon within the framework of her filter-attenuation theory. She proposed that extraction of the meaning of the *attended* message resulted in a lowering of the threshold for recognizing words most likely to follow. She was less clear about why subjects actually switch over to shadowing them, and why they switch back a short while later. Note, however, that at the point of a switch, the material on the *attended* channel does not make sense. It may be, therefore, that subjects sample the other channel even if they would not otherwise have done so. Thus, one cannot necessarily infer from these results that subjects *routinely* analyze the rejected message to the point of determining its meaning.

Other auditory studies employed even more subtle measures. One example is the autonomic response to words that were previously paired with shock. Corteen and Wood (1972) performed the first such experiment, which involved a conditioning phase and a testing phase. In the conditioning phase, subjects listened to a series of words through headphones. The words were drawn from a list of three different city names, and each was repeatedly paired with a mild but unpleasant electric shock. In the testing phase, the subjects shadowed a prose passage presented through the right ear while trying to ignore the contents of the left ear. Shock-conditioned city names (as well as new city names and unrelated nouns) were included in the unattended left-ear message. Conditioned galvanic skin responses (GSR) were detected for both shock-associated city names 38% of the time and for the other city names 23%; comparable GSR responses occurred only for about 10% of unrelated nouns. Shadowing errors did not increase when critical words occurred on the rejected channel, and on questioning, the subjects denied having noticed any shock-associated words in that channel. Corteen and Wood concluded that the contents of the unattended channel were processed to the point of semantic analysis.

The result of this test is widely cited in introductory textbooks as evidence that the meaning of unattended messages is fully analyzed. However, subsequent research weakened the case quite a bit. To start with, the observations sometimes proved difficult to replicate (Wardlaw and Kroll, 1976). Others raised questions about how the results should be interpreted. For example, von Wright, Anderson, and Stenman (1975) measured GSR responses to rejected words. They also compared the magnitude of GSR response to the critical words (conditioned words and associates of them) in the monitored and unmonitored channels. The mean GSR response to a critical word in the monitored channel was more than twice the response to such words in the unmonitored channel. These results involve averages over trials, and cannot tell us whether GSR responses to stimuli in the rejected channel occurred less frequently than responses to attended items, or whether they occurred equally often but were smaller in magnitude. What the results do show, however, is that the Corteen and Wood effect does not prove full processing.

Dawson and Schell (1982) analyzed the Corteen and Wood effect with unusual thoroughness. They replicated the original findings quite satisfactorily, and also employed additional measures to eliminate trials on which subjects lapsed in their selective monitoring of the relevant channel. These measures included shadowing errors, subjects' reports of having noticed items on the irrelevant channel, and, in one condition, overt detection responses (subjects were instructed to press a key whenever they heard one of the words).[2]

Dawson and Schell's main result was that when analysis was restricted to trials in which *none* of their measures indicated possible lapses, the GSR responses to the contents of the rejected channel were almost, but not completely, abolished. The data also showed an interaction with laterality: when the to-be-ignored material was played to the right ear, there were more signs of processing in the GSR than when it was present in the left ear. In light of these findings, it seems plausible that the Corteen and Wood effect simply shows that a subject's rejection of the distractor message occasionally lapses, voluntarily or involuntarily. To put it differently, the results do not force one to conclude that rejected as well as attended messages are identified fully in every trial. A filter that functioned as Broadbent suggested, but that was prone to lapses and switches, could certainly account for the results.

Another finding commonly taken to confirm semantic processing of rejected messages was reported by Lewis (1970). Lewis examined the speed (rather than accuracy) of individual shadowing responses to words in the attended channel as a function of the identity of the word occurring at the same time on the rejected channel. Shadowing response times (RTs) were slowed by about 30 msec when the rejected channel contained a synonym of the to-be-shadowed word; they were speeded up by about the same amount when the rejected channel contained an associate. This result does not seem to be terribly robust. Treisman, Squire, and Green (1974) confirmed the effect, but found that it occurred only early in the list. By the seventh word, no increase whatever could be detected. These authors suggested that lapses in monitoring occurred before subjects had a chance to occupy themselves fully with monitoring the relevant channel (p. 645).

Further evidence against completely unselective processing comes from an interesting experiment performed by W. A. Johnston and Dark (1982). The subjects' primary task was to monitor a dichotically presented word list for any target words (the names of states) and to repeat any words they heard from the target category. In the selective-attention condition, all the state names were in the message played to one ear, and subjects attempted to monitor only this ear. In the divided-attention condition, state names were distributed evenly in both ears, and the subjects attempted to monitor both. Occasionally, the subjects were interrupted with a visually presented probe word (e.g., bark) to which they were supposed to respond with an immediate free association (e.g., dog). Semantic processing of spoken words was revealed in subjects' word associate choice. Each probe word was homophonous with two entirely different meanings. Subjects' associations were scored according to which of these two meanings they were related to (e.g., dog and birch are examples of associations related to the two different meanings of the probe bark). Sometimes two prime words tending to favor one or other of the two meanings of the probe word (e.g., growl and noise) were presented in either the attended or the unattended ear.

Consider first the selective attention condition. When the two prime words were in the attended channel, subjects' associations followed the primes 69% of the time compared with a baseline of 50%. When the prime words were in the unattended channel, the subjects produced prime-related associations only 52% of the time, which was not significantly different from 50%. The corresponding measure in the divided-attention condition was at an intermediate level (59%). As Johnston and Dark point out, this priming measure is sensitive to processing of non-targets in the auditory monitoring task, but it does not support the idea that nontargets in attended and rejected spatial channels are processed to the same degree (see also Johnston and Wilson, 1980).

A study by MacKay (1973) provides a final illustration of the tendency for breakthrough of the unattended effects in audition to become less convincing as the effects are investigated more carefully. Subjects shadowed ambiguous sentences in one channel, while the contents of the other channel contained potentially disambiguating information. It appeared that the unattended material biased subjects toward the related reading of the sentence they were shadowing. For example, subjects tended to interpret the sentence "They threw stones toward the bank yesterday" as being about a financial institution when the word "money" was in the unattended channel, and as being about riverbanks when the unattended word was "river." Newstead and Dennis (1979), however, found that MacKay's effect occurred only when just a single word was in the unattended channel. When the unattended channel contained a series of words, the effect disappeared. They suggested, quite plausibly, that an unexpected isolated sound in the unattended channel may disrupt the ordinary state of channel selection.

What can be concluded from these studies about the extent of processing of unattended speech? Certainly, the indirect effects of the content of the rejected channels rule out any model claiming people can *always* and *completely* exclude speech sounds from anything more than simple physical processing. The meaning of rejected stimuli can affect listeners' behavior in quite diverse ways. What is lacking, however, is persuasive evidence that rejected message is analyzed to the *same* degree as attended message. The results are consistent with an alternative interpretation according to which semantic analysis occurs when selection lapses and/or is restricted to recognition of stimuli that are particularly salient (or primed, in Treisman's terminology). The unmistakable tendency has been for more careful studies to find less rather than more evidence for semantic analysis of unattended stimuli.

We now turn to visual selective attention, asking the corresponding questions about ease of selection and extent of processing of unattended stimuli.

Visual Selective Attention

Ease of Selection
What makes it easier or more difficult for a person to attend selectively to a particular visual stimulus and exclude others? As noted, in daily life we are typically aware of spatial selection only when we make an overt movement of our eyes. Reading, for example, obviously requires deliberately taking in information from different positions on the page at different times, and eye movements are an obvious manifestations of this selection process. They do not, however, *constitute* selection.

The most straightforward evidence that people can select visual stimuli without eye movement is obtained with visual filtering tasks. The instruction "tell me the name of the single red letter in the display of ten letters" would be an example. Here color (red) is the selection criterion and letter identity is the reported attribute. How can we compare the effectiveness of selection by different criteria? One way would be to determine how well an observer can perform visual filtering tasks as a function of which attribute serves as selection criterion, where the criterion is varied between blocks of trials while the displays and the reported attribute remain constant. (This sort of comparison was roughly accomplished by some of the early selective shadowing studies described in the preceding section.)

No one seems to have made explicit comparisons of this sort using either RT or accuracy as the dependent measure. Many studies examined RTs for selective report, but with spatial location serving as the selection criterion throughout (e.g., Eriksen and Hoffman, 1972a, 1972b). Other studies used accuracy measures to compare different selection criteria, but the goal was to examine visual sensory (iconic) memory, rather than the efficiency of selection per se. For that reason, cues were presented at variable intervals after the offset of the display (e.g., Averbach and Coriell, 1961; von Wright, 1970). For example, when color[3] was the selection attribute and letter identity was the reported attribute, the subject might see a brief display, knowing that either red *or* green items would have to be reported, but not which. Shortly after the display offset, a tone would sound, and its pitch would indicate whether red or green items would be reported. Accuracy was reasonably high so long as the cue was not delayed more than a few hundred milliseconds after display offset, reflecting sensory persistence from the display (usually termed iconic memory; see chapter 3). Selection from iconic memory probably involves the same process as selecting from a display that is still physically present (evidence for this will emerge throughout succeeding chapters). Assuming this is the case, iconic memory studies provide at least some comparative information about the effectiveness of different selection criteria.

The first comparison was carried out by Sperling (1960) in his classic partial-report studies. His subjects were shown a brief display of characters. After a variable interval, a tone indicated which subset of a display of letters and digits they should report. The selection criterion was either spatial location or category (letter vs digit). Accuracy was much better for location cueing than for category cueing. Von Wright (1970) performed a more systematic comparison in which a display of eight characters was presented for 100 msec. A high or low tone sounded as the display disappeared, cueing the subject to report a subset of the display, composed always of four items. Performance was excellent when the selection criterion was location, color, size, or brightness, but much worse when it consisted of an attribute that might plausibly depend on identification (e.g., orientation, letter vs digit, vowel vs consonant).

These observations were sometimes taken to show that information in iconic memory is precategorical, that is, that objects were not identified.

This interpretation of the results would be consistent with early selection but not late selection theories. As several authors pointed out (e.g., Allport, 1989; Duncan, 1981), however, the results do not require this interpretation. Even if the items were all identified, identity information might not be a good selection cue. Consider a filing system in an office, for example. One can easily retrieve file folders based on whatever is written on each file's tab, but this obviously does not mean that no other information is contained in the file itself. Indeed, later studies found that selection by category (letter vs digit) can yield a partial-report superiority effect (Merikle, 1980). Based on findings of this kind, some authors suggested that visual persistence *must* include categorical information; this inference is also dubious.

What, then, can be concluded about the question we started with: the relative ease of selection using different selection criteria? Selection by simple, physical attributes such as location, color, size, and brightness is clearly effective in filtering tasks involving brief visual displays. This closely mirrors findings from auditory selection discussed earlier in the chapter. Although this has been taken argue that unattended stimuli are not processed to any deeper level (Broadbent, 1958; Kahneman, 1973; Kahneman and Treisman, 1984), the argument is weak. Attended and unattended stimuli could even be processed to exactly the same extent, with only precategorical attributes facilitating selection.

Fate of Rejected Stimuli

Memory and Spontaneous Noticing   Moray's classic observations with word lists repeated over and over in the rejected ear in a shadowing task showed that people typically have little enduring memory for the contents of a rejected auditory channel. The same is true of rejected visual stimuli. Neisser (1976) had subjects read text in which alternating lines consisted of different prose passages, each written in a different color. Subjects had no difficulty reading only the red lines, and showed little memory of the unattended message.

There is little doubt, however, that a reader generally fixates directly on each attended line, giving the excluded lines a double disadvantage: greater eccentricity (hence poorer acuity) as well as attentional exclusion. Some studies used spatially overlapping forms to minimize this problem.

Rock and Guttman (1981) showed subjects series of pairs of overlapping forms (figure 2.2). Each pair was viewed for 1 second, and subjects reported their aesthetic judgment about the red figure. After viewing ten pairs, a surprise recognition memory test was given. Subjects were able to recognize the attended items almost as well as when no rejected item was present. The rejected items, however, were recognized at a level little better than chance. This was true even when the ignored line figure was the outline of a familiar object (e.g., house), or when subjects were asked about the contents of a display just 1 second after it had disappeared.

Following up on observations of Kolers (1972), Neisser and Becklen (1975) presented video images from two cathode-ray tube (CRT) displays to observers in such a way that the images appeared in the same part of their visual fields and at the same distance. This was achieved by placing a half-silvered mirror between the observer and one of the CRTs; the mirror reflected the image from the other CRT at equal contrast. The effect is described as similar to what one sees looking out a window from a well-lit room at dusk: the scene out the window and the reflection from the room are superimposed. Neisser and Becklen showed subjects video images of two types of events, one consisting of human hands interacting in a game, the other showing complete figures of people tossing around a ball (figure 2.3). Subjects were given the task of detecting particular events in the videos, such as a ball being thrown. They were able to monitor whichever video image they chose with only minimal interference from the other. However, they were extremely poor at monitoring

 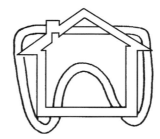

Figure 2.2
Examples of the overlapping forms used by Rock and Guttman (1981). Within each pair, one form was colored red. Reprinted with permission.

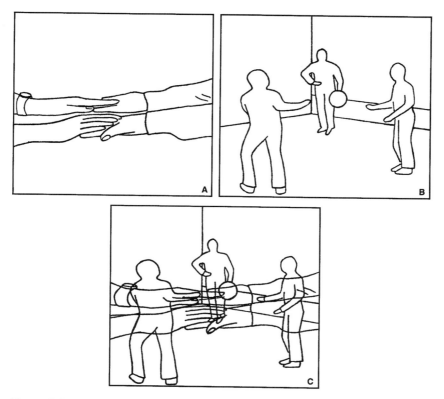

Figure 2.3
Outline tracings of typical video images of (a) a hand game alone, (b) a ballgame alone, and (c) hand game and ballgame superimposed. Reprinted from Neisser and Becklen (1975, figure 1) with permission.

both scenes. The results mirrored Cherry's findings with dichotic messages very closely.

Other findings mirrored Cherry's results as well. Just as Cherry tried changing the sounds played in the excluded ear, Neisser and Becklen placed various peculiar events in the videos (e.g., disappearance of the ball, substitutions of players). Only rarely did the observers who were monitoring the other video channel notice and report any of these events.

Indirect Measures of Identification We saw earlier that investigators have used a variety of indirect measures to assess the extent to which rejected auditory stimuli are perceptually analyzed, such as switching ears in shadowing and conditioned GSR changes. Even more diverse measures were employed to provide indirect evidence of processing of unattended visual stimuli. Most studies involved filtering tasks in which location was the selection criterion. Subjects made a deliberate response to a target stimulus at a fixed position. Excluded stimuli were presented at the same time or nearly so, usually in adjacent positions, but sometimes overlapping, as in Rock and Guttman's study. The critical evidence for processing of rejected stimuli consists of some sort of change in the speed or accuracy of responses to the target as a function of the relationship between the rejected stimulus and the target.

The best-known demonstration of this type is the *Stroop effect* and the large family of (apparently) related effects (Stroop, 1935; MacLeod, 1991). In the classic Stroop effect, the subject reads aloud the color of the ink in which a word is printed. When the word spells out the name of an incompatible color (e.g., GREEN printed in red ink), one is substantially slower to respond "red" than in a neutral condition (e.g., CHAIR printed in red ink). The difficulty caused by incompatibility is so large that it is quite noticeable when one reads through a long list of incompatible color/word stimuli. With long lists, overt errors as well as hesitations tend to occur. Most recent Stroop studies, however, have used individual computer-controlled trials, with a mixture of matching and mismatching color/word stimuli in different trials. Under these conditions, subjects can usually maintain high accuracy levels, and the effect of mismatches shows up as a slowing of response times on incompatible trials. A wide variety of effects at least somewhat analogous to the Stroop effect have been reported in the literature over the years. For example, if people report the number of characters on the screen, they are slower when these characters are numerals incompatible with the correct response, such as a display of four 3s (Flowers, Warner, and Polansky, 1979). Another Stroop-like task calls for the subject to say aloud the direction in which an arrow points; a left-pointing arrow is responded to more slowly when the word RIGHT is embedded in it, rather than the word LEFT (Shor, 1971).

The classic Stroop effect produces a substantial slowing on incompatible trials compared with neutral trials, often well over 100 msec difference. A speed-up in compatible trials is sometimes observed, although it is usually more modest. The slowing of RTs due to color/word mismatch can also be induced by a color word that is separated from the target color patch, although as Kahneman and Henik (1981) noted, the Stroop effect is larger in the standard case in which the word and the color belong to the same object. Gatti and Egeth (1978) presented a color word at eccentricities of 1 to 5 degrees from a central patch; the subjects named the color of the patch. Increases in spatial separation reduced the size of the Stroop effect, but even at 5 degrees, considerable interference remained (35 msec).

The classic Stroop effect certainly demonstrates that one cannot simply and completely turn off one's word-recognition machinery. Gatti and Egeth's results show that one cannot even completely prevent a word in a position known to be irrelevant from being read. As will emerge below, more ambitious inferences drawn from the effect are more problematic.

Analogous to the Stroop effect, but less colorful, are the so-called *flanker effects* observed in choice reaction-time tasks. Eriksen and Hoffman (1973) had subjects make a speeded response to a central letter, pressing the left key for an A or a U and the right key for an H or an M, for example. Next to this letter were other letters that the subject attempted to ignore. When these flankers were associated with the opposite response from the correct one on that trial (e.g., an H surrounding a target A), RTs to the target letter (here, A) were slowed, compared with the case when the distractors were associated with the correct response. Flanker effects are generally smaller than Stroop effects, which is not surprising given the effect of spatial separation noted by Gatti and Egeth. The size of the effect is reduced when the flankers are presented more than 1 degree from the central items, but this may be due to reduced acuity rather than complete selectivity at the greater distances (Egeth, 1977). Closely analogous flanker effects have also observed in tasks involving words. Shaffer and LaBerge (1979) presented two identical words above and below a central target word. The subject's response depended on the semantic category of the central word. When the flanking words were drawn from a different category than the target, RTs were slowed by about 40 msec.

Another indirect measure of perceptual processing which has been explored in many studies is *semantic priming*. Word recognition occurs more quickly when someone has just read a semantically associated word. Priming is commonly observed by presenting a *prime* word to which no response is made, followed by a target letter string to which subjects make a speeded *lexical decision,* indicating whether the letter string is a word or a nonword. The response to a target word is faster when the prime is semantically related to it (e.g., doctor-NURSE) rather than unrelated (e.g., chair-NURSE).

As with flanker and Stroop effects, semantic priming has sometimes been found when the prime is presented at the same time as a target word to which the subject responds. In one study of this kind, Dallas and Merikle (1976) had subjects name the word in a precued position, ignoring another word above or below it. Subjects were faster by about 20 msec when the two words were related rather than unrelated. It has been suggested that this sort of priming reflects automatic (unselective) processing of the prime word. If the primes are helpful to performance, however, one cannot assume that subjects really have an incentive to ignore them. In that case, such observations cannot test the idea of unselective processing as this concept was defined above. Other observations sometimes taken to support automatic perceptual analysis involve priming effects that occur when the target is not related to the prime in most trials. Since these primes convey no information about targets, some maintain, any processing of them must be obligatory rather than intentional or strategic (Neely, 1977; Posner and Snyder, 1975b; Tweedy and Lapinski, 1981). This argument is not compelling, either. In many of these priming experiments the prime is the only word present on the screen in a position that will be relevant to the subject's task; this would hardly seem to be an optimal condition for exclusion. In addition, the effects observed from primes that do not convey information is often restricted to beneficial effects on performance in related trials, with no decrement in unrelated trials. This means that observers have no obvious incentive to try to ignore them. These various priming results provide little or no basis for concluding that word identification is unselective. Stronger evidence would have to come from the Stroop and flanker effects when the task explicitly demands filtering.

Indirect Measures: A Closer Look   The diverse effects described in the preceding section seem to suggest that when people try to ignore familiar visual stimuli, these stimuli are nonetheless sometimes processed to the point of recognition. Such effects are often cited as evidence for unselective perception. That is, they occur because all stimuli undergo full processing to the point of recognition regardless of the observer's desires and regardless of what other stimuli are being identified at the same time.

As seen above, when indirect effects of rejected auditory stimuli were closely scrutinized, the evidence they provided for wholly unselective processing became less convincing. The same is true for effects of rejected visual stimuli. Consider first the obvious possibility that all such effects might simply reflect occasional lapses in selection, rather than completely unselective processing occurring whenever extraneous stimuli are presented. This possibility was raised in connection with several auditory findings, and it can be raised here as well. How can one be sure that flanker and Stroop effects, for example, reflect analysis of rejected stimuli that occurs in every trial or even in most trials? Oddly, this question has only rarely been tackled despite the large literature that deals with processing of rejected stimuli.

Eriksen, Eriksen, and Hoffman (1986) presented some relevant data. Their subjects performed a Sternberg memory-scanning task, deciding whether a centrally presented probe letter belonged to a memory set that was presented earlier. This probe item was flanked by other letters that sometimes did, and sometimes did not, belong to the memory set. Substantial flanker effects were observed (the exact nature of the effects is not presently relevant). Eriksen et al examined not just the mean RTs, but also the distribution of individual RTs in the compatible and incompatible conditions. Suppose that incompatible flankers produced a constant slowing of, say, 30 msec in every trial in that condition. In that case, one would expect that the cumulative distribution function for incompatible trials would be just like the distribution for compatible trials, but shifted to the right by 30 msec. By contrast, if the effect stemmed from, say, a 300-msec slowing that occurred only in one-tenth of the trials, the effect on mean RTs would be the same, but one would expect a different pattern in the RT distributions. The incompatible condition would include more very slow responses, and these would replace trials over most of the range of the compatible trials' distribution. Thus, the compatible and incompatible trials would differ little among the fastest RTs, and would diverge progressively more at the slower RTs. The data of Eriksen, Eriksen, and Hoffman appeared to fit the first prediction, not the second, suggesting that the incompatible flankers produce modest, reliable slowing, rather than large, occasional slowing. Nevertheless, further analyses are in order,[4] and the generality of the conclusion has to be verified. As the literature stands, many discussions of processing of rejected stimuli simply assume that effects of unattended stimuli reflect events occurring in every trial rather than just occasionally, but this has not been adequately demonstrated.

A second fact that weakens the interpretation of the indirect effects is that rejected stimuli almost invariably come from the same set as the relevant stimuli or at least from a set related to those stimuli. Therefore, it is quite reasonable to suspect that the subject may be primed for these stimuli, as suggested by Treisman. According to Treisman's proposal, unprimed stimuli would not produce the same effects, and thus the indirect effects simply do not reflect true stimulus identification. Some evidence on this point was reported by J. O. Miller (1987). His subjects made a speeded classification judgment to a central character that was flanked by other characters. Rather than employing flankers that belonged to the relevant set, as in the flanker experiments discussed earlier, Miller used letters that were not assigned to any response in the instructions given to the subjects. However, certain flanker letters were more often presented when one particular response was appropriate rather than another. This correlation meant that the response could be reasonably well, but not perfectly, predicted by knowing the identity of the flankers. Miller found that the speed of responses to the target was affected by the flankers, with faster responses occurring when the response was more likely given the flankers, and slower responses occurring with the less likely flanker-response combinations. Remarkably, subjects appeared to have little awareness of the correlation, although such assessments of awareness are notoriously treacherous (see, e.g., Brewer, 1974).

Miller stated that his results demonstrated semantic processing of unattended stimuli that were not "primed by task relevance" (p. 419). This conclusion may be questioned, however. The very fact that the flankers are correlated with the response means that subjects have no obvious incentive to ignore them. After all, they do convey information about what the correct response would be, albeit not as much as the central target. Thus, it might well be adaptive for subjects to base their response partly on whatever information they might have about the identity of the flankers, as well as information about the target itself, especially if the former happens to become available sooner than the latter in a given trial. This criticism was raised earlier regarding the idea that primes that convey no information about targets could only have effects because they are automatically processed. The general problem is this: to the degree one finds effects of processing distractor items that are mostly beneficial to performance, one cannot assume subjects are trying to exclude them. Of course, effects of correlated stimuli may have interesting implications for skill learning and other psychological issues.

Other evidence relevant to the selectivity of perception comes from several recent studies. Broadbent and Gathercole (1990) investigated the word-flanker effect first documented by Shaffer and LaBerge (1979). They successfully replicated the finding that nearby words produced flanker effects. However, when entirely novel words were used on each trial, the effects were eliminated. Lambert, Beard, and Thompson (1988) reached similar conclusions, although they were not able to eliminate the effect entirely when the two words were side by side. Broadbent and Gathercole suggested that once subjects had experienced a particular word, they may be able to identify it based on only partial cues, rather than full-blown word recognition. In line with this hypothesis (related to Treisman's idea of priming), it is interesting that the Stroop effect can be produced when only a few letters of an irrelevant color word are presented, such as OR or XXANGE[5] (Singer, Lappin, and Moore, 1975). These studies certainly weaken the argument for unselective processing based on indirect effects of rejected visual stimuli.

Further evidence along the same lines comes from experiments showing that these effects can be modulated either by adding additional stimuli or by changing task demands. Suppose the indirect measures of processing discussed here reflect wholly unselective and capacity-unlimited analysis undergone by *all* stimuli, limited only by acuity and other nonattentional factors. In that case, their magnitude should not be affected when the perceptual demands involved in the subject's voluntary task are altered; nor should they be changed when the number of unattended items present in the display is charged.

A number of careful studies carried out in the 1980s tested these predictions, and the results paint a fairly consistent picture. Kahneman and Chajczyk (1983) had subjects name the color of a patch of ink in the center of the screen. Above or below this patch were other stimuli. When a single incompatible color name was presented (e.g., RED above a green patch), the expected Stroop slowing was observed. In another condition, two words were presented, one above and one below the patch. Consider the case where one was the incompatible color name and the other was a completely irrelevant word (MOST). According to the unselective identification account, one would expect the Stroop effect to be unchanged, since the color name is identified regardless of the presence of the irrelevant word. However, the addition of the irrelevant word reduced the color/word incompatibility effect from 72 to 36 msec. In short, merely adding to the number of *unattended* channels reduced the impact of the contents of one of those channels.

Investigations of the letter-flanker effect yielded similar findings. Yantis and Johnston (1990) had their subjects decide whether a particular target letter (which varied from trial to trial) was present in a circular display of eight letters. The subjects only had to check one location, indicated by a spatial precue, because the target was always present in that location (if it was anywhere). Thus, each display contained seven rejected letters. Was each of these seven letters identified despite being rejected, as flankers apparently were in Eriksen and Hoffman's task? If so, when one of these seven letters was a copy of the target, one might expect to find a speed-up of the positive responses. A series of experiments with excellent statistical power showed, however, that redundant targets in noncued positions either had no effect or almost no effect (< 10 msec). There was no hint that the identity of distractors beyond those that immediately flanked the target made any difference whatever, despite the fact that with the circular arrays, acuity was constant for the different positions in the display. When positions were not cued, the redundant targets produced the expected speed-up. These results again show that the evidence for supposedly unselective processing can be made to virtually disappear when the number of rejected stimuli is increased and conditions for selection are optimized.

It should not be assumed, however, that the flanker effect is so fragile that it will disappear with any minor variation in the task. J. O. Miller (1991) tried five manipulations that he thought might have a chance of making the flanker effect disappear. He used flankers that did not have abrupt (possibly attention-grabbing) onsets, or he presented sequential displays to let the subject lock onto the center position, or he increased the number of *relevant* stimuli. None of these variables eliminated the effect. However, Miller did not examine the effect of increasing the load of *rejected* stimuli (as did Yantis and Johnston). Furthermore, some of the manipulations he examined did seem to reduce the flanker effect, so it is possible that if all of them had been used together, the effect would indeed have been eliminated.

Further evidence against the unselective processing hypothesis comes from recent investigations of semantic priming. W. A. Johnston and Dark (1985) presented four words for 67, 200, or 500 msec. Subjects attempted to report only the words in two prespecified positions among the four. Recognition memory for the words in the irrelevant locations, assessed at the end of the session, was essentially nil, in line with conclusions described earlier. In certain trials, however, an indirect measure of semantic processing was employed: the sequence of brief word presentations was interrupted for a probe test in which the subject tried to report a test word that slowly emerged from visual noise. When the test words were identical or related to the words that were present in the relevant positions in the report task, they were more easily identified (a form of priming). However, there was no priming for words that were presented in irrelevant locations in the report task (except for some marginally significant priming when the exposure durations were 500 msec—clearly so long that some relaxation of selectivity could well be expected).

Similarly, Hoffman and MacMillan (1985) presented a prime word very briefly, surrounded by several letters, and the subject had to search among these letters for a digit. Immediately thereafter, a target string for lexical decision was presented. The letter-search task virtually abolished the priming effect. Priming occurred, however, when the subject was instructed to ignore the letters and silently read the prime.

Thus, when only one or two letters are present in a display and subjects respond only to the one at a prespecified location, there is little doubt that the nontarget item(s) are processed at least to some degree, probably in most trials. Whether they would still be processed if (a) they were unrelated to the material the subject was attempting to process, and (b) the subject had no incentive to process them, seems to be an open question. However, the hypothesis of completely unselective processing fails when the number of rejected items is increased (in flanker and Stroop tasks), or the extent of concurrent visual processing is increased in studies involving words (in priming situations).

What conclusions can be drawn? There is good reason to doubt the claim that rejected visual stimuli are subject to full analysis. The measures used to support the hypothesis do not behave as one would expect once subjected to closer examination. Logically speaking, one could still contend that rejected stimuli *are* completely analyzed in every trial, but these measures just happen not to reveal it. It is indeed perfectly possible that such analysis occurs, but it is behaviorally silent. Although this view cannot be refuted, it deprives the unselective perception hypothesis of the support that was used previously to argue in its favor. In any case, the attractiveness of this dodge will be reduced further when we turn to the results of divided attention studies in chapter 3.

Do the data help in evaluating Treisman's (1960) suggestion that rejected stimuli are, in some not clearly defined sense, attenuated, and that once this attenuation has occurred, the only stimuli to be recognized are those that are primed in one way or another? Certainly, this hypothesis is broadly consistent with a number of facts reviewed above, especially those from more rigorous studies of recent years. However, the hypothesis cannot be said to have been decisively confirmed, either. The very nature of the indirect measures used in these studies makes the question difficult to answer conclusively. Ideally, one would like to know whether the brain has resolved the identities of stimuli that are unrelated to the task at hand. However, the indirect measures (e.g., Stroop, priming) consist of average differences between responses to related and unrelated stimuli—these provide no evidence about whether different possible unrelated stimuli were distinguished.

Negative Priming   Dalrymple-Alford and Budayr (1966) made an interesting observation about the color-naming task commonly used to elicit the Stroop effect. When a subject responds to the color of the ink in which a word is printed (say, red), the response is slowed if the word is, for example, GREEN (the basic Stroop effect). Dalrymple-Alford and Budayr found that when, in a given trial, the ink color is the same as the distractor on the previous trial, subjects are slower to respond "green" compared with an appropriate control. This effect—slower responses to a stimulus on trial n that was rejected in trial n-1—is termed *negative priming,* to distinguish it from the more common facilitatory priming effects.

Since that time, other examples of negative priming have been reported. Tipper and Driver (1988) showed subjects overlapping red and green figures, to which the subjects responded by identifying the red figures and ignoring the green ones. When the rejected (green) distractor in trial n was identical to the (red) target in trial n-1, responses in trial n were slowed. It was harder to select what had previously been rejected. Tipper and Driver also found the same inhibitory effect for responses to items that were semantically related, rather than identical, to the previous distractor, and the inhibition occurred even when a verbal response in trial n+1 followed a manual response in trial n (Tipper, MacQueen, and Brehaut, 1989).

Various researchers (e.g., Tipper and Driver, 1988; Allport, 1989) suggested the following view of negative priming. In each trial, perception is wholly unselective, with all elements semantically analyzed. The selection process in trial n works by inhibiting those activated codes that are associated with the distractor item. This inhibition persists until trial n+1, at which time it results in increased RTs when the inhibited code must now control the response. This theory, therefore, represents a novel variant of late selection theory.

No evidence conclusively rejects this account, but there are some reasons to doubt it. First, note that this hypothesis postulates identity-specific suppression of distractors that are excluded because of their position in the display or some other selection criterion such as color. The system could not know in advance which identities would have to be suppressed. To determine that, it is necessary to look up which items were present in each of the irrelevant positions. It is rather odd to suppose that the identities represented in each of the *irrelevant* locations are first sought out and then suppressed, when it would seem so much simpler to look up the identity of the single *relevant* item and use that for choosing a response. This was put forth in more conventional late selection theories, such as the one proposed by Duncan (1980b, 1981). The oddity of this inhibitory scenario becomes even greater when one considers a situation with one target in a prespecified location surrounded by twenty different distractors. It seems slightly bizarre to suppose that identity codes for all twenty distractors have to be activated, found, and squelched before the appropriate response can be made. If this were true, then the number of distractors should produce a sharp increase in RTs to respond to the target even when the position of the target is known in advance, which does not happen (e.g., Colegate, Hoffman, and Eriksen, 1973).

Of course, such arguments can never be decisive, partly because they rely on an argument from lack of imagination; the mere fact one finds it hard to think why something might happen does not disprove it. Better evidence against the unselective-perception interpretation of negative priming comes from more recent findings. Ruthruff and Miller (1995) observed that when uncertainty about the location of both targets and distractors was eliminated, negative priming disappeared. Furthermore, negative priming is consistent with other scenarios quite apart from the unselective-processing account described above. Whereas negative priming in trial n+1 does indicate that the distractor in trial n was identified before the response in trial n+1, it does not indicate that this happened before the response was made in trial n. Thus, negative priming cannot conclusively say how selection in trial n did or did not occur. Even a completely successful filtering operation as envisioned by Broadbent would be consistent with the data. Indeed, in his original formulation of filter theory, Broadbent (1958) remarked, "We considered . . . listening . . . as though a message which was rejected at the time of its arrival could never pass through the filter later. . . . This over-simplification was for expository purposes only" (p. 210).

Consider, then, the possibility that the distractor is analyzed some time *after* selection or even after response in trial n, perhaps during the intertrial interval. Why would inhibition be observed later in that case? Since the codes (partially) activated by the distractor proved to be unhelpful in trial n, they are likely to be unhelpful in the future. Thus, inhibition may result from a learning process that works to improve subsequent performance, perhaps using some sort of error-correction learning procedure (Hinton, 1989). In this account, negative priming would reflect not the process of selection that allowed the subject to perform correctly in trial n, but rather a tuning process working to improve performance on the present and subsequent trials.

Various findings make this concept plausible. For one thing, Tipper Weaver, Cameron, Brehaut, and Bastedo (1991) found that negative priming was undiminished after a delay of about 7 seconds, which is inconsistent with the possibility that it reflects a highly transient inhibitory state. Second, Tipper and Cranston (1985) observed that negative priming was eliminated when the target item, formerly a distractor in trial n, was presented without any accompanying distractor in trial n+1. The same result was reported with the Stroop version of the effect (D. G. Lowe, 1979). This is extremely difficult to reconcile with any account involving an inhibitory *attentional* mechanism. Context specificity may be more consistent with a learning account of the sort sketched above, although it can hardly be said to be predicted by that account.

In summary, negative priming effects have been cited as bolstering the hypothesis of unselective perception by providing evidence of processing of rejected stimuli even when the more conventional effects fail to do so (Driver and Tipper, 1989). However, the effects do not indicate *when* the distractors were identified, and it would not be surprising on any account (including Broadbent's original one) if, after selecting a response, distractors were sometimes processed more extensively. The source of the inhibition that shows up in the next trial is still an open question; the suggestions raised regarding learning are merely conjectures. One useful strategy for exploring negative priming further would be to see what happens when many distractors in trial n are present. If this eliminates negative priming, as Yantis and Johnston found with flanker effects, and as the results of Neumann and Deschepper (1992) with modest-size displays suggest may well occur, negative priming will no longer constitute any real support for unselective perception. If the effect remains, negative priming might challenge some of the conclusions reached above.

Physiological Measures   Thus far we have considered exclusively behavioral evidence about selective attention. At present, behavioral data provide the most direct evidence regarding attentional selection, but some intriguing physiological observations have emerged in the past several decades. Some of them involve humans and some involve monkeys.

A large fraction of the primate brain contains cells that respond to visual stimuli of some sort or another. In recent years, it has become common to divide the visual pathways in the primate cortex into two broad processing streams: the *dorsal* and *ventral pathways*. The dorsal pathway leads from the primary visual cortex in the occipital lobes into the parietal lobes. The areas along this pathway appear to be specialized for analysis of the location and trajectories of objects (Mishkin, Ungerleider, and Macko, 1983) and perhaps more specifically for the generation of plans actually to interact with these objects (Goodale and Milner, 1992). By contrast, recognition of objects of all sorts (including faces) seems to depend primarily on cortical areas lying along the ventral pathway, extending from the primary visual cortex called through extrastriate visual areas (e.g., V4 in the macaque) to the inferior temporal (IT) cortex. Lesions along this pathway produce impairment in recognition of object identities, colors, and other attributes, and often impair the apprehension of objects' shapes (Farah, 1990). Figure 2.4 shows a simplified outline of the anatomical layout of some of the structures lying along these two pathways.

Recent work has produced more fine-grained and bewilderingly complex maps of these areas (Van Essen, Anderson, and Felleman, 1992). As one moves along the ventral pathway, one encounters neurons with progressively larger receptive fields (the area in the visual field in which stimulation can affect the cell's firing rate). At the same time, the neurons tend to become more specific about the form of stimulation necessary to produce a response. For example, neurons in the primary visual cortex often respond well to oriented bars in narrow regions of the retina (Hubel and Wiesel, 1962), whereas those in IT and surrounding areas seem to respond selectively to complex stimulus configurations such as faces or facial expressions, with little regard to location in the visual field (Gross, 1971).

Moran and Desimone (1985) recorded from single neurons along the ventral pathway in alert macaque monkeys that were trained to perform

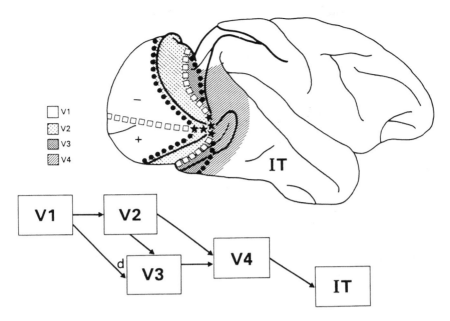

Figure 2.4
Overview of so-called ventral visual pathway from the striate cortex (V1) into
the inferior temporal lobe (IT). This pathway, which appears responsible for
object recognition, includes several extrastriate visual areas (V2–V4). Reprinted
from Desimone et al. (1985, figure 1), with permission.

tasks requiring spatial selection. The experiments used a *delayed match-
ing-to-sample task,* in which a *sample stimulus* was presented briefly, and
then after an interval, either the same or a different *test stimulus* was
presented in the same spot. The monkey was rewarded when it responded
quickly to just those test stimuli that matched the preceding sample
stimuli. In some trials, irrelevant stimuli were presented in different
locations together with the test stimuli, and the monkeys' behavioral
responses showed they were largely successful in ignoring these irrelevant
stimuli, basing their response on the test stimulus alone.

Moran and Desimone asked whether the responses of neurons in
different visual areas to a particular stimulus would differ depending on
whether or not the monkey was attending to that stimulus. In the primary
visual cortex, the responses did not differ. In V4, on the other hand,

responses to irrelevant stimuli were reduced by about two-thirds. Unexpectedly, Moran and Desimone also observed that this attenuation only occurred when an attended stimulus was located within the receptive field of the neuron. That is, a neuron that would ordinarily respond to a particular red bar would continue to respond when that bar was presented, but the monkey was attending to a different bar located *outside* the receptive field. In IT cortex, attenuation was always observed. Here the receptive fields were large enough that they included all stimuli, attended and unattended. Thus, the same generalization may apply to neurons in IT and V4, namely, that the response of a neuron is attenuated only when attention is directed elsewhere within the receptive field of that neuron (see Desimone and Duncan, 1995, for a review).

Corresponding experiments in auditory selection also showed a reduction in neural responses to unattended stimuli seemingly earlier in the processing stream. Benson and Hienz (1978) trained monkeys to respond to either the left ear or the right ear, depending on a visual signal, and ignore stimuli presented in the other ear. The firing rate of cells in the auditory cortex was recorded while tones and bursts of clicks or noise were played to both ears. Approximately two-thirds of the cells responded more strongly to stimuli in the attended ear. However, these attenuation effects appeared to be somewhat weaker than those observed by Moran and Desimone in extrastriate visual areas.

It is tempting to assume that the reduction in firing rate reflects attenuation of processing in something like the sense suggested by Treisman (1960). This interpretation is plausible but may not be right, because the functional significance of individual neurons' firing rate remains unclear. It has been proposed, for example, that the overall firing rate may not be as significant as the pattern of responses across many neurons (e.g., Richmond et al, 1987) or the temporal cross-correlations among individual action potentials (Gray et al, 1992). Reductions in overall firing rate do not necessarily indicate that signals are being blocked from passing beyond an early level. Visual areas in the ventral stream are highly interconnected, with large numbers of fibers running both forward toward the temporal lobes and backward toward the retina. Reduction in firing rate might therefore reflect joint activity in these forward and backward pathways, with higher as well as lower areas responding to the stimulus. Putting possible complications of this sort aside, the findings of Moran and Desimone and of Benson and Hienz are certainly congenial to the idea of attenuation. In fact, they might even be consistent with the strong conception of filtering envisioned by Broadbent. After all, the monkeys who show partial attenuation of neural responses are not achieving the high degree of behavioral selectivity that is typical in human observers, as shown by their error rates. (This may reflect inherent limits of monkeys compared with humans, or limits on what people can train monkeys to do in the laboratory.)

Another, more plentiful kind of physiological evidence about selective attention comes from studies recording electrical potentials from the scalps of people performing attentional tasks. The continuing electrical potential recorded from the scalp is referred to as the electroencephalo-gram (EEG). When a stimulus is presented and a person performs some sort of task involving this stimulus, the EEG record reflects both neural events involved in executing the task and those unrelated to the activity. In a raw EEG record, this noise generally overshadows signals from stimulus-related events. Fortunately, the noise can be reduced by taking EEG records from many trials and averaging them together, time-locked to the stimulus. That is, the potentials observed 1 msec after the stimulus in each trial are averaged across trials, then potentials at 2 msec are averaged, and so on. Signals unrelated to the stimulus have no particular temporal relationship to it, so this averaging process makes them cancel each other out, assuming, of course, that they combined linearly with the task-relevant signals in the first place.

This averaging procedure is the most common way of uncovering *event-related potentials* (ERPs). The ERP waveforms generally show several positive and negative voltage peaks after the presentation of a stimulus. These peaks are termed *ERP components,* and are believed to reflect synchronized postsynaptic activity in relatively large populations of neurons. Although there is no guarantee that neural activity critical for any particular information processing operation must be detectable in the ERP, these components nonetheless provide an intriguing source of clues about neural-mental operations.

Many studies have compared ERPs elicited by attended and unattended stimuli. They differ from most of the behavioral experiments described above in that the attended or unattended stimulus is usually, although not always, presented alone. This makes it easier to tell what stimulus elicited a given ERP component. In behavioral studies, on the other hand, both attended and unattended stimuli are usually presented at the same time, which is necessary when effects of unattended stimuli take the form of a modulation in the behavioral response to an attended stimulus.

The most basic finding of attention studies using ERP measures is that components arising very early after the presentation of a stimulus (within the first several hundred milliseconds) often differ as a function of whether the stimulus is attended or unattended (see Hillyard and Picton, 1987, and Naatanen, 1992, for reviews). In the auditory modality, the divergence between waveforms elicited by attended and unattended stimuli generally begins approximately 60 to 80 msec after presentation, and in some cases earlier divergence has been observed (Hillyard and Picton, 1987). The divergence is commonly known as the Nd, or negative-difference component (Hillyard et al., 1973). The time at which the Nd begins seems to depend on the difficulty of the discrimination required for selection and not response (Hansen and Hillyard, 1980): the harder the discrimination, the later the divergence.

It was initially proposed (Hillyard et al, 1973) that the Nd component simply represented a dampening of the exogenous N1 (first negative) components produced by unattended auditory stimuli (exogenous refers to components little affected by psychological state[6]). This would be consistent with the view that the Nd reflects reduced sensory and perceptual analysis of unattended stimuli or enhanced processing of attended stimuli. The fact the Nd begins earlier when the selection is easier fits with this interpretation. However, some investigators believe it may largely reflect an independent endogenous (psychologically influenced) component superimposed on the N1 (Teder et al., 1993; Woods, 1990). In this interpretation, when a stimulus is attended, the selection itself produces negativity, which is then added into the ERP waveform. If this is correct, the Nd effect might not reflect any change whatever in the perceptual analysis of unattended stimuli. Recent neuromagnetic studies that provide more detailed anatomical information suggest a measure of truth in both views, in that the Nd probably reflects both an endogenous selection-related effect and a reduction in exogenous responses beginning as early as 20 msec after the stimulus (Woldorff and Hillyard, 1991).

Effects of spatial selection on visual evoked responses have also been observed. Visual stimuli typically elicit two early components nicknamed P1 and N1, the first positive and negative components, generally occurring between about 100 and 200 msec after the stimulus. These effects are considered fairly exogenous, that is, they occur even when the subject passively watches stimuli flash by on the screen. Both the P1 and the N1 are smaller when a stimulus is ignored based on its location. Unlike the case of auditory attention, there seems to be little doubt that these changes reflect modulations in the magnitude of underlying exogenous components as a function of spatial attention, rather than selection-related components superimposed on the underlying exogenous ERP components.

A different and quite intriguing pattern of results is found with tasks requiring selection of visual stimuli based on color. Consider what happens when a subject is instructed to note only red bars and ignore green ones (responding on the basis of the length of the red bars). A red bar does not produce a bigger N1 or P1 than a green bar produces. Rather, as with auditory spatial selection, one sees an additional negativity superimposed on top of N1 and P1 for the color-relevant stimuli. Most remarkably, this color-selection component is greatly diminished when the stimulus is in an irrelevant spatial location (Hillyard and Münte, 1984). Thus, the ERP signatures of location and color selection are distinct and have a hierarchical arrangement, with location selection dominating color selection.

A rather appealing functional interpretation of these results would be as follows. The magnitude of N1 and P1 might reflect the degree of sensory and perceptual analysis (the more analysis, the bigger the component). Stimuli in unattended locations are not analyzed very deeply, because they are subject to early gating, hence, smaller N1 and P1; in fact, not even their color is analyzed. When stimuli are in the attended location, their color is analyzed, and if they are determined to be of the relevant color, a different selection process then takes place, indexed by the color-selection negativity.

This scheme fits the data quite well, but one should exercise some caution in accepting it. For one thing, the P1 and N1 components might not reflect perceptual analysis, but rather a selection process that fetches information from the perceptual machinery. The fact that the changes involve modulation of the magnitude of relatively exogenous components, which arise even during passive viewing, does not rule this out; even in passive viewing, a fetching process might occur. Other alternatives might also fit the data. For example, the N1 and P1 components could reflect collateral signals sent out by visual areas signaling other brain areas to get ready to receive information, or they might have "house-keeping" functions, readying the visual areas themselves to receive and process further sensory stimulation.

These alternatives demonstrate something that is rather obvious but easily overlooked: inferences about perceptual gating rely on a set of assumptions about the functional meaning of the components and their magnitudes. Reductions in N1 and P1 imply perceptual gating only if the magnitude of the components can be assumed to indicate the extent of processing. The fact that the underlying generators of the components can be localized to extrastriate visual areas where perceptual analysis is likely to be taking place (e.g., Mangun, Hillyard, and Luck, 1993) provides some evidence for this assumption; it is, however, equally consistent with several of the alternatives mentioned above. This basic problem applies equally to both auditory and visual ERP results, of course. This important caveat notwithstanding, the various ERP results are certainly congenial to the idea of early perceptual filtering, and can reasonably be described as converging evidence for it. If it were possible to test the usual assumptions about what the magnitude of an ERP component signifies, these results might provide compelling rather than congenial support.

In summary, both invasive and noninvasive neural measures suggest that rejected stimuli may undergo less extensive sensory/perceptual processing than attended stimuli, although the interpretation of physiological measures is in some ways an open question. This obviously implies no criticism of the investigators who carried out these technically difficult studies. It seems likely that physiological measures will provide increasingly important constraints on attention theories. Before this can happen, however, new evidence is required to clarify the relationship between information processing operations and the various physiological measures. Although physiological indexes do not yet provide unambiguous information about perceptual analysis of unattended stimuli, there is little doubt that further developments combining psychological and physiological measures and manipulations should provide stronger tests than either approach alone. Promising developments are emerging along these lines, such as studies combining psychophysical and single-unit recording observations in monkeys (e.g., Salzman et al., 1992).

Consequences for Early Visual Processes
The studies discussed thus far mostly focused on the process of identifying familiar objects. The visual system provides us with a great deal of information about our environment besides which familiar objects are present. Even in an abstract sculpture garden we readily and effortlessly perceive much about the spatial layout and reflectance characteristics of visible surfaces, and can even work out the three-dimensional positions of objects that are partly occluding each other (Marr, 1982; Rock, 1983). The majority of the stimuli and tasks studied by attention researchers place few demands on these perceptual mechanisms because they use stimuli such as high-contrast letters and digits in a fixed type font. Such stimuli are ecologically valid in the sense that reading is an important human activity; on the other hand, findings regarding identification of such impoverished stimuli may or may not generalize to other more demanding perceptual tasks.

It is an interesting fact about our visual system that we can identify objects whose contours are signaled by any of a large number of different cues (see Cavanagh, 1987). One illustration of this is the random-dot stereogram (Julesz, 1971) in which a portion of a random dot pattern is shifted in the pattern shown to the left eye compared with the pattern shown to the right eye. This produces the percept of an elevated (or recessed) surface. If the surface is shaped like the block letter B, for example, one can read the B without difficulty.

To identify three-dimensional objects, one might suppose the visual system normally computes an internal description of three-dimensional shape, and then compares this description to descriptions of familiar objects that are stored in memory (Marr, 1982; Biederman and Ju, 1988). The visual system may be more flexible than this, however. For one thing, the ability to analyze three-dimensional shapes and the ability to identify familiar objects tend to be lost together in visual agnosia (Farah, 1990). Farah suggests that computing a description of a shape and recognizing that shape are completely intertwined in the cortex. (Of course, the mechanisms might be anatomically intertwined but still functionally separate or sequential.) Another sign that the sequential model may be wrong is the fact that recognition of even three-dimensional objects such as faces can be achieved with images that provide little or no information about three-dimensional layout (Witkin and Tenenbaum, 1983). Therefore, one should not assume that analysis of three-dimensional form is an obligatory intermediate stage en route to object recognition, as Marr suggested.

Despite these caveats, the fact remains that a great many visual mechanisms are devoted to analyzing three-dimensional shape, and these mechanisms can provide input to object recognition. It is reasonable to ask how they are affected by attention. The unselective perception hypothesis, interpreted most broadly, would claim that they process excluded stimuli to the same extent and in the same way they process attended stimuli.

Few investigators have examined this issue, and those who have done so generally used visual aftereffects as their primary measure (e.g., Shulman, 1990). Prolonged viewing of stimuli that excite particular detectors in the visual system changes perception of subsequently presented stimuli (see Barlow, 1980). The best-known example is the motion aftereffect, commonly called the waterfall illusion. When one looked at an adapting display of continuous motion such as a waterfall for 30 seconds or so, and then views a static display such as an adjacent hillside, stationary contours appear to drift in the opposite direction. This effect probably originates at least partly in cells or synapses in area MT, the cortical area specialized for motion perception (Wenderoth, Bray, and Johnstone, 1988). Similar aftereffects can be observed for other visual dimensions such as orientation and spatial frequency (Graham, 1989).

Several studies asked whether the simple motion aftereffect can be reduced when subjects ignore the adapting field and attend to something else; they produced conflicting results. An early report by Wohlgemuth (1911) found no reduction in adaptation. Chaudhuri (1990) had subjects view a drifting texture with a small aperture in the center containing a character that changed several times a second. In the passive condition, subjects simply looked at the whole display; in the attention-diverted condition, subjects monitored the characters looking for the occasional digit to which they made a keypress response. The aftereffect was assessed by having observers view a stationary test field. The duration of the aftereffect was substantially reduced in the attention-diverted condition. Lankheet and Verstraten (1995) reached similar conclusions using three observers (themselves and one other individual) viewing displays of two-component transparent motion. Given the subjective nature nature of these judgments and the conflict with Wohlgemuth's findings, effects of selective attention on the motion aftereffect require further confirmation with larger numbers of naive observers.

In a series of interesting studies Shulman assessed the attentional modulation of aftereffects involving perception of three-dimensional structure. After prolonged viewing of a cube with a three-dimensional structure that is unambiguous, an ambiguous Necker cube tends to be seen as having a perspective opposite that of the adapting figure. During the adaptation phase of Shulman's experiment, twelve subjects viewed two superimposed unambiguous figures differing in size and color. They attended to only one of the figures, reporting any changes in its color. In the test phase, subjects' perception of the Necker figure tended to show an adaptation effect induced by the attending adapting figure rather than the unattended adapting figure (Shulman, 1993). Shulman obtained very similar results for ambiguous rotations in depth (Shulman, 1991) and ambiguous staircase figures (Shulman, 1992).

On the other hand, ignoring the adapting stimulus does not seem to reduce another visual aftereffect called the McCollough effect. This is is an orientation-specific color aftereffect that can be produced by viewing two grating patterns in opposite colors and different orientations, such as a green patch of horizontal stripes and a red patch of vertical stripes. After several minutes of adaptation, an observer will tend to see colorless grating patches as having a tint opposite that of the adapting patch that was presented at the same orientation. Houck and Hoffman (1986) had subjects view displays of colored grating patches, focusing their attention on some of the patches and ignoring others. The size of the adaptation effect was the same whether the patch was attended or not. The McCollough effect may stem from adaptation of mechanisms early in the visual pathway, before the site where information from the two eyes is brought together. Therefore, it may not be surprising that this effect would be unaffected by attention, whereas those mentioned in the previous paragraphs would be affected.

The observation that attentional instructions can determine the magnitude of perceptual aftereffects reinforces the other evidence described in this chapter that questions the idea that excluded stimuli are perceptually analyzed to the same degree as attended stimuli. To get a fuller picture, similar comparisons must be performed with a wider variety of aftereffects, including tilt and size. Most of the studies described above involve motion perception, which probably depends on processes occurring in the dorsal stream of visual processing, rather than the ventral stream most critically involved in object recognition. It seems plausible, therefore, that attentional gating may reduce or suppress perceptual analysis carried out in both cortical visual streams.

Visual Selection and Eye Movements

It has long been noted that people can attend away from the point of fixation and shift their attention without moving their eyes. Research conducted in this century attests to people's ability to shift from attending to one stimulus to another without making an overt eye movement (e.g., the partial-report experiments of Sperling, 1960). However, this does not imply that eye movements and shifts of attention are unrelated. In fact, there are obvious reasons why one would expect some functional ties between them. The acuity in the center of the fovea is far greater than at the periphery, so when visual input from a particular location in a scene is of special importance, it generally makes sense to foveate this location and improve the quality of information one acquires.

People are barely aware of making eye movements at all, so it is not surprising that they are usually unaware that the movements come in several varieties. Researchers commonly distinguish among five or more oculomotor systems, each with supposedly characteristic forms of eliciting stimuli, different movement trajectories, and different underlying neural systems. The three best-known types are saccadic, smooth-pursuit, and vergence eye movements. Saccadic eye movements are rapid and abrupt. Smooth-pursuit movements allow the eye to track relatively slowly moving stimuli up to about 20 or 30 degrees per second. With vergence eye movements, the two eyes move in opposite directions to permit fixation on stimuli farther or nearer along the line of sight. Recently, however, some theorists have challenged this proliferation of systems, proposing a more fundamental demarcation between the fast saccadic system and the slower smooth eye movement system, and arguing that finer taxonomies reflect different ways in which these systems can be driven (Steinman, Kowler, and Collewijn, 1990).

Until recently, most experts wrote about eye movements as if they were completely devoid of psychological content or interest. For the most part, investigators analyzed the (sensory) input and (eye movement) output of particular eye movement systems quantitatively, trying to characterize *the* input-output transformation achieved by the system. The experimental situations were expressly designed to minimize the role of attentional factors, together with anticipation or other mental processes. However, recent work demonstrates that eye movement control has rich interconnections with selective attention. We begin with saccadic eye movements.

Saccadic Eye Movements   We can voluntarily shift from attending to one spot in the visual field to another without producing a saccadic (or other) eye movement. Saccadic eye movements are at least potentially voluntary in the sense that one can will the eyes to move to a chosen point in the visual field and the movement will take place. Selecting a target for a willed or unwilled eye movement involves specifying an individual location in the visual field, probably based on some preliminary information about the stimuli present at that location. It seems reasonable, therefore, that shifts of attention to the intended destination of an eye movement might be involved in or necessary for preparation of a saccadic eye movement. This will be termed the mandatory shift hypothesis: a shift in attention is mandatory before execution of a saccade.

The matter seems straightforward enough, but initial studies painted a rather confusing picture. Remington (1980) used a peripheral target to summon the eye movement, and inserted a visual probe (requiring a speeded detection response) in the same or opposite direction as the eye movement to measure the allocation of visual attention (see chapter 4 for a discussion of this method). He found faster responses to probes that were located in the same direction as the eye movement compared with probes in the opposite direction. Under these conditions, though, the peripheral target might have produced the attention shift, rather than the preparation of the eye movement. A better test, therefore, would allow the subject to prepare to make an eye movement in a prespecified direction and then probe in some way to see if attention was indeed shifted to the destination.

Around the same time, Klein (1980) carried out an experiment in which subjects made either an eye movement (the direction was fixed throughout a block of trials) or a speeded detection response to a peripheral target. In dual-task blocks, subjects did not know which task they would have to perform, although they did know where the eye movement would go, if one should be called for. Responses were no faster when the peripheral target occurred at the position in which the eye movement would have been directed, compared with when the target appeared in the opposite position. On the basis of this finding, Klein rejected the mandatory shift hypothesis. However, it is worth noting that the subject only had to make an eye movement if an asterisk appeared, and the asterisk could appear on either side of the screen. Essentially, then, the subject was asked to prepare a leftward eye movement, and also to monitor both left and right positions for an asterisk, which would indicate that the eye movement should be executed. By the mandatory shift hypothesis, these requirements are inherently problematic. Therefore, one might well expect that subjects would not prepare the eye movement until they were sure it would be necessary. Consistent with this interpretation, saccadic latencies were unusually long for prepared eye movements.

More recent studies avoided these problems and yielded strong and direct support for the mandatory shift hypothesis. Shepherd, Findlay, and Hockey (1986) presented a central arrow cue indicating whether the subject should move the eyes leftward or rightward. After a delay (stimulus-onset asynchronies 70–550 msec), a square was illuminated either to the left or right of center, and the subject made a speeded button-push response on detecting this square. In some blocks of trials the square was usually to be found in the direction indicated by the arrow cue, placing it at the destination for the eye movement. In other blocks the arrow provided no information about where the square was likely to be, and in still others the square was usually located in the opposite direction from the one to which the arrow pointed. Detection responses were fastest when the square was in the location where the eye movement would go (the direction in which the arrow pointed). This was true even in blocks where the most probable position for the square was opposite the direction in which the arrow pointed. In control conditions where the arrow cue was present but no eye movements were required, detection responses were fastest on whichever side was most likely given the arrow. Thus, subjects were perfectly capable of using the arrow cue to shift attention either toward or away from where it pointed, but not when making an eye movement in the direction it pointed.

The findings of Shepherd et al certainly indicate that subjects cannot simultaneously move their eyes in the direction indicated by an arrow and (fully) shift their attention in the opposite direction, even when it would be to their advantage to do so. Furthermore, the fact that attention shifts toward the eye movement destination appear when the arrow says nothing about the likely position of the probe, is quite consistent with the mandatory shift hypothesis.

It would obviously strengthen the case if preparing an eye movement entailed an attention shift when the subject was not presented with such complicated demands. The probe-RT dependent measure used in these studies also raises problems of interpretation (see chapter 4). It would seem that an optimal and straightforward test of mandatory shift would combine rapid fixed-direction eye movements with an attentional measure that involved perceiving forms in a brief display.

Hoffman and Subramaniam (1995) recently carried out just such a test. They gave their subjects ample time to prepare to make an eye movement toward a prespecified one of the four corners of an imaginary square, and a tone provided a go signal for this eye movement. After a very brief interval from the tone onset (0, 50, or 100 msec), a display of four letters was briefly flashed. Subjects made the eye movement and then reported which of two possible targets was present in the display (search task). The targets for the search task were equally likely to be in any of the four positions. Nonetheless, subjects were substantially more accurate when targets were presented at the destination of the eye movement. Saccade latencies were very rapid, indicating that subjects were preparing the eye movement diligently. In another experiment, the subject always made saccades in a given fixed direction when the tone sounded (this direction did not change throughout the whole session). At the beginning of each trial, however, and shortly before the tone, an arrow cue indicated the most likely position of the target for the search task. As predicted by the mandatory shift hypothesis, target detection was most accurate when the target was located at the destination of the eye movement. Even more compelling was the fact that when the letter target was in a position *other than* where the eye moved, detection accuracy did not depend on whether or not this position had been cued. Deubel and Schneider (1996) confirmed these findings using a slightly different design. Kowler et al (1995) added further support, demonstrating that when people make a saccade in the direction of a pointer, the requirement to identify a letter not located at the target prolonged saccadic RTs by 50 to 70 msec.

These conclusions may be relevant to more naturalistic tasks such as reading. Inhoff and Brihl (1991) had subjects read passage presented in an upper line of text on a CRT while ignoring another passage contained in a line of text immediately below. Subjects were given multiple-choice questions about both relevant and irrelevant passages. Evidence suggested that subjects picked up material from the irrelevant material, but only on those occasions when they inadvertently fixated on that material.

In summary, evidence reveals that preparing to move the eye to a particular position in the visual field requires that visual attention first shifts to that position. Data suggest that this shift occurs during the time the system is actually preparing to produce the eye movement. Besides its theoretical interest, this conclusion raises intriguing questions about human performance in tasks requiring rapid responding. For example, drivers and pilots often glance toward instrument panels. Based on the results described, one might expect that a driver would be unable to detect an oncoming pedestrian for 100 msec or more preceding a glance, even if he or she was staring right at the person.[7] Since saccades often occur two or three times per second, one is led to wonder if, for a good portion of the time during which a person surveys a scene, the person is not really using information from the point of fixation.

An intriguing study by Blanchard et al. (1984) lends credence to this seemingly implausible speculation. The researchers monitored eye movements while subjects read computer-displayed text. A short time (50–120 msec) after the subject began to fixate a critical word (e.g., "tomb"), the display flickered to a mask (Xs replacing letters) for 30 msec, at which point new text appeared with a replacement word (e.g., "bomb") occupying the position formerly occupied by the critical word. Both the critical word and the replacement word made sense in the context of the sentence the subject was reading. Subjects were asked if they saw anything change and then given a recognition test for words from the passage. In the great majority of trials they appeared to have processed only one of the words, with the replacement affecting neither their recognition judgments nor their saccadic latencies. When the replacement occurred after 50 msec exposure of the first word, the word they recognized was usually the second word, but when the replacement occurred after 120 msec, it was usually the first.

Blanchard et al postulated a brief crucial period during a fixation in which the visual information is used. Given the research reviewed above, one explanation for this would be that during the later part of the fixation, planning the next eye movement requires a shift of visual attention away from the currently fixated word. Although this account may be correct, the data of Blanchard et al suggest that the picture cannot be quite that simple, since in 12% of trials in which the second word was reported, the replacement word was present only during the last 30 msec of the fixation.

Smooth-Pursuit and Vergence Eye Movements   The most striking difference between smooth-pursuit eye movements and saccades, aside from the fact the former occur more slowly, is that one cannot generate smooth eye movements by a sheer act of will in the absence of appropriate stimulation. The reader can verify this by simply staring at a wall and trying to make his or her eyes pan from left to right. The result is a series of short abrupt (saccadic) eye movements, rather than a smooth-pursuit movement.

The usual trigger for smooth-pursuit eye movements is a stimulus that slowly drifts along in the visual field. This does not mean that the smooth-pursuit system is devoid of psychological interest. On the contrary, these movements are intertwined with mental events in an intriguing way. For one thing, they can be driven by anticipation as well as direct sensory input. When a person expects a spot to begin moving at a certain time, the eye often begins moving before the spot does (Kowler and Steinman, 1979). Kowler (1989) carried out some elegant experiments pitting the expectation of the future path of the target against experience with its trajectory; the results showed that expectation rather than habit governed the eye movements. It may sound odd to say that these eye movements cannot be initiated voluntarily but that they are nonetheless driven by conscious expectations. Can one not form an expectation by sheer will? Apparently not, and other involuntary response systems also seem to illustrate the point. For example, changes in GSR are produced by conditioned stimuli that predicted shock in shock-conditioning experiments. These responses cannot be produced voluntarily and they depend on conscious expectations; however, when expectation is pitted against experience, expectation determines the response (Brewer, 1974).

More recent research, however, shows that anticipation of the trajectory of a stimulus is not a sufficient condition for eliciting a pursuit eye movement. An object must also be *attended* to be pursued. Kowler et al. (1984) showed subjects two superimposed fields of dots, one drifting and the other stationary. Observers could voluntarily choose which set of dots to track. This was true even when the density of the dots was so great that individual dots tended to be obscured by those from the other field. Variation in the relative luminance of the two sets of dots, and other stimulus factors, made little difference to the result. If subjects were indeed controlling which set of dots they tracked by selectively attending to the dots (in the same sense we spoke about attention in other contexts), then one would expect this to have perceptual consequences. Kowler and Zingale (1985) used essentially the same displays, but occasionally turned off a subset of one of the fields of dots. The subjects' task was to report when dots disappeared from either of the two fields. They were substantially faster and more accurate at doing this when dots disappeared from the field that was being tracked than from the untracked field. It might be objected that this difference could reflect the retinal smear of the untracked field. Kowler and Zingale recorded some plausible arguments against this possibility, but further investigation would be useful.

Older observations about voluntary control support the attentional interpretation. For example, try having someone move one hand in front of your eyes while you fixate directly on the hand; meanwhile, attempt to *prevent* your eye from tracking the hand. You will probably find that you can do this, but only by focusing your attention on objects in the surrounding field, as Mach noted in 1906 (cited by Kowler and Zingale, 1985). This would seem to imply that one can attend to outer regions of the field without attending to the central object (e.g., the hand). Can numerous noncontiguous elements actually elicit smooth pursuit even when the foveal stimulus follows a different trajectory?

Collewijn, Curio, and Grusser (1982) examined a form of pursuit eye movements induced by flashing, rather than moving stimuli, termed Sigma-pursuit movements (SPMs). In one condition, two horizontal rows of dots were presented in such a way that either one alone would induce SPMs at different velocities. The striking finding was that observers were able to foveate one of these inducing rows and yet, by attending to the other row, to produce SPMs appropriate for the other row.

Steven Yantis and I informally explored the limits of attentional control of ordinary smooth-pursuit eye movements using similar designs. We had people view two columns of spots moving from the top to the bottom of a CRT screen while a column of spots in between the two columns moved upward. The object was to attend to the outer columns and ignore the central column. In many cases, subjects' eyes appeared to move at the rate of the outer dots although the dots that were being fixated were moving in the opposite direction (Yantis and Pashler, unpublished observations). Most subjects found the task to be rather difficult. In summary, various observations, starting with those of Ernst Mach, demonstrate the fact that which stimuli guide pursuit eye movements depends to a great degree on voluntary control, which seems to be closely tied to attentional selection.

In vergence eye movements, the two eyes move in opposite directions to fixate on stimuli nearer or closer to the observer. Erkelens and Collewijn (1991) presented subjects with a pattern composed of multiple dots or sets of lines to each eye. The positions of various elements in the field differed slightly (to put it more technically, the elements had different retinal disparities). When the observers were instructed to attend to a particular form and its image in one eye was perturbed, that eye moved to maintain convergence on the form. These attention-dependent vergence movements could occur even when unattended stimuli were projecting onto the fovea.

In summary, it appears that the three most well-known types of eye movements—saccadic, smooth-pursuit, and vergence—are closely tied to visual selective attention. Preparation of saccadic eye movements seems to require shifting visual attention to the destination of the movements during a period of several hundred milliseconds immediately preceding the saccade. Combined motion and/or displacement signals from the elements in the display that are attended seem to combine to determine the path of smooth-pursuit eye movements. Vergence eye movements work to foveate attended, but not unattended, elements in the visual field. As Kowler and Zingale (1985) point out, the fact that smooth-pursuit eye movements provide an outward manifestation of selective attention suggests they may be a valuable tool for the study of visual attention. Researchers have barely begun to exploit this tool.

Bimodal Selective Attention

People are always (or almost always) subject to stimulation in different sensory modalities. In light of that fact, it is surprising that the relation between selection in one modality and selection in another has been relatively little investigated. The standard experimental paradigms in attention research use either visual stimuli or auditory stimuli, but not both, and most researchers have stuck to one or the other. Two issues are related to bimodal (or potentially multimodal) stimulation that are of obvious importance. The first is the relative difficulty of what one might call intramodal selection, selecting a stimulus in one modality and excluding other stimuli in the same modality, compared with intermodal selection, selecting a stimulus in one modality while excluding stimuli in a different modality. The second issue is whether simultaneous intramodal selection in different modalities is possible, and if so, how selection in one modality relates to selection in the other. For example, are they linked in space or some other way?

Intramodal versus intermodal selection can be addressed with filtering tasks that require selection of stimuli in one modality and rejection of stimuli in another. Anyone who has read a newspaper in a crowded subway or tried to work within earshot of a stereo can confirm that this issue has real-world validity. Obviously, we can accomplish this kind of selection with some success. What is not obvious is how effectively we can do it compared with excluding stimuli within the modality we are focusing on.

Various different hypotheses seem reasonably plausible. On the one hand, people might be capable of simply turning off processing in an unwanted modality more effectively than they can prevent processing of unwanted stimulation in a modality that they must simultaneously monitor. After all, we have seen that greater differences between selected and excluded stimuli tend to make selection easier, and intermodal selection could naturally be viewed as an even more gross basis for selection than, say, pitch or location. On the other hand, it has sometimes been suggested that rejected stimuli are more extensively processed when the selected channel contains little information to process, and thereby leaves resources idle (Helmholtz, 1867/1968; Kahneman, 1973, chapter 2). If this line of thought is valid, and if auditory and visual processing resources are at to some degree separate (a point that will be supported by evidence described in chapter 3), then excluding stimuli in a different modality might be less effective rather than more.

The few investigations that have been carried out do not seem to demonstrate that people are especially effective in shutting out stimuli in a particular modality when everything in that modality is irrelevant. To give one example, Greenwald (1970) played tapes to subjects while they read visually presented digits aloud. The tape contained either another digit or a tap at the same time as each visual digit. Subjects' responses to the visually presented digits were slowed by about 35 msec when accompanied by another digit, and the effect did not depend greatly on the rate at which the digits were spoken. Irrelevant speech substantially, although not massively, disrupts immediate memory for visually presented materials (Salame and Baddeley, 1982). Unfortunately, no data allow one to compare intra modal and intermodal selection. Doing so would undoubtedly be difficult, but the importance of the issue warrants trying.

A second broad issue about bimodal selective attention concerns the relationship between the mechanisms of selectivity within different modalities. Can people simultaneously select, say, the spoken messages coming to the left ear, ignoring the right ear message and the words colored in a CRT display, ignoring the green ones? Or is selectivity possible within only one modality at a time? Can someone process the visual stimulus coming from one location and the auditory stimulus coming from another location, ignoring distractors in each modality at the other location? The issue spans the topics of selective and divided attention; involving divided attention between modalities and selective attention within each modality.

In many mammalian species, even infants respond to unexpected sounds with an orienting response involving the whole body, triggered by the binaural localization of the sounds (Kelly and Potash, 1986). This response is hardly surprising from a functional point of view; sounds outside an animal's field of view may be very significant and vision is critical in determining this significance. Some authors even suggest that the evolution of auditory localization was largely driven by the demands of orienting attention (Heffner and Heffner, 1992). When one observes overt behavior, therefore, one sees plentiful evidence of cross-modal influences on attention. It does not follow, however, that these linkages are inherent and obligatory, much less that there is only a single supramodal spatial attention controller. The linkages that show up in orienting might merely reflect a default setting that can be overridden, or they might be restricted to unexpected sounds coming from locations out of view. To distinguish these possibilities, one must construct situations in which people have an incentive to avoid attending in the same way to visual and auditory stimulation.

Reisberg, Scheiber, and Potemken (1981) had subjects listen to a word list from one loudspeaker while another loudspeaker delivered distractor messages. Subjects were not able to remember as many of the relevant words and showed more intrusions of irrelevant words when they fixated their eyes on the loudspeaker playing distractors than when they fixated on the relevant loudspeaker or a silent speaker. However, the effect was small, and in a set of follow-up studies, Wolters and Schiano (1989) were unable to replicate the effect. Eye position (which of course is not the same as visual attention) is not apparently a potent determinant of auditory selection.

A more direct approach to this question is to present several signals in two modalities at once, and see if people can select auditory stimuli from one part of space while they select visual stimuli from another part. Driver and Spence (1994) carried out an experiment using two speakers and two CRT displays. One speaker and display sat at approximately the same location to the left of the subject, and the other pair sat at a corresponding position to the right. Two tasks were required: shadowing the message coming from one speaker while ignoring the message coming from the other, and monitoring a continuous visual display of characters on one of the CRT displays. A significant decrement in shadowing performance occurred when the visual display was on the opposite side as the speaker, rather than the same side. However, the magnitude of the difference was not especially large. Alfonso (1992) performed similar experiments in my laboratory. Using a slightly easier shadowing task, she found that subjects could readily attend to the visual stimulus on one side and the auditory stimulus on the other. Unlike the findings of Driver and Spence, there were no significant costs of attending visually to one side visually and auditorily to the other in this experiment, but the trend was in the same direction.

Another way of approaching the same issue is to present a cueing stimulus in one modality and a target requiring a response in another (the mechanisms behind these spatial cueing effects are explored in detail in chapter 4). In several studies of this type, responses to a visual target on the left or right of a screen were speeded up by auditory cues from speakers positioned on the corresponding side (Buchtel and Butter, 1988) and also by tactile cueing (Butter, Buchtel, and Santucci, 1989). As with the orienting behaviors, this result does not demonstrate an obligatory linkage: the cues predicted where the target would occur, and therefore subjects would have reason to select on this basis even in there were no intrinsic connections. (If the odor of camphor had indicated to subjects that a target on the right was likely, performance might have been improved; this would not implicate an obligatory olfactory-visual linkage.) Spence and Driver (1996) reported, however, that unpredictive auditory cues do produce a brief facilitation of responses to visual stimuli in adjacent positions. Of interest, they did not find visual cues to have the same effect, and suggested that this asymmetry may reflect the different functional roles of vision and audition alluded to above. Together, this evidence implies that some partial auditory-visual yoking is probably obligatory. Alfonso's experiment may have been insensitive to some small effect of this type.

The issue of supramodal attention has also been considered by neuropsychologists. Patients with damage to the parietal lobe frequently show a tendency to react weakly or slowly or not at all to information coming from the side of space opposite to their lesion (Heilman, Watson, and Valenstein, 1993). In many cases they are able to perceive a stimulus on their "bad" side as long as no other stimulus is presented, but when stimuli are presented to both sides, they do not perceive the stimulus on the bad side. This symptom, which may occur in various sensory modalities, is referred to as extinction. De Renzi, Gentilini, and Pattacini (1984) found that the severity of extinction in one modality did not very strongly predict the severity of extinction in another modality. By itself, this does not rule out the idea that a single center is responsible for orienting attention to space governing *all* sensory modalities, since the lack of correlation might be due to disconnection of attentional input to such a center, as pointed out by Farah et al. (1989). They found that extinction, as indicated by delayed responses to targets presented in the bad hemifield, could be induced by auditory as well as visual stimulation in the good hemifield. Unlike the experiments of Butters and colleagues, Farah et al. induced extinction with cues that did not predict the stimulation, so these results are not subject to the sorts of problems described earlier. These various results again suggest a fairly strong linkage between the machinery controlling attention to space in the two modalities.

Further study of this issue necessary before one can draw strong conclusions about how selectivity in different perceptual modalities is related. At present, evidence exists for some degree of obligatory linkage. Deliberately attending to objects in one location, or detecting auditory stimulation in a location, seems to favor selectivity in the other modality to that location. On the other hand, it seems clear people can decouple selection in two modalities to a substantial degree, arguing against a single supramodal spatial attention controller.

The Time Course of Selection

In many of the filtering studies the subject was informed about the criterion of selection by a stimulus of some sort. For example, in von Wright's studies, a bar marker next to a character indicated to the subject that this stimulus should be attended and other stimuli should be rejected. How long does it take to use such a cue to initiate selective processing by location? The best parametric information on the time course of selection comes from pioneering studies by Charles Eriksen and his colleagues. These researchers systematically examined spatial cueing in selection tasks involving arrays of characters; generally, subjects were asked to name or make a selective response to the cued character. These studies are especially useful because they provided converging evidence involving both response time and accuracy measures. Furthermore, unlike the more widely copied design involving simple detection of just a single spot (see chapter 4), the experiments required subjects to identify objects and to filter out distractors, which makes the attentional demands of the task much more apparent.

Eriksen and Collins (1969) presented subjects with brief circular displays of six letters, followed or preceded by an indicator of some kind that specified which letter should be reported. Various kinds of spatial cues were used, including indicators on the opposite side of the display from the cued position. Accuracy improved as the cues were presented earlier, up to around 100 msec before the display. Another experiment showed that the benefit seemed to reach a maximum value at approximately 200 msec. The RTs to vocalize the cued letter declined as the SOA from cue to display was increased to about 250 msec, and flattened off thereafter (Colegate, Hoffman, and Eriksen, 1973). Uninformative warning signs and spatial cues also were given at the same time as the display to show that this was not due to the alerting effects of the cues.

With displays of twelve items (Eriksen and Hoffman, 1973), RTs decreased substantially between probe-display SOAs of 150 and 250 msec. It seems possible, then, that the more spatial precision required, the longer it takes to set the selectivity in place. Eriksen and Rohrbaugh (1970) were able to find only equivocal support for this idea, however. Sperling and Reeves (1980) developed another, very ingenious, approach to measuring the time required for attention shifts. Subjects monitored a stream of sequentially presented characters looking for a target character. When they detected this target, they immediately attended to a second stream of characters and tried to remember the first several items they could "catch." By examining which items were reported from this second stream, Sperling and Reeves were able to compute the time between the onset of the character triggering the switch and the completion of the switch. This method yields slightly longer estimates of shifting time than the other approaches described, presumably because the task imposes greater perceptual and cognitive demands.

Together with some informative results, one unfortunate misimpression that came out of this research program deserves mention. In some articles, the authors suggested that the focus of attention might encompass a fixed extent, such as 1 degree of visual angle (e.g., Eriksen and Eriksen, 1974). This conclusion, based on observations regarding flanker effects and noise characters, has often been quoted. It is easily refuted without making detailed measurements in the laboratory. Consider a spatial-selection task like the one used by Eriksen and colleagues in which a bar probe sits next to one item in a display of eight letters. Observers with good eyesight can see such a display from such a long distance the *entire* display lies within 1 degree of visual angle, yet they can choose only the probed item. Readers with good visual acuity can verify this by holding this text several feet away and reading aloud the last letter in each word. Relative distance may affect the efficiency of selective attention and the exclusion of irrelevant stimuli, but spatial attention is far too flexible to be described by a single parameter in this way.

Conclusions

Selective Attention in Vision and Hearing

This section focused on perceptual filtering tasks in which numerous stimuli are presented, and an observer or listener attempts to identify just those that satisfy a simple, physical selection criterion such as spatial location, pitch, or color. Research has ranged over a wide variety of such tasks involving both visual and auditory modalities. Several basic generalizations can be stated with reasonable confidence. The first of these was well known to Cherry, who helped launch the modern era of attention studies, although it was not clear when he was writing how robust this generalization would prove to be.

1. When people try to focus on certain stimuli and ignore others, they generally notice and report only relatively gross physical properties of the rejected stimuli.

Generalization 1 seems to hold true over a wide range of different observation conditions, not only with speech presented to the two ears (Cherry's design), but also with such diverse stimuli as musical passages and overlapping video images. However, over the almost four decades that have elapsed since Cherry made his observations, a variety of subtle measures have been used to show that rejected stimuli are sometimes processed to a semantic level, findings sometimes described under the heading of breakthrough of the unattended. These examples illustrate a second generalization.

2. Under conditions that allow effective selection, as indicated by people's reports and lack of memory for unattended stimuli, it is often possible to show that *some* semantic analysis of rejected stimuli still occurs, at least in *some* trials.

At first, findings of this sort were taken to support the concept that identification of stimuli is wholly unselective, as late selection theorists proposed. However, many subsequent studies, using both auditory and visual stimuli, eroded this interpretation. A third generalization appears well supported.

3. When favorable conditions for attentional selectivity are provided, evidence of unselective processing is unconvincing.

Examples of factors that provide optimal conditions for selection include easy discrimination between relevant and irrelevant stimuli and adequate time to maintain a consistent criterion of selection. There is also moderate support for a further generalization.

4. Increasing the number of *rejected* stimuli reduces and even eliminates their effects, as indicated by the indirect measures.

The findings of Yantis and Johnston (1990) and Kahneman and Chajczyk (1983) provide the most clear-cut examples of this generalization, but there are others. This result argues against the hypothesis that perception is both unselective and free of capacity limitations (for a particularly clear exposition of this argument, see Hoffman, 1986). In some cases, increasing the difficulty of processing of the attended items eliminates effects of unattended stimuli, which also disagrees with this hypothesis. As a final example, evidence that rejected flanking words are identified seems to depend on repetition of words from trial to trial, which is congenial with Treisman's suggestion that priming may be a necessary condition for rejected stimuli to be identified.

These results make a good, although not watertight, case that the sensory and perceptual analyses of rejected stimuli are not full or complete. Physiological observations are also consistent with this interpretation. Single-unit recordings show that neural responses to rejected stimuli are reduced in the brain areas likely to be involved in quite early stages of object recognition. This has been observed in both visual and auditory cortices of primates. Studies of event-related potentials present a similar picture. The proposal that perception is unselective has also been challenged using selective adaptation effects as a dependent measure. When adapting stimuli are unattended, subsequent adaptation effects are sometimes much smaller than when they are attended. This has been noted with adaptation of the perception of motion, structure from motion, and three-dimensional shape from perspective cues. It does not seem to obtain with the McCollough effect, however.

Researchers have also elucidated linkages between selective attention and the mechanisms controlling eye movements. Visual selective attention appears to be tied intimately to eye movement control. Preparation of a saccadic eye movement seems to require a prior shift of visual selection to the destination of the eye movement. Smooth-pursuit and vergence movements are triggered, roughly speaking, by velocity and disparity signals, respectively, that originate in attended but not unattended parts of the visual field.

Despite the importance of the question, little is known about what happens when people select from among stimuli in different sensory modalities. It appears that when people monitor stimuli in one modality, they are no better at excluding stimuli in a different modality than stimuli within the same modality. Thus generalization 2 probably still holds when attended and rejected stimuli are in different modalities. It is not known, however, whether selection might actually be less efficient in this case, as one might hypothesize for various reasons. Little firm evidence exists about how selection within one modality affects selection within another modality. The direction of eye fixation and the spatial auditory selection may be tied together, but probably only rather weakly. Even casual observations disclose that people are capable of simultaneously maintaining separate modes of selectivity within each modality at the same time. It may be more difficult to maintain wholly incompatible forms of spatial selection within the two modalities, and some moderate linkage between spatial selection in one modality and another has been demonstrated. Evidence presently suggests, therefore, that attentional selectivity within each modality is probably largely, but not wholly, independent.

The focus here is on the consequences of selection for processing of unattended stimuli. A large set of studies points toward the conclusion that sensory/perceptual processing of rejected stimuli is ordinarily substantially curtailed. Given the rough framework depicted in figure 1-6, this is consistent with an early selection theory, but also with other, quite different possibilities as well, such as the controlled parallel processing model.

Space and the Process of Visual Selection
Although the question of what happens to rejected stimuli has a deservedly central place in studies of selective attention, other significant questions regarding selective attention have to be considered. One is whether different stimulus dimensions all play the same role in the process of selection: In considering this question, we focus on visual selection because there is little evidence regarding other modalities.

Under the heading of filtering tasks we encounter all situations requiring selection on the basis of a precategorical dimension. Usually, the response is based on postcategorical information (e.g., name the letter), although this does not have to be the case. The selection criteria can be quite diverse. Examples include location ("name the letter in the center"), color, and size. In audition, pitch and location work well as filtering criteria. The studies summarized above indicate that selection by spatial location is typically easier than selection by such criteria as color or size.

A variety of studies show that visual location is not just a more effective selection cue, but is in some sense a *primary* selection cue. There are several lines of converging evidence for this proposition. Some of these experiments take us outside the domain of filtering tasks, but since the topic is selection, the detour seems justified. First, consider what happens when people search a display for a target element, such as a letter T or a green element, reporting both the presence of the target and its location. (This is, strictly speaking, a divided-attention task, and properly belongs in the next chapter.) When an observer makes a genuine detection of a target as distinct from merely guessing its presence, it appears that the observer will be capable of reporting the target's location when offered a choice among the different locations occupied by stimuli. The most clear-cut evidence for this claim arises in forced-choice tasks in which one of n possible targets is always present and the observer must choose which it is. In this task, when the location is incorrectly reported, the probability of a correct target choice is found to be close to 1/n. This pattern was found by Shiffrin and Gardner (1972) and Johnston and Pashler (1991) involving brief masked displays. In threshold discriminations limited by contrast, essentially the same effects were also seen (Graham, 1989). Finally, when observers view two briefly presented objects side by side, their accuracy in choosing from among two possible targets is equal to their accuracy in saying where the target is located (D. M. Green, 1992).[8]

The conclusion that detection is accompanied by at least rough location information is controversial. Treisman and Gelade (1980) maintained that in the detection of simple features (pop-out search, which is discussed in chapter 3), people often report which feature was present without knowing anything of its location. This conclusion was based on an experiment in which people were able to make accurate forced-choice judgments about feature identity although their location reports were grossly erroneous. More recent evidence makes it likely that Treisman and Gelade's findings were caused by rather subtle guessing strategies that subjects employ when alternative targets differ in their detectability (Johnston and Pashler, 1991).[9] In summary, location is special in this sense: when an observer detects a target defined on *other* dimensions ranging from simple to relatively complex, this provides information about the location of the stimulus being detected. A simple metaphor conveys the essence of this idea: when someone reads out information from a channel selective for a particular target, the channel is labeled with at least rough location information (a term drawn from Watson and Robson, 1981). Of course, an observer may make many false alarms (e.g., reading from channels that responded spuriously to nontargets), but he or she will not be confused about the location of the channels from which activity is read, whether or not this activity corresponds to targets (Graham, 1989).

Location is also special in other respects, and this can be revealed with filtering tasks in which location is neither the criterion of selection nor the attribute being reported. Consider the task of reporting the identity of the single red item in a display of colored letters. Snyder (1972) examined the errors in such a task using circular displays of twelve letters, and reported that observers tended to report one of the two immediate neighbors of the red item on about 35% of error trials. If errors were equally likely to include all positions, this should have occurred on only about 18% of error trials. This suggests that when the selection attribute is color, selection involves two stages. In the first stage, the location at which the color is present is determined; in the second stage, this location is used as a cue to retrieve the form. If this is correct, one should also expect the observer to report the form accurately only when the location is available for report. Nissen (1985) confirmed the predicted dependency.[10]

Tsal and Lavie (1988) extended Snyder's work. In one of their experiments, subjects saw brief displays of nine letters, three each in red, green, and brown. Their task was to report one letter of a given color (say, red), and as many other letters as possible. The extra letters were more often nonred letters spatially adjacent to the red letter than they were other red letters in nonadjacent display positions.

Substantial evidence implies that spatial location plays a role in visual selection that is different from the role played by other attributes such as color and brightness. The simplest interpretation is that selection by location mediates selection by these other precategorical attributes. In chapter 5 we will see that the issue is rather more complicated than this, because nonspatial factors that determine what features or parts belong to the same object can also determine processing selectivity.

3

Divided Attention

Chapter 2 considered what happens when people try to focus on just one source of information and ignore other sources. We turn now to the general issue often termed *divided attention,* considering the portion of this broad area that pertains to perceptual processing and identification of stimuli (other issues of divided attention, including interference at the level of memory, thought and action, are taken up in chapter 7). This chapter asks what happens when a person attempts to take in sensory information from several sources at approximately the same time. The basic question here is whether the perceptual system(s) are limited in their ability to handle multiple inputs, and if so, how. The most extreme form of limitation would be a requirement to process inputs serially. As noted in chapter 1, however, graded capacity limitations are also possible; perceptual analysis of different objects might operate in parallel, with a reduction in speed or accuracy when the system is overloaded.

Several concepts and terms beyond those mentioned in chapter 1 must be introduced at this point. The identification of more than one stimulus is said to be subject to capacity limitations if the speed or efficiency of the processing is reduced when other stimuli are processed at the same time, compared with the case when only one stimulus is processed at a time. An extreme case of capacity limitation is serial processing: here the perceptual analysis of one stimulus must be completed before the analysis of the next stimulus can begin. Serial processing is of particular interest because it naturally suggests a mechanistic interpretation, namely, that only one mechanism is capable of carrying out the analysis. Processing is parallel if analysis of one stimulus can begin without waiting for processing of another to be completed. If there are no capacity limitations, parallel processing follows as a more or less automatic consequence. However, capacity limitations would not exclude parallel processing. Mental operations might occur simultaneously, but each might operate more slowly when other operations are under way at a given instant than would otherwise be the case (Townsend, 1974). Various hybrids of parallel and serial processing could also be considered; for example, a limitation might force processing of different items to begin at different times, but the processing of both could overlap in time (for a thoughtful discussion of various alternatives to simple serial and parallel conceptions, see Townsend and Ashby, 1983). For present purposes, however, the simpler taxonomy as described will be sufficient.

To determine empirically what limitations arise when people try to perceive and recognize numerous stimuli at once, one needs tasks that require a person to analyze the stimuli, or to process many bits of information from a single stimulus. A majority of the studies that have explored perceptual divided attention have used one of a few different tasks. To make these tasks concrete, suppose a display of eight digits is presented briefly to an individual. In a *report* task, the individual would be required to state what the digits were (3, 2, 7, etc.). In a *search* task, the individual would attempt to find one or more *target items,* if they are present: saying yes or no in a *presence/absence task,* or stating which of n alternative targets was present in an *n-alternative forced-choice search task.* The number of items being searched for is called the *target set size,* and the number of items in the display is the *display set size* (it is often called display size, but this sounds like it refers to the physical extent of the display, which is altogether a different variable).

Taking in Information from Brief Visual Displays

Report Tasks

The most obvious way to test how much visual information people can recognize in a briefly exposed scene is simply to ask them to state what they saw. With letters or digits, this task is usually termed the *full-report* or *whole-report* task. Sperling (1960), in his classic study of visual-report tasks, noted that the number of items reported was scarcely affected by variables that one would naturally have expected to make a big difference. Subjects are typically able to report four or five letters or digits regardless of how long the display remains present (over a range from 15 msec to 0.5 second), and regardless of the number of items present in the display, as long as the display contains more than five elements.[1]

Sperling made a powerful case that the whole-report limit is caused by a limitation in people's ability to retain or report more than four or five items. He proposed a simple model according to which the items are held in a short-term memory (STM) buffer with four or five slots. Delaying the whole report by a full second did not reduce the number reported, implying that information in this memory system is lost comparatively slowly, at least when the subject tries to maintain the information. Sperling's observations do not actually show that STM system contains a fixed number of discrete slots that exclusively store categorical information such as letter identity. Short-term memory might use some form of partial or distributed coding, and it may store continuous as well as categorical information. Indeed, delaying a partial-report cue has a deleterious effect on the precision with which people can report continuous dimensions such as line length (Palmer, 1988). The key implications of Sperling's data, then, are first that STM capacity can be used up, and second, that it does not lose much information over a period of seconds. These conclusions are now so familiar that they may even seem self-evident. In fact, they are not self-evident, and some of the alternatives they exclude would have seemed quite plausible a priori. For example, one could easily have supposed that each item in a display is registered in memory independent of how many other items are stored.

Although STM may fill up, Sperling (and around the same time, Averbach and Coriell, 1961) discovered another system that does not seem to fill up, at least in anything like the same way. This other system, usually termed *iconic memory,* holds a great deal of visual information but is subject to rapid decay. It is often characterized as a brief visible persistence that, at least under typical conditions, outlasts a display by a few hundred milliseconds. This is not long enough to allow a person to report much of anything, so the large capacity of iconic memory does not figure directly in the typical whole-report task. The original evidence for iconic persistence comes from Sperling's famous partial-report studies, which are undoubtedly familiar to most readers. Subjects were probed with a tone to report a subset of a 50-msec display. The tone sounded at some short interval after the display offset. In the most famous experiments, the pitch of the tone told the subject which row to report. Crucially, subjects did not know in advance which row would be cued on any given trial. If there were no memory system other than whatever short-term memory was responsible for whole report, subjects would have access to no more than four or five items in total once the display had disappeared. Thus, when the tone cued report of a particular row, the subject could succeed in reporting an item only in the lucky event that this was one of the items stored in short-term memory. Sperling's results refuted this account. As long as the probe was presented within about 0.5 second from the offset of the display, subjects had a good chance of reporting the probed item (performance was much better than would be expected if they only had four or five items available). Delay of the probe for just 1 second caused this performance advantage to disappear, however.

Sperling's findings argued that (a) subjects have a great deal more information available for a short period of time after the display offset (iconic persistence), and (b) they can transfer a selected subset of the information into STM as long as the cue arrives before this iconic persistence has faded away. This selective transfer is another manifestation of visual selective attention in the sense described in the previous chapter. As Coltheart (1977) points out, these phenomena are misunderstood surprisingly often. For example, it has sometimes been claimed that the limit on whole report is directly caused by the rapid decay of iconic memory. If this were so, then giving the subject more time to view the display should increase the number of items produced in whole report; as noted earlier, this does not happen. The discoveries of Sperling and Averbach and Coriell reveal the existence of two distinct memory systems: one, iconic memory, that is capable of holding on to a great deal of information but loses it very rapidly, and the other, short-term memory, that is easily filled to capacity but loses information quite slowly[2] (figure 3.1).

Sperling also found that he could drastically reduce performance in the partial-report task by presenting a bright field at the same time as the partial-report cue in the location formerly occupied by the characters,

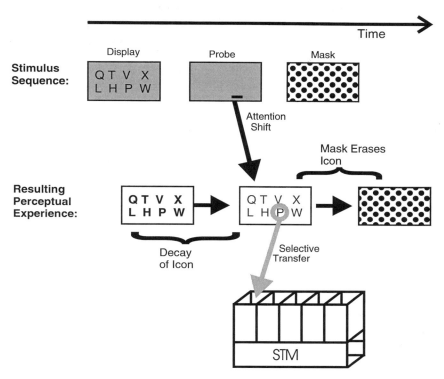

Figure 3.1
Conventional analysis of the sequence of mental events operating in a partial-report task. Iconic memory preserves a (weakened) sensory trace of the display; the probe triggers an attention shift (selective transfer of the sensory trace of the cued item into short-term memory [STM]). Presentation of an extraneous stimulus in the same retinal locus as the display abruptly erases iconic persistence.

something Baxt (1871) experimented with almost a century earlier. This phenomenon is now generally referred to as backward masking (Sperling, 1960; Turvey, 1973). Sperling inferred that the mask must be erasing iconic memory. Although controversy exists about the precise mechanisms of masking (Schultz and Eriksen, 1977; Turvey, 1973), this analysis has not been seriously challenged. As a consequence of their ability to erase iconic memory or prevent further processing of it, the effects of backward masks on whole-report performance are quite revealing. As the time between the display and the mask is lengthened, performance

improves, reaching an asymptotically high level (four or five items reported) at around a 50-msec delay (depending on stimulus parameters);
see figure 3.2 (Mackworth, 1963). Whereas the rate of transfer out of
iconic memory is not the limiting factor in partial-report performance, it
is the limiting factor in this kind of a whole-report task, where a legible
display is quickly followed by a mask.[3] The 50-msec figure therefore
reflects the time to transfer information into STM, although it does not
provide a direct estimate of that time, since the mask cannot be assumed
to terminate the transfer process instantaneously. Processing of both
display and mask may occur after somewhat different lags from their
respective onsets.

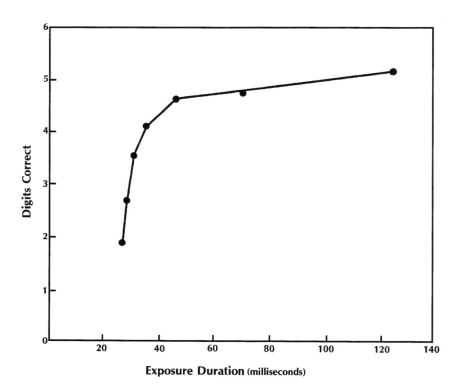

Figure 3.2
The number of items reported from a brief display followed by a bright masking
field. From Mackworth (1963, p. 64).

This analysis of information processing in brief displays was fully developed in the pioneering work of Sperling (1960) and Averbach and Coriell (1961). Although various questions about iconic memory have been hotly debated, the basic analysis of partial and whole reports has not been seriously challenged. Several researchers have questioned whether different measures of iconic memory really evaluate the same form of storage (Coltheart, 1980). In fact, there is little reason to doubt that visible persistence exists and that people can use it in carrying out partial reports, as the original iconic memory researchers proposed.[4] Nonetheless, important issues remain unresolved. One is the neural substrate of this persistence. The obvious candidate would be continued visual neuron firing after stimulus offset. This seems consistent with the rather scarce published data on the topic, which show persistence in at least some neurons in primary visual cortex lasting for at least 100 msec poststimulus offset (Duysens et al, 1985; Maunsell and Gibson, 1992). The behavioral data might have led one to expect longer persistence than that; perhaps neurons in higher visual areas maintain firing for longer periods.

Another unresolved question is what functional role, if any, iconic memory plays outside the laboratory. In some influential structural models of memory, iconic storage is depicted as an obligatory early *stage* in the processing of information (e.g., Atkinson and Shiffrin, 1968). This is somewhat odd, however, since, as has often been noted (e.g., Haber, 1985), the conditions under which iconic memory is observed in the laboratory are not typically encountered in natural environments (or even in most conventional memory experiments). Except perhaps for lightening storms, natural illumination does not disappear instantaneously. Usually, a fixation ends when the observer makes a saccadic eye movement to fixate some new object. When this happens, the portion of the retina previously fixated receives new input, rather than no input at all, as in the typical partial-report experiment. The new input is likely to mask the contents of the old fixation, because backward masking depends primarily on retinal overlap (Davidson, Fox, and Dick, 1973). Indeed, masking of one fixation by the next (rather than saccadic suppression) seems to be the real reason we do not see a great smear every time we move our eyes, even though the eye movement smears the retinal input[5] (Brooks,

Impelman, and Lum, 1981). Therefore, whereas iconic memory might seem to offer the potential for prolonging our access to a given fixation, this is probably prevented by masking caused by input from the subsequent fixation. These conclusions are consistent with findings showing that people have trouble detecting changes introduced between one fixation and the next (Carlson-Radavansky and Irwin, 1995); there is no reliable evidence that iconic memory lets us hold onto the contents of one fixation and compare them with the contents of the next.

If iconic memory is irrelevant within most fixations and useless for solving the problems generated by saccades, what possible function does it have? One may be left with exotic and seemingly trivial possibilities (e.g., reducing the impact of eyeblinks?) or the chance that it may be devoid of any function whatever. The STM system (or systems) that underlie whole report, on the other hand, are probably critical in our daily visual experience and behavior. For that reason, it seems ironic that the research effort devoted to iconic memory dwarfs that devoted to STM from brief visual displays (as in whole report).

From the research has been done, however, this STM has proved somewhat enigmatic. Many textbooks (e.g., Best, 1986) simply claim that whole-reported items are stored in "short-term memory," thereby implying, in line with Atkinson and Shiffrin (1968), that this is the same short-term memory used in tasks such as span memory (i.e., immediate serial recall of spoken material). In fact, this seems unlikely. Scarborough (1972) had subjects carry out a visual whole-report task of writing down letters they saw during an interval in which they also held onto a spoken set of digits. Remarkably, subjects performed both of these tasks in the dual-task condition about as well they could perform either one alone. Holding a concurrent spatial memory task does not reduce whole report, either (Henderson, 1972), and brain-damaged patients with severe impairment in short-term retention of spoken materials sometimes do reasonably at whole report tasks (Warrington and Shallice, 1969). The results point to the multiplicity of short-term memory systems, an issue that is discussed more generally in chapter 7.

If whole report does not depend on the articulatory-phonological memory people usually use to retain spoken material, what kind of memory system does it involve? One of the few investigators to consider the issue thoughtfully was Coltheart, who presented two very different formulations in a pair of carefully reasoned articles separated by eight years (1972, 1980). In the first formulation, Coltheart proposed that specifically visual short-term memory underlies whole report. In his second formulation, he suggested that the characters are stored in an abstract format, akin to a list of abstract (e.g., letter or digit) identities. As these vacillations suggest, available evidence was not conclusive and it still is not. Phenomenology appears to argue for a visual format, however: When observers perform a whole-report task, they usually report having an image of the items in the display in their correct spatial positions. However, one should not rule out the possibility of a hybrid storage involving both abstract and visual codes. The issue deserves further research, and the dual-task methodology of Scarborough and Henderson seems well-suited to this purpose.

Searching Brief Displays

The Problem of Statistical Noise   The studies described in the preceding section indicate that people cannot hold on to more than four or five items long enough to report them. Nonetheless, plenty of evidence shows that people can recognize far more than four or five characters in these kinds of brief displays. In his report on iconic memory, Sperling (1960) mentioned that investigators in the nineteenth century tended "enigmatically [to] insist that they have seen more than they can remember afterwards, that is, report afterwards" (p. 1). It is sometimes claimed that partial-report experiments themselves demonstrate that people see more than they can recall. If "seeing" implies having identified the stimuli, this inference seems unwarranted. The partial-report experiments demonstrate that a large amount of visual information can be retained for a very short time, and that from this information the identities of characters can be *recovered*. However, they do not indicate whether identification takes place before or after the report cue is presented, and thus they leave open the possibility that the uncued items were never identified.

To demonstrate that more objects can be identified than a person can report, and to determine what capacity limitations are involved in recognition, one requires a task that allows observers the opportunity to demonstrate that they have identified objects that they need not report. Estes and Taylor (1964) were the first to use visual search tasks for this purpose. Subjects were instructed to examine the entire display and report on the presence of only a single target character. Visual search is appropriate because finding a target element (or finding the target to be absent) shows that nontarget items were processed sufficiently to determine whether the items were targets or not. In Estes and Taylor's initial experiments, subjects made a forced-choice response indicating whether a C or an F was present in a display that contained variable numbers of consonants (one or other of the two targets was always presented). Figure 3.3 shows the number of elements successfully processed in the detection task as a function of the number of elements presented; the authors derived this using a simple correction-for-guessing procedure. For comparison, the figure also shows the number of items reported from the

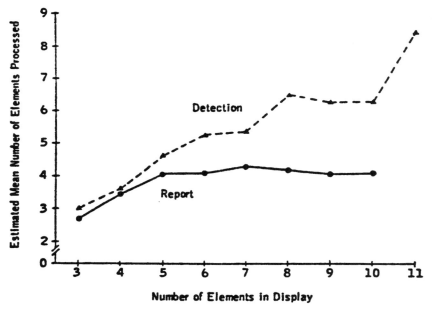

Figure 3.3
The number of items available from a brief display as a function of the number of items presented, assessed in a detection task or a report task. From Estes and Taylor (1964, p. 450).

same displays, which tops out at around four and thereafter does not grow with display set size, in agreement with Sperling. There is little doubt that whole report underestimates the amount of processing people can perform on a brief display, and that the degree of underestimation increases with display set size.

The gap between the processing that occurs and what is available to be reported is probably much greater in ordinary scenes viewed briefly outside the laboratory. Readers have probably seen many examples of this in the cinema and on television, whether or not they thought of them in this way. Movie directors and advertisers commonly flash sequences of scenes at rates ranging from about three to twenty per second (see Biedermann, Teitelbaum, and Mezzanotte, 1983). In one well-known example in the 1980s, the television show "Saturday Night Live" presented a sequence of famous faces (entertainers, politicians, etc.) at a rate of approximately ten frames per second. From my informal sample, just about everyone who watches this footage reported thinking they could recognize just about every one of these faces. (It is hard to see why anyone would find such a sequence amusing if it produced only confusion.) On the other hand, after viewing the sequences, one invariably has trouble recalling more than a few of the faces.

These impressions are confirmed by a number of interesting experiments with rapid picture perception. Potter (1976) showed subjects a series of eight pictures of scenes and objects at rates ranging from 133 to 333 msec per picture. Subjects did an excellent job of detecting the presence of a target object that was shown to them (or even just named for them) before they saw the sequence of pictures (almost 90% for 167-msec exposures). On the other hand, a memory test immediately after the display disclosed very little ability to report the objects in the sequence (less than 20% correct for 167-msec exposures). Thus, there is no doubt that people can often recognize much more than they can report in a brief display, whether the display involves characters or objects.

This still does not tell us whether or not identification of pictures or characters is subject to capacity limits. An obvious approach is to look at search accuracy while varying display set size. In several studies involving letters, Estes and Taylor (1965) presented displays of up to sixteen elements for search. The probability that someone could correctly detect a target fell with increasing numbers of items in the display, something that is not so apparent with the unmasked displays represented in figure 3.3. At first glance, a decrease in detection accuracy with display set size might seem to prove that people have severe capacity limitations in recognizing letters. If they could recognize each item just as well when it was surrounded by many other items, why should their detection accuracy fall as the number of items is increased? This argument sounds reasonable, but as a general proposition it is invalid.

Suppose the processes involved in search have unlimited capacity in a strict sense. That is, the quality of the processing that any particular item undergoes does not vary according to how many other items are processed at the same time. What will happen, then, to the overall accuracy of the observer's detection responses? Assuming that accuracy starts below ceiling (i.e., less than 100% with even the smallest displays), it is almost certain to decline as display set size increases, the unlimited capacity notwithstanding (Eriksen and Spencer, 1969; Duncan, 1980a; Tanner, 1961). The reason is purely statistical. Consider a search task in which an observer reports the presence or absence of a single target character. Assume that each element in the display has a nonzero probability of being confused with the target. Suppose, furthermore, that the subject declares that a target is present when even one element is taken to be a target. In a display containing n items and no target, the probability of at least one such confusion grows with n—the number of distractors. Assume that processing on each channel is statistically independent; that is, whether a confusion occurs on one channel tells one nothing about how likely a confusion is to occur on another channel. If the probability of (mistakenly) construing a nontarget as a target on any single channel is p, the probability of correctly realizing that there are no targets in a display of n elements is $(1 - p)^n$. Hence, the probability of incorrectly reporting that a target was present is just $1 - (1 - p)^n$. Since $1 - p$ is less than 1, $(1 - p)^n$ shrinks as n grows, causing the overall probability of a false alarm to rise. Of course, this is just the simplest model for a simple situation. The same statistical problem (which is referred to as *accumulation of decision noise*) is inherent in any system in which targets are sometimes confused with distractors.

One cannot easily get around this problem by changing one's assumptions about how information is combined in the decision process. For example, suppose the decision process gets more than just a discrete judgment of target versus nontarget from the perceptual system. Following along the lines of signal-detection theory, for example, one might assume that for each item in the display, an individual scalar value is transmitted, representing "how likely is this item to be a target." When no target is present, the likely value of the highest output will tend to grow as display set size grows.[6] If the observer's criterion for saying "yes" remains constant, the probability of a false alarm therefore increases. One might try to get around this by raising the criterion with display set size. The catch is that whereas this might hold constant the probability of a false alarm, it causes the probability of missing a target to rise as display set size grows. One way or another, the error rate in a search task must increase with the number of items to be processed.

This accumulation of decision noise does not occur in a task requiring an observer to make an *independent* report about each individual stimulus, however (see Sperling and Dosher, 1986, for an interesting discussion of this point). Of course, the reason for turning to search tasks in the first place is to reduce the amount of information reported, so this fact is not particularly helpful for present purposes. As described below, simply making an independent yes-no judgment on each channel tends to introduce some of the same additional processing limitations that arise with whole report.

For the sake of completeness, it should be noted that there are certain assumptions on which making a single response about the presence of a target in any of n channels might *not* yield the usual decision noise effect. Suppose the discrimination process sometimes results in a failure to detect a target that is actually present, but never mistakes a nontarget for a target—often termed a *high-threshold model*. In a high-threshold model, the probability of a miss remains constant as display set size grows, and the probability of a false alarm remains zero. High-threshold models have little plausibility as models of detection and discrimination of signals when performance is limited by reduced contrast (Graham, 1989). However, there are few data with which to assess their validity for discrimination tasks involving stimuli-like letters or words where accuracy is limited by masking. The fact that false alarms frequently occur in such tasks, however, would seem to make high-threshold models somewhat implausible.

Fortunately, these theoretical arguments, which admittedly border on the abstruse, have some clear implications regarding how various observations bear on underlying perceptual mechanisms. First, if the quality of stimulus analysis on any channel remains constant without regard to how many channels are to be processed (unlimited capacity), the error rate is still likely to increase along with display set size. Consequently, the observation that error rates do increase with display set size (e.g., Estes and Taylor, 1964) does not by itself imply capacity limitations. In the event that error rates did not increase with display set size, one would be forced to conclude two things: that a high-threshold model applies and that capacity limitations are absent.

If simply examining accuracy as a function of display set size is insufficient, where does this leave us in trying to determine whether there are capacity limits? Researchers have addressed this issue in two ways. One strategy involves confronting the decision noise problem head on and trying to work out how much accuracy should fall with increases in display set size, assuming the entire effect is due to decision noise. The first attempts along these lines used a three-state decision model and seemed to support independent, capacity-free processing (Burns, 1979). More sophisticated analyses using a multichannel version of signal detection theory were undertaken by Marilyn Shaw (1984). In her search task, observers saw brief displays of two or four items (targets could occur in any of the positions independently), and reported where they thought a target had occurred. Shaw assumed that when each location in the display was processed, the result was an output value reflecting the perceived likelihood that a target was present in that position. If a given item is a target, the output value is drawn from some particular (not directly observable) distribution. If the item is a distractor, it is drawn from a similar distribution that has a lower mean. The subject's response depends on picking the location with the highest output value, a procedure that is optimum in certain ways, as well as intuitively natural.

Suppose that subjects are able, under a given set of stimulus conditions, to achieve 90% accuracy in this task when the display set size is two. What should happen to performance when set size is increased to four?

Assuming the decision process just described, together with the assumption that the underlying distributions are Gaussian, Shaw calculated that the proportion of correct responses should fall by about 12% as display set size was increased. As she noted, however, the distribution might not be Gaussian, and she was able to place an upper bound on the size of the display set size cost on the assumption of no capacity limits, regardless of the shape of the distributions. When the task required subjects to detect a luminance increment, the display set size cost was very close to the predictions of the decision model with Gaussian distributions and no capacity limitations, and fell well below the upper bound for all distributions. When the task required detection of a target letter T among a set of distractors (F, ⊢, and ⊣), however, the cost exceeded the upper bound. From this, Shaw inferred that capacity limitations were present in the character task even when subjects searched for the same character over thirty sessions.

Shaw's work is impressive but it does depend heavily on several assumptions, some of which cannot be tested independently. One assumption is that when inputs on one channel triggers the decision that a target is present, the subject can report the location of the channel; this has good empirical support. A second assumption is that the decision process works by taking the scalar outputs from each channel and picking the highest. It sounds reasonable, but since it cannot be tested, this introduces some uncertainty into Shaw's inference that the letter-detection task is capacity limited.

Using slightly different assumptions than Shaw, Palmer (Palmer, Ames, and Lindsey, 1993; Palmer, 1994) compared the costs of display set size in accuracy to those predicted by a signal detection-based model postulating decision noise and no capacity limits. His work has also encompassed a much larger variety of stimuli and tasks. Palmer concluded that for tasks involving discriminations of line length, orientation, and certain judgments involving form, no capacity limitations exist. His displays involved no masks, however. For this reason, given the existence of sensory persistence, it is possible that observers were able to extract the same amount of information from small and large displays because they could allocate capacity to different items at different times.[7] This does not make the result uninteresting, of course, but it does change its implications for the time course of processing.

Simultaneous versus Successive Presentations   The work of Shaw and Palmer demonstrates that with ingenuity, one may be able to determine whether capacity limitations are present by examining how accuracy suffers when observers are forced to monitor greater numbers of channels. To make headway, however, strong assumptions have to be made about the nature of the processing and the nature of the decision. Another strategy is available that is simpler and involves fewer assumptions, and tends to involve assumptions that are more directly testable. In this strategy, developed by Eriksen and Spencer (1969) and Shiffrin and Gardner (1972), the number of items in the display is held constant; what is varied is the relative time at which each item is presented. If there are capacity limitations in processing the display, then subjects should be less accurate if all the items must be processed at the same time compared with a condition in which different items can be processed at different times. This approach was first tried by Eriksen and Spencer (1969). Their subjects detected the target letter A in displays of various numbers of letters, all presented extremely briefly without masks. When the number of items in the display was increased, the hit rate remained approximately constant and the false alarm rate increased. As described earlier, such an increase is to be expected from the accumulation of decision noise even in the absence of capacity limitations. In this critical experiment, subjects were presented displays of nine elements that were exposed either virtually simultaneously (5-msec interstimulus intervals) or successively, paced by the subjects themselves, at a rate of approximately 3 seconds between items. Remarkably, there was little difference in performance, indicating, as the authors put it, that the encoding device can "encode nine letters as efficiently in 50 msec as in 25 seconds" (p. 15).

Shiffrin and Gardner (1972) modified the design by following each display element with a mask and comparing simultaneous with successive displays. In the successive displays, four items were presented in a fixed order, so subjects always knew which item would appear next and where it would be. The procedure used in one of their experiments is shown in figure 3.4. In both the simultaneous (*SIM*) and successive (*SUCC*) conditions, four letters were presented, and subjects determined whether the display had an F or a T (one or the other was always there). Each item was presented for T msec (typically about 40 msec) and followed imme-

Successive Condition

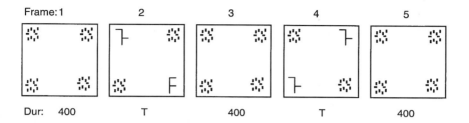

Simultaneous Condition

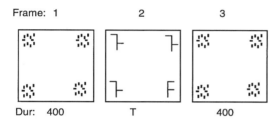

Figure 3.4
Method used in the experiment of Shiffrin and Gardner (1972) comparing successive and simultaneous exposures of search displays. The subject decides if an F or a T is present in a display that also contains three distractors (F-T hybrid characters). In the successive condition, the observer need only process two stimuli at a time, whereas in the simultaneous condition, all four items must be handled at the same time. Regardless of condition, each target or distractor stimulus is always masked after a delay of T msec (adjusted for each subject).

diately by a mask. In the successive condition the items were presented two at a time (each pair lying along a diagonal), with 0.5 second between pairs. (The purpose of the display geometry was to discourage eye movements.) In the simultaneous condition, by contrast, all four items were presented at the same time.

Subjects practiced for one day and then performed the task for three test sessions. The differences between SIM and SUCC performance were negligible. This result is of fundamental importance, and it is referred to frequently in the discussion that follows. Therefore, it is worth considering the method and the logic carefully. Empirically, the result is reliable, having been replicated several times (e.g., Foyle and Shiffrin, unpublished data; Duncan, 1980b; Gardner and Joseph, 1975), although, as Duncan pointed out, it is not uncommon to find tiny SUCC advantages that do not quite reach statistical significance. The inference that characters can be identified without any capacity limitations does rely on certain assumptions. One is that when a target is detected, it is equally likely to be reported in the SUCC and SIM conditions. Is it possible that the SUCC condition is unfairly handicapped because the subject must hold onto the target for an extra half second when the target appears in the first frame? If so, then targets in the first frame should be processed less accurately than targets in the second frame; Shiffrin and Gardner reported that no such effects occurred. Duncan (1980b, p. 285) also observed that performance in the successive condition was unchanged whether subjects were allowed to respond to targets in the first limb immediately, or were required to wait until both limbs had been presented. Thus, it seems unlikely that the delays inherent in the SUCC condition materially affect performance.

Another important assumption concerns the effects of the masks. The interpretation of Shiffrin and Gardner's findings (and many others discussed throughout this book) rests on the idea that the arrival of a mask abruptly halts continuing visual discriminations. If this were not the case, and if perceptual processing of masked stimuli took place without time pressure (suffering instead from poor-quality information), Shiffrin and Gardner's results could be reconciled with serial letter identification. One would merely suppose that even in SIM displays subjects actually identified each character well after the onset of the mask, perhaps one at a time. As Shiffrin and Gardner noted, Eriksen and Spencer's failure to employ masks made this possibility plausible in their study. However, when masks are employed, there is good reason to believe that processing is curtailed by time pressure. For example, consider what happens if offset of a display of letters is followed after a few hundred milliseconds by a mask, with a spatial probe indicating which item the observer should report. When the probe is delayed after offset of the display, error rates soar, which does not happen when there is no mask (Averbach and Coriell, 1961; Pashler, 1984a, 1989). If the mask merely degraded the input from the display, without curtailing the time for which the degraded information remained available, there is no obvious reason why this should happen.

Additional support for these conclusions comes from a study by Liss (1968), who compared the effects of backward masking using a letterlike mask with other ways of making letters difficult to read, such as presenting them extremely briefly or superimposing a mask directly on each character. Given comparable levels of letter identification performance, the backward mask shortened the perceived duration of the letter much more than either the concurrent mask or the brief presentation, so that even when the brief presentation was much briefer than the masked presentation (e.g., 7 vs 70 msec) it appeared to last longer. Backward masking did not reduce perceived brightness nearly as much as brief presentation, on the other hand. All of these results argue against the view that the backward mask sums with the character to produce a degraded montage that persists for some time. Other evidence that masks abbreviate processing comes from the nonmonotonic masking functions commonly found in letter-identification tasks: many masks, particularly those of low luminance, will reduce the identifiability of letters to a greater extent when they are delayed for a few tens of milliseconds rather than presented immediately after the offset of a letter (Purcell and Stewart, 1970). The likely explanation is that whereas stimuli occurring within a very brief time window are integrated, when two stimuli are separated in time by at least some tens of milliseconds, the second event replaces or interrupts processing of the first (Turvey, 1973). Some data suggest that interruption may not be the sole factor that operates under such conditions (Schultz and Eriksen, 1977), but what is critical for present purposes is that the masks do abbreviate processing time, causing errors in trials in which perceptual recognition happens to occur more slowly than average. This conclusion seems amply supported by the evidence just described.

A further assumption necessary for the interpretation of Shiffrin and Gardner's finding of equivalent performance in simultaneous and successive conditions is that the successive condition is not unfairly handicapped in some other way. Suppose, for instance, the masks themselves demanded visual-processing capacity. If this were the case, the successive condition might fail to show an advantage because, like the simultaneous condition, it effectively required recognition of four items at a time. Several sets of unpublished data that bear on this. For example, Peter Badgio and I replicated the basic Shiffrin and Gardner result using four letters and four masks, presenting just one mask after each target character.[8]

Shiffrin and Gardner's result appears to be a strong one, therefore, and indicates that the discrimination between two possible letter targets can be carried out in parallel and without capacity limitations for as many as four characters a time. Of course, detecting a target shows only that a discrimination between target and nontarget letters was successfully accomplished; it does not necessarily show that everything we would normally describe as "identification" or "reading" was accomplished.

Extensions and Limitations   The Shiffrin and Gardner result provides a powerful demonstration of parallel perceptual analysis without capacity limitations, albeit with a modest display load and a restricted type of task. Outside the laboratory, of course, people do not often encounter scenes as impoverished as these four-letter displays. An obvious research strategy, therefore, is to extend the technique to search tasks with greater perceptual loads.[9] If perceptual machinery truly has unlimited capacity (as Shiffrin and Gardner proposed), performance in SIM and SUCC displays should remain equal, however many discriminations are required and however difficult these discriminations are. If capacity is limited, with more complex discriminations a SUCC advantage should emerge.

A number of studies have used simultaneous/successive comparisons with more demanding tasks, and the equality of SIM and SUCC presentations breaks down beyond about four characters with zero or one target. Foyle and Shiffrin (unpublished data) varied the number of display elements in character search. With four characters, advantages for SUCC were negligible, as in Shiffrin and Gardner; for twelve character displays, on the other hand, the SUCC condition averaged 11% better than the SIM condition. Fisher (1984) required subjects to detect a target digit 5 in large displays[10] of 160 characters plus masks. In the simultaneous condition there were eight characters per frame, and in the successive condition there were four characters and four masks per frame. Frame durations ranged from 40 to 200 msec. Figure 3.5 shows the results: performance was much better with successive than simultaneous displays. In fact, accuracy with the simultaneous displays and a given exposure duration d is very close to that observed with successive displays and exposure duration 2d.

Kleiss and Lane (1986) used displays of four characters, but varied the difficulty of target-distractor discriminations. When the task required finding digit targets among letters, differences between simultaneous and successive displays were small. When the task required detecting Rs among Ps and Qs, constructed so that the Rs could be created by recombining the parts of the distractors, performance in the successive condition was superior. This task was motivated by Treisman's feature-integration theory, which is touched on below. A sizable advantage for the successive condition appeared, measuring about 14% correct, or a 50% reduction in d'.[11]

Similar results were found when the SIM/SUCC technique was applied with displays composed of words. Duncan (1987) had subjects search for a fixed target word (e.g., stab) among letter strings with some of the same bigrams (e.g., abst, stux, icab); performance was substantially better for successive compared with simultaneous presentations. Ling-Po Shiu and I also compared simultaneous and successive displays of words, requiring observers to perform a semantic detection task with orthographically unrelated words. In one experiment, subjects saw two words in each trial, and tried to tell whether a place name (e.g., Houston) was present in the display of nonplace name distractors (e.g., Remedy). In simultaneous trials, the two words appeared at the same time, above and below fixation. In the successive condition, a single word appeared either

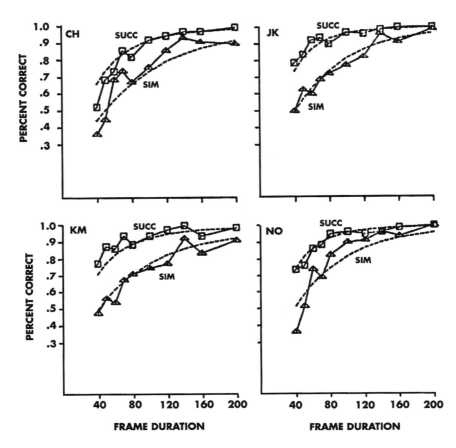

Figure 3.5
Performance of four subjects in Fisher's overload-simultaneous (SIM) and overload-successive (SUCC) conditions. Reprinted with permission from Fisher (1984, figure 3, p. 457).

above or below the fixation, followed by a mask, and after a half-second delay, the other word, followed by its mask (the position of the two words was independent and unpredictable). The error rate for the simultaneous presentations was 35.4%, close to double the 17.6% with successive presentations.[12] It can be seen that the SIM/SUCC method reveals severe capacity limitations for processing relatively complex stimuli such as words.

These conclusions are supported by some interesting observations reported by Kahneman and Treisman (1984), who required subjects to read a briefly presented upper-case word that was followed by a mask. Subjects were able to do this with 63% accuracy. When the display contained not only the upper-case word, but also a lower-case word or a scrambled upper-case word (either stimulus could be in either position), accuracy plummeted to 38% and 35%, respectively. As these investigators put it, "to a first approximation, . . . subjects were only able to process a single item" in the display (p. 52). Strictly speaking, one might dispute this conclusion, since this decrement could reflect accumulation of decision noise rather than capacity limitations, although its magnitude seems much larger than typical decision noise effects. Unfortunately, the SIM/SUCC methodology has not apparently been applied with displays of line drawings or photographs to assess capacity limits in something more like ordinary scene perception.

In summary, comparisons of subjects' accuracy in searching for pre-specified targets in simultaneous and successive displays provide a fairly satisfying, albeit still incomplete, picture of human beings' limitations in visual recognition. Despite a few inconsistencies, several conclusions are generally supported. With a handful of characters to be searched, there is no successive advantage, and thus no capacity limits, unless the discrimination is very difficult. Evidence for capacity limitations emerges once the difficulty of the discriminations is increased. This can be achieved by using highly confusable characters or characters that contain rearrangements of the features present in the other characters. When one uses words rather than letters, the advantage for the SUCC condition becomes very large, suggesting that the words are often read one at a time. Unfortunately, the method has not yet been applied to the perception of pictures or other nonlinguistic stimuli.

A promising new approach to exploring perceptual capacity limitations was described by Prinzmetal and colleagues (submitted). Instead of searching simultaneously or successively presented displays, subjects detected a letter target in a central display and noted the color of a peripheral dot; the letters and the dot were presented simultaneously or successively. Subjects indicated the color of the dot by placing a cursor on an essentially continuous color palette. The precision of the color judgment was lessened when letter and color displays were simultaneous, suggesting that the competing task increased the variability of the perceived color.

The Double-Detection Problem   It is not necessary to use a difficult target/distractor discrimination or a large displays set size to find instances in which successive displays are processed more effectively than simultaneous ones. Duncan (1980b) observed that presenting two targets in a search task was sufficient. His displays were similar to those of Shiffrin and Gardner (figure 3.4), with two limbs, each consisting of two characters and followed by masking characters. In successive displays, the limbs were separated by a half-second and occurred in a predictable order. The difference from the other experiments discussed here was that targets could be presented in each of the limbs (their occurrence was independent). In his combined task, Duncan's subjects specified whether one or more targets were present anywhere in the display. Here, they were more accurate when there were two targets rather than one, and the improvement in accuracy was well predicted from the single-target performance simply by assuming that targets were registered independently. (If the probability of detecting one target is p, the predicted probability of detecting two targets is $1 - (1 - p)^2$.) This independence is fully consistent with the equality, emphasized above, between simultaneous and successive displays, although the SIM/SUCC equality does not actually entail the independence.

In Duncan's separated task, subjects responded to each limb individually, indicating whether a target had been presented in that limb. When one target was presented, performance in the successive condition was not much different than in the simultaneous condition (the Shiffrin and Gardner result again). However, when two targets were presented, accuracy in the simultaneous condition was substantially worse than in successive condition. (Duncan did not put two targets in the same limb in the SUCC condition.)

At first blush, the results from the combined and separated tasks might sound contradictory: two targets are processed independently, yielding an increase in detection probabilities in the combined task; however, when the two targets must be reported independently, the detections are not independent. In fact, there is no contradiction here. Presenting two targets rather than one increases the chance of detection even if only one target can ever be detected. Analogously, buying two lottery tickets increases the chance you will be a first-place winner in the drawing, even though by definition there can be only one such winner.

But why should there be a problem detecting two targets at the same time? The fact that performance is comparable in SIM and SUCC (when at most one target is present) shows that there is no shortage of machinery for carrying out the processing necessary to discriminate targets from distractors. The problem is not caused by the need to make two separate overt responses: when subjects simply had to count the number of targets (one vs two targets present), the decrement remained. (In chapter 6 we will see further evidence that perceptual capacity limits are fundamentally different from response-related processing limitations.) This two-target effect does not seem to hinge on the requirement to make a complex symbolic discrimination such as letter versus digit, either: Duncan (1985) found essentially the same result when the targets were line segments tilted 45 degrees and the distractors were vertical line segments.

Duncan offered a reasonable interpretation: "no stimulus attribute can be overtly reported unless the target . . . gains access to [a] limited-capacity system" (p. 96). In this view, the process of figuring out whether something is a target does not run up against capacity limitations, but handling targets does. In this account, the limitation must occur *after* detection, since it pertains only to targets, not nontargets. Some explanation along these lines seems required, but the details can be disputed. Duncan formulated his statements within the broader framework of late selection theory (he proposed that stimulus analysis mechanisms were not only capacity free, but also unselective in their operation). As emphasized in chapter 1, claims about capacity limits and claims about selectivity are logically separable, and more recent work with simultaneous and successive displays (including work by Duncan himself) argues that capacity limitations do exist. But this does not reduce the interest in Duncan's finding that the need to process multiple targets can cause the appearance of processing limitations not caused by target/distractor discrimination.

The generality of the two-target problem was challenged by Braun and Sagi (1990, 1991). They found no interference when one of the tasks required only detection of a feature gradient, namely, a grating patch that differed in orientation from the surrounding elements in a dense texture field. The authors combined this task with various kinds of discrimination tasks involving a single stimulus embedded in the center of the texture field. Plotting accuracy as a function of stimulus-onset asynchrony (SOA) between display and mask, they found dual-task performance to be as good as single-task performance.

Braun and Sagi suggest that detecting discontinuities in dense textures may not be subject to the same limitations as object recognition. These discontinuities are often said to exhibit "pop-out," which the authors argue is truly preattentive and therefore avoids the limitations revealed by Duncan's work. Another interpretation is possible, however. In Braun and Sagi's single-task trials, the stimuli were just as in the dual-task trials, but subjects merely searched for the orientation singleton or performed the central discrimination. Although this procedure allows the stimulus conditions in the two tasks to be matched, it raises the possibility that subjects might have been unable to prevent the central target from being detected when they were searching for a break in the surrounding texture field, even in the single-task condition. Conceivably, then, rather than showing that Duncan's two-target decrement can be averted by using targets that pop out against a texture field, Braun and Sagi's results might perhaps indicate limits in selectivity. Further work on this point is necessary. At present, it is an open question whether certain primitive kinds of judgments and detections operate free of interference with, and cause no interference for, related visual tasks. Particularly plausible candidates would be the visual processes that underly postural adjustments and other behaviors that rarely engage our conscious thought, which may be handled by different visual machinery than that which is involved in object recognition (Trevarthen, 1968).

Reporting Different Properties of a Single Object   The special difficulty noted by Duncan in detecting two targets is robust, and occurs in auditory as well as visual monitoring tasks. In Duncan's (1980b) experiments, the several targets that had to be detected were different objects presented in different parts of the visual field. However, when an observer tries to report different attributes of a single briefly presented object (e.g., color, shape, texture), a different result is found. This brings us to a topic that was studied by investigators in the first part of the century: attention to multiple dimensions (e.g., Yokoyaka, described by Boring, 1942; see Egeth, 1967, for a review of early literature). The literature on discrimination of multiple attributes did not present a coherent picture until recently, probably because the early investigations were carried out before the role of memory limitations in reporting from brief displays was generally recognized.

Külpe (1904) carried out the best-known early work on the issue by presenting several different objects, each varying along dimensions such as color and form. Observers were required to report all the dimensions of each object. In different trials, varying emphasis was placed on being accurate with respect to one dimension or another. People were most accurate in reporting whatever dimension was most heavily emphasized, often substantially so. If subjects were capable of reporting two dimensions as effectively as they could report one with no capacity limits, there is no obvious reason why emphasis would have such an effect; thus, the results suggest a form of capacity limitation. Similar findings were obtained by Lawrence and LaBerge (1956), who varied the emphasis placed on different dimensions by means of a monetary reward. However, they observed a possible confounding of emphasis with order of report. Because the emphasized attribute is typically reported first, the less-emphasized attributes must be retained during the time the emphasized attributes are being reported. Responding to this objection, Harris and Haber (1963) controlled the order of report and still found some, albeit a fairly modest, effect of emphasis that apparently could not be attributed to the output factors mentioned above.

The proper interpretation of these studies depends on what factor or factors actually limit performance. Most of the experiments used highly discriminable colors and reasonably long exposure durations, with no postfield masks. With such stimuli, one would expect observers to be able to report all the attributes of a single item with almost perfect accuracy, or, for example, to find the discrepant color in a display composed of dozens of items. Therefore, the likely reason that performance was below ceiling in these tasks is that a considerable number of objects were displayed. When displays contain more information than can be retained in STM, emphasizing one attribute or another is bound to affect strategic decisions over which information to preserve. Therefore, results like those of Harris and Haber are consistent with the hypothesis that perceptual analysis itself is unaffected by emphasis; what they rule out is the rather improbable idea that different dimensions do not compete for either perceptual processing or storage space in STM.

To assess perceptual analysis per se, the obvious strategy is to present fewer objects (preferably just a single one) and to use brief exposures to limit performance. Several such experiments have been performed, and happily, the results are in good agreement. Allport (1971) presented brief displays of three colored shapes, followed by a mask (SOAs varied from 20 to 60 msec). In the color-only condition, subjects were to report all the colors, and in the shape-only condition, they were to report the shapes. The dual-task condition involved reporting all three shapes and then reporting all three colors. Reports of both color and shape in the dual-task condition were essentially as good as those of the same dimensions in the single-task condition.

Subsequent studies examined a variety of multidimensional discriminations using just a single object, requiring fairly subtle perceptual discriminations. Duncan (1984), for example, found identical dual- and single-judgment performance when combining judgments of tilt and texture of a line, or size of a box and position of a gap in the same box. In subsequent unpublished studies involving dimensions such as color, he found no significant single-task advantages with multiple attributes of the same object (Duncan, personal communication). The same observation was made for report of the orientation and spatial frequency of a patch of lines that was presented briefly and followed by a mask (Wing and Allport, 1972) and for report of these two attributes with sine wave grating patches presented at near-threshold contrast (Graham, 1989).

In summary, early studies appeared to indicate limitations in perception of multiple attributes of individual objects, but they probably demonstrated that (a) multiple attributes can, at least to some degree, compete for short-term memory storage, and (b) people have strategic control over what they put into short-term memory. Allport's results indicate that even when six attributes must be stored, neither perceptual nor memory storage competition may be important, since he found no dual-task decrements with such stimuli. With just a single object and discriminations that are time or contrast limited, the results are clear: observers can perceive and retain information on several attributes without any measurable interference. (This issue relates to further research that is discussed in chapter 5, bearing on a question sometimes as whether, as it is often put, attention is allocated to objects or to locations.)

A related and somewhat neglected question concerns the processing of *parts* of a single object, rather than multiple dimensions. Only one investigation of this sort appears in the literature, but its results are intriguing. Travers (1974) compared simultaneous and successive presentations of the individual letters composing a word. In successive displays, each letter was presented for 48 msec, at which point it was masked and the next letter appeared. In the simultaneous condition, all the letters were presented at the same time for 48 msec and then masked. Rather than producing any advantage, the successive whole-word presentations reduced recognition accuracy all the way to 34%, compared with 84% for the simultaneous displays. These results seem hard to reconcile with the idea that individual letters in a word are identified sequentially. The successive disadvantage implies that word identification requires simultaneous outputs from letter-detecting mechanisms, which is precluded in the successive displays. For the same reason, this result adds support to the assumption that masks rapidly terminate visual identification. If masked stimuli remained available for some time, albeit in a degraded form, this successive disadvantage would be hard to account for.

Spatial Interactions Between Detections   As described in the previous section, people have difficulty detecting two different targets even when they are perfectly capable of monitoring two different sources without interference. A detection on one channel makes a detection on another channel less likely. However, people can detect two different properties of a single object virtually without impairment. How can these result be reconciled? One possible clue may be found in several studies that investigated how detection on one channel affects monitoring performance on other channels as a function of the spatial relationship between the channels.

Hoffman, Nelson, and Houck (1983, experiment 1) had subjects perform two tasks: detect a digit in one of four locations in a masked display with letter distractors, and detect flicker, a momentary offset of a dot that was located adjacent to one of the characters. Subjects were substantially more accurate in detecting the digit target when it was adjacent to the flicker rather than in one of the other three locations. In another experiment the effect was somewhat larger when the digit task preceded the irrelevant visual discrimination task.

These observations are supported by the results of a slightly more complicated experiment by LaBerge (1983, experiment 2). This involved two successive frames in which subjects responded only if they detected a target in both frames. Targets were defined differently in the two frames, however. The first frame consisted of a row of five letters that remained present for 0.5 second. This was followed by a second display that also consisted of a row of five items, one character and four plus signs. The subject responded only if a target was present in the first display *and* the character in the second display was a 7. A target in the first display might be defined in one of two ways. In some blocks, the task required processing all five characters as a word (targets were first names and distractors were common nouns). Here, RTs (for detection of targets in both frames) depended very little on the location of the 7 in the second display. However, when a target in the first display was defined as the occurrence of a particular letter in the center position, RTs were much faster when the 7 in the *second* display also occurred near the center. Although retinal eccentricity was confounded with being located where the preceding target was in the initial experiments, the basic effect is not completely accounted for by that factor (LaBerge and Brown, 1989).

The results of Hoffman, Nelson, and Houck and LaBerge illustrate the existence of a spatial dependency between two visual detections; that is, people are better at taking in information from adjacent or coincident parts of the visual field than from more widely separated parts. This is less remarkable in the case of LaBerge task's, which explicitly demanded spatial selectivity in processing the first display. The results of Hoffman, Nelson, and Houck (1983), on the other hand, show something more: detection of a flicker is more impaired by detection of distant digit target than a nearby digit target, even though the subject could not possibly know where either one would be in advance of the trial. Cave and Pashler (1995) demonstrated a similar form of spatial dependence in a task in which detection was based on color. Subjects saw a series of frames, each containing a target digit of one color and a distractor digit of another color, and tried to name the highest digit of the target color. Subjects made fewer errors when successive targets appeared at the same location than when they appeared at different locations.

Still another illustration of the same point can be found in experiments requiring speeded detection of the conjunction of two targets. Moore and Osman (1993) had subjects search for both a color and a form target, pressing the yes key if an X and something red were present in the display, which remained present until response. When the two were in the same location (i.e., there was a red X in the display), the conjunction was detected almost as rapidly as either element was detected by itself in a disjunctive control search task (red or X). When red and X were both present, but in different locations, on the other hand, conjunction detection was substantially slower.

Processing Brief Displays: Summary and Interpretation   Despite a few lingering disagreements and uncertainties, several conclusions can be drawn from these studies examining limitations in simultaneous visual processing with brief displays. When people see a briefly exposed display, they have no means of remembering more than a small amount of information long enough to report it. With letters or digits, they can retain about four or five items. This storage is likely to be in a visual form rather than an articulatory or verbal form; at least it does not seem to compete with articulatory/phonological memory for spoken material. People have a high degree of voluntary control over what information they store in this limited-capacity short-term memory, however. If the display is followed by a dark postfield containing little information, a large amount of visual information (well over four or five items) remains available for a fraction of a second in a more capacious but transient memory system (iconic persistence). This prolongs the time that voluntary control can be exercised, permitting the partial-report advantage discovered by Sperling. Under ordinary viewing conditions, however, iconic memory is probably irrelevant because when stimulus input ceases, new input replaces it; normally, this happens when a saccadic eye movement occurs. Here, the contents of the postsaccadic field wipe out any iconic memory for the contents of the initial fixation.

Even with a very brief presentation, say, 100 or 200 msec, what an observer can actually report may greatly underestimate how much visual material the person will have identified. An observer searching for a target such as a luminance increment or a familiar simple figure has sufficient processing machinery to perform a target/nontarget discrimination on several items in parallel and with minimal capacity limitations. However, capacity limitations appear whenever more than one target must be detected and reported. Some evidence suggests that target detection results in a constriction in the uptake of visual information to the region of the visual field near where the target was present. Visual capacity limitations are also clearly apparent when the discrimination involves highly similar letters, or when people detect complex stimuli such as words or pictures. If the task requires reporting more than one attribute from a display rather than the presence of a single target, interference is usually found if the reported attributes reside in different objects. This interference seems to be avoided when the attributes are part of a single object.

An Empirical Illustration   Two experiments recently carried out in my laboratory illustrate a number of these points in a fairly transparent way (Pashler, 1994a). The procedure is shown in figure 3.6.

Subjects saw display 1, consisting of six characters, that remained on the screen for 200 msec, and then disappeared. After a delay of 800 msec, display 2 appeared. Display 2 was exactly the same as display 1, except that one character identity was switched to a new character with a probability of one-half. Display 2 remained present until the subject made an (unspeeded) same/different response. The overall error rate on the

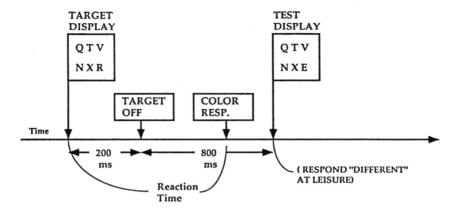

Figure 3.6
In the double-judgment experiments the subject sometimes responds to the color of elements in the target display, and always tries to remember elements in the target display, to determine whether a test display presented later is identical to the target display. Responses to colors in the target display are speeded; responses to the test display are not; the test display remains present until subject responds. Reprinted with permission from Pashler (1994a, p. 116).

same/different judgment was 26.4%, demonstrating storage of about the same amount of information as seen in whole report (see Pashler, 1988). Not surprisingly, subjects tended to miss a change more often than they misreported one. Other conditions required subjects to perform an additional task involving display 1. In one condition, the six characters in display 1 were all colored red or all green, and subjects made an immediate, speeded button-push response to this color (this response was almost always completed before display 2 even appeared).[13] This affected the error rate on the same/different judgments to display 2 only minimally, raising it to 32.0%. In a third condition, only *one* character in display 1 was red or green and the other five were light gray. The overall error rate was increased a bit more, to 35.1%.

Were subjects detecting the color and grabbing items for the same/different task independently? To answer this question, performance in the single-color-item condition was analyzed further. When the single-color character was the same character whose identity was changed in display 2 (which occurred no more often than chance), the change was detected

56.3% of the time, compared with only 29.4% of changes in the other positions. In short, detecting a target in one dimension (color) largely determined which objects were stored for the judgment in another dimension (i.e., form). This is consistent with the interpretation of the results of Duncan, Houck, and Hoffman and the others: the detection of any aspect of a target object directly entails storage of the multiple attributes of an object in visual short-term memory. This would claim that the effect is mandatory, but one might propose that it occurs merely for reasons of convenience: observers cannot store all the items, so they might as well include one of the items whose color is being detected. To see if the effect is strategic in this sense, additional experiments were carried out using the same two tasks—color classification in display 1, and same/different judgment—but with three of the six characters colored either all red or all green. Display 1 was replaced with a mask after 200 msec. In one-half of the sessions the sixteen subjects were informed that if a character in display 2 were to change, it would be in one of the colored letters, and it always was. The error rate on the same/different task was 20.9%. In another half of the sessions, they were informed that if a character were to change, it would be one of the uncolored letters. The error rate on the same/different task rose to 43.6%, not much better than chance. In short, observers had great difficulty registering the color of one set of letters while storing the other three in visual short-term memory.

The results reinforce most of the conclusions described earlier. The most important of these is that although the color discrimination is easy (the differences employed were undoubtedly gross enough to support pop-out), *using* the color information still had significant consequences for subsequent processing of information from the display. The main consequence appears to be a restriction of information uptake to the objects, or what is equivalent for present purposes, the locations of these objects (see chapter 5). Another implication is that the selection and production of a response produced fairly minor interference with the uptake of visual information from the display as a whole. Chapters 6 and 7 describe evidence suggesting that whereas selection of a speeded response produces profound interference at a central level, neither visual perception nor storing information in short-term memory is subject to this sort of central interference.

Speeded Visual Search

Slopes and Their Interpretation

The preceding sections focused on the accuracy with which people can report the contents of a briefly presented display or detect the presence of a target in such a display. In the past several years some of the most interesting studies of visual search have used speeded tasks in which displays remain present until response, with reaction time rather than accuracy serving as the key dependent measure. Usually, the focus in these studies is on how long it takes to detect targets (or the absence of targets) as a function of display set size. The basic rationale for this kind of study is simple and intuitive. If the subject can search all the items in a display in parallel without capacity limitations, then response times should not vary with display set size (i.e., what are often termed flat slopes or pop-out should be observed). On the other hand, if the subject must process items sequentially, RTs should increase linearly with display set size. A self-terminating search through the display (i.e., a search that terminates as soon as a target is found) would result in the target being found, on average, half-way through the search process. Therefore, it would predict that slopes for target-absent trials should be twice as great as slopes for target-present trials (Sternberg, 1969). Treisman and her colleagues applied this logic to speeded visual search using a diverse range of targets, distractors, and instructions (Treisman and Gelade, 1980); her research program and the feature-integration theory that developed out of it inspired much of the visual search research since the 1980s.

Before turning to the major findings in speeded visual search studies, a few methodological issues should be mentioned. The inference from parallel search to flat display set size functions can probably be inverted with a fair degree of confidence; that is, there is little doubt that flat slopes entail parallel search as well.[14] However, slopes that are not so flat, say, 20 or 30 msec per item, are trickier to interpret. One reason for this is that speeded search tasks are not immune to the problem of decision noise that was discussed above. Recall that when an observer analyzes each of a set of channels with equal accuracy regardless of display set size, overall accuracy is nonetheless almost sure to fall as set size grows, for purely statistical reasons. In studies using RTs as the primary dependent measure, accuracy is typically high, well over 90%.

Far from making the problem of decision noise go away, this may actually make it more problematic, as Wickelgren (1977) observed. To see why, suppose subjects seek to achieve approximately equal accuracy with both small and large display sets. To do this, they must acquire more information from each item in the larger displays to counteract the accumulation of decision noise. One way to do this would be to spend more time processing the display. Thus, an increase in RTs with display set size might arise even if an unlimited-capacity parallel search were taking place.

A second problem exists in interpreting slopes in search experiments: how to determine which mental operations are actually taking up the extra time associated with larger displays. An increase in RTs with display set size may reflect an increase in the time required for perceptual processing of the display items, but it need not. It might instead mean that subsequent decision or memory comparison processes take longer, for example. As usual, we have the problem of using a combination of common sense and previous empirical findings to work out the nature of the processing involved in carrying out the task. Thus, suppose all the items in a display of eight characters were identified in parallel as soon as the display was presented. Determining whether a target is present may require a further step of comparing the results with a stored representation of the target. The existence of a stage of this sort has been suggested from time to time; Schneider and Shiffrin (1977), for example, proposed a late selection theory (parallel visual analysis), but hypothesized an additional comparison stage (circumvented when the observer had enough practice searching for a given target set).

A third point that should be kept in mind is that search slopes do not cleanly partition themselves into two categories, steep or flat; observed values lie all along a continuum ranging from near zero to very steep (100 msec/item or more). Given these uncertainties, one has little choice but to follow Wolfe (in press) and characterize search slopes as more or less efficient, rather than trying to sort them into two categories (serial or parallel), as has been common practice since Treisman and Gelade (1980). Fourth, one might suspect that time taken for eye movements would be important in unspeeded search tasks. While it is true that subjects often make eye movements in more difficult search tasks with displays that remain present until response, this does not appear to play any critical role in generating search slopes (Klein and Farrell, 1989).

When speeded visual search tasks are carried out with alphanumeric characters as targets and distractors, slopes in the intermediate range of 20 to 30 msec per item are common (Atkinson, Holmgren, and Juola, 1969; Cavanagh and Chase, 1971). The display set size slopes are usually steeper for target-absent trials, suggesting some at least some degree of self-terminating search, especially when arrays are circular, eliminating the potential confounding of display set size and retinal eccentricity. Slopes can be essentially flat when people search for a single prespecified target letter among digits or vice versa, but here categorical differences seem to facilitate search only to the degree that they enhance the physical discriminability of target and background characters (Krueger, 1984; Duncan, 1983). What is impressive, though, is people's ability to search for an unspecified digit among letters or vice versa (Egeth, Jonides, and Wall, 1972; see also Sperling and Melchner, 1978). Slopes in this task are not completely flat, but search is not a great deal less efficient than searching for just a single target letter. Given the uncertainties in interpreting slopes, these results are consistent with the hypothesis of parallel identification of characters, but they fall short of proving it.

Feature Searches: Primary Findings   Although early studies of search concentrated mostly on letters and digits, recent research in this area more often used simple geometric figures and shapes, color patches, and other stimuli purposefully chosen to be unfamiliar to subjects and often for their relevance to Treisman's feature-integration hypotheses. Thus, discussion has not focused on capacity limitations in identification; after all, most of these stimuli are not well learned symbols in the first place. Instead, the question is whether the visual search process is serial or parallel. In the case of certain target/distractor combinations the results are clear. When the distractors are all identical and the target differs substantially from these distractors in color, brightness, size, or orientation, search is usually highly efficient; adding an extra item to a display costs the subject only a few milliseconds or perhaps none at all (Smith, 1962; Treisman and Gelade, 1980). This highly efficient search is undoubtedly parallel, and the effect is aptly termed pop-out. Pop-out can also be found when people search for a feature target among heterogeneous distractors. However, the exact conditions necessary to allow this to happen have not been fully worked out. Smallman and Boynton (1990) found flat search slopes using nine different colors in their displays (see also Moraglia et al, 1989). D'Zmura (1991) used two distractor colors and one target color, and found that the slopes depended on the relationship of the target and distractors in color space. Flat slopes were found only when the targets and distractors could be readily separated from each other by a single line drawn in color space. The difference probably hinges on the size of the target distractor differences involved, with D'Zmura's conclusions holding for closer separations than Smallman and Boynton's (Bauer, Jolicoeur, and Cowan, 1995).

In some cases, efficient search seems to depend on the existence of a categorical difference between targets and distractors, even though stimuli are arrayed on a continuum, geometrically speaking. For example, figure 3.7 illustrates an orientation search that was studied by Wolfe and colleagues (1992). In the left panel the target but none of the distractors would normally be described as steep, and search is quite efficient; in the right panel, both target and distractors are steep, and search is much less efficient, despite the fact that the figures are otherwise comparable. In

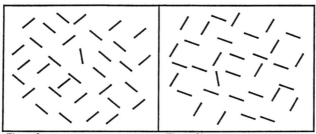

Figure 9a
T: -10 deg among D: -50 & +50 deg

Figure 9b
T: -10 deg among D: -70 & +30 deg

Figure 3.7
In left panel, searching for a −10-degree-oriented target among −50- and +50-degree distractors is easy. In right panel, searching for a −10-degree target among −70- and +30-degree distractors is hard. Note that in both figures the angular difference between target and the distractors is 40 or 60 degrees. Reprinted from Wolfe (1992, figure 9a/9b).

visual search based on color, however, categorization does not make any difference. People tend to agree about basic color categories, and these may be universal. Smallman and Boynton (1990) compared search involving basic versus nonbasic colors and found no difference. For some dimensions, search may be most efficient when the targets are extreme on a particular dimension. For example, search for medium-size targets among small and large distractors is not as easy as search for large *or* small targets (Treisman and Gelade, 1980).

Treisman and Souther (1985) found that it is far easier to find a target defined by the presence of a given feature than it is to report the absence of the same feature (see also Treisman and Gormican, 1988). For example, the left panel in figure 3.8 illustrates the difficulty of searching for a circle without a bisecting line, compared with the much easier search shown in the right panel where the target is a circle with a line. These researchers suggest that asymmetry between presence and absence searches may arise because the search process checks the total amount of activity anywhere in a feature map—a set of detector units that

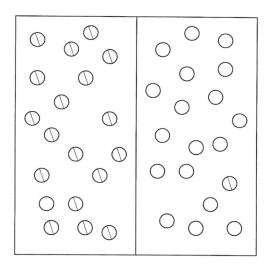

Figure 3.8
Search asymmetry. In left panel the target is an empty circle. This produces a difficult search compared with the right panel, in which the target is the circle with line. Redrawn with modification from Treisman and Souther (1985).

represent the presence of a particular feature type in various positions throughout the visual field. Naturally, it would be easier to distinguish some activity from no activity than it would be to distinguish activity in all relevant positions from activity in all but one. Regardless of the details,[15] search asymmetries are likely to provide a useful method for determining what visual attributes are and are not represented by elementary visual features. Of interest, the greater difficulty of detecting absence compared with presence is found with tactile as well as visual-detection tasks (Sathian and Burton, 1991). Similar asymmetries may arise with semantic as well as visual features; Lawrence (1971) found that people more readily detected an animal name in a list of nonanimal names than a nonanimal name in a list of animal names.

The visual findings naturally raise the question of whether the features revealed by this method can be identified with the neural detectors revealed by single-unit recording in the visual cortex. As a wider range of search tasks have been studied, it has emerged that the features that generate pop-out can depend on quite complicated perceptual analysis, raising doubts about any such simple correspondence. For example, Cavanagh, Arguin, and Treisman (1990) found pop-out for orientation differences even when the orientation was a property of an elongated region demarcated by differences in texture, rather than changes in luminance. To detect the orientation of this sort of texture region, the visual system must first locate the differences in individual texture elements that demarcate the boundary between regions. Pop-out can also arise as a result of differences in three-dimensional properties inferred from various depth cues. One example is shape from shading (Enns and Rensink, 1990). Another is size-distance scaling: when different objects are seen at different distances, their perceived size depends on both their perceived distance and their retinal extent (roughly speaking, it is proportional to the product of the two factors). Perceived size as well as retinal size can contribute to pop-out, suggesting that pop-out depends on comparisons that occur (or can occur) after size-distance scaling (Ramachandran, Pashler, and Plummer, 1990). These examples are just a few of the findings revealing that what is sometimes called higher-level vision contributes substantially to pop-out. One implication of these data is that these higher visual operations can operate in parallel across the visual field. Although this conclusion may frustrate any simple attempt to equate feature detectors with neurons, it makes some functional sense. Detecting boundaries in surfaces is likely to be critical for visual guidance of behavior, and it makes sense that whatever cues can help with this detection are likely to be used.

Conjunction Searches   When a task requires detecting a target composed of a conjunction of color and form, search is usually less efficient than feature search involving the same attributes. For example, finding a green T among green Os and red Ts produces steeper slopes than finding green things among red or finding Ts among Os. Treisman and Gelade (1980), in their original proposal of a feature-integration theory, suggested that detecting conjunctions always requires a self-terminating search through the elements of a display. Extensive evidence now shows that this need not be the case. For example, self-terminating search predicts that the variance of target-present RTs should grow sharply with display set size, outstripping variances on target-absent trials. The reason for this is that in target-present trials, the target might be found anywhere from the beginning to the end of the search, whereas target absence is always registered at the completion of search. In fact, target-present variances do not seem to increase in this fashion (Ward and McClelland, 1989). Even mean search latencies often fail to conform to what Treisman's account would predict.

For example, fine-grained analyses often disclose distinct nonlinearities (Pashler, 1987) and not uncommonly, slopes in color/form conjunctions turn out unexpectedly flat (Wolfe et al., 1989). Another observation that poses problems for feature-integration theory is that slopes for color-form conjunction sometimes depends only on the number of items having one of the desired features, not on the total number of items in the display (Egeth, Virzi, and Garbart, 1984).

Nonetheless, some kinds of conjunction searches clearly produce highly inefficient, laborious search that seems indisputably serial. This is often the case when search depends on the spatial arrangement of form features within the same object rather than on conjunctions across dimensions such as color and form. Figure 3.9 shows one example. The target (black above white) has reversed polarity from the distractors

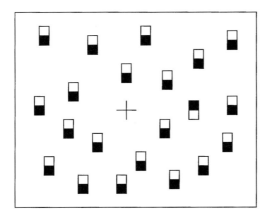

Figure 3.9
A difficult search: stare directly at the fixation point and find the item that differs from the rest. Heathcote and Mewhort (1993) reported data from a task very similar to this one.

(white above black); in a task very close to this, Heathcote and Mewhort (1993) found slopes of approximately 70 to 100 msec per item; performance improved greatly after a few thousand practice trials, however. Logan (1994) had subjects search for a plus above a dash (distractors were dashes above pluses) and found serial slopes on the order of 100 msec per item; even 6,000 trials of practice did not reduce these slopes much. Not every search depending on spatial arrangements of features turns out so difficult, however. In certain cases where the background is composed of homogeneous distractors (Humphreys, Quinlan, and Riddoch, 1989), or when the distractor items can be grouped into a common shape (Donnelly, Humphreys, and Riddoch, 1991), search seems relatively easy. Logan (1994) found some improvement with practice, albeit only a modest amount, when the plus and dash were connected rather than separate.

Conclusions   This very selective review of recent findings from speeded visual search studies yields a number of conclusions. When search slopes are nearly flat, search is obviously efficient and presumably parallel. This occurs when targets differ substantially from distractors along some simple featural dimension such as color or orientation. The differences that can produce efficient search need not be attributes coded in the early visual system; three-dimensional properties and other higher-order perceptual phenomena contribute as well. Feature search can be made as inefficient as one likes by decreasing the separation between target and distractors along a dimension such as color or orientation. Although conjunction targets are generally more difficult to detect than feature targets, finding conjunctions spanning different dimensions (e.g., color, form) does not necessarily involve serial search. Targets defined by spatial arrangements of objects or parts can yield strikingly difficult conjunction searches. Having homogeneous background elements and grouping background elements makes speeded search tasks easier, as do differences between background and target (Duncan and Humphreys, 1989).

It is no surprise, therefore, that recent attempts to model speeded visual search moved beyond Treisman's original proposal that conjunction search always operates serially. Perhaps the most fully developed model was proposed and has been periodically revised by Wolfe (1994). Labeled guided search, it is a two-stage model following early suggestions of Hoffman (1979). In the first, rather noisy stage of processing, individual target features are located across the entire visual field in parallel, and objects are compared with their neighbors in terms of these basic features. In the second stage, several kinds of information are brought together in parallel to guide a subsequent checking process. In this stage, a modest number of candidate target locations are interrogated one by one to determine if they contain a target. One source of information that guides the second-stage search is the differences between items and their neighbors detected in the first stage. Such differences constitute bottom-up support that increases the chance a given location will be checked. The most efficient pop-out searches can be done purely on the basis of this bottom-up support. Top-down guidance may also play a role in directing the second-stage checking, depending on exactly what the subject is looking for. If the target is a green T, for example, information about the location of green things and the location of T-like forms will be used in parallel to steer the checking process toward these locations. Because this guidance process relies on relatively noisy information, however, a target will not necessarily be the first item checked.

This theory accounts in a reasonable way for a broad range of search data. Its implications for the question of whether identification of highly familiar objects can proceed in parallel are not so clear, however. The fact that relatively difficult search based on spatial relationship of features becomes much easier with practice (Heathcote and Mewhort, 1993) is certainly consistent with the possibility that people may recognize objects simultaneously. The relative ease with which people search for unspecified letters among digits and vice versa, noted earlier, also suggests that semantic information can contribute to efficient search.

Beyond Search Slopes   Search slopes are inherently interesting because visual search is a ubiquitous human activity; knowledge of what makes it difficult or easy may be useful in a variety of practical contexts. However, for the reasons that emerged in the previous discussion, search slopes provide somewhat ambiguous evidence about serial versus parallel question. Is it possible to address this issue in the context of speeded search? Several methods can be applied if one can manipulate not only display set size but also the duration of the perceptual processing. One approach is to vary the visual quality of the display items as well as display set size. Pashler and Badgio (1985) had subjects perform search tasks involving from two to six item displays. In half the trials, all the elements in the display were visually degraded either by reducing their contrast or by superimposing dots on them. The effects of display set size and degradation were additive; that is, degradation added a constant onto RTs regardless of display set size. Assuming that the identification of each item is slowed by visual degradation, this finding clearly refutes the hypothesis of serial identification. If items were identified one after another, the extra time for identifying n degraded elements would be added into the total latency n times. Therefore, the effect of degradation should have been three times as large with displays of six items than it was with displays of two, for example, a multiplicative interaction of degradation and display set size. The additive pattern of effects has been seen not only in a visual search for a particular character, but also in a search task requiring people to find and name the highest digit in a display of digits. This task was selected to ensure that subjects would actually have to identify the characters as such, rather than just searching for a particular set of features. The fact that people are able to perform this task almost as readily as search suggests that parallel identification of alphanumeric characters is possible in divided attention tasks.

A related and in some ways complementary methodology was used by Egeth and Dagenbach (1991). Subjects searched displays composed of only two elements; each item could be visually degraded independent of the other. As the authors pointed out, if two searches proceeded in parallel, degrading both items should not add as much time to negative responses as the sum of the costs of degrading one or the other. To see why this is so, consider the following analogy: two chronically tardy individuals meet for lunch. If one friend is held up twenty minutes in traffic getting to the restaurant, and the other, driving from the opposite side of town, decides to stop en route to run a fifteen-minute errand, one would not predict that their lunch together would be delayed as much as thirty-five minutes. This form of subadditivity was observed by Egeth and Dagenbach in a letter search task, again confirming the hypothesis of parallel letter identification.

It seems clear, then, that the visual processing stages that are slowed by degrading alphanumeric characters operate in parallel when subjects perform search tasks with these stimuli. Unfortunately, it is not absolutely certain what these processing stages these are. If degradation affected only the earliest process of getting information to visual cortex, finding edges, and other early vision stages, the result might only show that these stages work in parallel; the actual identification of objects might still be serial. There is some reason to believe that degradation slows identification, however. For example, the effect of visual degradation interacts with stimulus probability, showing larger effects for low-probability characters compared with high-probability ones (Miller, 1979). Degradation also interacts with semantic priming in word recognition (Becker and Killion, 1977), having bigger effects on unprimed words than on primed ones. These results are hard to reconcile with the idea that degradation affects only stages before stimulus identification. These arguments notwithstanding, one would not want to claim that the locus of these effects is known with certainty.

In summary, studies of RTs suggest that in visual search tasks involving a modest number of characters, identification probably operates in parallel, even though other factors may contribute to RT slopes. This conclusion is consistent with the results of studies examining accuracy in simultaneous and successive displays (Shiffrin and Gardner, 1972) that were described earlier. The slopes observed in the speeded tasks also confirm that with greater display loads and subtler target/background discriminations, capacity limits may clearly emerge, which is also consistent with results of simultaneous/successive accuracy experiments (e.g., Kleiss and Lane, 1986). In short, despite the fact that each method of analyzing RTs and error rates has uncertainties associated with it, the conclusions reached from both methods are in reasonable agreement.

Search for Complex Stimuli: Words and Faces

The studies of accuracy with brief displays suggested that with words, capacity limits are severe enough to require sequential identification. A number of studies examined RTs in word search tasks. Karlin and Bower (1976) had subjects search for a specific target word in displays of up to six words. In a one-session experiment, slopes averaged 124 msec per item for target-absent trials (62 for target-present). Performance was unaffected by whether the distractors were in the same semantic category or a different one, although the different category distractors facilitated search when the target set consisted of several words. Flowers and Lohr (1985) had subjects search for a particular set of six target letter strings (three of them words) over thirteen sessions. When the target was a word and the distractors were composed of the same letters, slopes were 149 msec per item for target-absent trials and 80 msec per item for target-present.

Thus, speeded search for words (or comparable arbitrary letter strings) generates steep slopes suggestive of serial search, and this remains so even after subjects have had extensive practice. These results support the conclusions of accuracy experiments arguing for capacity limitations in recognition of simultaneously presented words (Duncan, 1984; Shiu and Pashler, unpublished observations), as described above.[16] In summary, the evidence of RT studies is consistent with the hypothesis that severe capacity limitations arise when people must read stimuli as complex as a pair of words. The results suggest that people probably read most words one at a time. Similar evidence of perceptual overload is found in search tasks requiring detection of faces or facial expressions (Nothdurft, 1993).

Multiple Attributes of a Single Object

An earlier section asked about capacity limits when people attempt to report several attributes of a single object such as color and form in a brief masked display. People are about as accurate in reporting multiple attributes as in reporting a single one, indicating that discriminations along several dimensions can be performed in parallel. A number of experiments looked at RTs to respond on the basis of several dimensions, and here again the results fit reasonably nicely with the conclusions from accuracy tasks.

Saraga and Shallice (1973) had subjects decide whether a colored shape fit a prememorized description that referred either to one dimension (red or square) or to two (red square). When subjects searched for something red, orange shapes were rejected more slowly than blue; when they searched for a square, a rectangle was rejected more slowly than a triangle. When people searched for red squares, however, they were able to reject both orange triangles and blue rectangles as fast as they could reject the easier component within each combination (triangles and blue) in the single-dimension condition. This argues against any account that would suppose that the two dimensions (color and shape) are tested in series (whether in a random or fixed order). It also suggests the absence of any capacity limitations in this kind of multidimensional processing task.

Most studies conducted to determine whether the several dimensions are compared sequentially or in parallel used same/different judgments. Usually, the subject's job is to say "yes" if two stimuli agree in all their attributes, otherwise "no." Obviously, this task requires the observer not merely to analyze each object along both dimensions, but also to compare the results. Nonetheless, various diagnostics indicate parallel processing across dimensions in this task. Several studies observed that responses are faster for different pairs that disagree in two dimensions compared with those that differ in only one dimension, where only this one dimension is relevant (Biederman and Checkosky, 1970; Egeth, 1966). This type of redundancy gain (benefit for extra information that favors the same decision) is expected if comparisons on each individual dimension operate in parallel and take a variable amount of time, with the different response being triggered as soon as a difference in any of the dimensions is detected. Applying slightly different logic, Downing and Gossman (1970) had subjects make same/different judgments on pairs of shapes differing in potentially as many as three dimensions. In some blocks and trials the objects could differ on any of three dimensions. In others they varied along only two dimensions (known to the subject). Eliminating the third dimension from consideration did not change the relative speed with which differences along the first two dimensions were detected. This again rejects the idea that subjects check the dimensions one by one.

These results argue that people can compare two objects along several dimensions at once. Of course, it should not be assumed that whenever people attend to a collection of objects their visual system compares all the different objects in the scene along all different dimensions. In fact, when people attend to a collection of more than two objects they find it surprisingly difficult to spot a match between some unspecified pair among the collection. Cavanagh and Parkman (1972) observed that even highly practiced subjects required substantially more time to detect pairs when additional item were added to the display. Oddly enough, spotting a match seems to be harder than finding the item that is most extreme on some abstract continuum like numeric value (as in the highest digit task described earlier). Perhaps when one tries to detect a pair in a display of more than two objects, it is necessary to take each candidate pair one at a time and exclude everything else to see if one has a match.

Divided Attention and Hearing

Report Tasks
One of the very earliest attempts to study auditory divided attention used a technique that came to be known as the split-span method, so named because the task is a variant of the familiar memory span task, but with the material split, half the items being presented to each ear. Broadbent (1954) presented two lists of three spoken digits, playing one to each ear at a rate of two items per second. For example, the message played to the left ear might be 3-5-8, and the message to right ear would be 9-2-6.

The listener's job was to repeat as much as possible. Broadbent found that people often reported the contents of one ear before reporting anything from the other ear (e.g., 3-5-8-9-2-6), rather than repeating pairwise (39-52-86). Anticipating the concept of echoic memory (discussed in chapter 7), Broadbent concluded that whereas the message to one ear was attended and repeated, the input to the other ear was held in preperceptual storage. When everything worked properly, the contents of the attended channel were reported first, followed by a switch of the filter to the other ear and retrieval of the other ear's message, which was waiting in the preperceptual storage. Consistent with this account, subjects were less accurate when they were instructed to report pairwise. Broadbent proposed that pairwise report required many time-consuming attention switches, thereby producing more errors. He observed essentially the same results when the channels were defined principally by pitch differences rather than differences in ear (Broadbent, 1956).

He proposed that information in preperceptual storage faded away rapidly, resulting in the split-span of six items approaching subjects' limits. Consistent with this, he tried an interesting variant of the split-span experiment. Six digits were presented to one ear and two digits to the other ear at some point during the time the six were being played. The listener's job was to report the six and then the two (Broadbent, 1957). Performance was good when the two arrived just before the end of the six, but poor when they arrived earlier. This result anticipated later but more widely cited studies of auditory sensory memory by Norman (1969).

According to other investigations that followed, grouping by ear is not the only way subjects can report dichotic presentations. Bartz, Satz, and Fennell (1967) used stimuli drawn from two different categories: digits and monosyllabic words excluding digits. When subjects were given no particular instructions about the order of report, they tended to report by ear, as in Broadbent's studies. Some subjects were instructed to recall the digits first and then the nondigits, and they proved capable of doing this about as accurately as they could report by ear. Gray and Wedderburn (1960) tried to use semantic cues to define channels with three-word phrases presented to alternating ears, and digits presented to the other ear. For example, the right ear heard "who-3-there" and the left ear heard

"2-goes-9." A number of subjects reported the familiar phrase (who goes there) as a unit. Many subjects reported by ear, as Broadbent originally described.

What conclusions can be drawn from the work with the split-span method? First, the results provide a convincing demonstration of brief auditory storage. Beyond that, however, it is difficult to reach firm conclusions about processing limitations. The fact that people are at least *capable* of reporting by category rather than ear (Bartz et al.) might seem to challenge Broadbent's analysis. After all, if a listener can recognize the contents of only one ear and simultaneously store the contents of the other ear in preperceptual storage, report by category should be relatively difficult. This is particularly likely given that the contents of preperceptual storage would be decaying rapidly, as other results demonstrated. Thus, the findings of Bartz et al. provide some evidence that listeners may succeed in identifying the contents of both ears and retaining the results.

This conclusion is sharpened by a partial-report study conducted by Massaro (1976) in which a list composed of a mixture of spoken letters and spoken words was played to each ear, four items per ear, spoken rapidly so that each list lasted only 1 second. When subjects were cued to report just the contents of one ear, they were much more accurate when the cue preceded the list rather than followed it. However, when the cue called for report by category (letter vs word), the timing of the cue had little effect. Furthermore, postcues specifying report by category were almost as effective as postcues calling for report by location. These results confirm that subjects can identify and categorize the contents of both channels to some degree, and use the category cue as the basis for selective retrieval. However, it should be noted that when postcued by category, subjects reported only about 60% of the items. Thus, the results do not prove that the number of items that can be identified exceeds the number presented to either ear alone.

Massaro drew a more radical conclusion from his results, however, claiming that they argued against the existence of preperceptual storage. This inference can be questioned. Subjects knew in advance whether they would be cued to retrieve by location or category. They may therefore have used different strategies in anticipation of the two different cue types. When a category cue was expected, they may have attempted to identify and remember all the items (with only moderate success, as noted above). When a location cue was expected, they may have proceeded essentially as Broadbent (1958) proposed, processing the contents of one ear immediately and then retrieving the other from preperceptual storage. Another observation from Massaro's study is consistent with this interpretation: the number of items reported was more variable with location cues than it was with category cues. Thus, the data provide no reason to doubt Broadbent's claim that we can store relatively unprocessed auditory information; this claim is in any case supported by other kinds of evidence (e.g., Guttman and Julesz, 1963; Norman, 1969; Warren and Bashford, 1981).

As the data stand presently, Broadbent's seminal analysis of the ordinary strategy in split-span report involving sensory storage and channel switching seems reasonable. What can be questioned is his assumption that this strategy rests on a basic inability to identify more than one signal in parallel; people may well be able to process both speech signals at once. (In chapter 5 it is maintained that this is in line with the usual empirical verdict on early versus late selection theory in many domains.)

Monitoring Tasks

Studies of visual search have provided a great deal of information beyond what could be gleaned from visual whole-report tasks, and similarly, studies of auditory monitoring tasks have added to what can be learned from auditory report studies. Auditory monitoring was the subject of systematic and lengthy research by several groups in the late 1960s and early 1970s. These studies give useful information about the limits of divided attention in hearing. Fortunately, the results mirror what has been found in studies with brief visual displays to a remarkable degree, something that is not widely appreciated.

A study by Pohlmann and Sorkin (1976) provides a good example of this literature. The study used channels defined by frequency rather than ear. Observers listened to sounds presented to one ear, trying to detect brief sinusoidal tone targets at three widely separated frequencies superimposed over broad band noise. In single-channel conditions, a target at a known frequency occurred in half the trials, and observers indicated whether it was present. In the three-channel monitoring task, each of the three targets could occur at the same instant (each with an independent probability of one-half), and the observers made three separate responses indicating whether each of the possible targets had been presented. When only one target was actually presented in three-channel monitoring, subjects were almost as good at detecting it as they were in the corresponding single-channel monitoring task, a 13% decrement in d'. In the subset of three-channel monitoring trials in which the subject correctly reported no targets present on the other two channels, there was no decrement whatever. Thus, subjects were capable of monitoring three frequencies as effectively as they could monitor one. However, when two or three targets were presented, detection accuracy fell, with d' decrements reaching 37% for three targets. It appeared from Pohlmann and Sorkin's analyses that the impairment caused by off-channel targets depended more on whether the observer reported that a target was present than on whether it was actually present, although they did not have enough data to resolve this issue.

These results are similar to what Duncan (1980b) later found with visual search. Comparable findings have also been obtained when subjects monitor two channels defined by ear (*binaural listening*). Some early binaural studies presented a rather different picture, suggesting substantial decrements (e.g., Moray, 1970), but discrepancies among these studies appear to have been resolved by Puleo and Pastore (1978). They had listeners monitor for a target of one frequency in one ear and a target of a different frequency in the other ear (the subjects knew which frequency could occur in which ear). Under monaural listening condition, targets occurred only in the ear the subjects monitored. In the selective-attention condition, targets could occur in either ear, but subjects attempted to detect only those in the monitored ear. Under divided-attention condition, targets could occur in either ear, and subjects reported on each ear independently.

When the frequency of the left-ear target was within the same critical band as the frequency of the right-ear target, the selective-attention condition was worse than the monaural condition. Here, subjects reported perceptual fusion of the two signals, and Puleo and Pastore attributed the failure of selective attention to this fusion. However, when the two targets were widely separated in frequency, no such fusion was reported, and performance in the selective-attention condition was as good as that under the monaural condition. In the divided-attention condition, overall detection accuracy was inferior to the other two conditions. However, as in Pohlmann and Sorkin's study, the decrement in one ear was contingent on whether the opposite ear contained a target. When the contralateral ear did not contain a target, detection was comparable with the selective and monaural conditions. Further experiments showed that monitoring for targets at two widely separated frequencies is approximately as good whether each target occurs only in one particular ear or all targets occur in the same ear (Sorkin, Pohlmann, and Gilliom, 1973; Sorkin, Pastore, and Pohlmann, 1972).

Together, these studies show that subjects can monitor multiple channels defined by either ear or frequency without loss, except when more than one target must be noted, or when the signals presented to different ears are perceptually fused. The absence of a decrement in the selective-attention condition shows, among other things, that the two-target problem is not due to sensory interactions. This is further demonstrated by the fact that a two-target decrement can occur when the target in one ear is defined as a gap rather than a tone (Gilliom and Mills, 1974, quoted in Pohlmann and Sorkin, 1976).

Neville Moray conducted a parallel research program examining dual-channel-monitoring tasks where subjects monitored continuous inputs rather than discrete observation intervals. Some of Moray's tasks involved speech rather than tones and had subjects listening for targets defined semantically; for example, dichotic monitoring for an unspecified spoken letter target among spoken digits. In a comprehensive review of work conducted in his laboratory, Moray (1975) described the main generalizations that emerged from these studies, and the pattern of results was essentially the same as that found by the Sorkin group: dual-channel monitoring is equivalent to single-channel monitoring except when a target is detected on the other channel.[17]

The Auditory Double-Detection Decrement
It will be recalled that the double-detection decrement observed in vision seemed to persist well after the time a detected target was physically

present. There is some indication that this may be true with auditory stimuli as well. Gilliom and Sorkin (1974) reported a number of studies examining the causes of the limitation in detecting two targets. In one binaural monitoring experiment, a 100-msec observation interval in the left ear immediately preceded a 100-msec observation interval in the right ear. A 630-Hz target was sometimes present in the left ear, and a 1400-Hz target was sometimes present in the right ear. Despite the fact that the two observation intervals were asynchronous, it was still difficult to detect the (later) right-ear target when the left ear had contained a target. Furthermore, performance did not differ depending on whether the order of observations was fixed throughout a block of trials or varied unpredictably from trial to trial.

It is not clear, however, whether the effect lasts longer than 100 msec. One piece of evidence suggesting that it might comes from Shaffer and Hardwick (1969), who had listeners monitor for an immediate repetition of a word in either the left or right channel (e.g., chair chair). When a target (repetition) was detected on one channel, it was much more likely that a target occurring during the following 1 second on the same channel would be detected, compared with a target occurring on the other channel during the same interval. Unfortunately, although, Shaffer and Hardwick's task was difficult, listeners were worse at detecting even a single target when monitoring two channels compared with one. Thus, the tendency to detect targets on a channel where a target was just detected may simply reflect the fact that subjects were monitoring one or the other channel preferentially. It would be interesting to know whether detecting a target on one channel tends to produce a constriction favoring further processing on the same channel, as the results of Hoffman, Nelson, and Houck and others suggest for vision.

Another apparent point of similarity between double detections in vision and hearing is the lack of any cost of divided attention when detecting two aspects of the same "object." In a carefully controlled experiment, Moore and Massaro (1973) had listeners judge the amplitude and/or quality of a brief tone, which was followed by a masking tone. The quality discrimination involved distinguishing between a triangular wave (sharp) and a sine wave (dull). Listeners were able to discriminate on both dimensions at the same time just about as well as they could discriminate on just one dimension. This result mirrors Duncan's (1984) findings with multiple attributes of briefly presented visual stimuli.

Another perspective on the double-detection decrement is provided by results of Puleo and Pastore (1978). The decrement that arises when two targets are detected can be fairly sizable when measured in terms of d' or detection probability. However, Puleo and Pastore assessed it in a different way. By varying signal intensities, they estimated how much the intensity of a signal presented simultaneously with a contralateral target would have to be increased to cancel out the two-target decrement. The estimated magnitudes were very small (1.5–2.5 db), leading them to suggest that the effect might not be "of sufficient behavioral importance to warrant further investigation" (p. 162). Although the theoretical significance of the effect may not depend on its magnitude, the fact that small increases in intensity readily compensate for it is intriguing.

With visual stimuli, people can monitor simultaneous and successive displays with equal efficiency only when the displays contain fairly modest numbers of simple stimuli, such as four letters and digits. Two visually presented words show clear signs of capacity limitations. What about auditory tasks that require identifying more than one word? Here, the picture is not as clear as one might hope. Ostry, Moray, and Marks (1976) had subjects monitor long lists of digits against white noise, attempting to detect unspecified letter targets that occurred rather infrequently. Subjects improved substantially over ten days, but at all levels of practice the detection rate was much greater when the contralateral channel contained no target (and no target was reported there). On the eleventh day, subjects performed the same task under focused attention conditions, with targets continuing to occur at the same rate in the (now unattended) contralateral channel. When no target was present in the contralateral channel, detection performance was about the same as on corresponding trials on the last day of divided attention testing. The same pattern of results was obtained in another experiment that involved five sessions of monitoring for animal names, even though here the targets were chosen from a set of seventy different words.

What conclusions can be drawn from these studies? As far as one can tell, the main conclusions of studies of visual divided attention apply also to auditory divided attention. Relatively simple discriminations appear to proceed in parallel without evident capacity limitation except when a target is detected on another channel. More complex discriminations, such as those involving the identity of spoken words, sometimes reveal capacity limitations, however. It should be noted that auditory monitoring studies do not provide terribly compelling evidence on the time course of processing. The reason for this is that echoic memory (discussed in chapter 7) could potentially extend the time over which auditory signals remain available to be processed, and later-arriving signals do not appear to mask earlier-arriving ones in the same way as with visual stimuli.[18] The continuous monitoring tasks of Moray may avoid this problem by providing a constant stream of inputs to be processed; here, a buffer-and-identify strategy would presumably be fallible.

A nice final illustration of some of these points comes from a study by Ninio and Kahneman (1974) who had subjects monitor dichotic word lists for animal names. Each list contained ten pairs of words spoken simultaneously at about two pairs per second. Subjects in a focused-attention condition performed almost as well as those hearing only one of the lists, indicating that binaural masking was minimal. In the focused-attention condition, however, when an animal name occurred on the irrelevant contralateral channel prior to a target on the relevant channel, a modest (4–6%) increase was seen in the tendency to miss the target. Of most interest, however, was the substantial increase in the miss rate in the divided-attention condition, where subjects monitored both lists (the miss rate rose to 23% from about 4% in the selective-attention condition). This cannot be attributed to the dual-target decrement, since only one target was ever presented per trial in the divided-attention condition. Accompanying this tendency to miss targets was a slight increase in the false alarm rate and a marked (136 msec) increase in the response time for detections. Ninio and Kahneman noted that if subjects were simply monitoring one channel at a time and switching between channels, the fastest RTs in the divided-attention condition should be comparable with the fastest RTs in the focused-attention condition, reflecting the trials in which they were monitoring the channel on which the target occurred. However, the slowing in the divided-attention condition affected the fastest RTs as well as the slower ones, with only 3.5% of the divided-attention RTs being as fast as the fastest 14% of the focused-attention RTs.

In subsequent sections, we will examine the question of how these capacity limitations are to be understood. One obvious and fundamental question about these limitations is whether they are taxed only by stimulation within a given sensory modality. The next section addresses this question.

Perceiving Bimodal Stimuli

What happens when people attempt to monitor streams of information arriving in different sensory systems? The question is important because many human activities do require people to take in information from a multitude of sources. It is odd, however, that the issue has been investigated only intermittently over the past thirty years. As we will see, the studies that were carried out used extremely diverse methods and stimuli. Unfortunately, these methods raise methodological problems that become somewhat convoluted, and readers interested more in conclusions than in methodology may wish to skip to the concluding paragraph of this section.

Eijkman and Vendrik (1965) conducted what seems to have been the earliest study, requiring subjects to detect increments in the intensity of lights and tones. The increments lasted 1 second, and subjects tried to detect increments in the light, the tone, or both simultaneously. Subjects were able to detect increments in one modality with essentially no interference from monitoring the other modality. Furthermore, performance (measured with d') was comparable with that obtained when monitoring only the visual or only the auditory stimuli. (Of interest, detection of increments in *duration* of the same stimuli [lights or tones] show marked interference, suggesting that temporal judgments may depend on a single processing system.) Of course, 1 second is plenty of time for switching between channels.

A number of well-conducted studies found the same result with brief presentations. Shiffrin and Grantham (1974) required subjects independently to detect brief auditory, tactile, and visual signals. In the SIM condition, all three occurred simultaneously. In the SUCC condition, there were three observation intervals, with the constraint that the visual signal occurred in the first interval, the auditory in the second, and the tactile in the third. There was no advantage for the SUCC condition; in fact, performance was slightly better in the SIM condition. Gescheider, Sager, and Ruffolo (1975) combined simultaneous auditory and tactile judgments. The auditory task required pitch discrimination and the tactile task involved detecting vibration of the finger. The authors examined only dual-task conditions, varying the relative emphasis of the two tasks (payoffs of 4:1 or 1:4). The emphasis manipulation had no significant effects.

Other studies combining auditory and visual discrimination tasks observed decrements in monitoring for signals in different modalities. Consider an early study by Tulving and Lindsay (1967). Subjects heard a tone and saw a circular patch of light. The intensity of each was independently varied in small steps. In the single-task conditions, subjects judged the intensity of either the tone or the light. In the dual-task conditions, they judged the intensity of both. Simply presenting the tone did not impair single-task judgments of the light, nor did the light impair single-task tone judgments. However, performance (calculated in terms of information transmitted) was slightly inferior in the dual-task condition compared with the single-task condition. Results were quite similar in another experiment in which subjects judged the intensity of the light and the pitch of the tone.

These decrements were fairly modest (under 10% measured in information transmitted). Long (1976) observed similarly modest decrements in a task requiring a pitch judgment and two judgments regarding visual stimuli (intensity and length of a line), also exposed for 1 second. Each judgment involved a choice between two alternatives, and accuracy was approximately 6% less in the triple-task condition than in the single-task control. Long noted, however, that this decrement was much less than one would expect if subjects could monitor only one of the three attributes in any given trial.

These cases differ from the bulk of the studies described earlier in the chapter in that they involved magnitude judgments rather than categorical judgments. In this task, performance may be severely limited by subjects' difficulty in maintaining a standard in memory against which to judge inputs. Therefore, it seems plausible that inadequate preparation for the task, rather than difficulty actually processing the stimuli, may be the source of the dual-task decrements. This is potentially testable;

preparatory differences should affect performance in trials in which subjects prepare for all three tasks but are required to perform only one.

A study by Lindsay, Taylor, and Forbes (1968) has probably been cited more than any other experiment reporting interference across sensory modalities. The stimuli consisted of a brief tone and a spot presented on a CRT, followed after a 500-msec ISI by another tone and spot. A trial could involve any of four judgment tasks, two relating to the tones and two relating to the spots. The tone tasks involved deciding which of the two tones was higher in pitch or in intensity. The visual tasks involved deciding which of the two spots was higher or leftward of the other. Within a block of trials, subjects performed one, two, or all four of these tasks. Accuracy was worse the more judgments a subject had to make. However, when performing two tasks, subjects were no less accurate when judging two within-modality attributes (pitch and intensity of the tone) compared with two between-modality attributes (pitch of the tone, vertical position of the spot). The authors concluded that capacity limits seem to handicap within-modality and between modality divided attention comparably. As the reader will probably have noticed, however, the within-modality combinations also required processing the same objects; as described above, this tends to improve performance and may therefore have spuriously elevated performance in this condition.

In one case at least one of the tasks involved classifying stimuli into well-learned categories, and costs were nonetheless observed in between-modality conditions. Massaro and Warner (1977) presented subjects with a tone and a letter, each followed by its own mask. Subjects chose between two alternatives for the frequency of the tone and two for the letter identity. Single-judgment performance was substantially better than dual-judgment performance. In another experiment, Massaro and Warner compared simultaneous and successive discrimination performance. Under these conditions, identification of the tone was substantially better with successive than simultaneous presentations. For the categorical judgment about letter identity, on the other hand, no difference was apparent. The authors concluded that discriminating patterns in the two modalities draws on a common pool of limited processing resources. However, the nature of the successive condition may call this into question. The letter always preceded the tone, and by an interval that was appreciably longer than is customary in such studies (1.5 seconds, rather than, say, 0.5 second in Shiffrin and Gardner, 1972). It seems quite possible that this successive condition affords subjects the opportunity to prepare optimally for the stimuli as in a single-task condition, particularly benefiting the second stimulus presented.[19] (In principle, it might benefit either or both stimuli.)

For present purposes, the most revealing comparison of within- versus between-modality divided attention would involve difficult classification of complex stimuli into well-learned categories, and substantial display loads on both tasks. Treisman and Davies (1973) performed the only study that comes close. Subjects monitored four streams of words, two presented visually and two presented auditorily to different ears. In one condition, subjects searched for words containing the sound (or string) "end" (e.g., lender, pretend). In another condition, subjects searched for animal names. Only one target was presented in each trial. Subjects detected fewer targets when monitoring two streams compared with one stream. However, performance was much worse when subjects monitored two visual or two auditory streams compared with the between-modality task. In short, perceptual overload was much more severe within rather than across modalities.

Despite the aggravating diversity of methods and interpretations found in this literature, the bimodal discrimination literature does support a few tentative conclusions. Difficult categorical judgments (though not magnitude estimation) in two modalities can sometimes at least be carried out simultaneously with no evident interference. Probably, this is the case with the same kinds of judgments that would produce within-modality interference, although this has not been clearly demonstrated. When experiments require a classification that is specific to the experiment and that requires keeping a standard in memory, as in magnitude estimation, dual-task costs are observed; these costs may well reflect preparatory limitations, though this idea remains to be tested. Even fairly simple judgments probably involve at least a tiny preparatory cost, however. It seems quite likely, admittedly based on little other than Treisman and Davies' study, that the resource limitations that arise with concurrent difficult discriminations are at least primarily a within-modality phenomenon. This topic plainly requires further work. A comparison of simultaneous and (rapid) successive presentations using different kinds of difficult bimodal discriminations, perhaps with continuous monitoring in both modalities, would be necessary to allow strong conclusions on this fundamental question about human processing limitations.

A Summary of Divided Attention

What can be concluded from this review of the literature on divided attention in perception and recognition? One crucial point, which is sometimes overlooked, is that decision noise, purely statistical in origin, can masquerade as a capacity limit. When people make one response to an ensemble of stimuli, increasing the number of stimuli may result in a decrease in accuracy even if no capacity limitations are present, that is, even if increasing the number of items does not change how effectively each individual item is processed (Duncan, 1980a; Sperling and Dosher, 1986). The only conditions under which this kind of decision noise will not increase error rates would be if a high-threshold model applied, which is, as far we know, not ordinarily the case.

The decision noise problem makes inadequate the obvious strategy of simply comparing accuracy in monitoring one or a few channels with accuracy in monitoring many channels. Less obviously, it also raises doubts about the many studies that examined effects of display set size on reaction times (search slopes), since these slopes may reflect extra time being taken to compensate for the noise-based increase in errors, rather than true capacity limitations. Another point that endangers the usual interpretation of RT slopes is the fact that the slopes themselves might reflect time taken for mental operations that occur *after* the item in the display have been identified.

Several techniques seem able to circumvent these problems. One involves comparing accuracy with simultaneous and successive displays that consist of a fixed number of items. The results of such comparisons have, encouragingly enough, been similar in both the visual and auditory domains. First, accuracy is usually comparable in the two conditions when the task requires fairly simple stimuli such as letters or phonemes and only a single target is presented. Second, when the stimuli become more complex and discriminations become more difficult, performance in the simultaneous condition can become markedly inferior to that in the successive condition. Third, when more than one target is presented, detection almost invariably suffers.

Within both the visual and auditory modalities, it appears that capacity limits do exist beyond a certain point; with stimulus load below this level, processing appears to be parallel and free of capacity limits. It seems likely, however, that more parallel processing can occur than Broadbent envisioned in his original filter (early selection) theory. The two-target effect, occurring in both the auditory and visual modalities, indicates a second form of capacity limitation that cannot be attributed to limitations in the machinery that discriminates targets from distractors. The implications of this effect are discussed more extensively in chapter 5.

Given that perceptual capacity limitations do arise in divided-attention tasks, a fundamental and fairly obvious question is whether stimuli in different modalities draw on the same single-capacity limitation. Unfortunately, the literature on bimodal detection is too meager and unsystematic to provide a very satisfying answer. It has been documented in at least one case, however, that when the load is divided between modalities, performance is better than when everything is in the same modality (Treisman and Davies, 1973). The literature does not specifically address the question of whether the two-target decrement arises with targets present in different modalities.

The Nature of Perceptual Capacity Limits

The preceding sections documented the existence of capacity limitations in perceptual processing. Thus far, however, only a few conclusions have been drawn about what actually causes these limitations. First, it was suggested that—at least within a modality such as vision or hearing—increasing the total complexity of the required calculations beyond some modest level causes capacity limitations to appear. Obviously, this is vague, and one wants to know: What sort of complexity? Second, it appears that the difficulty in processing more than one target has a different source than the limitation arising with difficult discriminations and only a single target among distractors (see Duncan, 1985).

Before considering hypotheses about the causes of perceptual capacity limitations, it may be useful to summarize the results slightly differently, holding theory at bay insofar as possible. It sounds like a truism that if a task is made harder, this will make it hard to do it at the same time one does some other task. Have we learned anything that takes us beyond this? We can consider different ways in which a discrimination task can be made harder, and ask which ones cause capacity limitations to appear, where hardness is construed operationally, to refer to any change in stimuli or task that increases error rates. Does increased difficulty always cause capacity limitations to show up, with variation in the number of items causing a decrement in performance not attributable to statistical noise?

One way to make a perceptual task more difficult is to reduce the SOA between display and a mask. By itself, this does not suffice to reveal capacity limitations: the clearest demonstration of capacity-free search (Shiffrin and Gardner, 1972) involved tasks with reasonably high error rates caused by presentation of pattern masks shortly after the stimuli. This is consistent, of course, with the idea that presenting the mask earlier reduces the time during which the machinery is available to process the stimuli without changing the nature of the perceptual work that is required.

A second way to make a discrimination more difficult is to reduce the contrast of a stimulus, or equivalently, to reduce its exposure duration when it is flashed briefly and followed by a field containing few contours. This by itself does not seem to reveal capacity limitations. That it does not is suggested by the work of Shaw on lightness increments, by the work of Palmer (1994; Palmer, Ames, and Lindsey, 1993) on unmasked discriminations, and by studies of location uncertainty in threshold tasks that will be described in chapter 4.[20]

A different pattern is observed when discriminations are made more difficult by requiring more *precise* discrimination along a basic dimension such as orientation, color, or size. An example would be discriminating a line oriented at 40 degrees from one oriented at 42 degrees rather than 60 degrees. The same is true for a fourth way of increasing difficulty: imposing a task that requires the *relative spatial arrangement* of different parts of the object to be accurately registered. An example would be discriminating a black bar above a white bar from a white bar above a black bar (see figure 3.9).

The evidence that increasing the required precision of discrimination can by itself increase capacity demands is fairly strong. Some of the results of Kleiss and Lane (1986) described earlier seem to show capacity limitations with fine target/background discriminations, for example as do the observations by Prinzmetal and colleagues with continuous color judgments. Accuracy can be much better for successive compared to simultaneous displays in line length and line orientation searches involving very fine differences between targets and distractors (Shiu and Pashler, unpublished observations). In speeded tasks, slopes are often quite steep when target/background discriminability is low (Treisman, 1991). The evidence for capacity limitations in registering the spatial arrangement of parts is also demonstrated in the successive advantage found in lexical search tasks (Duncan, 1986) and in the RT slopes found with certain speeded search tasks. It seems reasonably certain, then, that requiring either precise discrimination along a single featural dimension *or* accurate determination of the spatial arrangement of a set of parts can increase demands on perceptual capacity limitations beyond the total available resources (holding constant the number of objects in the field).

Why do these kinds of difficulties produce overload? Some authors seek to characterize the underlying limitations in terms of information transmission. Nakayama (1990) speculated that any given attentive fixation might transmit something on the order of 100 bits of information to visual recognition. Along similar lines, Verghese and Pelli (1992) suggested 30 to 60 bits per fixation. Information can be measured only relative to some coding scheme, however, and these estimates depend on what authors admit to be highly informal conceptions of the coding that is involved. Another idea that naturally suggests itself to researchers exploring artificial neural networks is that perceptual overload might stem from cross-talk or interference between similar patterns represented within the same network. For example, Mozer (1991) offered a model of visual object recognition that predicts that multiple objects could degrade the processing of other items that were simultaneously input into the same network.

Both of these approaches are intriguing and point toward the possibility of a functional analysis of visual processing limitations that would replace such vague notions as difficulty, complexity, and capacity. At present, it is difficult to tell whether any of them is likely to be illuminating. To tell, one must have answers to a number of empirical questions, of which the following are some of the more obvious examples.

1. How is the two-target limitation related to the perceptual capacity limits that appear when difficult discriminations are required with only a single target? Are the effects of a concurrent detection and the effects of a concurrent difficult discrimination indistinguishable? This issue bears critically on the idea that capacity limits depend on information transmission; after all, detection of a target on another channel can presumably be represented with just one or a few bits of information.

2. Does the two-target effect arise when the two targets are in different sensory modalities? If it does, then it may be that the effect operates at a completely different level from perceptual overload per se, making it indifferent to the costs of complexity and difficulty.

3. Does the interference between two perceptual tasks depend on the similarity of the processing required in each task? The connectionist approach (e.g., Mozer, 1991) suggests that similarity might be crucial. Just about all the studies of visual divided attention reviewed in this chapter involve search or report tasks, in which the subject's job with respect to each item or channel is essentially the same. When display load is increased, so too is the number of similar discriminations to be performed. Duncan et al. (1995) examined the role of similarity and found that interference between a color discrimination and a form discrimination was comparable in magnitude with the interference between two color discriminations. If this finding generalizes, it would suggest that similarity has nothing to do with capacity limitations. In these experiments, however, subjects had to report the identity of both elements, and at least some of the interference presumably reflects the two-target effect rather than the possibly different processing limitation associated with making difficult discriminations. It is conceivable that this latter form of perceptual interference might depend heavily on similarity of stimuli or discriminations. In chapter 5 we will return to the topic of perceptual capacity limits and the nature of the two-target problem.

4

Attentional Set

In previous sections we examined what happens when someone tries to take in information from certain channels and ignore information from others (chapter 2), and what happens when they set out to process information on multiple channels (chapter 3). We now turn to another classic issue in the study of attention: whether having advance information about a stimulus can help one perceive that stimulus more effectively. One can pose the question of how advance information affects perception in relation to many different types of stimuli and many different sorts of advance information. For example, to take a very simple kind of task, what is the effect of knowing the frequency of a tone on a listener's ability to detect that tone superimposed on noise? Or, to take a more complex one, can an observer recognize a scene composed of objects such as tables and chairs more quickly if he or she knows that it will be a kitchen rather than a street scene?

Benefits of advance information about stimuli have often been termed perceptual set effects. The word "set" has been used in different ways for a long time (see Gibson, 1941, and Haber, 1966 for discussions of early literature). The idea behind this term is that people may be able to set their perceptual system to process certain stimuli or carry out certain discriminations more effectively than would otherwise be possible. This chapter asks whether this actually takes place, and if so, what can be concluded about the mechanisms of set effects. (One phenomenon traditionally classified under the heading of set, task set, deals with broad issues of cognitive control, rather than the interaction of perception and attention; task set is discussed in chapter 8.)

The discussion starts with set effects involving advance information about stimulus attributes that are logically orthogonal to the discrimination the person is trying to perform. In this context, orthogonal means the information the person is given provides no information about the judgment the individual is trying to make. The first example has been studied extensively in recent years: information about the location of a stimulus in the visual field. How are judgments about the form or identity of a stimulus affected by knowledge of where the stimulus will be? It has often been suggested that location knowledge permits a person to allocate processing capacity to a location (or strictly speaking, to the internal channels that process information from that location) in advance of the stimulus, and that doing so enhances perception.

After reviewing the effects of advance knowledge about orthogonal stimulus attributes, we turn to advance information about the likely attributes of the stimulus along whatever dimension the person *is* trying to discriminate. Knowing that a letter will be drawn from a set of two particular alternatives, for example, can the observer tune his or her letter detectors to do a better job of distinguishing among these particular alternatives than if all twenty-six letters were possible?

Before turning to the findings, a few comments about methods will be useful. Generally speaking, advance information about a stimulus can be provided in one of two ways. The first is by *cueing*, giving the observer explicit information about the likely attributes of the stimulus that follows. When the cues are usually but not always accurate, one can compare performance in the majority of trials in which the cue is *valid* with performance in the minority of trials in which the cue is *invalid*. Performance in both of these conditions can also be compared with *neutral* trials in which some sort of uninformative cue is provided. When cues are completely omitted, performance could be affected by the absence of information the experimenter did not intend the cues to transmit, such as when the stimulus will appear (cf. Jonides and Mack, 1984).

A different way to look for effects of advance information is to compare blocks of trials in which the relevant attribute is held constant and is therefore predictable to the observer, with the performance in blocks of trials in which the attribute varies from one trial to the next. Studies of this kind are typically described as measuring *uncertainty effects*.

Basically, the issues are the same as in cueing studies. However, the constant blocks not only provide information to the observer, but also ensure that the attribute is repeated from trial to trial. Repetition can potentially have facilitating (or, conceivably, inhibitory) effects above and beyond the effects of prior information per se.

Cueing Orthogonal Attributes—Potential Benefits

Before looking at what effects prior information does have, it is worth considering what sorts of effects it might have. Consider what happens when subjects are told about a dimension of a stimulus that is orthogonal to the judgment they will make about the stimulus. In one way in which prior information might affect processing, the cue allows limited-capacity resources to be devoted to the processing of the signal more quickly than would have otherwise been possible. This widely accepted account is illustrated in figure 4.1, which refers to location cueing; the top panel shows the valid-cue condition and the bottom panel shows the no-cue condition. After the cue appears, indicating that the second position is likely to contain the stimulus, capacity available to the second channel is increased. This is represented as a widening of that channel, and has the consequence that the stimulus is recognized more quickly than it would otherwise be (seen by comparison with the bottom panel). An extreme version of this hypothesis would postulate a discrete rather than a graded shift of resources, where capacity must be shifted completely before processing can proceed. Many investigators suggested accounts of this kind for advance information about the location of a visual stimulus (Posner, Snyder, and Davidson, 1980; Johnston, McCann, and Remington, 1996). This general type of explanation for cueing effects will be referred to as a *capacity-allocation mechanism*.

   Advance information about location might facilitate performance in another, quite different way. This mechanism could arise whenever the advance information allows the observer to disregard channels containing *noise;* that is, information that could degrade a decision process if allowed to influence the decision. In chapter 3 it was noted that monitoring more channels, regardless of how they are defined, can reduce accuracy in a search task even if the system has no capacity limits

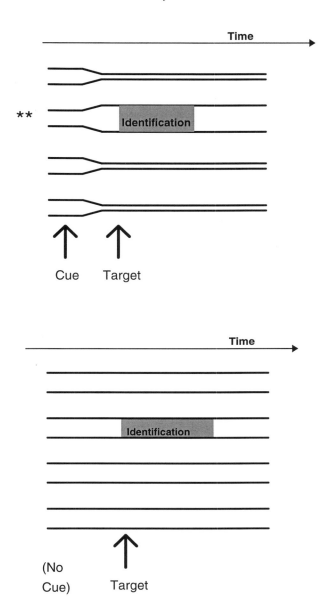

Figure 4.1
Capacity allocation explanation for the cueing effect. Top panel. A valid cue causes more capacity to be allocated to the channel. Stars represent cues. Bottom panel. No cue is present, so all channels have equal capacity.

whatever. The cost arises for purely statistical reasons. In a detection task it arises whenever the processing of information in channels excluded by the cue would have some chance of yielding a false alarm. In a discrimination task it will arise whenever these uncued channels are capable of producing an output that is mistake for one of the possible targets. The critical point is that a decrease in the number of channels to be monitored inevitably improves accuracy, even if each channel produces outputs that are completely independent how many channels are processed (i.e., if no capacity limits exist).

Figure 4.2A shows a simple version of a noise-reduction account applied to a yes/no detection task. This account is formulated in a signal-detection theory framework, although it is by no means the only way that theory might be applied to multichannel tasks. Perception of a given stimulus yields some output that has some variability; hence, it is represented by a bell-shaped distribution (a rightward movement along the X axis indicates more evidence in favor of a target being present). Naturally, the evidence tends to be greater when the stimulus is a target. This is represented by the fact that solid (target) distributions are shifted rightward compared with dashed (nontarget) distributions. The stimulus analysis process that is represented here might or might not be task specific, something that happens only when the person decides to carry out a monitoring task; this question lies outside the scope of the theory. When no cue is presented (panel A), the decision is made by comparing each output with a threshold, resulting in a positive decision if any of the channels exceed this threshold. When the cue is presented (bottom panel), stimulus recognition is unaffected, as reflected in the fact that the distribution for a target following a cue is no higher than for an uncued target. However, only the output of the appropriate channel is compared with the threshold value. This reduces the chance of a false alarm from the inappropriate channels, and thereby improves performance. This kind of account is called a *noise-reduction* mechanism.

The remaining panels in the figure show other possible mechanisms whereby spatial cues could produce a benefit through noise reduction. For example, subjects could derive the same benefit by blocking perception of uncued stimuli (panel D). Raising the threshold for detection of a target on each of the uncued channels (panel C) could also produce a

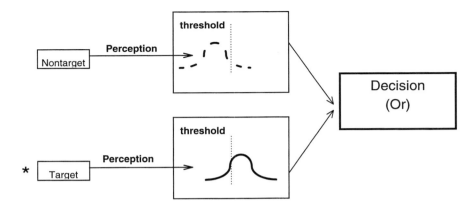

Panel A.

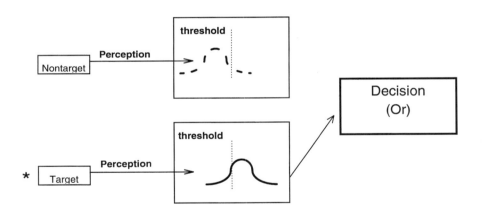

Panel B.

Figure 4.2
(A) A possible signal detection analysis of two-channel monitoring. Perception takes target or nontarget as input and produces an output reflecting evidence for target, where this output is a random variable with a bell-shaped distribution. The central tendency of distribution is higher for targets than for nontargets, however. A separate decision is made on each channel by comparing output with criterion (vertical dotted line). The final task decision involves saying "yes" if

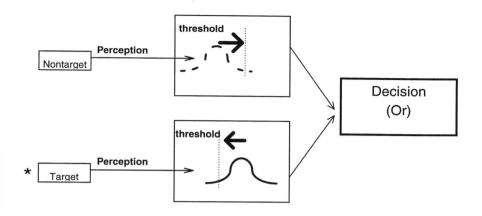

Panel C.

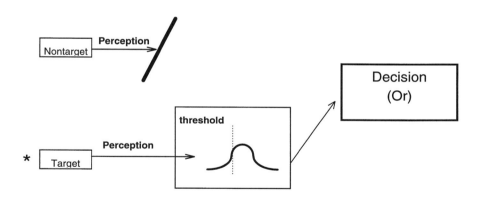

Panel D.

either channel exceeded its respective threshold (an or gate). (B) In response to cue (*), the decision from the uncued channel is not considered in the final or decision. (C) In response to cue (*), the threshold is raised on the uncued channel and lowered on the cued channel. (D) Perception of the nontarget is blocked before computing its value.

noise-reduction effect. This would effectively reduce the chance of a false alarm arising from these channels. Since the cues are always (or usually) valid, this will have the effect of improving the observer's overall detection performance, as measured by d', for example. This illustrates the more general observation that changes in the criterion within a single part of a system can affect the sensitivity of the system as a whole (Shulman and Posner, 1988). Of course, if the cue provided an absolute guarantee that the uncued channels will not contain a target, then it would be optimal to shut out these channels completely, as depicted in panels B and D. Formally, this would be equivalent to setting an infinite threshold on the uncued channels in the model shown in panel C.

An analogy may help to clarify the difference between noise reduction and capacity allocation as explanations of cueing effects. Suppose you are the chief of police in a small town, investigating an important murder case. You have a large number of suspects, with various degrees of circumstantial evidence implicating each of them. Each bit of evidence has to be followed up. What happens if you receive a credible anonymous tip saying that the culprit is under 5 foot 10 inches in height? (Never mind where the tip comes from, and why you choose to believe it; we assume that you know it to be true.) Would the tip aid you in pursuing your investigation? It might well, by allowing you to assign all your detectives to follow leads implicating shorter suspects. In this way, you would collect better information on each of these individuals, and catch the culprit more quickly. This is a straightforward case of capacity allocation. On the other hand, suppose for some reason you *cannot* reallocate detectives (capacity), or suppose you already have more resources than you can use (perhaps—as it used to be said about the former East Germany—the number of people working for the police is as great as the number of other residents in the town). In that case, if you put more detectives on any given suspect they may end up tripping over each other. Does this mean the tip is of no benefit to you? Not necessarily; you may still gain from it if there is any chance your investigation might end up implicating an innocent person. This is because when you put all your evidence together, you can disregard anything that implicates tall suspects. Since that evidence is sure to be misleading, excluding it can only improve your decision. This form of benefit is a noise-reduction benefit.

It should be noted that there is one set of assumptions under which one would not expect a noise-reduction benefit: if for some reason the clues turned up by the detectives could not, under any circumstances, implicate innocent individuals. This is equivalent to what psychophysicists call a high-threshold model, and it predicts no effects of uncertainty. Here, one simply must wait for positive evidence to turn up. Noise-reduction gains could be achieved at different processing stages in both the criminal investigation and the monitoring task. In the former case, if there are no resource limitations, it is not necessary to prevent tall suspects from being investigated (panel D) except perhaps to reduce strain and confusion. The noise-reduction benefit can be obtained after the detectives have made their reports simply by disregarding any evidence implicating tall suspects (panel B). In perceptual monitoring, noise reduction might involve perceptual suppression, but it need not.

The implications for perceptual monitoring for targets can be summarized as follows. Regardless of whether there are any capacity limits in monitoring multiple channels, one should expect a noise-reduction benefit as long as (a) there is some confusability of nontargets with targets, and (b) advance information can be used to exclude confusable nontargets from consideration in the decision process. Assumption b could obviously depend on the cues becoming available in time to use them in guiding the decision. Noise reduction could be carried out by blocking processing on to-be-excluded channels (pulling the detectives off tall suspects), or by letting the processing occur but then discounting it in the decision (letting the detectives investigate tall suspects but disregarding their findings). Some noise-reduction benefit can also be achieved by raising the threshold on uncued channels. The upshot of all this is that one should probably expect to find benefits of precueing any attribute that designates a channel that can be selectively monitored in a decision as long as the nondesignated channels are likely to contain noise; such findings do not necessarily indicate capacity allocation.

Noise reduction and capacity allocation are by no means mutually exclusive, however. One might use information about the likely location of a stimulus both to discard outputs of channels processing nontargets and to enhance processing on channels dealing with likely target positions. Logically speaking, the two issues are not completely independent. If a shift of resources to a channel is necessary before any processing whatsoever can take place (e.g., as proposed by Johnston, McCann, and Remington, in press, then capacity allocation would simultaneously accomplish noise reduction of the sort shown in panel C.

Location Cueing and Uncertainty Effects in Vision

The most extensively studied type of set effect involves advance information about the spatial position of a visual stimulus. This has been investigated in a variety of detection and discrimination tasks, both speeded and unspeeded.

With discrimination tasks involving stimuli-like letters and displays that are composed of many items, cueing the location at which a target is likely to appear can produce dramatic benefits (Colegate, Hoffman, and Eriksen, 1973). Here, the uncued channels obviously contain distractor stimuli that are confusable with the target. Under these conditions, noise reduction would be expected to produce a benefit whether or not capacity allocation occurs. To put the point slightly differently, cueing effects with crowded displays might be attributable exclusively to noise reduction, although they are frequently thought to entail capacity allocation. Of course, these effects are also consistent with capacity allocation. A critical test of whether location information affects perception through capacity allocation requires presenting a target in a situation where the uncued channels contain no information potentially confusable with the target. As we will see, achieving this goal involves subtler issues than one might have expected.

Detection and Discrimination at Threshold

Numerous psychophysical studies demonstrate that location uncertainty reduces performance in tasks requiring detection of a single low-intensity or low-contrast stimulus presented against a blank field (for lucid reviews, see Graham, 1985, 1989). Cohn and Lasley (1974) were among the first to investigate the spatial uncertainty effects arising in detection of luminance increments. Subjects fixated in the center of a display surrounded by four light-emitting diodes. In one of the two observation intervals, the intensity of one of the diodes was increased for 8 to 20 msec, and subjects stated which interval they thought it was. In the uncertain location condition, any one of the four diodes might contain the signal, whereas in the certain location condition only a prespecified diode could contain it. Detectability measured by d' was reduced approximately in half by the increase in spatial uncertainty from one position to four.

The results might seem to imply capacity allocation, but the blank field is confusable with a near-threshold stimulus (that is, after all, what being near threshold means). Therefore, noise reduction alone predicts uncertainty effects. It turns out that the magnitude of the observed uncertainty effect approximates what would be predicted by a straightforward signal-detection model that postulates no capacity limitations but allows for statistical noise (Nolte and Jaarsma, 1967). That is, the magnitude of the uncertainty effect is approximately that predicted for an "ideal observer" who optimally integrates information from sensory channels, with the quality of the information on any given channel being unaffected by the number of channels to be monitored. This ideal observer still makes errors in the task, of course, because the output of each channel is only probabilistically related to what stimulus was presented. Pelli (1981) reported finding the same thing when observers had to monitor 10,000 possible locations in space and time. It should be noted that when overall performance is analyzed using signal-detection theory, noise reduction may increase d' (Bashinski and Bacharach, 1980) even if the quality of processing for signals coming from the cued location is not enhanced.[1]

Uncertainty about where a stimulus will appear can also be eliminated by cueing the location. If subjects can act rapidly and flexibly to exclude noisy channels from their decision, this should facilitate detection through noise reduction. When Davis, Kramer, and Graham (1983) had subjects detect gratings at threshold, position cueing substantially aided performance. Again, the size of this improvement was consistent with what would be expected from an ideal observer not subject to capacity limitations. It should not be thought that this type of experiment is in some way incapable of demonstrating decrements beyond those attributable to noise reduction. Sekuler and Ball (1977), for example, had observers detect the presence of moving dots at threshold contrast, and found a decrement in performance when the direction of motion was uncertain. The size of this uncertainty effect exceeded the noise-reduction predictions, suggesting that observers are incapable of monitoring for dots moving in either of two opposing directions at once (a capacity limit).

What about discriminating among several possible faint stimuli presented against a blank field? To the degree that the blank field is confusable with the stimuli to be discriminated, location cueing should produce a benefit just by noise reduction. An interesting case is the discrimination of the spatial frequency of gratings presented at low contrast with widely separated spatial frequencies. Evidence indicates that different analyzers or sets of analyzers respond to particular spatial frequencies at particular locations (Graham, 1989). Here, performance in discrimination and detection tasks is generally comparable, when appropriately measured (Thomas, 1985). This is illustrated most clearly in the so-called two-by-two paradigm (Nachmias and Weber, 1975) in which one of two possible signals is presented in one of two successive observation intervals. The observer is required to guess which interval contains a signal and what that signal is. When the discrimination is between two gratings widely separated in spatial frequency, observers perform equally in the two judgments (Watson and Robson, 1981). Furthermore, when the observer is wrong about which interval contained the signal, he or she is at chance about which signal was presented. This pattern makes sense on the following account.

Suppose that the most sensitive analyzers responsive to these stimuli are effectively labeled as to their spatial frequency. That is, whenever basing a response on the output of a particular analyzer, the observer can tell, essentially without error, which of the two spatial frequencies that analyzer detects. In that case, when stimulus contrast is lowered to the extent that discrimination becomes error prone, the blank positions will become confusable with the alternatives to be discriminated. If observers can monitor a chosen subset of the analyzers simultaneously for the purpose of making their discrimination, then uncertainty effects should arise here just as in detection tasks. In fact, they do arise. When the task involves choosing among widely separated spatial frequencies, increasing the number of alternative spatial frequencies impaired discrimination as well as detection (Yager et al., 1984). Yager et al also found that the magnitude of this improvement was consistent with the predictions of a model that assumes a person capable of monitoring several noisy spatial frequency-tuned channels. Here, too, uncertainty seems to reflect an accumulation of decision noise rather than capacity allocation.

One could also ask what happens when more complex stimuli, like words or pictures are presented at sufficiently low contrast to affect discrimination performance adversely. Naturally, one can detect a word one cannot read, because a few gross features may suffice to tell that a word is present. Therefore, reducing the contrast of a word just enough to cause errors in word identification would probably not make the word confusable with the blank field. If cueing effects operate solely through noise reduction, therefore, one would expect that location knowledge would not be helpful in this type of task. Unfortunately, this experiment does not seem to have been tried.

Spatial Cueing in Simple Reaction Time

Probably the best-known work on spatial cueing effects involves detection of stimuli presented well above threshold, with speed rather than accuracy serving as the primary dependent variable, commonly known as simple reaction time. The first studies of this type were reported by Posner et al. (1980), who observed large speed-ups from location precues. In a typical experiment, a signal consisted of turning on one of four light-emitting diodes. Subjects pressed a key as soon as this happened. One-sixth of the trials were catch trials in which no signal was presented. In cued blocks, a digit presented in advance of the signal told the subjects which position was the most likely. Subjects were more than 50 msec faster to respond to stimuli in the expected position. The authors interpreted their result as indicating that capacity is allocated to positions in space, enhancing processing (as in figure 4.1).

At first glance, the fact that subjects are significantly faster in responding in the cued location would seem to confirm that early perceptual processing can be speeded up by spatial cueing, apparently by an average of 50 msec. The very magnitude of the effect should arouse some degree of suspicion, however. If the most primitive sensory information is available approximately 50 msec earlier when its location is known in advance, one might expect to see dramatic effects of cueing in recognizing letters or words. For example, 50 msec extra, when provided by delaying the onset of a mask, is often sufficient to bring accuracy from a level near chance to virtually perfect (Sperling, 1963; Turvey, 1973). As will be seen shortly, spatial cues do not produce effects of this magnitude in identification tasks.

If capacity allocation produces such a sizable speed-up in processing an element against a blank field, one also wonders why it does not facilitate threshold detection to a greater extent than would be predicted by noise reduction alone. Superficially, at least, threshold detection and simple RT seem to demand about the same, rather minimal degree of stimulus processing. One possible explanation is that threshold tasks without masks are not necessarily severely time limited.

Suppose the cueing effect in simple reaction time is not caused by capacity allocation; what other factors might be producing the speed-up? As Mulligan and Shaw (1981) pointed out, subjects could reduce their criterion for how much sensory information from the cued location must be registered before triggering a response. The simple RT task requires the subject to respond as soon as enough sensory information has been accumulated to make it clear that a stimulus is present. After a little time has passed, a suprathreshold stimulus presumably produces enough sensory activity to make this discrimination unambiguous (figure 4.3). However, to respond *as fast as possible,* one ought to respond as soon as one has enough evidence to make this discrimination with adequate reliability. Waiting until there is no doubt means not responding as fast as possible. It seems plausible that a criterion must be set for how much information will be required before triggering a response. It also seems plausible that different criteria can be set for each channel, at least for channels corresponding to location of a visual stimulus. If the goal is to reduce response times while minimizing the probability of a false alarm on catch trials, it would be adaptive to set the criterion level lower on any channel where the probability of a target is higher, and to raise the criterion on low-probability channels. This will produce faster respond-

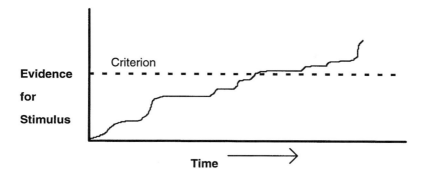

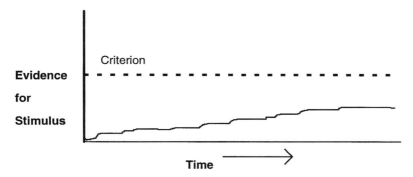

Figure 4.3
Possible analysis of a simple RT task. Evidence for the presence of the stimulus builds up over time, albeit with noise; detection is contingent on evidence crossing an adjustable criterion. The top panel shows a typical case where a stimulus is present. The bottom panel shows a typical catch trail where the stimulus is absent.

ing to stimuli on high-probability channels compared with low-probability channels.

If cues speed up simple RT because they induce people to lower their response criteria, as Mulligan and Shaw (1981), supposed, one might expect to see a corresponding increase in the false alarm rate. This need not be the case. If subjects lower their criterion for the high-probability channel and raise it for the low-probability channels, the *overall* false alarm rate may not rise at all. It is true that the probability of a false alarm originating from the high-probability channel would rise, but given the nature of the simple RT task, false alarms are not labeled as to which channel(s) triggered them; thus, signal-detection analysis cannot be applied directly here.

Several recent studies used more elaborate detection tasks designed to allow signal-detection analyses to be applied with the goal of distinguishing sensory enhancement due to capacity allocation from criterion adjustment. These studies involved detecting simple targets that could occur in one of a number of different positions, sometimes preceded by informative cues. Hawkins et al (1990) required subjects to detect a small white target spot in one of four boxes. Cues (valid about three-fourths of the time) consisted of an accentuation of one of the boxes, occurring 166 msec before the spot. After the spot was presented, all four positions were masked, and 500 msec later a report probe appeared next to a single location that might or might not have been the location that was cued. The observer's task was to report whether a target had been present in the position marked by the report probe. Sensitivity (assessed by d') was better when a cued location rather than an uncued location was probed. The authors interpreted their results as showing that cue validity effects "cannot be accounted for entirely by changes in decision bias alone."

These results do not necessarily contradict a decision bias account. The authors theorize that if the cue had no effect on the quality of the sensory information arriving from the cued position, cues should not improve accuracy of response to the report probe. Notice, however, that this hinges on the assumption that outputs of analyzers processing information from all four positions are still available at the time the delayed report probe is presented. Recall, however, that this is a half-second *after* the display has been replaced by masks. There is direct evidence that people cannot hold onto all the information from even *two* detectors when both are masked: for example, Duncan's (1980b) two-target effect and other effects discussed in chapter 3. For that reason, it seems more plausible that when a display is followed by masks, observers usually retain just a single estimate of the likelihood of a target being present and the location of the most likely candidate target, having stored this information within a short time after the masks appeared. If this is the case, the observation that performance is better when the report probe appears in a cued location does not suggest perceptual enhancement at all; it merely indicates that observers make use of cues at the moment they are forced to make a decision (i.e., when the masks appeared), achieving benefits through noise reduction.[2]

In summary, presenting a delayed report probe for a single position sounds like something that allows criterion and sensitivity effects to be analyzed separately for cued and uncued positions. However, the problem is that these estimates reflect whatever information can be *retained* from all the positions, not the information available at the time the decision was made. One knows quite independently that the former can be far less than the latter.[3] Other studies also used delayed probes and reported similar observations (Muller and Humphreys, 1991; Downing, 1988),[4] and their findings have similar problems of interpretation. (In some cases additional problems arose because several rather than single positions were cued.)

Does the criterion adjustment account for spatial cueing in simple RT make any specific and distinctive predictions of its own? Suppose subjects reduce the response criterion for the most likely channels, as suggested by Mulligan and Shaw. The slower the rate at which the outputs of these channels build up, the greater the savings in RT (figure 4.4). Therefore, any sensory manipulation that reduces the rate of buildup of evidence should interact with cueing, producing bigger cueing effects for stimuli producing a slower buildup. An obvious variable to reduce the buildup of evidence is a reduction in target energy, in this case, visual luminance. Two groups of investigators confirmed this interaction (Backus and Sternberg, 1988; Hawkins, Shafto, and Richardson, 1988).[5]

Mulligan and Shaw's account suggests that the effects of spatial uncertainty might be quite similar to the effects of temporal uncertainty. As

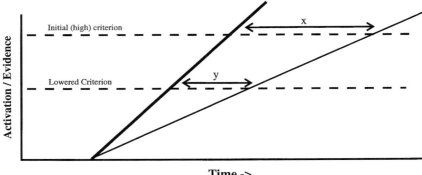

Figure 4.4
Lowered criterion of evidence and reduction in the rate of accumulation of evidence have interactive effects on the time taken to reach criterion. The thick line represents fast buildup of activation from a high-intensity stimulus, while the thinner line shows slower buildup from low-intensity stimulus. The difference in the time at which these two accumulation processes cross a high threshold (upper dotted line) is x. The difference in the time at which they cross a lowered criterion (lower dotted line) is y. As the figure illustrates, y is smaller than x.

with spatial uncertainty, uncertainty about when a near-threshold stimulus will appear produces a substantial decrement in detection accuracy (Lowe, 1967; Lasley and Cohn, 1981). Also, the magnitude of this effect corresponds well with what one would predict by assuming decision noise without any additional capacity limitations. (Here, capacity limits would mean inability to maintain a constant level of performance throughout the observation interval.) Simple RTs are quite sensitive to temporal uncertainty, with faster responses to stimuli that occurs at the most probable time within an interval (Karlin, 1959). As with the speed-ups in simple RT produced by spatial cues, the effects of temporal cues may reflect strategic changes in criteria for producing a response.

To summarize, the spatial attention task most intensively studied involves cueing in simple RT, and the effects of cues in this situation are often assumed to reflect perceptual enhancement, as shown in figure 4.1. Perhaps they do, but Mulligan and Shaw's criterion account offers a reasonable alternative that seems consistent with a broader range of evidence.

Discrimination Accuracy in Brief Masked Displays

Neither speeded detection tasks nor detection of stimuli at threshold provides a clear test of capacity allocation, because information about location might facilitate performance by reducing decision noise or inducing subjects to lower response criteria. If the capacity allocation account is correct, one should be able to perceive an isolated stimulus (e.g., letter or word) against an otherwise blank field more quickly when its location is known in advance. To demonstrate this speedup one needs a task in which subjects' accuracy of responding is limited by the time available for perception so that a delay or slowing in perception will show up as a change in accuracy. This naturally recommends an experiment in which a single stimulus is presented at a contrast well above threshold followed by a mask. Are people more accurate in identifying single masked items against a blank field when they know their location in advance? If they are, it will be difficult to explain solely in terms of noise reduction.

Before considering empirical findings of this type, it is worth recalling two important findings from divided-attention studies that were described in the preceding chapter. First, in a visual search task, people can recognize a handful of letters in parallel without any evident capacity limitations (e.g., Shiffrin and Gardner, 1972), whereas they show obvious capacity limits in carrying out more demanding form discriminations (e.g., reading two words). Second, even when the search can be performed without any capacity limitations, adding more elements to a display can reduce accuracy simply due to accumulation of statistical decision noise. Eriksen and Spencer (1969) demonstrated that decision noise can limit performance in a situation in which capacity limitations are absent.

These two conclusions suggest it would be somewhat peculiar, although not impossible, for advance information to greatly facilitate identification of an isolated character. To see why, suppose a single letter *were* processed more quickly when its location was known in advance. In that case, in a successive display of two letters, with the order of presentation fixed, as in Shiffrin and Gardner's experiment, one of the letters in each frame should benefit from this enhancement effect. By contrast, in the simultaneous condition, at most *one* item could benefit from enhancement. Thus, if perception of items in known locations were enhanced, a successive advantage would be expected, and yet none occurs.[6]

Thus, divided-attention studies make it seem a little unlikely that discrimination accuracy could be much improved by telling an observer in advance where an object will appear when it appears in an otherwise blank display. However, the situation is completely different when the item appears together with nontarget characters or other confusable stimuli. In that case, cueing is almost bound to produce a benefit because it effectively reduces the display size from four to one, thereby counteracting the accumulation of statistical noise in the decision process. For such a cueing effect to occur, the cues must appear early enough for the decision process to access the appropriate channels selectively while the critical information is still available.

Grindley and Townsend (1968) were among the first to examine accuracy with brief displays. They required subjects to report which of four possible forms was presented (shaped like the letter T in four different possible orientations). A form appeared in one of the four corners of the display, and subjects were told in advance which corner it would be (with crude, but seemingly effective monitoring of eye movements). No benefit was evident when observers knew in advance where the form would appear. This study can be criticized, however, for relatively low experimental power (Henderson, 1996).

Several recent studies found beneficial effects of position cueing. In one study that found a large benefit, subjects had to distinguish a single X or O (Henderson, 1991). An arrow cue preceded the character, which was presented for 50 msec in one of eight possible locations. The single-item display was followed by eight masks located in each of the locations. Accuracy for validly cued targets exceeded that for invalidly cued targets by more than 20%, very different from Grindley and Townsend's results. Similar results were reported by J. C. Johnston (1981), who used a verbal cue for a forced-choice letter-identification task with displays of four letters.

Studies conducted by Ling-Po Shiu and me (1994) suggest that the use of multiple masks, as in Henderson's (1991) study, can greatly inflate the effects of cueing. We had subjects identify a target letter presented in one of four positions, preceded by a 75% valid spatial cue. In blocks where the target was followed by four masks in all the possible positions (as in Henderson's and Johnston's studies), a sizable cueing effect was observed. However, when only a single mask appeared in the position formerly occupied by the target, spatial cueing effects were negligible. This pattern of results did not depend on whether the cues were central arrows or transient flickers adjacent to the position of the target. We found essentially the same result with a vernier acuity task. Subjects detected the direction of offset of a pair of line segments. Spatial precues did not improve discrimination when the line segments appeared alone and were followed by a single task. A cueing effect was found when the display also included three distractor lines, each individually masked (Shiu and Pashler, 1995).

The effects of number of masks can be readily understood in terms of statistical noise: a blank patch followed by a mask is confusable with a masked target stimulus, thereby introducing decision noise that can be eliminated by precueing. Several aspects of the data supported this interpretation. For one thing, when subjects were required to locate as well as identify a target stimulus, they often reported a target present in the position occupied solely by a mask. What is more, the false location reports associated with invalid cues tended to involve reporting a target at a cued position; if cues enhanced perception of the cued position, one might have expected something quite different. Other observations suggesting relatively negligible cueing effects for a single item followed by a single mask were reported by van der Heijden (1992) and Nazir (1992).

More recent results paint a somewhat confusing picture. Luck et al. (1996) replicated the findings of Shiu and me (1994) using letter discrimination with single and multiple masks. When they used slightly longer cue-target intervals and a cue that consisted of a brightening of four dots surrounding a given location, however, substantial cueing effects emerged, even with only a single mask. These experiments did not have a neutral condition, however. Shiu and I recently replicated the findings of Luck et al. and also found differences between valid and invalid cues using longer cue-target intervals and cues surrounding the target. When we added a neutral baseline condition (brightening at all positions), the results showed a cost (difference between neutral and invalid) but no benefit (difference between neutral and valid). Recent data of Bacon,

Johnston, and Remington (1995) complicate the picture even more: they found both cost and benefit with a paradigm almost identical to the one used in the two studies just described. The only difference was in the use of a mask composed of fragments of the items to be discriminated, rather than unrelated visual features.

Together, these results create a rather unappetizing empirical stalemate. Further research exploring a number of different factors within the same experiment will be needed to figure out whether cueing in single-item displays enhances processing or merely reduces noise due to extraneous stimuli and perhaps introduces other artifacts. Despite the stalemate, we can draw at least a few conclusions. The benefit of valid cues compared to neutral baseline must be modest, if one exists. Invalid cues, on the other hand, do seem to cause worse performance than a neutral baseline, at least with reasonably long cue-target intervals. Should it turn out, as seems plausible, that there is a true cost of invalid cues but no enhancement from valid cues, this would indicate that cues can trigger attentional responses that are basically maladaptive, at least for performing the task at hand. This possibility, which will be discussed further below, is not terribly surprising given certain other attentional phenomena described above, in particular the dual-target effect reported by Duncan (1980b). However, it is also possible that there is a true benefit from valid cueing, as one study suggests (Bacon et al., 1994). In that case, the experiments showing no benefit must have been insensitive in ways that are not presently understood.

Speeded Discrimination Tasks

A few studies have examined the effects of location precueing on speeded discrimination responses to single visual stimuli. Posner et al. (1980) required letter versus digit discrimination, and preceded the displays with arrow cues indicating the most probable quadrant. Responses to stimuli in the expected position were about 30 msec faster than those to stimuli in unexpected positions. Several other studies observed effects of similarly modest magnitude (e.g., McCann, Folk, and Johnston, 1992).

Can speedup in choice RT be attributed to a reduction in the criteria, as, it was argued above, seems to be the case with simple RT? In a speeded choice task one is responding only when sufficient information is available to indicate which of the alternatives is present, unlike simple RT where one is simply waiting to be sure there is something rather than nothing. One can assume that separate channels represent evidence for the different possible targets at each of the positions (e.g., eight channels to be checked if there are two alternatives and four locations), and that one can vary criteria on each of these separately. However, unlike in the simple RT situation, it is not possible to reduce criteria without increasing overall error rates. Empirically, it turns out that in some cases (e.g., Kingstone, 1992) the speedup produced by valid cueing is indeed accompanied by an increase in error rates. Thus, the benefits of cueing can be associated with a speed-accuracy tradeoff. Posner et al. (1980) reported that in a go–no-go paradigm, valid cues increased error rates on no-go trials to a remarkable extent; they commented that "subjects found it very difficult to withhold responding when a nontarget occurred in the expected position" (p. 169). In other studies using choice RTs, however (e.g., McCann, Folk, and Johnston, 1992), no tradeoff effects were found. It is difficult to detect speed-accuracy tradeoffs when subjects are operating at very high levels of accuracy, as in almost all these studies (Pachella, 1974), so subtle ones may easily be missed in these situations.

Shiu and I recently investigated the issue using spatial cues in a speeded letter-discrimination task (Shiu and Pashler, 1993). Subjects decided whether a single letter was an F or a T, making a speeded button-push response. When we used ordinary speeded instructions, placing moderate emphasis on accuracy, we found a small benefit of valid precues with a slight decrease in accuracy (speed-accuracy tradeoff). When extreme speed pressure was applied, valid cues produced a sizable decrease in accuracy and about a 30-msec speedup in responding. It would appear, then, that for some unknown reason subjects take the validity of a spatial cue as an indication that it is time to respond. When we computed the speed-accuracy microtradeoff curve, examining accuracy as a function of response speed for a given subject's responses, we found no evidence that, compared with neutral trials, valid cues led to better accuracy for any given speed. However, we saw some evidence of cost—reduced accuracy for a given speed on invalid trials compared with neutral trials. Recall that the discrimination accuracy studies also suggested that cues may produce cost without benefit; while this apparent convergence is certainly intriguing, it requires further testing and verification.

What can be concluded about spatial cueing and discrimination RTs? Here too, costs and benefits of cueing are certainly not large, rarely exceeding 20 or 30 msec. It is possible that the benefits are real, but these speedups may be artifacts of speed-accuracy tradeoffs, in which case they provide no evidence for capacity allocation.

Advance Knowledge about Location: Conclusions

What can be concluded from studies of location cueing in a wide variety of different experimental paradigms? Studies of detection and discrimination at contrast threshold provide no evidence for benefits of location knowledge beyond those attributable to statistical decision noise, which arises because the blank field is confusable with the stimulus in a threshold situation, by definition. Valid cues are often associated with faster simple RTs, but these might well reflect a change in criterion: subjects demand less information on whatever channels are likely to contain evidence for the presence of the imperative stimulus. Tasks that measure accuracy of identifying a suprathreshold stimulus followed by a mask offer potentially the most sensitive test of capacity-allocation accounts, because here accuracy depends on carrying out perceptual analysis without delay. Despite a recent flurry of research on this question, the issue remains unsettled. It seems clear that invalid peripheral cues are capable of reducing subjects' accuracy, but evidence for a true benefit (improved performance in valid trials compared with neutral trials) remains spotty at best.

Chamberlin's method of multiple working hypotheses (1897) may offer a useful approach in stalemates of this kind. Chamberlin believed that rather than aiming to declare one theory the victor, one ought rather to consider how each theory might be developed to account for existing results, anticipating that one of these paths will ultimately prove fruitless. Following this advice, suppose that capacity allocation is not possible and that statistical noise reduction accounts for all true benefits of location cueing. This plainly explains the absence of capacity limitations in divided-attention tasks involving several masked characters (Shiffrin and

Gardner, 1972). It also readily predicts the excellent fit of ideal-observer models to uncertainty effects at threshold (Mulligan and Shaw, 1981; Shaw, 1984; Cohn and Lasley, 1974). It would have to be supplemented, however, with an explanation of why an invalid peripheral cue could sometimes produce a cost compared with a neutral cue (e.g., Luck et al, 1995). Since the possibility of information *exclusion* is uncontroversial, and is required in explaining effects of cueing with crowded displays, one might posit that an exogenous cue involuntarily triggers some reduction of information uptake from distant regions. None of this amounts to capacity allocation as depicted in figure 1.8.

Suppose, on the other hand, capacity allocation does occur as in figure 1.8. To account for the absence of true benefits in threshold detection and discrimination results, one could postulate that capacity is simply not used in the earliest detection operations. Presumably the same would be true for the simple RT task as well; thus, the cueing effect there might be accounted for in terms of criterion reduction, as Mulligan and Shaw proposed. Of interest, then, it seems that if capacity allocation does occur, it may play no role in the tasks cited as providing evidence for capacity allocation. In this view, failures to observe cueing effects with masked stimuli would still have to be explained. If this line of argument is correct, these experiments must be insensitive for reasons that remain to be worked out.

Visual Stimuli: Set for Nonspatial Attributes

Spatial Frequency and Size
The most careful studies of set involve not retinal extent, but the closely related dimension of spatial frequency, which is usually described in terms of the number of cycles of a grating per degree of visual angle. The existence of spatial frequency uncertainty effects in discrimination tasks was mentioned above. The converse of the uncertainty effect can be observed as well: at threshold, subjects' detection of gratings is substantially improved when they know the spatial frequency of the grating in advance (Davis, Kramer, and Graham, 1983). The magnitude of the improvement is consistent with what is to be expected from the accumulation of decision noise: when subjects are uncertain about spatial

frequency, they must monitor several channels, and in so doing incur an increased probability of a false alarm from a channel that contains no target. As with spatial position, this decrement in accuracy appears too small to reflect any absolute inability to monitor more than one spatial frequency-selective mechanism. In the Davis et al study, when spatial frequency was uncertain, spatial position was fixed; thus, these studies gave no direct evidence that observers can actually monitor for gratings of a single spatial frequency over a range of spatial positions. This ability would be especially intriguing, since it might well reflect monitoring of visual analyzers that are distributed over different cortical visual areas,[7] which is less likely to be true of the other threshold-monitoring phenomena discussed here. In any case, it appears that observers also have the ability to monitor two relatively distant spatial frequencies (1 and 16 cycles/degree) without monitoring intermediate spatial frequencies (Davis, 1981).

What about recognizing stimuli of variable size presented well above threshold? Folk and Egeth (1985) asked whether letter recognition would be speeded when the size of the letters was fixed and thus could be anticipated by the subject, rather than varied. In each trial, the subject named a single letter as quickly as possible. The letters were either large or small (large letters were bigger by a factor of 4 on each dimension). Subjects were no faster in pure-size blocks than in mixed-size blocks. The only case in which size made any difference was when displays in a search task contained elements of both sizes; here there was some degree of slowing when the target was smaller than the distractor. Farell and Pelli (1993) had people search for characters in displays of 32 characters of homogeneous or mixed size, examining accuracy with brief displays. When subjects had to detect and identify a target, mixing sizes did not reduce accuracy. On the other hand, location reports did show some cost. It is not clear what to make of the decrement in location accuracy. It might be that people have more difficulty translating between their internal representation of location and position in the array when the size is mixed and, hence, irregular. In any case, the comparable performance in identifying the targets rules out quite convincingly the hypothesis that people cannot attend to large and small simultaneously.

The results of Graham and colleagues with gratings of different spatial frequencies presented at threshold, and findings of Folk and Egeth's and Farell and Pelli's with suprathreshold stimuli closely mirror the pattern of results found with location cueing. For size as well as location, observers appear able to monitor selectively analyzers that are tuned to particular values of the dimension, producing detection or discrimination responses on the basis of the outputs of these analyzers. This selective monitoring prevents the quality of perceptual decisions from being degraded by noise contained in the irrelevant channels. However, when a large suprathreshold letter is presented, there is no reason to expect that analyzers selective for small letters (assuming that these even exist) would contain spurious signals. Thus, as perhaps with spatial location, there is no facilitation for discrimination of a suprathreshold stimulus when the value on the dimension is specified in advance. Models proposing that limited processing capacity can be allocated in advance to size-dependent channels, thereby allowing processing to start more quickly or proceed more efficiently, receive no support from the data.

What about information that is present at different scales in the same object? Here, it seems that the apparent ability to monitor at small and large scales breaks down. Consider, for example, a study by Ward (1985). He presented single large letters made up of many repetitions of a particular small letter (so-called bilevel stimuli). Subjects searched for either of two possible target letters; the target could be either the local or the global constituent in the form presented. When emphasis was placed on monitoring one level (global or local), subjects were much faster for that dimension and much slower on the other dimension, compared with an equal-emphasis condition. The magnitude of the effect was large (cost + benefit = 300–400 msec). It is perhaps conceivable that this could reflect a decision noise effect, but given that the effect is so much larger than the costs found with different objects of different sizes, that possibility seems unlikely. Ward reported that observers subjectively felt unable to process the letters at both size scales simultaneously, and the objective data are certainly consistent with these reports.

Ward's effects also seem much larger than those observed by Folk and Egeth, whose subjects searched two different letters presented side by side at different scales. Unfortunately, one cannot reach any definite conclusions until a comparison is made between observers' ability to search forms at both sizes when (a) a small letter is next to a big letter (made up of, say, asterisks) versus (b) the same big letter composed out of the small letter (Ward's stimuli). If the different size/same object task is indeed much harder, this would show that it is not merely processing at different scales that causes the breakdown. In that case, the problem in Ward's task may be in parsing one region of visual space in two different (and incompatible) ways.

In summary, it appears that the visual system does not have to be, and indeed cannot be, tuned to recognize a form at a particular spatial scale. No evidence, for example, suggests that processing capacity can be pre-allocated to detectors that respond only to stimuli of particular sizes. Nonetheless, in detecting near-threshold stimuli people appear able to monitor selectively elementary visual analyzers that respond to stimuli at different spatial scales. This selective monitoring improves detection or discrimination accuracy, probably by reducing decision noise, as discussed in preceding chapters. Although it is evidently of no benefit to know in advance the size of a suprathreshold stimulus, it may be slightly difficult to search for target features defined at two different spatial scales. A much more severe problem seems to arise in computing or accessing form information from the *same* region of visual space at different spatial scales. This may reflect basic parsing operations that take place before object recognition or cooperatively with it. On this account, it is difficult to adopt two different parsings of the same region of the visual field simultaneously. That might be akin to the difficulty in simultaneously resolving classic ambiguous figures such as the duck-rabbit and the crone-maiden.

Orientation of Familiar Objects

People are often capable of recognizing objects that are tilted with respect to the retina, but recognition is often less efficient as a consequence. The reader can immediately verify this by rotating this book 90 degrees and continuing to read. It is harder to read, but certainly not impossible. People can recognize an individual letter at different orientations with almost no slowing, although careful measurements examining accuracy with masked characters show a subtle decrement at nonvertical orientations (Jolicoeur and Landau, 1984). The slowing of identification due to disorientation becomes much more noticeable with more complex stimuli such as words (Koriat and Norman, 1984). When faces are turned upside down, it is difficult to recognize them at all (A. Johnston, Hill, and Carman, 1992). These difficulties depend on retinal rather than gravitational disorientation. To verify this, the reader can take a magazine, turn it upside down, and open it to some pictures of familiar people. They will be difficult to recognize. Now stand up, hold the magazine in your hand so you are looking straight at it, and (continuing to keep the magazine in the same position relative to your head) lower your head toward the floor as if you were performing a toe touch. In this way, you cn make the magazine upright in gravitational coordinates and upside down in retinal coordinates. Having done so, you will probably find the difficulty recognizing the faces to be every bit as severe, indicating that it is retinal rather than gravitational disorientation that impairs object recognition.

This should not be taken to mean that gravitational coordinates have no effect on perception. Irvin Rock's pioneering studies of orientation and form perception demonstrated that the shape we perceive and remember after viewing an unfamiliar form often depends on the subjective top-bottom axis we assign to the object, which is often determined by gravitational axes (Rock, 1973). As evidence of this, Rock tilted observers and had then view some novel shapes. Later he showed the observers, who were now upright, the same shapes, along with some foils, and had them perform recognition judgments (old vs new). Recognition was best for shapes whose actual (i.e., gravitational) orientation was the same at the initial viewing and test, even though this meant that the retinal image of these objects was different on the two occasions.

These results led Rock to suppose that an observer typically imposes a frame of reference that assigns top and bottom to whatever is in the highest and lowest position in gravitational coordinates, respectively, even when this is not aligned with retinal top and bottom. The internal descriptions of the form that are then stored are relative to this axis. What is even more intriguing is the fact that by sheer force of will an observer can impose a top-bottom frame that does not conform to either the gravitational or the retinal coordinates. This is illustrated by the diamond/square ambiguity: if you look at a square that is resting along one of its edges you can make yourself see it as a diamond with its top in what you formerly saw as the upper right or upper left corner of the square. Much harder, but sometimes possible, is seeing one of the bottom corners as the top.

The fact that an act of will can determine what one sees as the top and bottom of an object would make plausible a set effect for orientation: with advance knowledge of how an object will be oriented, one might prepare a frame of reference, thereby facilitating identification of appropriately aligned objects. Accordingly, one might expect the observer to have less difficulty identifying disoriented stimuli when they are cued in advance about the orientation. The literature does not seem to contain any reports of this kind of set effect. Koriat and Norman (1984) found no benefit when two different words were presented at the same particular disorientation on two successive trials (one might have expected that repetition would automatically produce selective preparation for the same orientation, even if the orientation in one trial did not predict the orientation in the next). Cooper and Shepard (1973) had subjects judge whether a rotated letter was a mirror image or normal letter, sometimes cueing them about the rotation but not the letter. Observers were not able to prepare the frame of reference in advance and circumvent the rotation. However, mirror-image judgments probably require different processes from those involved in identifying objects (e.g., Corballis, 1988), so these results may not address quite the same question.

Unconvinced by these failures, William Wright and I carried out a series of experiments trying to find a set effect for orientation in the recognition of words and pictures. In one experiment, subjects made a speeded semantic judgment deciding whether or not a word was a place name. The word could appear at any of five orientations. In some trials subjects were presented with what seemed to be an optimal cue to let them lock onto the appropriate frame of reference for the upcoming word. The cue was a cartoon face that appeared briefly in the same position and orientation as the subsequent word. The face then disappeared and was replaced by the word. Disorientation of the word caused the same slowing regardless of whether subjects had been cued with the face. Other attempts to find evidence for a voluntarily preset frame of reference also failed. The one case in which orientation cueing confers a benefit is when the task requires judging the symmetry of a dot pattern; cueing the axis of symmetry facilitates performance (Pashler, 1990a).

In summary, Rock's results, and common observation, demonstrate that with a voluntary act of will one can arbitrarily select a top-bottom axis, thereby changing the perceived form of an object. However, the difficulty one has recognizing retinally disoriented stimuli remains even when the orientation is known in advance. It does not appear that one can prepare a general reference frame in advance of the stimulus to facilitate recognition of the stimulus in a particular orientation.

Auditory Stimuli

Set for Frequency
Hearing researchers have extensively studied the detection of a relatively brief tone superimposed on a background of noise. Just as uncertainty about spatial position reduces detection for visual events at threshold, uncertainty about frequency reduces tone detection (Green, 1961). The simplest account of these uncertainty effects is that listeners are unable to monitor more than one frequency at a time (sometimes termed a single band model in the auditory literature). Given that speech recognition depends on brief events occurring simultaneously in different parts of the frequency spectrum, such a limitation would be rather surprising. In fact, the uncertainty effect in detection is far smaller than what the single band model would predict (Veniar, 1958). Furthermore, recall that in chapter 3 we discussed results by Sorkin, Gilliom, and co-workers that strongly argued for parallel processing of different frequency channels in tone detection. The most straightforward evidence for parallel monitoring is the fact that subjects can monitor for a low- or high-frequency target in the same observation interval just as effectively as they can monitor for a low-frequency target in one observation interval and a high-frequency target in a second shortly later (D. M. Johnson and Hafter, 1980). Therefore, uncertainty effects in simple auditory as well as visual detection probably reflect accumulation of decision noise rather than genuine capacity limitations. The noise appears to be attributable to both

variation in the stimuli and to internal noise that arises during neural processing (Siegel and Colburn, 1989).

Recall that visual uncertainty effects can be reduced by cueing the subject about stimulus location in individual trials in a block containing targets of mixed frequency. Similarly, cueing can reduce frequency uncertainty effects in hearing. Gilliom and Mills (1976) found that auditory precues presented well above threshold caused performance to improve near the level achieved in monitoring for a single known frequency.

In the past decade or two, researchers investigating attentional effects in auditory signal detection have favored a technique known as the probe-signal method. This technique defies the organization of this book, because it could be reasonably classified as a selective-attention task, a divided-attention task, or a perceptual set manipulation. In the basic procedure developed by Greenberg and Larkin (1968), subjects listen for targets (which they call probes), usually in a two-interval forced-choice paradigm (did the first or second observation interval contain the target?). In the early experiments, subjects always believed that all probes would be fixed at a particular frequency throughout the experiment, called the primary frequency. However, in fewer than one-fourth of the trials, a probe at a different frequency was presented. Under conditions where the probe was detected in 80% or 90% of trials, these distant-frequency probes were often detected at near-chance levels in the two interval procedures. Evidently, subjects monitor almost exclusively at or near the primary frequency.

Research with the probe-signal method has addressed several issues. The first is the precise nature of the frequency-selective mechanism being monitored. Auditory scientists refer to the critical band as the fundamental frequency-sensitive channel in the peripheral auditory system. Do subjects monitor the critical band centered at the primary frequency? Dai, Scharf, and Buus (1991) found that the shape of the critical bands and the attention bands differed. Furthermore, the effective attenuation for probes distant from the primary is about 7 db, whereas the sensitivity of the auditory filter falls off much faster for distant frequencies. Evidently, listeners do not restrict their monitoring to a single critical band, although they nonetheless achieve a great deal of frequency selectivity.

As noted, subjects can monitor for targets at two different frequencies in a single observation interval as well as they can when each target can only appear in one of two successive observation intervals (D. M. Johnson and Hafter, 1980). This indicates that they can monitor two frequency intervals at the same time. Can they monitor for signals at the two widely spaced frequencies *without* also monitoring the intervening frequencies? If not, performance in simultaneous monitoring should suffer because of statistical noise on the intervening frequency channels. Therefore, the equality of simultaneous and successive monitoring found by Johnson and Hafter provides some evidence people can monitor two noncontiguous locations on the frequency dimension.

Converging evidence for this conclusion is provided by a probe-signal investigation performed by MacMillan and Schwartz (1975). Their subjects listened for primary tones, which occurred in 77% of trials. In some blocks the tones could occur at either 1000 or 2300 Hz. Probes at unexpected frequencies were detected much less often, even when their frequency was between the primary tone frequencies. Subjects detected either primary tone in well over half the trials, so it is not likely that listeners monitor for one pitch in one trial and another pitch in another.

The reader may wonder whether, in probe-primary research, listeners miss probe tones because they are consciously aware of them but decline to report them. Scharf et al. (1987) pointed out several sorts of evidence against this, which they named the heard-but-not-heeded hypothesis. For one thing, when subjects are told that there will be tones at frequencies other than the primary, they still tend to miss them, although not quite so often. Scharf et al also tried probes consisting of complex tones with energy at the frequency of the primary. These probes were generally well detected, even though the authors report that they do not sound quite the same as the primaries. If people missed target-distant probes simply because they reject atypical-sounding tones, one would expect them to reject these probes as well. Even more interesting, Scharf et al. had subjects monitor for primaries at 400 Hz, but occasionally inserted a probe with energy at three frequencies—1,600, 2,000, and 2,400 Hz. This complex tone sounds much like a 400-Hz pitch due to the phenomenon of filling in the missing fundamental. Nonetheless, subjects performed poorly at detecting this complex, suggesting that they actually monitor for energy around 400 Hz, rather than simply rejecting signals that sound different in pitch from the usual primaries. This suggests that listeners in threshold tasks may base their responses on activity in detectors that register more primitive information than the discriminations that constitute ordinary above-threshold hearing.

Further tests of the heard-but-not-heeded hypothesis could make use of the dual-target effect noted by Sorkin and colleagues. Suppose subjects listened for tones at 1,000 and 2,300 Hz, as in MacMillan and Schwartz's study. Consider a probe at 1500 Hz presented simultaneously with a primary at 1000 Hz. If the probe is heard but not heeded, its detection should reduce the probability of detecting the 1,000-Hz primary just as another target at 2,300 Hz would. If the 1,500-Hz tone does not produce such a decrement, this would go some way to objectively confirming Scharf et al's rejection of the heard-but-not-heeded hypothesis.

Set for Location and Other Attributes

Does uncertainty about spatial position affect hearing in the same way as uncertainty about frequency, and conversely, does cueing facilitate it? As stated in chapter 2, selective-attention studies tend to show similar benefits for selection when messages are segregated by either frequency or spatial position. However, uncertainty and cueing effects with single stimuli do not paint such a clear picture. Lowe (1968) presented tone signals through either of two loudspeakers on the subject's left or right. Meanwhile, noise was presented from two speakers in front and behind the listener. Sensitivity was only barely improved when the 1,000-Hz tone burst always originated from the left speaker, or always from the right speaker, compared with the condition where it might originate from either speaker, and the overall uncertainty effect was not significant.

An outright negative result was reported by Scharf et al. (1986) who used the probe-and-primary technique. They presented 80% of their signals from a loudspeaker located on the subject's left, and only 20% from the loudspeaker on the right. Detection of probes in the two speakers was not measurably different.

Neither of these results provides compelling evidence against a location-uncertainty effect analogous to the frequency-uncertainty effects discussed above. Big effects of frequency uncertainty occur when the listener is not sure which frequency to monitor and the noise contains components at that frequency. Typically, the target energy level is low enough in these situations that internal noise is significant as well. However, in Lowe's experiment, the signal was always presented from a different location than the noise. Lowe's finding basically shows that it does not help to know which of two locations the signal will come from, when the noise comes from *yet other* locations. Similarly, Scharf et al. presented both the noise and the signal from the same speaker and found that it did not help if the subject knew which speaker it was.

To compare the results with the frequency uncertainty and cueing studies, one needs an experiment in which noise is played in the left ear and uncorrelated noise is played in the right ear. In some blocks of trials, the signal always comes in one ear, whereas in other blocks it may be presented in both ears. Unfortunately, no data have been reported of this type. However, the fact that detection thresholds are reduced when interaural phase produces a spatial separation of signal and noise (the masking level difference effect mentioned briefly in chapter 2) would make it seem pretty plausible that an uncertainty effect would be found here.

There was one positive finding with location cueing, but unfortunately this study is useful mainly as an illustration of methodological pitfalls. Rhodes (1987) placed nine small speakers in a circle around a listener. When a suprathreshold tone was played, the listener indicated which speaker it was coming from, using numbers ranging from one to nine. More often than chance, a tone in trial n+1 came from the same speaker as in trial n. This was done to provide subjects an incentive to "keep their attention on the location of each sound until the next one occurred" (p. 2). Subjects were as much as 350 msec faster to respond to tones that occurred at the same location as in the previous trial, compared with tones occurring in distant locations. Furthermore, there was a monotonic increase in RTs as this distance was increased. Rhodes concluded that attention moved from point to point in a continuous fashion. It seems implausible that changes in the perception of a tone of this kind could produce such a large speed-up. Furthermore, one would naturally have expected repetition of the stimulus in a difficult choice RT tasks to speed the response selection stage of the task (Pashler and Baylis, 1991). In fact, other findings of Rhodes directly indicate this: when subjects had to respond with arbitrary names for the speakers (Smith, Jones, etc.), the distance effect was even larger, favoring a response selection locus by the logic of the additive factors method (Sternberg, 1969).

Spence and Driver (1994), on the other hand, found evidence for an effect of spatial cues on pitch discrimination in a task involving speeded responses to suprathreshold tones. For example, in experiment 6, a 2,000-Hz cue preceded a target tone of either 345 or 375 Hz; 75% of the time, the target came from the same speaker as the cue. Responses on validly cued trials were slightly faster and more accurate than responses on invalidly cued trials (20–40 msec difference). As noted above, differences between valid and invalid peripheral cueing may reflect costs caused by invalid cues, rather than benefits caused by valid cues, and the experiments do not allow us to distinguish among these alternatives.

In summary, knowing spatial position may or may not have some beneficial effect on pitch discrimination. Future research could profitably examine this question further using both threshold and suprathreshold discrimination tasks.

Tactile Perception and Pain

Two studies of set effects in tactile stimulation at threshold produced results comparable with those found with faint visual and auditory stimulation. Meyer, Gross, and Teuber (1963) determined that uncertainty of site of stimulation affected the threshold for detecting light pressure on the skin. Thresholds for detecting a filament passing over the skin were significantly higher when, for example, the stimulation could occur on either the left or right palm, compared with when the subject knew the stimulation would occur only on one palm or the other. Whang, Burton, and Shulman (1991) reported similar site-of-stimulation uncertainty effects in a task requiring detection of amplitude change in vibratory stimulation of the fingertips.

Similar results were observed in detection of painful thermal stimulation. Bushnell et al. (1985) placed two thermodes above the lips of subjects who were required to detect a modest increase in the already uncomfortable temperature of one of the thermodes. The increase might occur at any point in a 5-second period. When subjects were accurately cued about the side on which the painful stimulation was most likely, their responses were faster and more accurate. Using a similar experimental setup, Miron, Duncan, and Bushnell (1989) found that subjects' rated the intensity and unpleasantness of painful thermal stimulation as greater when they were accurately cued to expect thermal rather than visual stimulation.

In each of the studies discussed here except the last, improvements in detection may reflect reduction in noise from uncued location and, in some cases, changes in criteria for detecting signals against a noisy background. The effect of uncertainty on ratings of painfulness is of course not directly comparable with detection of a threshold stimulus and is perhaps not attributable to the same mechanism.

Set for Object Identity and Perceptual Readiness

The preceding sections explored what happens when an observer is provided advance information about an incidental aspect of a stimulus that is to be identified—incidental in the sense that it provides no clue about the attribute of the stimulus the observer must determine, e.g., its identity. We turn now to advance information that does provide a hint about the identity of a stimulus. The issue, in simple terms, is whether we perceive things better when we do know what to expect than when we do not. According to Hatfield (in press), in the first century B.C. Lucretius claimed that things are not seen sharply "save those for which the mind has prepared itself." In modern laboratory contexts, we can allow people to prepare their minds by giving them one or more likely candidates or otherwise constraining the set of alternatives.

Potential Benefits

What happens when the observer is notified of the set of possible alternative stimuli he or she will be asked to discriminate before a target stimulus is presented? From a computational perspective, object recognition can be viewed as a problem of searching an extremely large number of candidate identities to find the best match to the current input. The size of the search that is actually carried out could potentially be reduced when advance information is available that shrinks the number of options worth considering. Researchers in the field of artificial intelligence and machine vision have argued that recognition must be strongly guided by top-down information, that is, by prior expectations and any contextual information that might be obtained from processing in different parts of a scene (Minsky, 1968). Various psychologists followed Lucretius and endorsed this assumption with regard to human recognition processes. For example, Hochberg (1978) and Neisser (1976) described perception as an interactive process of interrogating the visual image to verify particular cognitively generated expectations. These views all suggest that advance information should profoundly improve our ability to distinguish among possibilities we expect, compared with possibilities we do not expect.

If the hypothesis-testing metaphor correctly describes human object recognition, advance information about likely alternatives could facilitate perception in several ways. The greatest benefits of top-down information would be expected if different perceptual hypotheses were ordinarily tested against the input sequentially. In that case, prior knowledge would allow the system to consider correct candidates at or near the beginning of the search, potentially producing enormous benefits (Becker, 1976). Given the speed with which people can recognize objects without advance information, the number of candidate visual objects that people can recognize, and the fact that individual neural operations are relatively slow (Sejnowski, 1986), this sort of serial processing seems highly implausible. Advance information could also yield large benefits for a parallel search, however. For example, it might be possible to allocate limited processing resources to different analyzers (specialized for recognizing different objects), thereby increasing their efficiency.

Advance information about alternatives might also increase the overall accuracy of recognition even without affecting the evidence gathered about different alternatives, as envisioned in the schemes just described. Suppose that recognition of identities of such familiar objects as words, tables, or chairs involved checking the outputs of higher-order detectors that function like the lower-order detectors implicated in studies of detection of threshold patterns (as discussed above; cf Graham, 1985).

Assume also some overlap between the possible outputs of the chair detector when a chair is present and when a chair is not present. In this case (the bare essentials of a signal-detection analysis), providing alternatives in advance could improve accuracy by allowing an observer to monitor only those detectors relevant to the specified alternatives. As described, such changes have been confirmed in tasks requiring discriminations of spatial frequency near the contrast threshold.

As the reader will have noticed, these two explanations, allocation of capacity to analyzers and selectivity in decision, correspond to the general classes of alternatives described in connection with the effects of cueing on orthogonal dimensions. Of course, we have no a priori reason to believe that conclusions must be the same in the two domains.

Before versus Before and After

The two views just described both predict that, at least under some circumstances, discrimination accuracy should improve markedly when advance information about alternatives is provided. This issue has been studied over many decades. It was noted some time ago that comparing advance presentation of alternatives with *no* presentation of alternatives may not be appropriate. Having alternatives might lead to better recognition accuracy than not having alternatives, even if the alternatives had their effects after perception was completed. Consider an extreme example. Suppose an experimenter briefly flashes a picture; the observer suspects he saw a rhinoceros, but with little confidence. Asked what he saw, the observer would say "rhinoceros." On the other hand, if told that the object was either a hippopotamus and ashtray, the observer would undoubtedly say "hippo." On average, then, providing the alternatives at time of test facilitates performance. The improvement obviously cannot reflect enhancement of perception, since the alternatives were not available until long after the stimulus was gone. Indeed, providing alternatives after the offset of a visual display can produced this sort of benefit (Lawrence and Coles, 1954). It has generally been thought, therefore, that if providing alternatives facilitates performance by allowing the perceptual system to be tuned appropriately by changing the order in which hypotheses are verified, or by allowing monitoring of noisy detectors as with simple patterns at threshold, for example, there should be an additional benefit when the alternatives are provided in advance compared with presenting them afterward.

Several studies precued subjects with a fairly large number of alternatives or with abstract information about the class of stimuli that would be briefly presented. Lawrence and Coles (1954) showed subjects pictures of familiar objects in a tachistoscope for exposure durations ranging from 20 to 500 msec. A set of four alternative objects labels was provided either after or before and after the picture, and subjects chose from this set. No additional benefit was found in the before-and-after condition. Similarly, Long, Henneman, and Garvey (1960) reported no advantage for recognition of blurred words from advance presentation of the four possible alternative letters. J. C. Johnston (1981) presented a letter followed by pattern masks, and offered the subject two choices in a forced-choice task. He found no extra benefit when these choices were provided before as well as after the display. Neither did Smith and Fabri (1973) in several carefully conducted studies that also involved letter discrimination. Other studies provided more abstract, semantic information about the subsequent stimuli. Biederman et al. (1983) had subjects detect incongruities in scenes depicted in briefly exposed line-drawings (e.g., a fire hydrant sitting on a mailbox); they observed no improvement when the subject was cued in advance about what sort of scene would be presented (e.g., downtown city street).

Thus, knowing the set of possible alternative objects does not seem to facilitate recognition of a briefly presented and masked item drawn from the set. However, highly specific information about alternatives can sometimes improve discrimination accuracy. Egeth and Smith (1967) briefly exposed pictures of common objects (e.g., a shoe) and had observers choose among four pictures. When the four objects were similar (e.g., different styles of men's shoes) prior exposure to the alternatives produced a fairly substantial benefit. This was not the case when the four objects were dissimilar in appearance. Pachella (1974) confirmed that prior presentation of pictorial, but not verbal, alternatives facilitates recognition of pictures, and showed that alternatives retrieved from memory in advance of the stimulus worked about as well as those directly provided by the experimenter. With briefly presented letters (distorted but not masked) Long, Reid, and Henneman (1960) observed a modest benefit when the set of alternatives was restricted to just two letters.

Facilitation seems to be the rare result, and to arise only in situations involving a complex discrimination task (e.g., picture identification), when the advance information is likely to permit the observer to select a small set of critical features in advance. This kind of information transforms the discrimination task to be performed. For example, if the different men's shoes in Egeth and Smith's study happened to differ only in a few particulars (e.g., laces, the size of the heel), subjects could improve their performance by basing their responses solely on these features, disregarding other information. Therefore, these studies do not reveal that observers can allocate capacity to the appropriate detectors or give appropriate detectors top priority in any general way.

A few findings in the literature might seem not to conform completely to this conclusion, however, such as Long, Reid, and Henneman's observation of modest benefit with letter discrimination (differing from the results of Johnston and of Smith and Fabri). Why the different result? An intriguing study reported a few years later by J. C. Johnston and Hale (1984) may help pinpoint the critical factor. Subjects saw or heard a single word as a precue, followed by a single word and then a pattern mask. Subjects were offered a test stimulus and decided whether it matched the word presented (yes or no). In half of the trials the precue was identical to the word actually presented, and in the others it was identical to the alternative offered the subject after the target. Thus, the (cue)-target-test? sequence might be (fish)-CHAIR-fish? (correct answer "no") or (fish)-FISH-fish? (correct answer "yes"). In the corresponding no-cue trials, the target-test sequence can be abbreviated CHAIR-fish? or CHAIR-chair?. A signal-detection measure was employed: responding "yes" to (fish)-FISH-fish? counted as a hit, and responding "yes" to (fish)-CHAIR-fish? counted as a false alarm.

In three experiments that used this design with a pattern-masked target, Johnston and Hale found no benefits of cueing, although a small benefit was observed when the stimuli were presented briefly at low energy and not followed by a mask. This situation is more similar to the method of Long, Reid, and Henneman (1960), which also produced some cueing effect. Therefore, a reasonable summary of the findings would be as follows: when a stimulus is available for several hundred milliseconds because it was presented briefly or at low contrast, but not masked, there may be time for some limited hypothesis-driven identification to take place. When a pattern mask abruptly terminates identification, on the other hand, no evidence exists that hypothesis-driven processing can take place. People are often successful in comprehending scenes exposed for periods as short as, say, 150 msec and followed by a mask (Biederman, Mezzanotte, and Rabinowitz, 1982). Therefore the results argue against suggestions of Minsky, Hochberg, and other perceptual theorists (as well as numerous textbook writers) who assume that top-down expectations are essential in guiding perception. Evidently, one should not underestimate the capacity of the visual system to carry out purely bottom-up object recognition.

Bias and the Benefits of Set
In Johnston and Hale's study, presenting a precue did produce a drastic effect on performance, not yet described. Rather than a benefit, the effect took the form of a strong bias toward choosing the precued alternative. That is, when the precued alternative was (fish) and the target was CHAIR, subjects were more likely to say "yes" to the query "fish?" than if the precue was not presented. This bias effect was present whether or not the target was masked. Ratcliff, McKoon, and Verwoerd (1989) found that repetition priming, a much longer-lasting facilitation in identifying briefly presented words, also works the same way.

How should bias effects of this sort be understood? The simplest view would be that detectors are preactivated or, equivalently, that thresholds are lowered, as in Morton's (1969) logogen model of word recognition. Morton postulated detectors for each individual word that accumulate evidence favoring the presence of that word. The evidence can come both from the context (e.g., preceding words in a sentence) and from stimulus input. If certain alternatives are likely, the detector may be preactivated to some extent, in which case less stimulus information will be necessary for recognition to operate. This interpretation is supported by the fact that semantic context effects in word-identification tasks are greater when target words are degraded with superimposed fine dots (Meyer,

Schvaneveldt, and Ruddy, 1974) or reduced in intensity (Becker and Killion, 1977). This interaction is readily predicted by two assumptions: that detectors for expected words are preactivated, and that stimulus quality affects the rate at which sensory information builds up in the detectors (the logic is the same as shown in figure 4.4). The same type of interaction was observed between visual intensity and manipulations of the probability with which individual letters appear in choice reaction-time tasks (Miller, 1979), which would also plausibly lead to a perceptual bias.

The results described earlier suggest that when an object is available for prolonged viewing (as with an unmasked display), one can observe top-down effects not attributable to bias. With brief exposures, on the other hand, only bias seems to show up. This conclusion is supported by an elegant study of Schvaneveldt and MacDonald (1981) who examined the effects of primes on different sorts of lexical decision tasks. In one experiment, the prime "doctor" could be followed by a related word ("nurse") or by a nonword constructed from a related word by switching a single letter ("nerse"). If the prime induces a simple bias effect toward recognizing related words on the basis of less sensory input, one would expect an increased rate of false alarms for these primed misspellings. Indeed, when the target words were masked and the accuracy of un-speeded lexical decision was examined, this was exactly what happened, with no improvement in detectability. On the other hand, when the targets remained on the screen until response, and subjects made the lexical decision response as quickly as possible, they were both faster and more accurate in catching misspellings such as "nerse." Schvaneveldt and MacDonald concluded that the "initial analysis of sensory information . . . is not directly affected by semantic context," and a secondary analysis of stimulus information is possible involving a "memory-driven process in which hypotheses about the identity of the stimulus are tested by comparing actual stimulus characteristics with those predicted by the hypothesis" (p. 685).

In summary, studies of set for identity (perceptual readiness) present an interesting, and in some ways counterintuitive, picture of how expectations guide perceptual recognition. Perhaps most interesting is that expectations at a conceptual level do not seem to allow more efficient hypothesis testing to take place in the early stages of perception with brief displays. It seems that the initial identification processes are inflexible (or modular) in this important sense.

In this case, as with many phenomena related to attention, it may be tempting to summarize these conclusions as indicating that perceptual processes (e.g., word recognition) are automatic. This would be imprecise and downright misleading. At its core, the idea of automaticity implies that the processing is involuntary and free of capacity limitations. Neither of these claims received much empirical support from the studies reviewed in earlier chapters, and findings regarding set have little bearing on those issues. Although word recognition cannot evidently be *tuned* by conscious expectations in certain ways, it can nonetheless be voluntarily turned off or at least attenuated (see chapter 2), and it also clearly competes with other visual processing (chapter 3). Therefore, the issues regarding set effects are better kept separate from empirically dubious claims about automaticity.

The results reviewed here also suggest that discrimination can be made more sensitive when alternatives are known in advance under certain limited conditions. One case is when highly similar and visually complex alternatives must be distinguished. Here the advance information may actually allow the observer to transform the task. This seems likely to involve a strategy of monitoring different detectors, rather than tuning existing detectors or changing the order in which perceptual hypotheses are evaluated. A second case in set effects have been found that are not reducible to bias is in the case of recognition of degraded stimuli that remain available for some time. Outside the laboratory, one often has an impaired view of a stimulus but rarely is the stimulus replaced by a mask, so this situation is not uninteresting. On the other hand, people typically make several fixations per second, with the contents of each fixation masking the previous ones (Davidson, Fox, and Dick, 1973), and therefore masking may be more representative of many real-life perceptual challenges than are low-contrast stimuli that are viewed continuously or, perhaps equivalently, extremely briefly exposed but unmasked stimuli (J. C. Johnston and McClelland, 1973).

Set and Subjective Clarity

Early investigators of set effects, such as Chapman and Kulpe, focused on how a person's advance knowledge of a stimulus might affect the subjective experience of perceiving it. It was widely agreed that stimuli that match prior expectations are perceived with greater clarity or vividness. Contemporary introspections seem to agree; for example, one of the most recent groups to investigate the topic (Ratcliff, McKoon, and Verwoerd, 1989) noted that "subjects report that a previously presented word 'jumps' out of the display" (p. 384). As the preceding section disclosed, recent investigators have focused almost exclusively on how set may affect discrimination performance, rather than subjective experience. Given the orientation of modern psychology and psychophysics (sometimes termed methodological behaviorism), this is undoubtedly to be expected, but it has occasionally led to discomfort even among practitioners. Pachella (1975) concluded his study of set in the perception of briefly presented pictures with the interesting complaint that that objective measures seemed to be missing the most important aspect of the phenomenon. Having failed to find objective benefits of set, he proposed that the "nature of the effect of set on tachistoscopic recognition is to facilitate the act of perceiving and not necessarily to facilitate veridical judgments about the state of the world" (p. 148). According to Pachella, even if set did not improve the quality of information extracted, it might permit the subject to form a clearer percept. This is not a distinction that many present-day experimenters would feel comfortable with, and the only evidence Pachella offered to bolster the suggestion was a not terribly compelling tendency for subjects to claim higher confidence when they said the picture matched the prespecified alternative.

Pachella's suggestion that set could affect subjective clarity without facilitating the extraction of veridical information should not be dismissed. There are, of course, good reasons to be wary of purely anecdotal reports. For one thing, they might reflect a kind of experimental demand effect. Alternatively, subjective confidence judgments might be based on the observer's vague sense of harmony or disharmony between expectation and reality, possibly arising only after completing the task, rather than a genuine change in perceptual experience occurring during trial. One approach to measuring possible changes in perceptual experience is to try to find stimulus properties that subjects will mistake for the effect in question (see Brindley, 1970, for a general discussion).

We tried a simple and preliminary experiment of this sort in my laboratory in an attempt to see whether observers might conflate the effects of set with changes in stimulus contrast. In each trial, a word was presented briefly against a black background at one of five randomly chosen contrast levels. The observers' task was to judge contrast (five-alternative magnitude estimation). They received no feedback on their performance, although they were intermittently shown samples of the five contrast levels to remind them of what they were trying to discriminate. The word was preceded by a 1-second preview of XXXX's (unprimed) or a preview of the word itself (primed). A temporal gap separated the prime, which was green, from the brief target, which varied from dark gray to light gray; this was what the subjects responded to. The word primes were 100% valid, but only half the targets were preceded by informative primes.

The results showed no effect whatsoever of priming on judged contrast. This suggests that however perceptual expectations may affect the experience of seeing a briefly presented word, these effects are quite distinguishable from variations in stimulus contrast. If this result proves to generalize to other stimulus dimensions that might be related to clarity, one might conclude that set effects alter (if anything) only nonsensory processing. The result described is certainly not exhaustive and conclusive, however.[8] At present, then, we have no evidence to back up claims that expected stimuli look or seem clearer than unexpected ones, but the fact that so many observers make such statements suggests that an interesting phenomenon may remain to be unraveled.

Conclusions about Set

This chapter described findings involving a wide variety of different perceptual judgments ranging from detection of faint tones and barely detectable gratings to decisions about whether strings of letters spell words and identification of pictures of natural objects. In each case, the general issue is how perceptual processes are affected when the perceiver has prior information about the stimulus. Despite the diversity of tasks, and some empirical disagreements, a fairly simple and consistent picture can be maintained, although its validity requires further testing. When an observer has to carry out a detection or discrimination involving a difficult-to-see or difficult-to-hear stimulus, prior information about the stimulus can often improve performance substantially, whether measured in terms of accuracy or speed. Advance information can therefore be said to facilitate perception in the broadest sense, but this is not so when perceptual facilitation is defined more narrowly. A number of plausible hypotheses about how advance information might facilitate perception of an isolated stimulus are questioned by the evidence. First, the idea that location information directly enhances discrimination mechanisms or facilitates recognition by allowing limited-capacity resources to be allocated in advance to the proper channel does receive some support, but the balance of the evidence seems unfavorable to it. For example, it is often thought that knowing the location of a single visual stimulus in advance lets one allocate capacity to the appropriate channels, resulting in faster or more efficient processing of signals on those channels. The evidence shows that effects of this kind are weak and possibly nonexistent.

Another idea that has struck many people, especially computer scientists, as highly plausible is that top-down knowledge about what objects are likely to be present in a scene is essential in letting the system carry out just the necessary discriminations (or give extra capacity to the appropriate analyzers). Data show that advance information about alternatives to be discriminated does not generally improve the categorization of briefly presented visual stimuli compared with presentation of the alternatives afterward. This conclusion is subject to several important limitations. One, implicit in choice of the word "categorization," is that all of this pertains to determining which familiar categories a stimulus belongs to. There is no disputing the fact that prior information may lead a person to rely on *different* discriminations to perform a given judgment (e.g., Egeth and Smith, 1967). Furthermore, outside of the realm of well-learned categories, it is likely that various ad hoc judgments regarding stimuli may be carried out on a piecemeal and voluntary basis; the visual routines for computing certain spatial relations, suggested by Ull-man (1984), are examples. To consider a concrete example, suppose an observer sees a briefly exposed grid of 50 colored squares and is asked whether any red square sits directly above any blue square; for such a task, accuracy undoubtedly will be better when the question is asked before, rather than after, the presentation. What seems questionable is whether schemes of categorization for which the person already has detectors or analyzers are enhanced when the person knows in advance that they will be relevant to the task at hand. A second limitation of this conclusion is that within about a third- or half-second after a visual stimulus is presented, should it remain present for that long, advance information does appear to enhance discrimination somewhat. Obvi-ously, most objects we see are not masked after a few hundred millisec-onds, so one might argue that the effects found with stimuli that remain present are of at least as much importance as results with masked stimuli. On the other hand, we can evidently comprehend most scenes within a few hundred milliseconds (Biederman et al., 1983), and people often make a succession of rapid fixations, with each stimulus masking the preceding one.

These conclusions have interesting and far-reaching implications re-garding the flexibility of mental machinery. It has been suggested that human information processing is so enormously flexible that the search for simple processing limitations is hopeless and misguided (Neisser, 1976). The phenomenon of set is one of few areas in which one can empirically assess just how flexible our mental apparatus is at a micro-scopic scale. It appears much less flexible than Neisser's descriptions would suggest. The results described here do nonetheless show that set can affect performance in important ways, even with briefly presented stimuli. It appears that advance knowledge can aid perception in two ways. First, information on channels not likely to bear useful informa-tion, but that would contribute noise were they allowed to influence the decision, can be excluded. When a stimulus is near threshold, it is by definition confusable with no stimulus at all, and therefore advance information may provide benefits even when no other signal is presented. In threshold vision, channels that can be selectively monitored include those specific to location and spatial frequency, but not contrast, and in threshold hearing, the channels appear selective for frequency (evidence regarding location selectivity is ambiguous). When a brief visual stimulus is followed by a mask, recognizing the stimulus in the allotted time is problematic, but a stimulus is not readily confused with the absence of a stimulus as long as only a single mask is presented. Here, prior knowledge about location provides no substantial or consistent benefit, although a small benefit may exist. One way of summarizing the picture that emerges is to say that an important subset of the phenomena described in chapter 4 (set) may reflect the operation of the same selective mechanisms revealed in filtering tasks that were the focus in chapter 2 (selective attention). This line of thought will be pursued further in the next chapter.

The other mechanism that produces a benefit from prior information occurs when the information indicates the most likely identity of a stimulus. Typically, this triggers a bias toward the more probable or expected stimulus. The stimulus will then be recognized on the basis of less information than would otherwise be required, resulting in a greater likelihood of falsely detecting the expected stimulus should something else be presented. One might think of this as being accomplished either by lowering the threshold for detecting a stimulus or by preactivating detectors. As for the idea of expectations driving top-down hypothesis testing, there is little evidence that this happens during the initial processing of a brief stimulus, but some findings (e.g., Schvaneveldt and MacDonald, 1981) suggest that it can occur with more prolonged stimulus input.

Biasing of perceptual judgments on the basis of cues about the likelihood of encountering different kinds of objects is likely to be useful from a Bayesian perspective. In some sense, therefore, it is not very surprising that it occurs. On the other hand, people are often insensitive to base-rate information when solving verbally presented problems requiring probabilistic reasoning (Lyon and Slovic, 1976). The ideas that are most directly challenged by these findings—that prior expectations are a precondition for perception and a guiding force in its operation—seem to have emerged primarily from attempts to simulate object recognition using digital computers. Because computers have very different computational strengths and weaknesses than the brain, it should perhaps not be surprising that the perspectives of would-be simulators proved misleading. The conclusions described in this chapter also bear on the doctrine of modularity, which has engendered fierce debate in the area of language processing. Fodor (1983) argued that visual, auditory, lexical, and syntactic analyses are all carried out by subsystems that are not penetrable by general-purpose cognitive processes, including inferences and expectations about what is likely. The word "penetrable" is vague, but it conjures up an image of a central processor monkeying with the inner workings of perceptual and linguistic machinery. Indeed, some of the top-down hypotheses described earlier come close to fitting that description (e.g., shifting resources to different analyzers, changing the order in which hypotheses are tested), and the results described above argue against this sort of penetrability. It is not clear whether one should count a bias toward one stimulus and against another as an example of penetration, but in any case, biasing may provide effective control over the border between perception on the one hand and thought and action on the other.

5

Capacity and Selection: Theorizing about Attention

Ten Generalizations: A Summary of Chapters 2 through 4

The preceding chapters addressed many aspects of attention as it relates to perception, proceeding in a piecemeal fashion, staying clear of broad theoretical issues and shunning the word "attention" itself. This chapter goes beyond specific empirical questions to try to sketch out some general principles of attention and perception. The first six sections attempt to make sense of the findings of the last three chapters. The general theoretical perspective that emerges is then used to address several other issues regarding the control of perceptual attention and its consequences. The final two sections examine empirical findings that were not discussed earlier regarding the control and consequences of attention, issues that have broad implications for the nature of perceptual attention.

As a preliminary, we start by reviewing the more basic and robust generalizations that emerged from the research described in the preceding chapters. These conclusions are numbered so that they can be referred to conveniently in the discussion that follows.

Selective Attention

In most of the experiments described in chapter 2, subjects performed some sort of filtering task; that is, they judged and responded only to stimuli that satisfied a prespecified selection criterion, ignoring those that did not satisfy the criterion. In some cases subjects were explicitly told to ignore these other stimuli, and in others they were given an incentive to focus on the relevant stimuli. Three key findings were as follows.

1. When the selection criterion is a highly discriminable physical attribute such as visual location or auditory pitch, people often have no long-term memory for the identity of to-be-ignored stimuli.

2. Difficulty of selection depends on discriminability, with selection by simple physical dimensions easier than by semantic dimensions.

3. Although indirect behavioral measures sometimes suggest that to-be-ignored stimuli are analyzed to a semantic level, the totality of the evidence does *not* favor the view that complete analysis takes place on every occasion.

Divided Attention   In most of the divided-attention studies reviewed in chapter 3, subjects tried to process information arriving on more than one channel at a time with the goal of monitoring the contents of all the channels or to detect the presence of a target. The following main generalizations emerged.

4. When targets differ from nontargets along a simple featural dimension (and the difference is substantial), many elements can be processed in parallel without evident capacity limits, although due to statistical decision noise, accuracy may fall as display set size is increased.

5. Parallel, unlimited-capacity search also seems possible when targets are defined by membership in a well-learned symbolic category, and the target/nontarget discrimination does not require extensive perceptual analysis (e.g., a letter among digits).

6. Capacity limits are evident when the task requires discriminating targets defined by complex discriminations (e.g., reading a word); the requirement for fine featural discriminations or correct processing of spatial configuration are examples of difficulty in this sense.

7. Detection of a target impairs one's ability to detect other targets for a relatively short period thereafter.

Perceptual Set
In most of the experiments on set described in chapter 4, a single stimulus was presented. The question was how the analysis of this stimulus changed when the subject had advance information about some properties of the stimulus. Three generalizations emerged.

8. Advance information about an attribute orthogonal to the discrimination the subject performed (e.g., location in a task requiring a form discrimination) produces either no benefit or a rather small benefit; when

the advance information allows the subject to exclude irrelevant stimuli that are potentially confusable with targets, however, benefits can be large.

9. When the task requires categorizing a briefly presented stimulus, advance information about the most probable category or categories produces a bias toward the likely category, without improving subjects' actual discrimination ability.

10. Advance information (of the type described in (9) produces a modest benefit in discrimination when stimuli remain available for prolonged observation.

Classic Theories Revisited

Chapter 1 described several classic theories of attention, theories that motivated much of the behavioral attention research carried out since the late 1970s. It was maintained that these theories do not exhaust the reasonable accounts of attention and perception that have to be considered. Given the ten conclusions above, none of these theories can be defended in a strong form, which is hardly a startling conclusion. It is instructive, however, to see exactly how they fail. Table 5.1 shows the main generalizations described thus far and their relationship to these theories.

Early Selection Theory

In his original filter theory, Broadbent proposed that people have a limited ability to carry out multiple discriminations in parallel. He suggested, first of all, that only physical featural analyses could be carried out in parallel. Just about all contemporary textbooks of cognitive psychology claim that findings of selective-attention studies refute the filter theory, citing examples of breakthrough of to-be-ignored stimuli. Older examples include conscious noticing of one's own name in an unattended channel (Moray, 1959) or shadowing that switches channels to follow the message (Treisman, 1960). As stated in chapter 2, these data are not necessarily fatal for a theory such as Broadbent's, because the rejected material may be analyzed only occasionally and partially, reflecting lapses in selection rather than its absence. What are much more problematic for Broadbent's theory are findings of divided-attention studies. These

Table 5.1
Key empirical generalizations and their relationship to classic theories of attention

	Theory	
Result	Late Selection	Early Selection
1. Selection by discriminable criterion attribute results in no memory for TBI stimuli.	C	C
2. Physical discriminability facilitates selection.	C	C
3. Under favorable conditions for selection, evidence for full perceptual analysis of TBI disappears.	I	C
4. Parallel search for feature targets.	C	C
5. Parallel categorization involving perceptually simple discriminations.	C	I
6. Capacity limits with complex discriminations.	I	C
7. Detection of one target impairs detection of another.	C	C
8a. Cuing orthogonal attribute produces no benefit in absence of noise.	C	C
8b. Cuing orthogonal attribute produces benefit in presence of noise.	C	C
9/10. Cuing likely identity produces bias, not increase in sensitivity.	C	C
11. Indirect evidence of analysis of TBI reduced as number of TBI is increased.	I	C
12. Capacity limits in perceptual processing apply to attended, not TBI, stimuli.	I	C

TBI = to-be-ignored stimuli; C = consistent; I = inconsistent.

results show that people are capable of fairly extensive parallel processing. For example, in letter search tasks, comparable detection with simultaneous and successive displays of letters implies strongly, although
perhaps not infallibly, that people can extract several letter identities in
parallel. The findings of set studies are clearly consistent with early
selection theories.

Late Selection Theory

Late selection theories as proposed by Deutsch and Deutsch (1963) and
Duncan (1980b) hold that perceptual analysis operates without capacity
limitations and without voluntary control. The case against this theory
was already fairly strong by the early 1980s (Kahneman and Treisman,
1984), and the more recent results described in chapter 2 make that case
even stronger. The theory claims that even when a subject in a filtering
tasks tries to ignore a stimulus, the stimulus is fully analyzed anyway,
assuming adequate sensory input. Evidence for this almost invariably
involves some indirect measure of processing such as a Stroop effect or
a priming effect. Whereas these results are sometimes taken to imply that
to-be-ignored stimuli are invariably processed to the level of semantic
identification, the research reviewed in chapter 2 does not support this.
These effects partly or even completely disappear when more optimal
conditions for filtering are provided. Of course, even if rejected stimuli
are analyzed fully, this need not be revealed with any given measure,
or, indeed, with any available measure. Therefore, the lack of evidence
for processing of ignored stimuli might merely reflect insensitivity of
measures.

As we will see shortly, we do not have to be content with a stalemate
here. Several findings show that indirect measures of recognition can be
modulated by factors that should not, according to the theory, have any
such effect. Consider, for example, the Stroop effect. The effect is much
larger when the irrelevant color name is the object whose color the
subject names rather than lying adjacent to a patch of color (Kahneman
and Chajczyk, 1983). This could still be reconciled with late selection
theory, since indirect effects of irrelevant attributes might be magnified
when an object is selected for further processing. Accessing a file

containing both relevant and irrelevant information about an object could amplify effects of the irrelevant information. In short, just as late selection theory need not insist that any particular measure will reveal putative unconscious processing, neither must it claim that any putative measure is a pure measure that reflects *only* involuntary processing.

Although one might suspect that the theory has been granted enough wiggling room to avoid any possible empirical refutation, fortunately this is not the case. Several studies examined the effect of the *rejected* stimulus load, that is, the number of stimuli to be ignored, and found that this reduced indirect measures of processing of the unattended. Kahneman and Chajczyk (1983) found that the Stroop effect was attenuated when a wholly irrelevant neutral word was added to a display containing a color word and a central color patch (with the subject overtly responding to the color patch). Similarly, Yantis and Johnston (1990) determined that the effect of irrelevant flankers on speeded responses to a centrally presented letter was attenuated when the number of flankers was increased. These findings are summarized in the following generalization, which overlaps the domains of selected and divided attention.

11. Evidence for analysis of to-be-ignored stimuli is reduced when the number of these stimuli is increased.

This finding is particularly problematic for late selection theory, which claims that perceptual analysis is *both* involuntary and capacity free. To account for this one would have to abandon one or other of the most essential claims of late selection theory. Therefore, the results of selective-attention studies make a fairly strong case against the theory, which would have to be modified beyond recognition to account for the totality of findings.

Results of divided-attention studies, in which people try to process several inputs at once, tighten the noose around late selection theory even further. First, capacity limits emerge when target/nontarget discriminations become sufficiently complex. When the task requires reading several words, recognizing particular letter combinations, or discriminating fine orientation differences, for example, accuracy is much worse when the stimuli are presented simultaneously rather than successively. This result

implies the existence of capacity limitations (and probably serial processing) and cannot be attributed to statistical decision noise. The two-target
effect (point 7) by itself *would* be consistent with late selection theory,
however. Indeed, Duncan (1980b) formulated one version of the theory
around precisely this phenomenon. According to him, capacity limits did
not arise in target-distractor discrimination, but in a later processing
stage to which only targets were subjected.

What about the perceptual set findings described in chapter 4? They
also have implications for late selection theory. The fact that benefits of
advance information depend on the possibility of excluding target-con-
fusable information (8) implies that irrelevant information can be excluded from the *decision*. By itself, this does not necessarily mean that
perceptual analysis can be voluntarily curtailed: decision noise might or
might not be reduced by that means. Therefore, these findings are consistent with late selection theory. The absence of a benefit of spatial
precuing when no noise is present to be excluded (8) is certainly consistent with the theory, as are bias effects produced by cueing subjects about
alternatives to be discriminated (9).

In summary, late selection theory is refuted by the existence of capacity
limitations in perceptual analysis (6 and especially 11), and would have
great difficulty accounting for findings of selective-attention studies (3).

Selection and Capacity: Controlled Parallel Processing Revisited

Having concluded, perhaps as no surprise, that neither of the traditional
theories is quite right, we now return to the general theoretical issues
first raised in chapter 1 in the hope of being able to achieve some more
positive conclusions. It was proposed in chapter 1 that, as a matter of
logic, early and late selection theories should not be looked on as two
alternatives that exhaust the set of possible or even reasonable theories.
Nor, in fact, do they represent two end points of a continuum of possible
theories, as many people have supposed. Rather, they represent different
cells in a two-by-two matrix of possibilities (see figure 1.6). The rows
and columns of this matrix are defined by the answers to two questions:
whether parallel processing is possible, and whether perceptual gating is
possible. Results (1) through (11) imply that the correct account is

actually in the lower righthand corner of the matrix, asserting that capacity limits *and* perceptual gating both characterize human perceptual processing. This account was termed *controlled parallel processing (CPP)*, and as noted there, it is a rather commonsensical view that often occurs to people when they first encounter the issues posed by attention theories. For some reason it has been widely, although not universally, overlooked in the attention literature. This theory claims that parallel processing of different objects is achievable, counter to early selection theory, but it is optional, contrary to late selection theory. If someone chooses to process a number of stimuli at the same time, it is possible to do so. If the person chooses to process only one, that is possible, too, and largely prevents other stimuli from undergoing full perceptual analysis.

In the CPP view, we should expect to find evidence of parallel processing in divided attention tasks where such processing would be advantageous (5), and evidence of perceptual selectivity when gating is beneficial to performance (3). This concretely illustrates the observation that evidence for parallel processing is not, except in the weakest possible sense, evidence for late selection theory, as it is often construed. Similarly, evidence for perceptual gating is not evidence for early selection theory, either. This is demonstrated by the fact that both kinds of evidence are wholly consistent with CPP.

On balance, then, CPP is supported by a range of empirical evidence, but it provides only the roughest scaffolding for a general account of perceptual attention, with many questions remaining to be addressed. The theory postulates both capacity limits and perceptual gating, so a question that naturally arises is how capacity limits are related to attentional selectivity. Does perceptual gating determine which stimuli compete for capacity?

A proper test of this issue requires a monitoring task where (a) nontargets are numerous enough or require complex enough discriminations to produce signs of capacity limitations, and (b) it is possible to compare the costs introduced by relevant nontargets and irrelevant nontargets. The literature contains several hybrid divided- and selective-attention experiments that satisfy these requirements, although they were not necessarily carried out for the purpose. Happily, the results of all of them are in essential agreement.

Consider a study by Holmgren (1974), in which subjects searched displays of one to five letters for a target character. In some trials, a single bar marker cue was presented next to one of the characters. When a target was present, it was always in the cued position, so subjects should have restricted their search to that position (if they could). Holmgren concluded that the cues greatly reduced the effect of display size. The effect was not totally eliminated, however; possibly, cues that *preceded* the displays might have eliminated the display size effect altogether.

Duncan (1979) presented subjects with relevant and irrelevant nontargets in spatially interleaved positions. Subjects searched circular displays of either one or eight letters for a target letter Q. When the display size was eight, there were only four relevant positions in alternating spots around the circle, and the subjects knew that the other positions would not contain targets. The difficulty of rejecting distractors was varied by changing the relationship of the distractors to the targets. When the distractors were O and C, the task was relatively easy, but it was relatively more difficult when the distractors were O and K, presumably due to the potential of featural recombination that could form Qs (Treisman and Gelade, 1980). Duncan independently varied the difficulty of the distractors in the four relevant and the four irrelevant positions. When the relevant position distractors were made difficult, search times were slowed, but when the irrelevant position distractors were made difficult, performance was unaffected.

Johnston and Heinz (1979) performed analogous experiments with auditory stimuli. Subjects listened to a series of binaural word pairs, one word spoken in a male voice, the other in a female voice. One word in each pair was a target word drawn from a set of four prespecified words, and the subjects' job was to repeat the target word in each pair and make no response to the nontarget word. In some blocks, target words were always spoken in a male voice and nontarget words were always spoken in a female voice. The difficulty of discriminating nontargets at a semantic level was also varied (difficult nontargets were semantically related to the target words). The results showed that the semantic difficulty made no difference when the voice cue was available to discriminate.

Finally, Palmer (1994) had observers judge the relative orientation of pairs of dots, each consisting of one white and one black dot. In this task, increasing display set size produced effects whose magnitude argued for capacity limitations, as we would expect given the perceptual demands of the task. However, observers were able to exclude items in uncued locations, as shown by the fact that performance when only a subset of a large display was cued was comparable to performance when only that subset was present.

These studies offer an intuitive and reasonable answer to the question of how selectivity relates to the capacity limitations mentioned in (6):

12. The capacity limits in perceptual processing (6) depend on the attended stimulus load and hardly at all on the ignored stimuli.

Results (1) through (12) favor the following interpretation, which rests comfortably within the CPP category. People can usually exercise control over what stimuli undergo extensive perceptual analysis, including, on occasion, selecting multiple stimuli for analysis. When this takes place, the stimuli that are selected compete for limited capacity. If the total load of stimulus processing does not exceed a certain threshold, parallel processing occurs without any detectable reduction in efficiency. Above this threshold, efficiency is reduced by the load of attended stimuli, and processing may sometimes operate sequentially, perhaps as a strategy to minimize loss of accuracy. Figure 5.1 shows the sequence of operations implied by this view.

Attention: Exclusion or Capacity Allocation?

The scheme in figure 5.1 shows both a capacity limitation and a gating mechanism. Should one speak of either of these as "attention"? Is such a concept useful at this point? As noted in chapter 1, that term is used by ordinary speakers and by many psychologists in ways that suggest it refers to both a selection mechanism and a limited capacity resource. If either early or late selection theory were correct, it would be possible to maintain both conceptions simultaneously. This is because, according to both theories, gating is possible only at the point at which parallel processing becomes impossible. One cannot, in either of these views, choose to prevent processing that is possible given the capacity limits of the system. Corresponding to this presumption, there is a widespread tendency in the literature to assume that whenever some perceptual

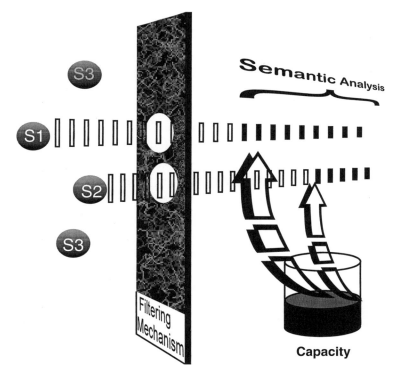

Figure 5.1
A proposed controlled parallel scheme whereby selected stimuli compete for limited capacity. If the total load of stimulus processing does not exceed the maximum available, parallel processing occurs with no detectable reduction in efficiency. Above this threshold, efficiency is reduced by attended stimulus load.

operations are shown to operate in parallel across the visual field in tasks such as search, they can be described as preattentive. This inference appears to rest on the unwarranted assumption just described. In fact, the empirical findings listed above suggest that this assumption is not just unwarranted but wrong: selection *can* prevent stimuli from being analyzed to a semantic level (3) even when our processing machinery is perfectly capable of analyzing all the stimuli to this level in parallel when it is desirable (5).

Unlike either early selection or late selection theory, the analysis shown in figure 5.1 postulates both a gating mechanism and a resource limitation; the distinction between the two is substantive and not merely semantic. There is still an issue of interpretation, however; if one chooses to retain the term "attention," one must decide whether it should be identified with the gating mechanism or with the resource. An *exclusionary interpretation* would regard the mechanism that reduces processing of irrelevant stimuli as attention. The perceptual machinery that performs the recognition sits *behind* the perceptual filter and deals with information that passes through this filter is not, in this view, to be referred to as attention. As we have seen, it manifests capacity limits as reflected in the fact that overload reduces the efficiency with which any one stimulus is processed: generalization (12) from hybrid selective- and divided-attention experiments clearly entails that the filter (attention) sits in front of the capacity limitation, rather than behind it. This interpretation, wherein attention is identified with a purely exclusionary mechanism, and capacity limitations are attributed to the perceptual machinery, is in keeping with Broadbent's classic work (1957) and some more recent writings as well (e.g., Green, 1991; Pashler and Badgio, 1985). More loosely, the notion of attention as a purely inhibitory process was considered in the early literature, although the evidence that figured in this debate was quite different from the evidence assayed here (Pillsbury, 1908).

The other alternative is to construe the limited processing resource rather than the filtering device as attention. In that case, the process of determining what receives this resource—gating—is equated with capacity allocation. The *resource interpretation* suggests that when visual attention is allocated to an item, it is perceptually analyzed; when it is allocated to several items, they are processed in parallel, but if the capacity limits are exceeded, processing becomes less efficient. The general concept of resource allocation has been advocated by writers such as Kahneman (1973) and Wickens (1984). Analyses of cueing effects in crowded displays such as Eriksen's zoom lens model (e.g., Eriksen and St. James, 1986) did not focus so much on traditional questions about selectivity, but their approach is broadly consistent with this view.

We are confronted with several choices. We can dispense with attention as a theoretical construct and say that a functional analysis of human information-processing has to postulate both gating mechanisms and capacity limitations (as in figure 5.1). Or, we can try to hold onto the word attention, equating it with either the limited capacity resource or the gating mechanism. In either case, it is probably best to speak of perceptual attention, for reasons that will emerge below. In light of the results described earlier, however, one thing we cannot choose is to maintain the presuppositions inherent in commonsense talk and in early and late selection theories that selectivity and capacity limitation are inherent features of the very same process or mechanism.

Assuming that we do choose to maintain the word attention, is the choice between the exclusionary interpretation and the resource interpretation merely one of linguistic taste, or is there some genuine difference of fact? Before trying to answer this question, it may be instructive to relate the two proposed interpretations to some findings described in earlier chapters, and a few new ones as well.

The Two-Target Effect Revisited
In many kinds of monitoring tasks involving brief stimuli, detecting one target makes it more difficult to detect another target for some short period of time, even when the person is capable of carrying out the multiple target-distractor discriminations in parallel (7). In the exclusionary interpretation, how should this two-target effect be understood? One straightforward interpretation would be as follows. At the start of a trial, attention is distributed broadly, giving all stimuli have access to perceptual machinery; therefore, perceptual analysis proceeds on all channels at once. When a target is detected, attention (the gating mechanism) narrows down to filter out everything except the target, and possibly stimuli in nearby locations. This makes it possible to report attributes of the target beside those that triggered its detection (Duncan, 1984), but makes it less likely that other targets will be detected. This contraction is not strategic in any obvious way, since it harms performance in the task. Of course, it may (and one would suspect, does) have useful consequences in other situations.

This interpretation is quite different from the (late selection) interpretation offered by Duncan (1980b). Duncan identified attention with the process of *reading out* information from channels processing information from the target location. Processing in the channels themselves was devoid of capacity limits, but had no effect on conscious awareness unless a later stage of read-out was successfully accomplished.

How could the resource interpretation of attention be reconciled with the two-target effect? Given that the resource is necessary to discriminate targets and nontargets, it must be allocated to all stimuli at the outset; presumably, it is then withdrawn from locations other than the target once the target is detected. With respect to the two-target effect, therefore the two accounts simply mimic each other.

Set Revisited

In chapter 4 it was suggested that knowing the location of a stimulus clearly improves discrimination performance when such information allows the subject to exclude stimuli that are potentially confusable with the targets or possible targets defined for that task. If signals are gated out and thereby denied perceptual analysis, they obviously do not contribute noise to the decision. On the other hand, when there is nothing to be excluded, the effects are certainly much smaller and sometimes take the form of a cost of invalid cueing without a corresponding benefit of valid cueing; it remains unclear whether a true benefit effect occurs, although some evidence suggests it could (McCann, Folk, and Johnston, 1992). What does a resource interpretation say about this? If knowing the location in advance produced a benefit in processing a stimulus presented against a blank field, this would plainly be compatible with the resource interpretation: resources can be allocated to a location channel in advance, producing a benefit. Suppose there is no real benefit, as suggested in chapter 4, although admittedly without benefit of fully conclusive data. Can *that* conclusion be reconciled with a resource interpretation? To do so, one would have to suppose that resources can be allocated to a stimulus quickly enough to become available as soon as they are needed. The larger benefits found when confusable distractors are present would still have to be accounted for, and here one could reasonably appeal to noise reduction. Indeed, if the channels that are denied capacity are not considered to be candidates for the presence of a target, as one would readily suppose, noise reduction more or less follows from this analysis.

Summary: Conceptualizing Attention

It seems pretty clear that the results described in the preceding chapters can be accounted for by conceiving of attention either as an exclusionary process or as a pool of resources to be allocated to different channels or stimuli. Table 5.2 shows the sort of modifications required to account for the facts in each of these formulations. How should one choose between these seemingly different ways of thinking?

If we understood the neural circuitry and neural operations that underlie these processes in detail, would one of the two accounts emerge as the obviously superior choice? Perhaps. Consider the idea of a resource. Suppose the limitations in the brain's ability to perceive different stimuli reflected the limited availability of something concrete, such as a chemical or neural tissue. By as-yet unknown means, this resource could be used to analyze whatever stimuli were selected; for example, the chemical might be shunted to different locations in the brain, or information from different stimuli could be sent to a particular neural mechanism by a process akin to multiplexing. In that case, one would be inclined to prefer the resource framework. On the other hand, suppose that which neural tissue is responsible for processing a given object depends purely on the location of this stimulus, and limitations in handling multiple stimuli arise because of cross-talk between different neural modules. In that case, the gating interpretation would seem more natural. There are few data available to help choose between these two conceptions. However, Luck and his colleagues (1994) observed that split-brain patients can independently search displays presented to the two hemifields, with each search proceeding at a normal rate; this seems to argue for the second of the two possible neural interpretations mentioned. From a more abstract standpoint, however, either neural reality could be described within either an exclusionary or a resource framework. For example, shutting out cross-talk can reasonably be described as allocating a resource, namely, interference-free processing. Once these two accounts are elaborated appropriately, therefore, they may be simply notational variants of each other with the real empirical content embodied in the twelve constraints described above.

Attention or Attentions?

We have seen that the main conclusions about attention and perception require postulating capacity limitations and gating mechanisms, and that attention can be reasonably equated with either the processing capacity

Table 5.2
Suggested ways of accounting for empirical results assuming either gating or resource interpretation

	Conception of Attention	
Result	Gating Interpretation	Resource Interpretation
2. Under favorable conditions, selection can prevent full perceptual analysis.	Ignored stimuli filtered out.	Ignored stimuli denied resources.
3. Parallel search for feature targets.	All stimuli allowed past filter.	a. Preattentive (does not use resource).
		b. Demands less than total available resources.
5. Capacity limits with complex discriminations.	Consistent (limited resources).	Consistent.
7. Cuing orthogonal attribute produces no benefit in absence of noise.	Directly predicted.	Resources become available as quickly as they are needed.
8. Cuing orthogonal attribute produces benefit in presence of noise.	Directly predicted.	Consistent.
11. Indirect evidence of analysis of TBI reduced as number of TBI is increased.	Directly predicted.	Consistent.
12. Capacity limits in perceptual processing apply to attended, not TBI, stimuli.	TBI stimuli filtered our before they grab resources.	TBI stimuli denied resources.

TBI = to-be-ignored stimuli.

or the gating mechanism. In trying to arrive at some general picture of perceptual attention, one obviously needs to decide whether there are separate perceptual attention systems associated with different sensory modalities, or a unified polymodal attention system. Should we speak of visual attention and auditory attention, or are these really the same thing? Evidence that is relevant to this issue was described in chapters 2 through 4; the following are most pertinent.

13. People appear capable of selecting visual stimuli in one part of space and auditory stimuli in another part.

14. Capacity limits in recognition appear to be more severe when processing multiple stimuli presented through a single modality compared with multiple modalities.

Both of these results tend to favor modality-specific perceptual attention systems. On the other hand, modality specificity may be a graded rather than absolute property. Recall, for example, that Driver and Spence (1994) found that attending to one visible object produced some very modest degree of bias in the system toward processing sounds coming from the same location.

Following the exclusionary interpretation, modality specificity leads us to suppose that the entire scheme shown in figure 5.1 is multiplied for the separate modalities. That is, separate attentional gating systems exist for separate sensory modalities, and the capacity limitations associated with perceptual analysis in different modalities are also distinct (processing load in one modality does not disrupt processing in another).

It will be seen in chapter 6 that in addition to these separate perceptual analysis mechanism, we have to postulate attentional limitations at a more central level, where cognitive machinery manipulates the outputs of perceptual analysis, chooses actions, and does other things as well. These limitations, we will see, can be indifferent to whether two stimuli originate in the same modality or in different modalities.

Despite being partially elaborated, the view sketched so far is still more a skeleton of a theory of perceptual attention than it is a full-fledged account. The next two sections add more meat to the bones, asking how attention is controlled, and inquiring about the various consequences of attending for the internal representation of the world. In previous chapters the austere tasks studied in attention laboratories were ideal for the limited questions we asked, but as we try to relate perceptual attention to broader questions about the functioning of the mind, this austerity severely limits the conclusions we can draw.

The Scope of the Preattentive

In various situations people evidently search displays in parallel (4 and 5). In the exclusionary interpretation, one is led to suppose that attention is distributed as widely as possible (i.e., nothing is excluded from processing) at the time the search commences; subsequently, of course, it may be narrowed involuntarily. In the resource interpretation, equivalently, attentional resources are said to be distributed broadly. One might go one step further and propose that certain kinds of processing (e.g., basic features) occur regardless of (prior to) gating. In the common vernacular, they would be preattentive in either conception of attention. Many researchers routinely assumed that parallel search (pop-out) implies that features such as color and orientation are coded preattentively, as Treisman proposed in her theory. For reasons belabored earlier, this inference is invalid, although pop-out is perfectly consistent with such a possibility.

What does the evidence for the reality of filtering (chapter 3) say about possible preattentive extraction of primitive features? Most of the data pertained to semantic discriminations, especially letter identity and word name. Even if we can block the extraction of these higher-level descriptions, it by no means follows that the operations involved in featural analysis can be prevented. Fortunately, some of the evidence described in chapter 3 was not restricted to letter or word identification (e.g., adaptation effects); some suggested that noncategorical visual analysis is also subject to attentional suppression. The biological evidence (ERPs, single-unit data) strongly suggests that some visual processing is selective, but one cannot draw good conclusions about particular types of analysis from those data. The other evidence that bears on this issue is the study by Braun and Sagi (1990), who found that a concurrent search did not impede detection of peripheral pop-out; assuming this is not a problem of insensitivity, it may provide the strongest support for preattentive processing currently available. In short, despite the enormous popularity of the notion of preattentive featural processing, only a very small amount of evidence even bears on it, and these data are somewhat equivocal.

Control of Attention

We turn now to some major questions about the allocation of attention: whether capacity is allocated in a graded or discrete fashion, whether visual attention is allocated to objects or to locations, involuntary influences on attention allocation, and how voluntary control of attention relates to other mental events. The remainder of this chapter describes empirical findings in these areas that were not described earlier. The findings do not fit neatly into the restricted scope of the last three chapters, but they have broad implications for the theory of perceptual attention.

Competition for Resources: Sharing versus Switching

We saw in chapter 3 that when we try to perceive complex stimuli at the same time (e.g., words), capacity limitations may be exceeded and the efficiency of processing may be reduced. In tasks requiring perception of brief displays, for example, accuracy may be reduced with simultaneous compared with successive displays (e.g., Kleiss and Lane, 1986). In speeded search tasks, competition for resources is probably the main reason for increases in search times associated with increases in display set size.[1] Several ways of thinking about these increases were discussed earlier, including cross-talk and limitations in informational capacity. A major question that has not been considered is exactly what happens when the limits are exceeded: are resources shared in a graded fashion? If so, how is the allocation predetermined—is it determined on line, as a function of the difficulty of the discriminations actually required? Is there a discrete processing bottleneck, with resources first allocated to one object and then switched to the next?

Duncan, Ward, and Shapiro (1994) argued against switching based on the slow time course of interference. Combining two difficult visual discriminations, each requiring a separate judgment, they concluded that interference lasted out to SOAs of several hundred milliseconds despite the fact that each stimulus was promptly masked. They proposed that the competition for visual processing resources is temporally extended because stimuli are slow to relinquish these resources—far too slow to be reconciled with the serial scanning that theorists sometimes envisioned.

Another kind of information that bears on this issue is the correlation between accuracy in two simultaneous judgments. Switching between two channels should tend to make accurate judgments on one channel go together with inaccurate judgments on the other. As Sperling and Melchner (1978) noted, the situation is analogous to that of a student who wishes to attend two lectures held simultaneously. Since he cannot attend all of both lectures, the more time he spends in one the less he can spend in the other. What predictions follow from graded sharing of capacity? If the allocation of capacity were fixed from trial to trial with accuracy depending on other factors (e.g., internal neural noise), there should be no correlation. If the allocation of capacity varied from trial to trial, this should tend to produce a negative correlation.

Applying this logic, Sperling and Melchner had subjects search a series of displays containing one patch of small letters and a surrounding patch of large letters, and make an independent judgment on each. This task evidently overloaded subjects' perceptual capacity. The results showed some negative correlation between the accuracy of judgments on each patch, suggesting switching or variable capacity allocation. By contrast, Miller and Bonnel (1994) had observers carry out two line-length comparisons on a single display of four lines: two pairs of lines were flashed at the same instant and then masked, and subjects stated which was longer in each pair. Accuracy on one pair was uncorrelated with accuracy on the other. This remained true even when the duration of total presentation was varied from trial to trial.[2]

These data obviously do not resolve the issue. It would be interesting to explore correlations with more complex stimuli such as words, where simultaneous displays are processed much less efficiently than successive ones. Under these conditions, subjects may perhaps have the option of processing both at once, but the cost of doing so may be so great as to favor a strategy of switching, at comparatively modest rates, of course. Whatever the outcome, it is true here as it is everywhere that correlations do not provide a strong basis for drawing conclusions about causation. Suppose, for example, that subjects are simply more alert in some trials than in others. This will help or harm both judgments in tandem, thereby superimposing a positive correlation on top of whatever negative correlation may or may not be caused by switching or variability in graded allocation. This sort of equilibrium could account for the different results of the experiments described above. An alternative strategy that might allow one to draw stronger conclusions would be to make one discrimination more difficult and see how it affects another, concurrent discrimination. This has barely been tried in the realm of difficult perceptual discriminations,[3] although in chapter 6 we will see that it has been used extensively with tasks that require more than one response selection or memory retrieval.

Attentional Blink

This brings us to an intriguing phenomenon, sometimes nicknamed the attentional blink, that is clearly relevant to the present issue. The blink effect occurs when people view rapid serial visual presentations of a series of stimuli presented in the same location, usually at rates of approximately 100 msec per item, in tasks requiring them to detect and report several target items. One way to elicit the effect is to require an observer to report the (only) red item (T1) in a display of letters and also a digit (T2), which appears at some point in the sequence after the red item. The blink effect refers to a decrement in detection or report of T2 when it appears after T1. Remarkably, the decrement is often greatest when T2 occurs not immediately after T1 (position n+1), but rather somewhere around positions n+2 through n+5. This effect seems to have been discovered by Broadbent and Broadbent (1987), using sequences of words. The choice of stimuli does not seem to be critical, however; the effect also occurs with letters (Shapiro, Raymond, and Arnell, 1994) and with nonsymbolic figures (Horlitz, Johnston, and Remington, 1992)

Several simple explanations for the effect are easily refuted. For example, one might propose that it takes time to switch set between searching for one kind of target (red in the above example) and searching for another (digit). This cannot explain the effect, however, because it also appears when the same defining criterion is used to pick out both T1 and

T2 (e.g., both are digits; Raymond, Shapiro, and Arnell, 1994). Alternatively, one might imagine that the problem is in maintaining a visual image of T1 while new information arrives from the same spatial location; perhaps new information on the same channels tends to overwrite the image. One problem for this view is that the blink effect can be observed when the subject has to detect T1 without reporting its identity. Logically, at least, the subject is only required to store one bit of information: T1 target found.

The effect has several counterintuitive features. The first is that T2 is often better reported in position n+1 than it is in position N+2 (Shapiro, Raymond, and Arnell, 1994; Horlitz, Johnston, and Remington, 1992); that is, there is no monotonic recovery of processing ability after a detection, at least at first glance. The second feature is that manipulations that make T1 easier to report seem to reduce the effect. For example, introducing a blank after T1 (i.e., extra time without any new items) attenuates the reduction in T2 accuracy (Raymond, Shapiro, and Arnell, 1992). One naturally expects the blank to improve the accuracy of T1 report, of course, because it weakens the masking of T1. What is hardly obvious is why it should make T2 easier to detect; one might have imagined it would strengthen T1 and exacerbating any competitive interaction with T2. Another way of making T2 easier to detect is to require only easy color discrimination; this seems to cause the blink virtually to disappear (Horlitz, Johnston, and Remington, 1992). It is not clear if this observation occurs because of the difference in dimension, or simply because the color judgment is easier.

One interpretation of the blink effect is that the subjects are still identifying the initial item (T1) at the point at which the blink effect reaches its maximum (Chun and Potter, 1995). This readily explains the dependence on T1 difficulty, but does not so easily explain the nonmonotonic time course. It also conflicts with the assumption that successive visual displays interrupt identification, for which there is a fair amount of support. The relatively better performance when T2 comes in position n+1 might occur because in that case, both T1 and T2 can be preserved in the same "snapshot" (presumably, a record in visual short-term memory). We will see in chapter 6 that the blink effect is probably not attributable to the kind of central interference that shows up in dual-response experiments.

What possibilities are left? One that has not been much considered, perhaps because it is unappealing in some ways, is that the reduction in T2 accuracy might be an aftereffect of already completed processing of T1 rather than a reflection of continuing competition for access to processing resources or mechanisms. Conceivably, it might even have a different origin from the two-target effect, despite obvious similarities to that effect. A systematic examination of two-target limitations, manipulating both temporal and spatial relationships of stimuli, appears necessary to determine the relationship of these phenomena.

Attending to Objects or to Locations

Chapter 2 described several pieces of evidence that seem to indicate that when people carry out a filtering task that involves a selection criterion other than location (e.g., reading only the red items in a brief display), selection involves a two-stage process: first, the locations of objects having the specified color are determined, and second, filtering by location takes place. Some researchers propose, however, that it is objects rather than locations to which visual attention is allocated (Duncan, 1984; Vecera and Farah, 1994).

Distinguishing attention to objects from attention to locations on an empirical basis is not as straightforward as it might sound, because the concept of an object and the concept of a location are conceptually intertwined. To start with, the concept of an object implies spatial contiguity or connectedness; consider how odd it sounds to speak of two wholly disconnected bits of matter being a single object. It may be even odder to speak of two different physical objects occupying exactly the same position in three-dimensional space. Whether or not such statements involve a self-contradiction, they are certainly difficult to understand. The same difficulty arises in distinguishing visible surfaces from the location of these surfaces in the visual field. Although a line extending from a viewer's eye may contact many different objects visible to the viewer, it can intersect only one visible surface (transparent surfaces are one special exception). Given that objects and locations are conceptually intertwined, perhaps one may not sensibly ask whether attention is allocated to objects or locations. If two objects cannot occupy a single location, attending selectively to an object *implies* attending to everything in that location, in which case attention could equally well be described as allocated to the location.

One point seems clear enough, however. Visual attention is not necessarily allocated to gross, spatially convex regions in space, as popular metaphors such as spotlights and zoom lenses might suggest. This is especially clear when there are objects in a scene, rather than merely blank space prior to the arrival of a stimulus. The most compelling evidence comes from a study mentioned earlier that actually predates the current interest in object-based attention: Neisser and Becklen's (1975) demonstration that people can attend to one of two spatially overlapping, dynamically changing figures. People are able to track one of these objects with little awareness or memory for the superimposed figure that they ignore. Some researchers contend that two discontinuous regions cannot be attended to at the same time (LaBerge and Brown, 1989; Posner, Snyder, and Davidson, 1980), but the evidence for this has never been compelling. A simple demonstration suggests its implausibility. If one views a display of, say, eight characters (two rows of four) presented for 100 msec and followed by a mask, one can, of course, report only four or five characters (see chapter 3). Of interest, one can decide in advance to attend only to the four characters at the extreme corners of the display, and after the display is flashed, one is left with a single clear image of these four characters, everything else being hazy. Phenomenology can be misleading, of course, but it seems extremely difficult to understand this on the assumption that perceptual attention is restricted to continuous regions of visual space. Kramer and Hahn (1995) provided more objective evidence for the fact that people can split the spatial allocation of attention. Of course, to say that visual attention can be allocated to spatially discontinuous elements is not to deny it may have some general preference or default favoring contiguous regions. If visual attention can be allocated to two separate locations simultaneously, one would also expect that it could switch from one location to another without traversing intermediate positions; the evidence generally supports this hypothesis (Yantis, 1988).

A variety of evidence has been used to prove the primacy of objects over locations in visual attention. It involves both divided- and selective-attention tasks, mostly using simpler methods than Neisser and Becklen's. In the area of divided attention, Duncan (1984) had subjects report two attributes from a brief display composed of two spatially overlapping objects; one was a line of a certain orientation, the other a boxlike shape. When a judgment concerned two aspects of the box, accuracy was noticeably better than when it concerned different objects, even though the spatial separation was at least as great in the same-object condition (see also Vecera and Farah, 1994).

In the area of selective attention, the interference paradigms discussed in chapter 2 yield evidence taken to favor the allocation of attention to objects rather than locations. When subjects respond to a central object and seek to ignore a flanker, interference from the flanker is sometimes amplified when the flanker and the central target are embedded in common objects (Kramer and Jacobson, 1991) or grouped by Gestalt principles; for example, when they share a color (Baylis and Driver, 1992) or a common direction of motion (Driver and Baylis, 1989; but see Berry and Klein, 1993; Kramer, Tham, and Yeh, 1991). It may be a mistake, however, to assume that when a collection of elements is grouped by the Gestalt principles this makes them a single perceptual object. As Palmer and Rock (1994) point out, the visible stuff making up a single object is usually bound by a stronger principle that they call uniform connectedness; phenomenologically, Gestalt grouping principles cause one to see objects as a collection, with each retaining its status as an object.

Given the inherent confounding of space and locations, the findings described here could be accounted for by supposing that attention is allocated to locations, or, more precisely, to channels representing different locations in the visual field. The exact locations to which attention is allocated, however, may vary to conform to regions whose boundaries are located by figure-ground grouping mechanisms; this is essentially the analysis proposed by Treisman (1982).[4] The Gestalt grouping mechanisms may make it easier to divide attention over a collection of different locations without making them a single object.

One intriguing study suggests that this formulation may not do justice to the role of objecthood in divided attention. Yantis (1992) showed observers a display composed of objects moving quasi-randomly around a display, rather like a swarm of flies (a task first used by Pylyshyn and Storm, 1988). Subjects tracked only a subset of these elements. To assess their tracking ability, an item was occasionally probed, requiring observers to indicate whether it belonged to the subset being tracked. Subjects were fairly successful at tracking three or four objects in such displays. Yantis observed, however, that performance was noticeably better when the tracked items could be seen as occupying the corners of a single imaginary convex (although not rigid) polygon; inversions that made it impossible to maintain such a representation impaired performance. It would seem, therefore, that although people may be able to attend selectively to several discontinuous objects, this can be accomplished only, or at least, best, by viewing the objects as part of a single, superordinate object. One is reminded of William James' claim: "however numerous the things [to which one attends], they can only be known in a single pulse of consciousness for which they form one complex 'object'" (1890/1950, p. 405).

Involuntary Shifts of Attention

Virtually all of the early attention theorists commented on the fact that people sometimes find their attention grabbed by a stimulus even when they would prefer that this would not happen. Titchener (1908) noted that any sudden change or movement, including a change in pitch, could distract someone from concentration on something else (p. 192). James (1890) made similar observations, and stated that the sheer intensity of a stimulus was sufficient to draw attention involuntarily. A number of writers from the same era (e.g., Titchener, 1908, p. 199) also noted that attention is often summoned by the termination of a stimulus that was previously unnoticed (air conditioners offer a compelling example in the present day). James thought all these phenomena significant enough to distinguish *passive sensorial attention* as a separate and distinct type of attention.

Recent studies of involuntary attention shifts mostly used visual search tasks to measure attention shifts. An abrupt visual onset shifts attention toward a location even when the person has an incentive to prevent the shift from taking place, as indexed by harmful (or at least unhelpful) effects on performance in the search task. Consider, for example, a task requiring someone to search a display containing several distractor elements. A flicker occurring before the display, in a position where a search target could possibly occur, generally enhances detection if a target appears in its neighborhood and impairs detection of distant targets, even when there is an no incentive for the subject to allow the shift (Yantis, 1994; Yantis and Hillstrom, 1994). Remington, Johnston, and Yantis (1992) confirmed this using blocks of trials in which the flicker was never adjacent to the position of the target, providing maximum incentive to ignore the flicker. Yantis (1994) maintained that involuntary orienting is not triggered by just any kind of moving or flickering stimulus, however, but only by changes heralding the appearance of a new object in the visual field. For example, when just one item in a display moves, and it is no more likely to be a target than is any other item, there is apparently no advantage in having the target move (Hillstrom and Yantis, 1994). On the other hand, when the motion triggers the appearance of a new object, involuntary shifts do occur, producing better detection for rapid-onset targets.

Some controversy exists as to whether a static element in a display that stands out because it is unique in a feature such as color (e.g., a red object against a field of green objects) is also capable of inducing a shift. If a person is searching for a target element defined by uniqueness in one dimension—say, orientation (e.g., the only / among \s)—then a distractor that is unique in color causes substantial interference, presumably by summoning attention (Pashler, 1988). This does not always happen when what defines the target is not a singleton in some featural dimension, but some more abstract criterion (e.g., a particular specified letter among distractor letters; Folk and Annett, 1994). Todd and Kramer (1994) proposed that whether irrelevant singletons interfere with search for abstractly defined targets depends on display size: with four element displays, irrelevant uniqueness in color made no difference, whereas with twenty-five-item displays it slowed RTs by about 10%. In summary, certainly irrelevant events often trigger a shift of attention even when no incentive favors such a shift. The appearance of a new object seems to do this quite reliably. An object that is unique and therefore stands out against its background definitely intrudes on a person who is trying to search for something that is unique in some other feature, and seems to have a weaker tendency to interfere with a search for something other than a singleton.

Are shifts to abrupt onsets truly automatic, in the sense of being completely unsuppressible? Apparently not. For one thing, a moderate amount of practice weakens them to the point at which they may be undetectable (Warner, Juola, and Koshino, 1990). Second, abrupt visual onsets occurring in regions where no target will appear (and the subject knows no target will appear) do not seem to trigger shifts (Yantis and Jonides, 1990). If this were not the case, people might be incapable of carrying out many routine tasks. Railings next to a highway, for example, often generate a train of abrupt onsets in a driver's peripheral vision, but produce no obvious interference with attention to the road. Common sense suggests, however, that under certain conditions abruptly arriving stimuli may grab attention even when they are not in relevant locations; for example, a loud noise. Indeed, the examples of intruding stimuli noted by the early attention theorists usually occurred in spatial locations that were not relevant to the observer's task (to the extent they had one). It seems unlikely that if a photoflash were unexpectedly set off while a subject performed the visual search tasks described above, the subject would have sat oblivious and undisturbed. What differentiates these situations from the cases where sudden-onset stimuli in irrelevant positions produce no effects? The intensity of the stimulus, the unexpectedness of the event, or the potential of the event to signify a threat are all factors that might make a difference. One reason there are so few data on such basic questions may simply be because few investigators are inclined to carry out experiments that yield only a single observation per subject.

Within the visual search context, further controversy surrounds the extent to which involuntary attention effects are independent of task set. Folk, Remington, and Johnston (1992) suggested that even the effects of abrupt onsets may depend to some degree on the subject's set. In one of their experiments, subjects saw a display composed of three green items and one red one. Their job was to make a choice response to the red item. Under these conditions, an abrupt-onset cue with no predictive value presented slightly before the display had no effect, whereas an irrelevant patch that was also colored red did have an effect. When the task was to respond to a single character, bearing its own abrupt onset, the situation was reversed: the abrupt-onset cue was disruptive and the red-colored patch was not. Folk et al proposed that there might be nothing special at all about abrupt visual onsets. The true generalization, according to these authors might be that subjects cannot help shift their attention to any attribute that characterizes the target they desire to attend to. In this view, there is no automatic grabbing of attention by onsets, but rather a general inability to have one set control shifts of attention at one moment and another set a very short time later. Their data clearly reveal that when a person adopts a set to search for a target defined by a certain attribute, the person cannot avoid shifting to immediately preceding cues bearing this attribute. As Yantis (1993) pointed out, however, abrupt onsets produce involuntary shifts of attention even when the display is composed of many items and the target is defined by form; according to the view proposed by Folk et al, one should expect no involuntary shifts here. The effects of unique but static distractors also suggest that the hypothesis of Folk et al cannot be the whole story: although searching for a singleton enhances the disruptive effects of singletons, recall that Todd and Kramer (1994) reported that singletons can disrupt abstract searches as well, when display sizes are large.

Another possibly involuntary influence on attention is a tendency to shift attention to stimuli that are novel or unexpected. Novel stimuli or changes in predictable sequences of stimuli often elicit overt orienting responses in people and other animals. These orienting responses include eye and head movements that facilitate gaining additional sensory information about a stimulus together with various psychophysiological changes (Hinde, 1966; Rohrbaugh, 1984). As described in chapter 2, changes in the physical properties of unattended stimuli (e.g., the pitch of an unattended voice in a dichotic listening experiment) are often noticed and sometimes produce at least brief signs of orienting.

Sokolov (1963) suggested that the orienting response to stimulus change or novelty implies the existence of a neural model of the sensory environment against which new stimuli are compared. In his conception, a neural model is built up as a consequence of repeated stimulation, and it represents the expected properties of the stimulation. When new stimulation deviates from the model, orienting reactions occur. There is voluminous literature describing behavioral and psychophysiological aspects of the orienting reaction caused by novel stimuli. These observations are usually made in situations where animals or people have no incentive to avoid orienting, however, and therefore the results do not necessarily tell us about *involuntary* orienting. The same can be said about observations of Berlyne (1957), who gave people the option of responding to any of several different stimuli in a display; subjects tended to respond to whatever stimulus different from habituating stimuli they had been exposed to previously.

Some data from distraction paradigms provide evidence that familiar stimuli are easier to ignore than novel and unexpected ones. Several studies preexposed people to certain stimuli and found that this reduced their distracting potential in a subsequent test in which they had to be ignored. Waters, McDonald, and Koresko (1977) played a tape of a female voice pronouncing numbers and arithmetic signs. When subjects later solved arithmetic problems spoken in a male voice and the numbers and arithmetic signs were presented as distractors, preexposed subjects showed smaller distraction effects. Similarly, Lorch, Anderson, and Well (1984) preexposed people to stimuli subsequently presented in a classification task. The preexposure somewhat reduced the interfering effect of irrelevant variation.[5] The effects of novelty that are demonstrated by these experiments are statistically significant but not terribly large, and they may not play a very strong role in determining the ease of selection under most circumstances (see Cowan, 1988, for an alternative perspective).

Another intuitively plausible suggestion is that emotionally charged stimuli may involuntarily attract attention, perhaps especially in states of anxiety or emotional disturbance (according to Hatfield, in press, Augustine of Hippo noted this in the fifth century). It has often been observed, for example, that people have difficulty avoiding attending to such stimuli even in conversations they are ignoring. The effect that is most widely interpreted as evidence of orienting to emotional stimuli is the so-called emotional Stroop effect. In this design, the subject of a remarkably voluminous literature, subjects attempt to say the color of a word as fast as possible (Eysenck, 1992; Mathews and MacLeod, 1985).

In some situations, responses to emotional words (e.g., panic) are slower than responses to nonemotional words (e.g., flute). The effect has been extensively replicated with anxious individuals, but it only occurs intermittently with normal individuals.

The range of emotional stimuli that produce the effect seems variable. Martin, Williams, and Clark (1991) found that patients with general anxiety disorder showed slowing to highly positive as well as negative words, but Dalgleish (1995) failed to find such an effect under some conditions. The most commonly suggested interpretation of the emotional Stroop effect claims that the emotionality of a word causes more attention to be devoted to processing the identity of the word, increasing the extent of response competition between the name of the word and the color name. This might be correct, but there seems to be little direct evidence for it, and various alternatives seem fairly plausible also. For example, an emotional stimulus might produce a defensive emotional reaction that retards motor responses (cf De Ruiter and Brosschot, 1994, for a related suggestion). Alternatively, familiarity rather than emotionality might be the critical factor. Dalgleish (1995) observed that ornithologists were slow to name the color in which bird names were printed; perhaps anxious subjects show greater interest in or acquaintance with the concepts that retard their color naming than nonanxious subjects.

However, more direct evidence exists that emotional stimuli can attract visual spatial attention in studies presenting emotional words and requiring responses to other stimuli. Stormark, Nordby, and Hugdahl (1995) showed subjects a word that was either emotional or neutral, followed usually by a dot in the same or a different location; subjects made a simple RT response to the dot. The position of the word predicted the position of the dot on most trials. A greater priming effect was seen (speeding of the response to the dot in the same position as the word) when the word was emotional than when it was neutral. MacLeod, Matthews, and Tata (1986) reported a similar effect: when an emotional and nonemotional word were presented at the same time, subjects were faster to respond to a probe stimulus that replaced the emotional word. Broadbent and Broadbent (1988) replicated this effect, and found that among normal subjects, the effect was larger among those with more signs of anxiety. Of course, an emotion-laden word is not an extremely powerful emotional stimulus. Pictures of emotionally disturbing scenes elicit quite stronger emotional reactions (Lang et al, 1993), and such stimuli might have larger effects on attention. From the point of view of attention theory, effects of emotionality should probably be understood as biasing factors that typically alter the deployment of visual attention from an initially wide allocation to a narrower distribution. The observations described here do not dispute the claim that unattended stimuli are generally excluded from full analysis (chapter 2), because the stimuli were not generally presented in situations designed to facilitate such exclusion.

Voluntary Control of Sensory Attention

The preceding chapters were mostly concerned with perceptual processing that occurs in the context of the constrained goals of a laboratory task. In this context, the subject usually tries to process one signal while ignoring a predictable number of other stimuli, and these stimuli are typically drawn from a limited set (chapter 2); in divided-attention experiments, the subject tries to process several inputs at once with the goal of detecting some prespecified target (chapter 3). People exhibit a remarkable degree of control over the processing of stimuli under these conditions, demonstrating both the capability for gating and, at least under conditions of moderate discrimination load, for parallel processing.

These laboratory tasks have reasonable ecological validity: people frequently focus on one voice and ignore others, search for a toothbrush on a cluttered countertop, or read a pageful of text in an orderly fashion, for example. However, our goals and intentions are often more fluid. We simply survey a scene not looking for anything in particular, we listen to a symphony, or we walk around a cluttered scene relying on visual guidance. One might say this last activity involves search, but one would be hard pressed to say what kind of search; is it for obstacles to avoid bumping into them, or is it for a clear pathway? In short, the set that people adopt in many routine activities is much more nebulous than what is demanded by a typical discrete laboratory task.

Despite these differences, one would hope that laboratory research could nonetheless illuminate these other situations as well. Studies of fixation patterns when people freely view pictures (Antes, 1974) are one step in this direction. The general finding is that people tend to fixate on informative regions of the display that are most likely to contain easily identifiable objects (Antes, Singsaas, and Metzger, 1978). Objects that are improbable given their identity and the surrounding context are more often fixated than other objects (Loftus and Mackworth, 1978). Unfortunately, it is not clear to what extent this occurs because these objects were identified before the fixation takes place. As described in chapter 3, there is good evidence that object identification and localization can be accomplished in parallel, subject to capacity limits; one could therefore hypothesize that subjects pick up the gist of the scene based on a parallel analysis (limited, of course, by the poor acuity for more peripheral objects) and direct subsequent fixations to objects that either fit with, or conflict with, this gist.

This brings us to the general question of how the control of perceptual attention is affected by the content of ongoing mentation, a question that has been little investigated. Matthew Remuzzi and I explored this issue by trying to determine whether creating an image *forces* attention to be directed to a picture of the type of object being imagined. The experiment began by giving subjects an object word or phrase, such as "fish" or "swimming pool" and instructing them to form a complete, clear mental image of it. Having done so, they pressed a key that triggered a rapid sequential presentation of pictures. They had only one task while viewing the pictures: to search for a digit interpolated among the pictures; in fact, they were told to let the image go in order to focus on the digit search. The subjects guessed what digit was present at the end of the sequence. Analysis of performance as a function of lag between the picture and digit revealed an attentional blink effect (poorer digit detection shortly after the pictured item), suggesting that subjects adopted a set to detect whatever they had just formed an image of, even when it was disadvantageous to their primary task. This result would not have surprised W. B. Pillsbury (1908), who said:

Searching for anything consists ordinarily of nothing more than walking about the place where the object is supposed to be, with the idea of the object kept prominently in mind, and thereby standing ready to facilitate the entrance of the perception when it offers itself. It is for that reason too that it is much easier to find an object again after finding it once, because you can look with a more definite image and can apply it more accurately.

This preliminary study suggests that forming a visual image entails searching. A more interesting hypothesis would be that any mental manipulation of conceptual (not merely visual) representation primes the system to search for instances of the concept.[6] It would be interesting, therefore to see if people can comprehend a story on a certain topic without tending to fixate on objects semantically related to the topic. This hypothesis would suggest that the meandering of visual attention (and, on its heels, saccadic eye movements) in routine activities may tend to track stimuli that activate detectors for concepts semantically related to ongoing trains of thought. The ability to search for and find targets may be a strategy for using a system wired up to draw our attention to stimuli that resonate with central activity. This tendency was suggested by Norman (1968) and is illustrated by the well-known "breakthrough of the unattended" experiment of Treisman (1960), described in chapter 2. There, it will be recalled, people shadowing words in one message will switch over and shadow the unattended message when it completes the sentence they have been shadowing.

A certain conceptual tension exists between the idea that attention tends to shift toward stimuli that resonate with ongoing thought and another idea that was discussed earlier, namely, that attention tends to be drawn to novel stimuli. Is attention drawn to what fits, or to what does not fit? There is no necessary contradiction here. In general, what one is thinking *about* is not necessarily what one *expects*. The familiar distractors that are more effectively ignored are not likely what the subjects in Lorch et al's experiments were deliberately imagining or thinking about, for example. An unconscious comparison of inputs against a neural model driving orienting reactions (as suggested by Sokolov, 1963) could coexist with a tendency for attention to be drawn to inputs that activate already activated conceptual nodes. Before pursuing such speculations further, though, it would be useful to have some empirical clarification of the relationship between the tendencies. For one thing, there is no evidence that these two tendencies in fact operate at the same time. The question would seem to be testable within relatively traditional paradigms; for example, can a person simultaneously be set to look both for an unspecified novel stimulus and for some specified target object, detecting whichever happened to appear? It is possible that detection of novelty and detection of stimuli that resonate with thoughts are in fact incompatible modes of functioning, rather than tendencies that coexist at any given instant.

Consequences of Attention

Knowledge of the World

According to the conclusions suggested earlier in this chapter, a person can voluntarily decide whether to analyze exclusively a single stimulus or many stimuli at a given instant; excluded signals are not fully analyzed, nor are the results considered in making decisions in detection tasks. But what is the consequence of allocating attention to many channels at once, that is, to a whole scene? For what purposes are the results of these analyses available? What functional role does divided attention play outside of the laboratory? The discussion of divided attention in chapter 3 focused almost entirely on documenting capacity limits in monitoring tasks. The data indicated that target-distractor discriminations can be performed in parallel and without capacity limitations up to some combined level of complexity, as long as only a single target is presented.

What does this tell us about what happens when a person looks at a natural scene and tries to take it in at a glance? One would naturally assume that visual attention typically starts out divided, allowing parallel (capacity-limited) analysis to occur, even though the person has no set to detect any particular target. One would expect this analysis to yield progressively more refined information about the different objects in the scene, their identities and their locations, although naturally this information might be quickly lost. Suppose, then, a person looks at a scene for a second or two and something in the scene is abruptly changed? Will the change be detected? In a series of elegant experiments, Phillips gave subjects the task of detecting changes in matrix patterns composed of light and dark squares; a variable interstimulus interval (ISI) separated the initial pattern and the possibly different test pattern. When the ISI was just a few milliseconds or tens of milliseconds, the observers saw flicker or motion in the position of the change, and easily caught almost all of the changes (e.g., Phillips, 1974, 1983). Phillips suggested that detectors located early in the visual system underlie this performance.

When the ISI was longer, however, the flicker or transient activity arose throughout the visual field, in which case flicker no longer provided a cue to the occurrence of change. At this point, detection of change became relatively poor. Here, the complexity of the pattern had a large effect on performance, suggesting that whatever change-detection people did accomplish was based on limited-capacity visual short-term memory.

Similar results can be found with displays of meaningful objects. Using displays of ten letters and an ISI of 67 msec, I found that people's performance in detecting single-letter changes was surprisingly poor, equivalent to fewer than five letters retained, or roughly the span of whole report (Pashler, 1988). McConkie and colleagues tried similar experiments with pictures of natural scenes, introducing the changes while the observer was executing a saccadic eye movement. People were remarkably poor at detecting such changes (Currie et al., 1995; see also Carlson-Radavansky and Irwin, 1995). This has the rather provocative implication that our experience of the stability of the visual world when we make saccadic eye movements (sometimes called space constancy) may not arise because our visual system checks that things are not changed, compensating for the eye movement (cf. MacKay, 1973). Of course, eye movements might flush visual representations that would have remained present if the eye was stationary; are people insensitive to changes in displays of natural scenes, as well as scenes composed of letters? Allen Lu, Ling-Po Shiu, and I assessed people's ability to spot changes in doctored photographs of scenes that were fairly similar to those used by McConkie's group (e.g., the color of a shirt worn by one of several individuals standing prominently in the scene might change from red to blue). With a 100-msec ISI, people saw flicker but detected relatively few changes (see also Simons, 1996). All of these results suggest that when observers attend to an entire scene, they do not, and presumably cannot, form a representation that allows them to keep track of each object in the scene and its identity, its appearance, and its location. At most, it seems, they can keep track of whatever they can hold in visual short-term memory.

There is another way to assess how much information a person can pick up about the objects in a scene when they have the opportunity to attend it. Consider the following situation. An observer looks at a display; after some time of preview, a cue appears (a bar marker next to one of the objects) requiring the observer to call out the name of the cued object (figure 5.2). The task is similar to partial report, except, first, the display remains present up to the time the cue appears, and second, the observer must respond as fast as possible. Suppose that while the observer previews the display a mental representation is constructed that includes the identities of all the objects in the display together with their locations. Suppose further, that the appearance of the probe initiates the retrieval of the *outcome* of this identification process (late selection in the strongest sense). This account makes a strong prediction: response times to name the object, measured from the time the cue is presented, should not depend on any variable that lengthens the time taken to identify the object. The identification process lengthens is already over and done with by the time the cue appears, so any variation in how long this identification took should be absorbed.

The first experiments using this method consisted of displays of eight letters and two different forms of degradation, reducing the intensity of the letters and increasing their confusability (Pashler, 1984a). The effects of degradation on RTs were not eliminated by stimulus preview; in fact, discriminability effects were sometimes larger than those observed when a probe appeared before the display (i.e., no preview). The results argue that even when observers have the opportunity to preview a display and every incentive to process as many items as possible, they still identify the probed item *after* the probe arrives. Mewhort et al. (1991) confirmed this basic result (persistence of the degradation effect after preview) using a different and in some ways superior manipulation of degradation: dots superimposed on top of characters.[7] More recently, however, Fera, Jolicoeur, and Besner (1994) found the effects of intensity to be reduced in the preview condition using several typefonts, but not the font used in the original experiments; with that, they replicated our observations. It is rather maddening to find results depending on which font one chooses! However, reducing visual intensity slows transmission of information early in the visual pathway, even before the visual cortex (Vaughan, Costa, and Gilden, 1966).

Whatever portion of the intensity effect arises at this early stage is bound to be absorbed into preview, since visual input can hardly sit

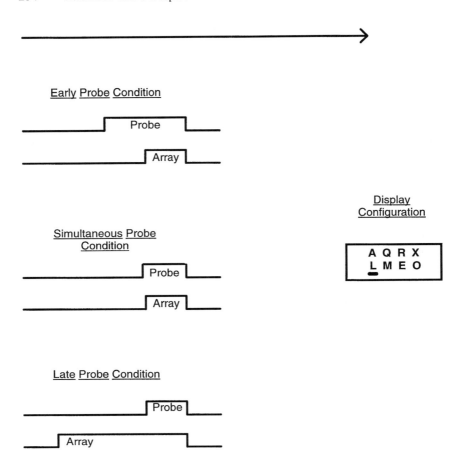

Figure 5.2
Design for analysis of perceptual processing during preview. In the preview (late probe) condition, the array appears for 400 msec before the probe, while in the early probe condition, the probe appears 150 msec before the array. The RTs shown on the next page are always measured from the first instant at which both probe and array are present; these data are from an unpublished replication of Pashler (1984a) conducted at the University of California, San Diego.

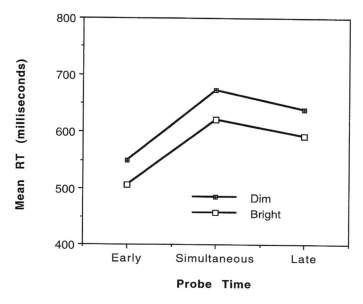

Figure 5.2 (continued)

waiting at the retina until more central mechanisms call for it. This does not explain why interactions of intensity and preview should depend on typefont, but it does suggest that letter confusability and noise degradation (as used by Mewhort et al) are more suitable than intensity for this experimental design. With these variables, preview has not been found to reduce the effects of visual identification time on RTs.

On balance, then, the evidence favors the view that identification takes place after detection of the cue. This conclusion is further supported by patterns of error rates. Error rates are noticeably higher when discriminability is low (hardly surprising). More interesting, these rates do not change depending on whether the probe comes after the display (preview condition) or simultaneously with it. This is consistent with the view that no effective identification of the to-be-probed item occurs during preview. One might contend that a data quality limitation puts a ceiling on performance levels with the low-discriminability items, but error rates were much lower when the cue appeared before the display. This provides an independent validation of the hypothesis that the probed items are generally identified after the probe appears, not before.

In summary, when we stare at a display of letters in anticipation of a cue telling us which one to report, we evidently lack the ability to work out the identity of each letter and keep that information at the ready. What is striking about this is the fact that we do *not* lack the ability to identify more than one letter simultaneously when our purpose is to find a target. After all, recall that when people view a display of letters and search for a target, visual degradation and display set size have *additive* effects. This demonstrates that in the search task, the processing stages retarded by degradation are performed on all the objects in parallel. Yet the experiments described above reveal that people cannot finish these stages while they preview a display in anticipation of a cue indicating which letter to report. This seemingly paradoxical state of affairs does not seem to reflect technical differences; Badgio (1987) confirmed both effects (absence of preview-X-degradation interaction, additivity of degradation and display set size) using the same types of displays and the same type of visual degradation.

The change-detection experiments and the studies of preview and degradation both suggest that observing a scene (with maximally divided attention, one assumes) accomplishes less than one might have assumed. Our awareness of the contents of the scene does not seem to provide us with the information we might have expected it would, or if the information is there, it is apparently not usable for as wide a range of purposes as we would have supposed.[8] To compound the puzzle, parallel identification of objects seems possible for some purposes but not others. How can these various findings and impressions be reconciled? There are a number of possibilities to consider. Dennett (1991) offers some radical suggestions focusing on our lack of awareness of the fact that our visual acuity falls off badly for stimuli more distant from the fovea. Ordinarily, he points out we do not have any sense that our visual periphery is blurry or indistinct, yet the quality of the input is very poor indeed. Our sense that we have a richly detailed inner representation of a scene may be entirely illusory. Rather than reflecting our possession of an inner representation of the details of the scene, he suggests, our visual awareness may merely reflect our recognition that we have the potential to *access* such information should we need it by shifting our eyes. Similarly, one might say that our sense of knowing about the contents of a scene reflects our ability to shift our attention to whatever interests us and identify it, precisely the sequence implicated by the display preview experiments described earlier. Dennet's proposal does not obviously help explain why parallel identification contributes to search tasks, however.

Another possibility is that our awareness of a scene does reflect our possession of detailed internal representations of it, but these representations are not of the sort required for object identification or change detection.

Along these lines, Iwasaki (1993) suggested that what he calls background consciousness depends on processing in the dorsal stream of the cortical visual system (leading from the primary visual cortex into the parietal lobes). Selective impairments in background consciousness are seen in syndromes like simultanagnosia (a disrupted ability to process a scene with more than one object present). Background consciousness would reflect the operation of a system specialized for analyzing the locations of objects for the purposes of action planning (Goodale and Milner, 1992) rather than working out the identities of objects. Perhaps, therefore, one should not expect awareness to confer any ability to identify cued objects or to detect changes in a scene. One thing that should be noted, however, is that people do a poor job of detecting not only changes in object identity, but also simple additions or deletions (Simons, 1996) that could be picked out without identifying anything. Thus, if our seemingly rich visual awareness reflects workings of the dorsal processing stream, one would still have to assume that the visual attributes computed in this system are not retained and compared over brief offsets.

Still another possibility is that when we attend to an entire scene we *do* create a mental representation of the objects along with their identities to the extent visual acuity permits. However, our subsequent access to this information may be limited in ways that make it useless for the change-detection and preview tasks. One example of such a limitation is if our internal description of the scene amounted to a set of one-directional pointers from object identities to object locations, with no pointers running in the opposite direction (Pashler, 1984a). This kind of representation would allow us to process the objects in a scene in parallel to detect and locate targets. However, to say what object was present in a cued location, a new round of visual processing, restricted to the relevant location, would be necessary; hence the results of the preview experiments. This kind of representation would not readily support change detection, either. This suggestion makes some testable predictions that differ from the other hypotheses considered above: if the representation includes identity->location pointers, people should be able to verify that an element is present in a scene once they have been staring at it for some time.[9]

Attention and the Perception of Time

What are the consequences of attention for the perception of time? An old and intriguing idea is that when a person attends to a stimulus, he or she perceives it as having occurred earlier in time than they would if he or she was not attending to it. The existence of such a phenomenon, often called *prior entry,* has been claimed for over a century. Titchener (1908) even included the law of prior entry among his half-dozen laws of attention: "the stimulus for which we are predisposed requires less time than a like stimulus, for which we are unprepared, to produce its full conscious effect" (p. 251). Many popular theoretical claims about attention seem to make prior entry reasonable and even likely. For example, it is commonly assumed that attending to a stimulus is a necessary precondition for becoming aware of it. It is natural to assume that the time one perceives a stimulus as having occurred is the very first instant at which one becomes aware of it. From these two assumptions, it follows that judgments of temporal order ought to depend on when a stimulus is attended. Another common assumption is that limited attentional resources can be allocated to stimuli in a graded fashion, determining the speed at which the stimuli are processed. If capacity allocation affects the duration of processing stages before the point at which the brain determines the arrival time of a stimulus, a prior entry effect is also to be expected.

For over a century, prior entry effects have been reported in a variety of different laboratory tasks. Interest in the question of how attention affects temporal perception started before experimental psychology itself. Early astronomers had to record the exact time at which they observed celestial events. Their problems have a close laboratory analogue in the so-called *complication experiment* (Boring, 1957). In one version of this experiment the subject watches a pointer revolving around a clock face. At some point a tone sounds, and the observer tries to say where the pointer was at that instant. It has been claimed that an observer who focuses attention on the bell will judge that it occurred before the actual time of presentation (a counterclockwise error; e.g., Leatherman, 1940). However, the most careful studies of this effect by Cairney (1975b) showed that although counterclockwise errors sometimes occur, attention-dependent prior entry is unlikely to be the cause.

Most investigators interested in prior entry effects used more austere tasks in which the observer simply judged the relative temporal order of a few stimuli (*temporal order judgments,* or *TOJs*). The simplest test for prior entry involves presenting two stimuli A and B at the same time and inducing the observer to attend to one stimulus more than to the other. If prior entry occurs, the observer should judge that the more-attended stimulus occurred earlier than the less-attended one. The literature using this kind of method presents a confusing picture, unfortunately. Several investigators reported prior entry effects (e.g., Stone, 1926; Sternberg, Knoll, and Gates, 1971; Stelmach and Herdman, 1991), and many negative results have also been reported, starting with Hamlin (1895) and continuing to the present (e.g., Jaskowski, 1993).

If prior entry is a real phenomenon, one could obviously fail to find evidence for it by failing to induce subjects to allocate their attention in the desired way. However, several studies reporting negative results used seemingly strong manipulations of attention. Van der Haeghen and Bertelson (1974) presented a tactile stimulus as a reference, and had subjects make a speeded response to the occurrence of another stimulus, indicating whether it was visual or auditory. After making the speeded response, subjects indicated whether the tactile stimulus appeared before or after the other stimulus. Attention was manipulated by changing the relative frequency of auditory versus visual stimuli. Responses to the more frequent stimulus were faster, confirming that the manipulation was effective, but TOJs were not affected. It could be argued that responses to high-frequency stimuli are faster not due to perceptual attention, but rather to a speedup of response selection (but see Miller and Anbar, 1981). Cairney (1975a) manipulated perceptual attention in a different way, having subjects judge the relative order of a visual stimulus (a pair of lines) and an auditory stimulus. In some blocks of trials, subjects were induced to give attentional priority to the lines by requiring them to first make a speeded response to their length. This task, which would seem to be a powerful attentional manipulation, reduced the accuracy of the TOJ, but produced no reliable tendency to claim the lines occurred before the sounds.

As noted earlier, other studies did yield the sort of evidence expected on the prior entry view. Unfortunately, most of them appear susceptible to fairly severe kinds of response bias. Consider, for example, the situation in which two visual stimuli occur at approximately the same time, with an arrow presented before one of the stimuli to provide an attention cue (Stelmach and Herdman, 1991, experiment 1). The observer's only task is to report which stimulus came first. A tendency to report the cued stimulus as being first, which Stelmach and Herdman observed, might reflect a genuine prior entry effect. On the other hand, it could reflect a demand effect induced by the arrow. Subjects presented with two stimuli and an arrow pointing at one of them might pick the cued stimulus as having any characteristic they were asked to judge—arriving first, being brighter, or perhaps even arriving last. In several other studies reporting prior entry effects, attention was manipulated by presenting a visual cue immediately before the to-be-attended stimulus and in the same location (Hikosaka, Miyauchi, and Shimojo, 1993; Neumann, et al., 1993). In this case, reports consistent with prior entry might arise because the cues themselves are confused or perceptually amalgamated with the cued stimulus, causing people to report the cue-stimulus complex as leading.[10]

At present, the empirical evidence for prior entry is unconvincing. The various failures to find the effect in what appear to be reasonable studies suggests at the very least that it is not very powerful. Of course, one certainly cannot rule out the existence of some effect. Future demonstrations of prior entry, if they are to be convincing, will have to include careful precautions to minimize response biases.[11]

If prior entry does not occur, as the data suggest but certainly do not prove, one wonders why this should be the case. As noted earlier, one might expect prior entry, based on seemingly plausible assumptions about attention. Does delaying attention to a stimulus not delay the moment at which the person becomes aware of the stimulus? Is the time of awareness not the time the person perceives the stimulus as having occurred? Reasonable though it may sound, the second of these propositions is not necessarily true. Here, attention is likened to a clerk in an office who admits incoming mail to the office and places a time stamp on each letter. The time stamp indicates not when the mail carrier brought the letter, but when the clerk got around to opening it. As Dennett (1991) observes, the code that the brain uses to represent time need not be time itself. One can see this is so by considering a perceptual feature such as color; this attribute *must* be represented by something other than itself, which shows that it is neither absurd nor self-contradictory to suppose that the brain might represent time with a neural code other than time itself.

To be more concrete, prior entry might not occur because the event of our being aware of a stimulus (occurring, say, at time t) may represent the proposition that the stimulus occurred at an earlier time t-k. To return to the postal analogy, the mail clerk may have an assistant who places a time stamp on the mail indicating when the mail reaches the office; at a later time, when the clerk opens the mail, he behaves as if he received it at that time. This is, of course, exactly what happens in many offices. Something of this kind must happen in the act of recollecting events from long-term memory: when we remember an event from last week we do not believe that the event is occurring at the moment we are doing the recollecting. In short, one should not be surprised by the idea that the representation of a stimulus would include a specification of its time of arrival, and that this representation could be before (or backdated from) from the time at which the stimulus is first analyzed to the point that we ordinarily call awareness, if indeed there is such a single point.[12]

II

Attention, Memory, and Action

In part II we move beyond perception of stimuli to consider attentional limitations in higher cognitive processes and motor control. In chapter 6 we will focus on studies that examine limits that arise when people try to perform two or more concurrent tasks that require some form of thought and action, the area commonly termed dual-task interference. Chapter 7 discusses attentional limitations in memory and learning. It is often assumed that speaking of dual-task limitations as attentional implies that they reflect the same resource or mechanism (attention) involved in perceptual phenomena described in part I, an idea first mentioned in the discussion of folk psychology in chapter 1. Many of the results described in chapters 6 and 7 directly question that assumption, suggesting that distinct resources or mechanisms underlie these phenomena. However, there are still reasons to describe the limitations on performance discussed here as attentional. First, they ordinarily depend on voluntary choice or action (the mere presentation of multiple stimuli does not elicit most of the types of interferences that are described). Second, the limitations clearly do not stem from the structure of our motor or sensory apparatus per se. Limitations that do, such as our inability to touch-type and drink a cup of coffee at the same time, are not discussed. Chapter 8 surveys three broad concepts often linked with attention: automaticity, mental effort, and the control of cognitive processes.

6

Central Processing Limitations in Sensorimotor Tasks

Theorizing about Central Attentional Limitations

Before turning to empirical findings about dual-task performance, it may be useful to consider some possible theoretical accounts of dual-task interference that have been proposed at one time or another. These ideas are logically distinct but not always mutually exclusive.

Commonsense Theories

People do not generally have strong intuitions about many of the issues addressed in the first five chapters of this book, such as whether visual search is serial or parallel or how advance information affects perception. However, they do often have some beliefs about their ability to carry out different activities at the same time. In ordinary talk, activities are usually classified at a comparatively molar level, such as driving, talking, and eating. Speaking at this level, people frequently claim to do two things at the same time, such as drive and have a conversation, or talk and walk. Commonsense notions might be taken to assume that when interference does arise, it reflects limits on a single underlying resource (attention) that is shared in a graded fashion. For example, people often speak of devoting more or less attention to some task or activity, as if they were dividing up a commodity such as money (pay more attention to your driving).[1] They also often remark that practicing an activity allows them to carry it out with less attention (or, they sometimes say, with no attention whatsoever). The issue of practice is discussed in detail in chapter 8.

Capacity Theories

Several theorists tried to develop a general account of dual-task interference that shares many of the assumptions of the folk psychological ideas just described. For example, Kahneman (1973) concluded that dual-task interference could be understood in terms of graded sharing of a single pool of mental resources (or capacity). Others accepted the idea of graded sharing but argued for multiple resources (Wickens, 1984; see Kramer and Spinks, 1991, for a review). Two key ideas characterize virtually all capacity theories. The first is that processing in the two tasks operates in parallel, with its efficiency dependent on the amount of resources allocated to the tasks. The second is that the person can usually vary the allocation more or less at will. Many psychologists have equated general processing capacity with short-term memory capacity, a point that is specifically discussed in chapter 7.

Bottleneck Theories

Beginning with Kenneth Craik and Alan T. Welford in the late 1940s and early 1950s, a more discrete view of dual-task interference has sometimes been advocated. Craik (1947) conducted some of the first studies of visual-manual tracking, having subjects try to keep a hand-held pointer on top of a meandering line exposed by a moving drum. He suggested that although tracking appeared continuous, people were actually making intermittent correction responses, about twice per second, to minimize the error in the position of the pointer, functioning as what he called an intermittent correction servo (see Pew, 1974, for a discussion). Welford (1952, 1967) pursued the study of intermittency using discrete speeded tasks, and concluded that certain types of mental processing cannot be carried out simultaneously in two tasks, thereby creating a discrete processing bottleneck. The approach is sometimes called single-channel theory (see Bertelson, 1966, and Smith, 1967a, for excellent early reviews). Bottleneck theorists usually claimed that queuing is associated with one or more of the stages of processing in a choice reaction-time task, such as memory retrieval, decision, response selection, response initiation, or response execution. In principle, however, bottleneck models would not have to be built around stages or types of processing; whether two mental operations have to queue up might depend instead on the difficulty of the operation, the extent to which the person has practiced it, or some other factor.

Crosstalk and Task Similarity

Another influential idea is that limitations on doing tasks at the same time may depend on the similarity of the tasks themselves, or the similarity of the information being processed in each task. Logically speaking, similarity could either facilitate or impair dual-task performance. For example, if only one type of processor can be active within any brief period of time, it might be easier to carry out two tasks that use the same processor than two tasks that require different processors (just as it is easier to have several plumbing problems taken care of on a given day than it is to get both plumbing and electrical problems fixed). However, beginning at least with the writings of Paulhan (cited by James, 1890/1950), it has generally been suggested that similarity exacerbates rather than reduces dual-task interference. In one formulation, Navon and Miller (1987) attributed dual-task interference to what they called *outcome conflict,* in which one task "produces outputs, throughputs, or side effects that are harmful to the processing of the [other task]" (p. 435).

Neural Theories of Dual-Task Interference

The theories mentioned so far all suggest that the determinants of dual-task interference can be characterized in psychological terms. It is quite conceivable, however, that interference patterns might make sense only in light of neural structures and their functions. One interesting idea along these lines, proposed by Kinsbourne (1981), was that the ease with which tasks could be combined depended on the physical distance between the cortical circuits that carry them out. This predicts that dual-task interference will be modulated by purely anatomical facts such as the distance between the areas in motor cortex that control particular movements. Other researchers combined this with the idea of capacity sharing; for example, Friedman and Polson (1981) proposed that the left and right cerebral hemispheres constitute at least partially separate pools of processing resources. This theory predicts that it should be easier to carry out a pair of tasks when one can be carried out by the left hemisphere and the other by the right, compared with those that must both be done by the same hemisphere.

Empirical Evidence: Continuous Dual-Task Performance

A great deal of research on dual-task performance used tasks that are, in a loose and intuitive sense, continuous. Examples are visual-manual tracking, copy typing, shadowing, and taking dictation. In studies involving continuous dual-task performance, subjects typically produce a stream of behavior lasting roughly 30 seconds to several minutes, and aggregate performance over the whole interval is assessed (e.g., total number of errors in copy typing, average deviation from perfect tracking). Several important conclusions have been drawn from these studies.

In some cases involving highly practiced tasks, dual-task performance is comparable with single-task performance. For example, a skilled typist was able to type visually presented text and shadow a message played through earphones with essentially no interference (Shaffer, 1975). Peterson (1969) found that people could add numbers they heard while reading characters aloud, with little decrement. Spelke, Hirst, and Neisser (1976) had subjects listen to words and write them down (i.e., take dictation) while reading unrelated stories for an hour a day for fourteen weeks. After the training, the subjects appeared able to carry out both activities simultaneously with no decrement in reading speed or comprehension. These results are sometimes cited as evidence for automaticity, a topic that is discussed in more detail in chapter 8.

Second, it is often the case that when tasks are made more similar in some respect, be it sharing an input modality, an output modality, or the type of choice or judgment required, dual-task interference is increased (Allport, Antonis, and Reynolds, 1972; Bornemann, 1942; Wickens, 1984; Wickens, Sandry, and Vidulich, 1983). The third observation, often taken as decisive evidence for graded capacity-sharing models, is that when interference arises, instructing subjects to vary how much emphasis they place on each task often results in a fairly smooth-looking tradeoff function. Tradeoff functions are usually depicted with what is called an attention operating characteristic (AOC) curve, a convenient representation that seems to have been developed independently by Bornemann[2] (1942), writing in German, and later by Sperling and Melchner (1978) and Gopher, Brickner, and Navon (1982). In an AOC curve, performance on the two tasks is represented as a point in X-Y space (figure 6.1); the value on the X axis represents performance on one task and the value on the Y axis represents performance on the other task. In different instructional conditions, subjects are told to give different amounts of emphasis to each task (e.g., 100% to task A, or 60% to task B). Performance in a given condition is represented by a single data point; all the points representing different instructional conditions are linked to trace out the AOC curve.

Suppose the subjects can perform tasks A and B together with no dual-task impairment. In that case, they do as well on task A when they give 50% emphasis to that task and 50% to task B as they would if they gave 100% emphasis to task A. This results in a data point at the upper righthand corner of the AOC space, giving a right-angled AOC curve as shown by the dotted line in the figure. When the tasks interfere with each

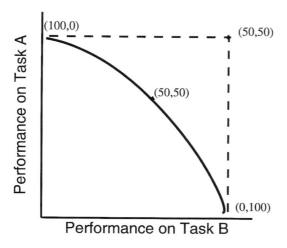

Figure 6.1
An attention operating characteristic (AOC) curve; numbers in parentheses are relative emphasis on Task A and Task B, respectively. The broken line shows an atypical case where equal emphasis on both tasks (50,50) produces no sacrifice in performance. More commonly, performance on both tasks is impaired (unbroken line).

other, however, the AOC curve looks more like the unbroken line: a fairly smooth tradeoff whereby increased emphasis on task A improves task A at the expense of task B. It is common to find tradeoff functions that look something like this.

What can be inferred from the findings involving continuous dual-task performance just mentioned? Investigators who used continuous tasks and AOC curves tended to favor some kind of capacity-sharing account, hypothesizing sharing of one or more resources (e.g., Gopher and Navon, 1980). Commonly, they assumed that resources are shared in a graded way, with the allocation remaining constant throughout a given performance[3] (Navon and Gopher, 1979). It seems likely, however, that even when they involved apparently continuous streams of behavior, most sensorimotor tasks actually required intermittent or discontinuous processing at central stages. In a task such as copy typing, for example, the finger movements may never cease, but planning these movements may involve intermittent discrete processes. One piece of evidence for this idea is the eye-hand span—the lag between the character fixated and the character typed at any given moment—which well exceeds a single character for a skilled typist (Salthouse and Saults, 1987), strongly suggesting that at some level the task is handled in chunks larger than a character. Skilled typists also type more quickly when the material is composed of words than of letter strings that do not form words (Fendrick, 1937). These findings make it seem likely that central processing is intermittent. Other tasks such as reading aloud also show an input-output span (Levin, 1979).

This likelihood of intermittent processing drastically affects the interpretation of the continuous task results described. To start with, when a task such as copy typing can be combined with a secondary task without any interference, this may only mean that the demands the two tasks place on limited mechanisms are scheduled to occur at different times. It does not imply that either task or both make no demands (cf Schouten, Kalsbeek, and Leopold, 1960; Broadbent, 1982; S. Fisher, 1975). This issue is discussed in more detail in chapter 8 in connection with the issue of automaticity.

The possibility of underlying intermittent processing in apparently continuous tasks also has important bearing on the interpretation of AOC curves. As noted, smooth tradeoff functions are often seen as direct evidence for graded changes in capacity allocation. However, suppose a continuous task requires exclusive but intermittent access to central decision-making machinery (a dual-task bottleneck). In that case, interference would arise to the extent that each task simultaneously requires access to the limited mechanism(s). What would have to be allocated would be access time, rather than any continuously divisible resource (time sharing rather than resource sharing). Given that AOC functions are averages computed across many operations and usually more than one subject, time sharing would be bound to produce smooth tradeoff curves. Therefore, smooth tradeoffs are just as consistent with underlying bottleneck models as they are with graded resource sharing. They can also be reconciled with other types of dual-task theories described above.

The general conclusion to be drawn is that aggregate measures of continuous performance are not very useful in discriminating among different underlying causes of interference, because they are simply too gross. The absence of interference may reflect adroit scheduling of processes that interfere with each other discretely, albeit intermittently. Smooth tradeoffs in aggregate performance may reflect time sharing of limited central mechanisms, rather than sharing of any resource akin to fuel or processing capacity.

Empirical Evidence: Dual-Task Interference in Simple Tasks

The ambiguities inherent in studies of continuous tasks suggest that to understand dual-task interference at a mechanistic level, more fine-grained analyses are necessary. For this purpose, it is useful to have people perform punctate tasks and measure the time involved in performing each one. This makes it possible to determine more directly whether two tasks rely on the same mechanisms or resources, and if so, what these mechanisms or resources are doing. This strategy leads us to one of the earliest and most basic experimental designs used to study dual-task interference: the *psychological refractory period (PRP)* procedure.

Dual Speeded Responses: The PRP Effect

A simple way to examine dual-task performance limitations is to have a person carry out two tasks, each of which requires making a speeded response to an individual stimulus. Starting with Telford (1931) and

Vince (1949), it has been found that the time it takes to respond to the second stimulus generally becomes greater when the interval between the stimuli becomes very short. Telford termed this slowing the psychological refractory period (*PRP effect*), on analogy to the refractory period of neurons. Although the analogy is flawed in some ways, the term has stuck. In the typical PRP experiment, two stimuli are presented, S1 and S2, separated by an SOA. The person responds to each stimulus, R1 and R2, respectively. Figure 6.2 shows the PRP effect whereby the time between S2 and R2 (denoted RT2) becomes greater as the SOA is shortened, whereas the time between S1 and R1 (RT1) often remains relatively unaffected. In some cases the slope reaches −1, implying that further reductions in SOA simply increase RT2 correspondingly. Equivalently, one could say that presenting S2 closer in time to S1 (beyond a certain minimum) sometimes fails to result in R2 being produced any earlier. However, the total time for both tasks (the interval between S1 and R2) is often significantly less than the sum of the time required to complete each task by itself.

The PRP effect has been observed in many different tasks, including simple RT as in Telford's studies, and choice RT tasks (e.g., Creamer, 1963). Most of the earliest PRP experiments used two manual responses, sometimes made with the same finger, sometimes with different fingers. However, PRP effects can be found even with pairs of tasks that involve diverse kinds of responses. Examples are manual and eye-movement responses (Pashler, Carrier, and Hoffman, 1993), manual and vocal responses (Pashler, 1990), manual and foot responses (Osman and Moore, 1993), and vocal and foot responses (Pashler and Christian, 1994). Although many response combinations have not been tried, the effect appears robust across a wide range of output modalities. Almost all PRP studies used auditory and/or visual stimuli, but at least one used tactile stimulation and found the usual results. Brebner (1977) stimulated one finger on each of the subjects' hands with an upward movement of a key driven by a solenoid. Subjects responded by pressing the key, and a substantial PRP effect was observed. The PRP effect is commonly found even when S1 and S2 use different input modalities. For example, Creamer (1963) and Borger (1963), among the first investigators to examine PRP effects with choice reaction tasks, combined a visual with

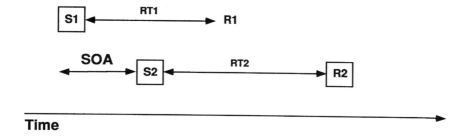

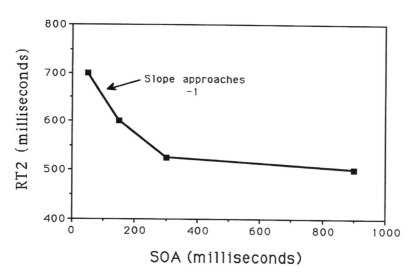

Figure 6.2
The psychological refractory period (PRP) effect. (Top) S1 precedes S2 by a variable stimulus-onset asynchrony (SOA). (Bottom) Typical slowing of RT to task 2, which increases as SOA is reduced; the slope often approaches −1.

an auditory stimulus. There is no good evidence that R2 slowing is greater when S1 and S2 are in the same modality, but this possibility is hard to assess because changes in input modality are usually confounded with changes in stimulus-response compatibility.

The existence of the PRP effect by itself challenges the commonsense theory, which suggests that only cognitively demanding tasks interfere with each other. With certain extremely simple tasks, however, the effect sometimes seems to disappear. This was found with tasks requiring a saccadic eye movement toward a spot (Pashler, Carrier, and Hoffman, 1993) and repeating a spoken word, or shadowing (Greenwald and Shulman, 1973; McLeod and Posner, 1984). Greenwald and Shulman (1973) suggested that the key might be ideomotor compatibility (roughly, when the stimulus is the same as the feedback that one experiences from producing the response). This would not seem to apply to the case of saccadic eye movements, nor does it fit another recently reported case. Using a visual-manual mapping with very high stimulus-response compatibility Koch (1994) reported that refractoriness was eliminated. More remains to be learned about the conditions under which the PRP effect disappears, however—for example, whether it depends on properties of both tasks, or only one. It does seem clear that the situations in which dual-task interference in punctate tasks is eliminated are quite narrow; interference is often found even with what one would intuitively describe as easy or simple mappings.

Preparation and Temporal Warning   Several early investigators suggested that the PRP effect is caused by subjects' uncertainty about when S2 will appear. In tasks involving response choice, this is clearly incorrect. For one thing, RT2 is often slowed even when there is no temporal unpredictability at all because SOA is held constant over a whole block of trials (e.g., Bertelson, 1967; Broadbent and Gregory, 1967). In Bertelson's study, two lights, one adjacent to a lefthand key, one adjacent to a righthand key, were illuminated and the subject pressed the appropriate keys as rapidly as possible. The second response was substantially delayed, and this slowing was about the same whether the interval varied randomly from trial to trial or remained constant. For another, when the first stimulus was presented but no response was required (SOAs vary from trial to trial), there was very little slowing of the response to the second stimulus[4] (e.g., Pashler and Johnston, 1989).

Of interest, neither of these points applies when the second task involves simple RT. Temporal uncertainty has a big effect on simple RT (Klemmer, 1957), and R2 is sometimes slowed to the same degree regardless of whether a response is required to the first stimulus (R. Davis, 1959; Koster and van Schuur, 1973). Thus, temporal uncertainty may play a special role in simple RT, which is hardly surprising in view of the fact that simple RT involves temporal uncertainty to the exclusion of any other kind of uncertainty.

Even though temporal uncertainty is not likely to be the prime cause of dual-task slowing found with choice tasks, another aspect of preparation has to be considered. The PRP effect could reflect limitations in people's ability to keep two tasks prepared at the same time, rather than a limited ability actually to carry out the tasks. This could slow performance regardless of whether people know when the stimuli will arrive. It is often suggested that this form of preparatory limit contributes some portion of the slowing found in the PRP situation (e.g., Pashler, 1984b). From time to time, though, it has been suggested that dual-task interference might be explained principally by this factor (e.g., Gottsdanker, 1980; Koch, 1994; Neumann, 1987). To get the purest measure of preparation cost, one must force subjects to prepare two tasks but to perform only one of them. This is easily accomplished simply by presenting only one stimulus. Figure 6.3 illustrates one study of this type that compared the condition just described with conventional single-task and dual-task conditions. The results showed that although the preparation factor was indeed responsible for some slowing, actually having to perform both tasks produced substantial slowing above and beyond that.

Converging Evidence for a Central Bottleneck

The investigators who first explored the PRP effect generally favored some kind of central bottleneck as the primary explanation for the effect. Figure 6.4 provides a graphic illustration of how a central bottleneck would account for slowing in the PRP task: the decision-related stages of task 2 cannot commence until the corresponding stages in task 1 have been completed,[5] resulting in a slowing of RT2 that increases as SOA is

Type of Block	Tone Task	Color Task
Tone Task alone	605 msec	---
Color Task alone	---	538 msec
Tone or Color Task	732 msec	599 msec
Tone and Color Task	847 msec	728 msec

Figure 6.3
Mean response times in an experiment examining cost of preparing for, versus actually performing, a concurrent task (data from 13 subjects). Color task required naming color of patch aloud; tone task required making one of three keypress responses depending on pitch of tone (300, 600, or 900 Hz). In Tone Task alone and Color Task alone blocks, the subject performed only one task. In Tone or Color Task blocks, tone or color patch was presented (not both), but subjects did not know which it would be. In Tone and Color Task blocks, both tasks were performed (stimuli were simultaneous and response order was unspecified) (Ruthruff and Pashler, unpublished observations).

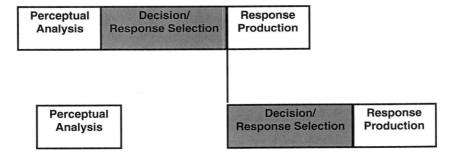

Figure 6.4
Central bottleneck model of PRP effect. The shaded portion of task 2 cannot begin until the shaded portion of task 1 is complete. Nonshaded stages can overlap with the other task, however.

reduced. The fact that the bottleneck encompasses only part of each task predicts that the sum of the times to perform the two tasks alone should be greater than the time between S1 and R2; this is usually the case, as noted above. The central bottleneck is, therefore, a hybrid serial/parallel information-processing model.

The earliest proponent of a central bottleneck theory was Alan Welford (1952). Noting that the PRP effect can be observed even with tasks involving two very different kinds of responses, or two different stimulus modalities, Welford reasoned that the effect must originate in a central process he termed S-R translation (more commonly called response selection since the work of Sternberg, 1969).[6] Welford thought that the execution of the response was not a part of the bottleneck, but he did suspect that monitoring feedback from the response sometimes occupied the same single-channel mechanism for a second time.

A rather unusual PRP experiment by Van Galen and ten Hoopen (1976) provides a nice example of the early evidence consistent with a single-channel bottleneck. Subjects first saw a letter (S1); if it was a P they said the Dutch word *periodiek* and if it was an M they said *magistraal*. After an ISI ranging between 60 and 1630 msec, they saw another letter (S2), and responded with a righthand button push that depended on the identity of this letter. Three subjects carried out the task for ten sessions, producing vocal response as fast as possible. The authors divided trials into three different bins depending on whether S2 occurred during the interval between S1 and the time the person began pronouncing the word (R1), during the pronunciation process, or later. Within each of these bins, trials were further subdivided according to which portion of this interval the stimulus arrived in. As figure 6.5 shows, reaction times were unaffected when S2 arrived during the articulation itself, but they were substantially elevated when the stimulus arrived during the preceding "decision" stage. The authors did not analyze the relationship between the production of the two responses. Similar experiments disclosed that the production of the two responses often overlap in time (Pashler and Christian, 1994). Consistent with this, casual observation often reveals that people make simultaneous movements of different effectors (e.g., talk while raising a cup of coffee toward their mouth). Such observations suggest that even if there is a bottleneck or capacity

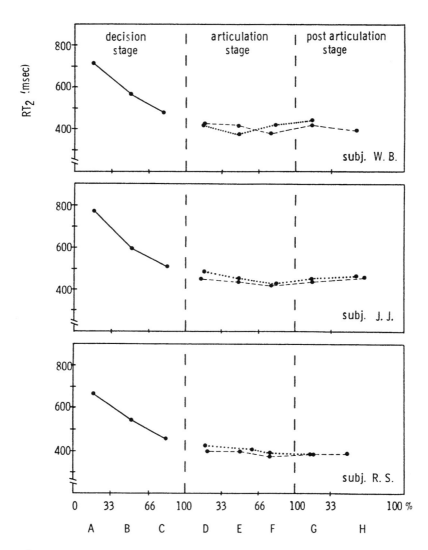

Figure 6.5
Reaction time for button-push response to a letter (S2) as a function of whether
S2 occurred during the interval between S1 and the vocal response to S1 (decision
stage), during the articulation of this response, or later. Data from three subjects'
last eight sessions; reprinted from van Galen and ten Hoopen (1976, figure 2),
with permission.

limit in central decision making, several distinct motor responses can be executed in parallel. The results do not specify the locus of any processing bottleneck with much precision, of course.

Strategies for Testing Bottleneck Models   The PRP paradigm is well suited for determining the locus of any possible processing bottlenecks. Models that postulate a bottleneck associated with particular processing stages make distinctive predictions that can be tested by manipulating the duration of different stages of each task. Most of the experiments to be discussed were conducted with instructions that emphasized the speed of the first task; without such instructions, subjects often emit responses in the two tasks in a fixed temporal sequence, often called grouping.[7] Suppose a bottleneck is present in some central stage, as shown in figure 6.4. Four types of predictions follow, each illustrated in one of the four panels of figure 6.6; the critical (bottleneck) stage is shaded. Each panel shows what happens when a particular stage of either task 1 or task 2 is slowed down by some experimental manipulation (reducing the intensity of a stimulus, changing the stimulus-response mapping, or whatever). Panels 1 through 4 correspond to predictions 1 through 4 described below. The figure always illustrates the situation where the SOA is short enough that the critical stages of one task do actually postpone the critical stages of the other.

Prediction 1   If a stage of task 1 up to or including the bottleneck is prolonged, both RT1 and RT2 are slowed, and to the same degree. One might say that the slowing in the first task is propagated onto the second task. Of course if the SOA were long enough, this propagation should not occur. This principle is familiar in another context: if you enter a bank right ahead of another customer, and only one teller is on duty, the teller represents a bottleneck. Principle 1 says that if you dawdle and chat with the teller, both you and the second customer will be delayed, and to the same extent.

Prediction 2   If stages of task 1 *after* the bottleneck are slowed, RT1 is increased but RT2 is not, since task 2 is not directly waiting for these stages. (If the first customer takes extra time to count money but is considerate enough to do so after leaving the teller's window, the second customer will not be delayed.)

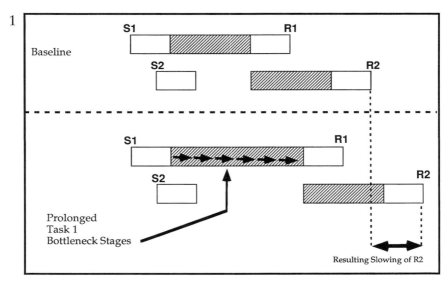

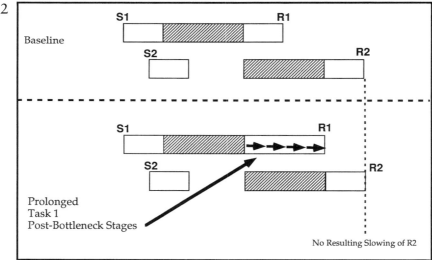

Figure 6.6
Predictions of a central bottleneck (in shaded stage) for experiments in which a particular stage of one or other task (the stage with superimposed ->->->->->) is prolonged by an experimental variable. (Panel 1) Prolonging the bottleneck stage in task 1 delays both R1 and R2 correspondingly. (Panel 2) Prolonging the postbottleneck stage in task 1 does not delay R2 at all. (Panel 3) Prolonging the prebottleneck stage in task 2 does not delay either R1 or R2. (Panel 4) Prolonging the task 2 bottleneck stage adds a constant onto R2 (no effect on R1). Reprinted from Pashler (1994e) with permission.

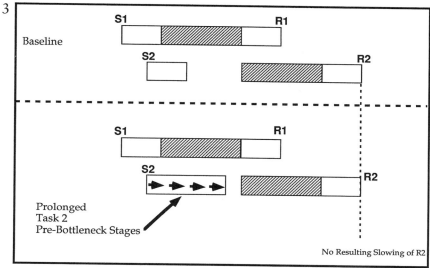

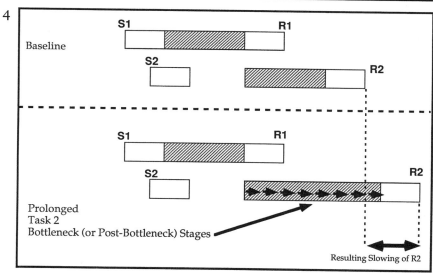

Prediction 3   This is a particularly interesting prediction. If stages of task 2 *prior to* the bottleneck are slowed by a certain amount, RT2 is not increased correspondingly. This is because, at short SOAs, the second task does not have to wait for completion of stages in task 2 before stage B, but only for the critical stages in task 2 to be completed. (If the teller is working with the first customer, you can saunter in without prolonging your stay in the bank.)

Prediction 4   Manipulating the duration of stages at or after the bottleneck in task 2 to a given extent will slow RT2 to just that extent, regardless of the SOA; naturally, this has no effect on RT1, however. (If you spend three extra minutes talking with the teller, the customer before you is not slowed down, but you will assuredly spend three more minutes in the bank.)

These four predictions involve large and distinctive interactions, and they have the virtue that they are likely to hold even if additional slowing is added by extraneous factors, such as the preparatory limitation mentioned earlier. Schweickert and colleagues (1978; Schweickert and Townsend, 1989) showed that formalisms from operations research can be used to represent and derive predictions such as these as well as more complex ones; the single-bottleneck model considered here is a simple example of the types of structures they studied.

A fair number of published studies can be used to assess these four basic predictions from the bottleneck model. The results described below come from typical PRP experiments using choice tasks rather than simple RT. The studies generally avoided having difficult perceptual discriminations in the same sensory modality (e.g., reading a word and categorizing a shape). Often, although not always, subjects were instructed to produce the first response as quickly as possible. This practice has been used, beginning with Creamer (1963) to avert grouping of responses, a strategy of emitting the two responses at the same time. The results reviewed below argue that at least under these conditions, the PRP effect generally reflects a bottleneck in response selection and perhaps associated decision-making stages, as first suggested by K. W. J. Craik (1947) and Welford (1952, 1980). The results also rule out a bottleneck located exclusively in an earlier or later stage.

Empirical Results   If there is a bottleneck in response selection, then increasing the duration of that stage (or prior stages) in task 1 should increase RT2 as well as RT1 when the SOA is short (prediction 1). Karlin and Kestenbaum (1968) and Smith (1969) confirmed this prediction when they manipulated the number of alternatives[8] in a choice RT task, as did Hawkins, Church, and de Lemos (1978, experiment 1) using stimulus probability.[9] Broadbent and Gregory (1967) found a slightly greater effect of S1 probability on task 2 compared with task 1, however.

By prediction 2, a bottleneck in response selection should entail that when the production of the already-selected R1 is slowed, RT2 will not increase. Pashler and Christian (1994) varied the complexity of the task 1 response. In one case, subjects had to produce either a single key press or a sequence of three key presses, depending on the identity of S1. The time taken to produce the first key press was approximately the same regardless of whether the response consisted of one key press or three. Obviously, though, it took longer to complete three key presses—about 489 msec longer in one experiment. The main question was how much of this slowing would propagate to produce a corresponding slowing of the (vocal) RT2. Only 64 msec of slowing showed up on RT2. Thus, actually producing the sequence, including whatever central and peripheral motor control processes may be operating up until the last key press, does *not* hold up the second task. On the other hand, the 64-msec slowing, although small in relation to effects on RT1, suggests that some delays may not be purely attributable to decision and response selection. It is possible, for example, that response production normally proceeds without interfering with task 2, but on the occasional trial, response corrections are necessary, and these corrections interfere with task 2.

Prediction 3 offers the most distinctive predictions for testing the response-selection bottleneck theory: increasing the time for prebottleneck perceptual processing of S2 should have *smaller* effects in the dual-task condition when the SOA becomes short. Several experiments manipulated stimulus intensity and confirmed this prediction (Pashler, 1984b; Pashler and Johnston, 1989; de Jong, 1993). Because of the uncertainty as to how far into the system intensity continues to have effects (Miller, 1979), these results might be consistent with a bottleneck that encompasses not only response selection, but also later stages of perception, say, object recognition, as well. Other results discussed below provide some evidence against this possibility, however.

By prediction 4, a response-selection bottleneck implies that increases in the duration of task 2 response selection should have a constant effect on RT2 regardless of SOA. Many studies confirmed this result, as the following examples illustrate.

Pashler and Johnston (1989) observed that the effects of stimulus repetition were additive with SOA; that is when S2 in trial n was identical to S2 in trial n-1, RT2 was faster, but to the same degree at short and long SOAs. In relatively unpracticed choice RT tasks with easily recognizable stimuli, repetition primarily affects the time required to select a response (Pashler and Baylis, 1991).

Pashler (1989) had subjects perform a second task involving naming the highest digit in a display of digits (experiment 4) or making a button push response indicating its identity (experiment 3). Naturally, response selection is easier in the vocal task, and RT2 was over 100 msec quicker in that task. The SOA effect was similar in the two tasks.

McCann and Johnston (1992) devised a second task in which subjects pressed one of two response keys depending on the identity of a visual stimulus. In the compatible condition, the stimuli (shapes of increasing size) were mapped onto an array of response keys in an orderly fashion; in the incompatible condition, the mapping was shuffled. In the incompatible condition, RT2 was about 60 msec slower than in the compatible condition. This effect was additive with SOA (figure 6.7).

Other cases of additivity are reported by Pashler (1984b, experiments 1 and 2, target presence/absence), Fagot and Pashler (1992, experiment 7, Stroop effect), and Hawkins, Church, and de Lemos (1978, number of stimuli per response[10]).

Response Production Bottlenecks?
Over the years, many investigators have suggested that the PRP effect is caused by motoric rather than cognitive limitations. Keele (1973) and Norman and Shallice (1986) argued for a bottleneck in initiating or producing responses. The hypothesis of a bottleneck located *exclusively* in response initiation and/or production clearly implies (by prediction 3)

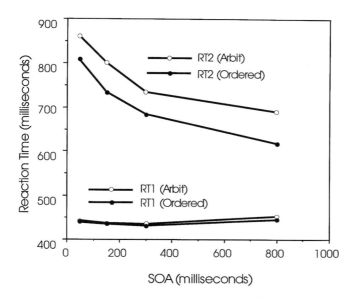

Figure 6.7
Additive effects of second-task stimulus-response compatibility and SOAs on RTs in a PRP experiment (from McCann and Johnston, 1992). In the high-compatibility condition, the size of boxes is mapped onto buttons in an ordered way; in the low-compatibility condition, the mapping is arbitrary (Arbit).

a strong prediction regarding factors that increase the duration of any stage in task 2 before response initiation (e.g., factors increasing time for response selection). The prediction is that when SOA is reduced, these factors should have a progressively smaller effect on R2 latency. As described above, many experiments failed to confirm this prediction: response-selection difficulty factors such as compatibility generally add a constant to RT2 regardless of the SOA; that is, the effect of response selection difficulty is additive with dual-task slowing.[11]

This does not rule out the idea that, under special circumstances, response production might represent a bottleneck. Consider a task in which subjects are required to produce a sequence of key press responses with one hand (the whole sequence being R1) and a single key press response with the other hand (R2) (Pashler and Christian, 1994). Rather than producing R2 while the R1 sequence is under way, as usually happens when R2 is vocal, the manual R2 is typically delayed until just after the last key press in the R1 sequence has been emitted. That is, producing a rapid sequence of manual responses with one hand seems to prevent the emission of a response with the other hand (or foot). This is consistent with other demonstrations of interference between manual responses. Netick and Klapp (1994) reported that when subjects do a visuomanual tracking task with a righthand joystick response (trying to keep a cursor within a target region), they often hesitate in their tracking responses when a lefthand response is required (signaled by a tone). It seems that producing certain kinds of motor movements with hands or feet is sometimes subject to a separate bottleneck[12] (see also Heuer, 1985; McLeod, 1978, 1980; McLeod and Mierop, 1979). This is not the same as saying it is part of the central bottleneck.[13] Perhaps for the same underlying reason, when two slow hand movements are executed simultaneously, they show a tendency to become spatially coupled (e.g., Franz, Zalaznik, and McCabe, 1991; Chan and Chan, 1995).

This limitation on finger and foot movements does not seem likely to play much role in the standard PRP experiments, even when two separate finger responses are required. This is because in the typical choice task involving two individual key press responses, the R1 key press is probably finished well before the second response is ready to emit. Thus, the inferred inability to produce two simultaneous independent finger responses probably affects response latencies only when the first task involves an extended sequence of responses, as in the studies of Pashler and Christian and Netick and Klapp, or when the second task is extremely brief (de Jong, 1993). To summarize, the data argue for a response modality-independent bottleneck in selection of responses, and they also favor at least one specific (i.e., effector-dependent) bottleneck in response execution that prevents certain kinds of independently selected movements from being produced simultaneously. Although this second limitation is unlikely to play a very important role in the laboratory tasks using key press responses, it may be important outside the laboratory, for example, when musicians execute sequences of complex finger movements with both hands, or when drivers move a steering wheel with one hand and try to adjust a radio with another (McLeod and Mierop, 1979).

It is not known whether this manual response-related bottleneck encompasses all actions involving the limbs, or whether there are additional response-related limitations tied to particular types of action. As we have already seen, producing speech does not seem to interfere with manual response execution. Producing speech does not seem to interfere with perception of unrelated speech, either, as some "motor" theories of speech perception would predict. It has been observed that simultaneous translators are both speaking and listening for more than half the time they are at work (cf. Gerver, 1974), and ordinary individuals have little difficulty reading words aloud while monitoring unrelated speech for semantically defined targets (Shallice, McLeod and Lewis, 1985).

Evaluating Theories of Dual-Task Interference

The results of these studies of simple discrete tasks have various implications for the five kinds of theories of dual-task interference described at the beginning of the chapter.

Commonsense Theories

The commonsense theory of dual-task interference would lead one to expect that seemingly trivial tasks would not interfere with each other as profoundly as they do in the PRP task. The fact that people do not ordinarily notice dual-task interference is interesting in its own right. One reason for this may be that people are simply oblivious to any brief delay that does not seriously disrupt performance. It may be possible to put many routine tasks on hold for a short time, and then resume them without performance suffering. There is not much research on task interruption per se, but the little that does exist seems to confirm that even after relatively long interruptions, people can usually pick up where they left off with little or no cost. Gillie and Broadbent (1989), for example, had subjects play a computer game and interrupted them to perform mental arithmetic for 30 seconds. Subjects resumed the game with no detectable cost. The subjective feeling people have that they can have a conversation at the same time they are driving has to be considered in light of such findings. If driving occasionally delays the planning of an utterance for, say, a half-second or so every 5 or 10 seconds, one might well fail to notice this altogether and mistakenly conclude that the driving was automatic (a notion that is discussed further in chapter 8).

The commonsense theory also suggests that practice eliminates dual-task interference. As yet not enough data are available to tell whether this is correct or not. The PRP effects sometimes persists even after a great deal of practice (Gottsdanker and Stelmach, 1971), but these experiments involved manual responses and interresponse intervals that became very short, so the interference that persisted might conceivably have reflected the difficulty with simultaneous manual response production noted above. It is possible, then, that after sufficient practice response selection can operate simultaneously with other mental operations. Even if this is not the case, practice might make interference less salient for other reasons. For one thing, it may reduce the demands of task preparation. Thus, a novice driver may have to remind himself or herself of each of the different subtasks (braking for pedestrians, steering to stay on the road, etc.), whereas the expert prepares all these behaviors as a unit ("I'm driving now"). Second, a series of motor movements that have been performed together many times may be selected as a single chunk. For example, instead of selecting each motor action involved in changing gears one at a time, the experienced driver may be able to choose the entire sequence as a single unit. Together, these phenomena may leave us with the (incorrect) feeling that practiced activities can truly be run on autopilot. This issue is discussed further in chapter 8.

Graded Capacity Sharing

The results of PRP studies discussed above provide little direct support for graded capacity sharing (parallel processing at a reduced efficiency that depends on some proportional allocation). Experiments that posit a central processing bottleneck in the PRP task do not completely rule out that possibility, on the other hand. It is common in PRP studies to ask subjects to produce R1 as quickly as possible; subjects are occasionally told to produce the responses in a fixed order, but this seems less common. Even if graded capacity sharing were possible, assigning top priority to task 1 might lead people to allocate all available capacity to that task until it has been completed, and only then allocate full capacity to task 2. If one modified the shared capacity model to suppose that capacity is only required for central stages, this model could mimic the predictions of the central bottleneck hypothesis.

An obvious way to test this idea is to stop requiring rapid responding in task 1. In some cases this has been done, and the results still suggest a central bottleneck by virtue of prediction 4 (Carrier and Pashler, 1995; Ruthruff, Miller, and Lachmann, 1995). This should warrant some skepticism about graded capacity sharing. Are there other ways to test the capacity-sharing hypothesis? A specific version, proposed by McLeod (1977), assumed that each task consumes a fixed amount of capacity. It is possible to show that in this particular model, increases in task 1's difficulty should have greater effects on RT1 in the dual-task situation than they have in the single task; this prediction does not seem to hold (Pashler, 1984b). However, capacity sharing need not involve such restrictive assumptions, so these data do not speak against capacity sharing in general.

Better tests require giving the subject incentives to share capacity in a graded fashion and seeing whether such sharing does take place. In one initial experiment along these lines, subjects were required to perform two choice RT tasks with stimuli separated by intervals of −1000, −500, 0, 500, and 1000 msec[14] (Pashler, 1994d). The instructions asked subjects to divide their capacity equally between the two tasks. If this were possible, it seems reasonable to expect that in the zero SOA condition at least some subjects would divide capacity in a fairly equitable way, carrying out central processes in parallel, albeit more slowly than normal. If there is a structural bottleneck, on the other hand, subjects should have no choice but to carry out central stages of one task before the other, producing a bimodal distribution of responses. In fact, subjects fell into two groups. Some clearly produced grouped responses, indicated by interresponse intervals near zero with extremely low variability, thus neither supporting nor refuting the structural bottleneck theory. Most subjects, however, produced the bimodal distribution of interresponse intervals predicted by the structural bottleneck.

Of course, a single study cannot rule out the possibility of graded capacity sharing in general. It is especially critical to know if the result holds up with tasks that use different response modalities and more difficult requirements for response selection. The plausibility of capacity sharing as a strategic option can be dismissed only after many experiments are carried out, looking at situations in which capacity sharing could have been expected to show up and it still fails to materialize. As the matter stands presently, the most one can say is that no convincing evidence from PRP designs indicates that people are capable of graded capacity sharing, even though a reasonable opportunity has been provided for such a capability to be demonstrated.

Another point that should be mentioned concerns the relationship between capacity sharing and preparation. It was suggested above that variation in the extent to which subjects prepare for tasks in advance can account for some proportion of observed dual-task slowing. If preparation can be allocated in a graded fashion, this could provide an additional explanation for the smooth tradeoffs in task performance described above (in addition to time sharing, that is). Fortunately, the contribution of preparatory factors to dual-task slowing (or to effects of task emphasis and tradeoff) could be independently assessed by means of catch trials in which only one task is presented (see figure 6.3).

These conclusions have implications for several widely applied methodologies. One is the common practice of having subjects hold onto a short-term memory load to examine how performance of some task is affected by a reduction in available capacity; this is discussed further in chapter 7. Another capacity-based methodology that has been used in many areas of psychology is often called the probe RT method. The basic idea is to use increases in a concurrent simple RT as a measure of attentional demands. The idea is actually an old one (see, e.g., Swift, 1892), but contemporary probe RT studies began with the work of Posner and Boies (1971). As a primary task, their subjects had to determine whether or not two successively presented letters were identical, making a rapid button push response shortly after the second letter appeared. (The two letters are referred to as sample and test letters.) In half of the trials, a tone sounded at some point and the subject responded by pressing a key with the other hand as rapidly as possible. The instructions stressed rapid performance of letter matching as the primary task, however.

Posner and Boies assumed that the speed of the response to the probe provided an index of the amount of spare capacity left unoccupied by the primary task. As shown in figure 6.8, probe RTs were not much elevated when the probe was presented within a short time of the sample letter. Therefore, the authors believed that the perception of the sample letter could not have used up more than a very small amount of capacity.

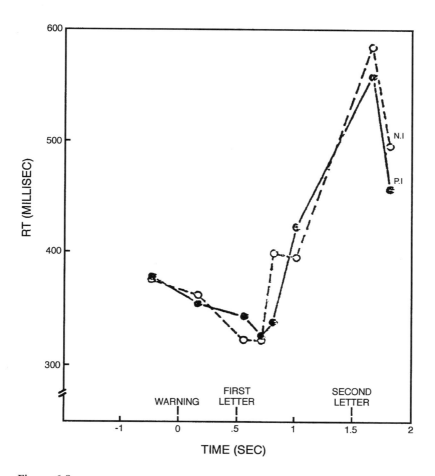

Figure 6.8
RTs to respond to a probe that occurs at some time during a letter matching task. Reprinted from Posner and Boies (1971) with permission.

The RTs to probes were elevated beginning after the presentation of the sample letter and around the time the test letter was presented. Posner and Boies concluded that whereas encoding of the test letter did not require central capacity, "generation of distinctive features for testing" during the interval between the letters and the response phase of the matching task both did require capacity (p. 407).

The results described earlier point up problems with these inferences. First, the idea of shared capacity, which is assumed rather than tested in probe RT studies, is itself questionable. Second, the probe method usually involves simple RT, so the peculiar sensitivities of that task, especially to temporal uncertainty, could masquerade as evidence of capacity limits (Goodrich et al, 1990). Third, the task allows fairly long periods of empty time, so people may alter their preparation for the probe task, again producing changes that could be mistaken for a change in capacity allocation. Nonetheless, the conclusions reached by Posner and Boies are broadly similar to those from PRP experiments involving choice tasks. The concept of response phase, however, would seem to include both choosing and carrying out responses, activities that, according to PRP studies, play quite different roles in dual-task performance.

Subsequent studies using the probe RT method challenged Posner and Boies' conclusions. Instead of presenting the sample letter for a full half-second of view, Comstock (1973) presented it briefly followed by a mask (100-msec SOA), and found that this produced an abrupt increase in probe RTs when the probe was presented 100 msec after the letter. This is not necessarily inconsistent with Posner and Boies' conclusion that encoding did not require central capacity, since when they expect a mask, people might begin generating test features immediately.

The possible capacity demands of perceptual processing were also addressed in a probe RT study reported by Thompson (1987) in which the primary task involved visual search rather than matching. Subjects searched an array either for a single feature or for a conjunction of features (primary task). They did not have to make any immediate response to the array; they simply had to remember it, and after 2 seconds a pair of target alternatives appeared from which the subjects chose. The RTs to probes presented at the time of the display or 50 msec after it were elevated to some fairly small degree. However, given that simple RT is elevated by a previous stimulus that does not require any response at all (R. Davis, 1959), the results (or similar findings, such as those of Johnson et al, 1983) do not make any strong case for central demands of the search process itself. It is less surprising that when a visual search task does require an immediate response, probe RT is elevated (Logan, 1978a).

Actually *producing* a manual reaching response also delays concurrent manual probe RTs more than it delays concurrent vocal probe RTs (McLeod, 1980), consistent with suggestions above regarding modality-specific conflicts. In summary, the results of the probe studies are consistent with the conclusions from PRP studies. In fact, if those conclusions are correct, the bottleneck to which the PRP effect has been attributed must surely be a major cause of slowing in probe RT studies as well. Since the order of responding and the relationship between probe and primary-task RTs are not examined on a trial-to-trial basis, however, this conjecture cannot be assessed from published data.

Bottleneck Theories
With respect to bottleneck models, the results described above are clearly supportive, confirming that central processing operations including response selection are often subject to a bottleneck. However, as noted, results of studies have not yet proved that this bottleneck is a fixed, structural feature of the information-processing system. They also intimate that production of finger and foot movements may sometimes be subject to what appears to be a separate response-execution bottleneck. The conclusion that there is a central bottleneck that arises in selection of action should not, of course, be confused with the early and late selection debate described in chapter 1. The finding that people seem unable to select two responses at the same time does not dispute the fact that they also have limitations in perceptual processing and, in addition, have available the option of excluding stimuli from perceptual analysis. The relationship between the central bottleneck and these other aspects of attention are discussed later in this chapter.

Crosstalk and Task Similarity
Data from studies of simple tasks show that two tasks do not have to be similar in any obvious way to interfere with each other. For example, pressing a button depending on the pitch of a tone is not in any obvious

way similar to naming the highest digit in a display (Pashler, 1989, experiment 3) or to verbalizing the response element of a set of paired-associate words (Carrier and Pashler, 1995), or to moving the eye one direction if a central color patch is red and another direction if the patch is green (Pashler, Carrier, and Hoffman, 1993). Similarly, making a foot response to a tone and making a hand response to a letter seem intuitively dissimilar (Osman and Moore, 1993). In each of these cases, however, reducing the interval between the stimuli increased RTs for the second task. Therefore, attributing all dual-task interference to crosstalk, or to some optional strategy chosen to prevent crosstalk, does not seem promising.

But even if crosstalk is not the sole cause of dual-task interference, it might sometimes modulate the magnitude of interference. Indeed, there is little doubt that task similarity can exacerbate interference. Navon and Miller (1987) created two tasks that dealt with semantically overlapping materials and observed disruption. The tasks required searching two words on one diagonal for a boy's name and searching another display for a city name. In the dual-task condition, responses in task A were slower when the distractor in task B was a target in task A (or was semantically associated with it). Hirst and Kalmar (1987) had subjects monitor dichotically presented speech that consisted of sequences of words, letters, or numbers on each channel. For example, one task required verifying that a sequence of letters correctly spelled out a pre-specified target word, or verifying that each number in a sequence was equal to the previous number plus two. When the same type of task was performed on both channels (e.g., verifying one number sequence on the left and another on the right), subjects performed much worse than when a different task was performed on each channel.

These manipulations of similarity are obviously rather extreme, and for this reason they may not say much about the role of similarity in more ordinary situations. Hirst and Kalmar's task required holding onto the accumulated partial results of each task in short-term memory, and similarity is known to impair short-term memory (Baddeley, 1966). The use of similar distractors in Navon and Miller's task may fundamentally change the task from searching for words from a particular category to the more difficult task of searching for words satisfying a conjunction of semantic and spatial features.

Does a more moderate increase in the similarity of content in two tasks modulate interference? Some data reported by Pashler and O'Brien (1993), although not collected for that purpose, suggest that it may not. In several experiments, the first stimulus was a disk presented either above or below the fixation point, to which the subject responded by pressing one of two response keys arrayed in a corresponding fashion, using fingers of the left hand. In one case the second task involved making a righthand response to a disk (identical task) and in another it entailed responding to the identity of a letter, also using the right hand (different task). There was little difference in the extent of interference (PRP effect). At the moment, then, there is no sign in studies of discrete tasks that similarity exacerbates dual-task interference except when the similarity transforms the tasks or when the tasks require storing and accessing information from short-term memory.

This brings us back to the distinction noted earlier between the molar-level description of behavior in which a task is something like driving or having a conversation, and the microlevel description of information processing operations occurring over short time spans. Similarity may matter most for concurrent performance of molar-level tasks, which, it has been proposed, probably relies heavily on switching. People may be able to switch into and out of an activity quite smoothly as long as these activities do not write on top of the memory stores that hold information necessary for one or other activity. For this reason, similarity may be a key determinant of performance whenever people switch back and forth between tasks. This may be one reason why similarity has important effects in laboratory studies of continuous task performance[15] and, one suspects, in real-world dual-task performance also, despite the fact that its effects are hard to demonstrate with combinations of discrete laboratory tasks.

These suggestions may possibly help to illuminate the well-known experiments carried out by Lee Brooks (1968, 1970). In one task, people held a sentence in memory (a bird in the hand is not in the bush) and reported whether or not each word in the sentence was a noun. When responses were made verbally (no, yes, no, no, yes, . . .), the task was very difficult, much more so than if responses were made manually. Evidently, formulating verbal responses interfered substantially with the articulatory/verbal STM representation of the sentence. Similarly, people have little difficulty making a series of spatial judgments about an image of a block letter and reporting these judgments verbally, but using a spatial mode of report produces interference in this case. In an interesting extension of Brooks' work, Saariluoma (1992) showed that concurrent articulation had little effect on chess players' ability to judge whether checkmate was imminent on a displayed chess board, whereas a variation of Brooks's spatial letter task proved very disruptive. It seems that similarity and overlap of codes can indeed be a severe problem when the contents of STM must be consulted repeatedly. These factors are likely, therefore, to be of special importance for practical issues in the design of human-machine systems.

Neural Theories

Various writers have suggested that hemispheric specialization may have strong implications for people's ability to perform two tasks at the same time. For example, Friedman and Polson (1981) proposed a multiple-resources model according to which "the left and right hemispheres together form a system of two mutually inaccessible and finite pools of resources" (p. 1031). In this rather extreme view, when a person tries to carry out two tasks simultaneously and each task requires resources from a separate hemisphere, one should not expect to find interference. A related idea is the functional distance theory (Kinsbourne, 1981; Kinsbourne and Hicks, 1978) that proposes that two tasks can be combined most efficiently when they are carried out by brain areas that are functionally distant, with the two hemispheres being an extreme case of distant structures.

A number of experiments yielded results supporting these theories, manipulating cortical or hemispheric involvement by varying the nature of the processing required or the laterality of presentation or response. When one examines these studies, one notices that at least one task (and usually both) do not require independent response choice. Consider some examples. Hiscock (1982) reported that reciting tongue twisters (presumably heavily left-hemisphere loaded) interfered more with righthanded tapping than with lefthanded tapping. Other studies confirmed similar patterns of effects on tapping combined with verbal and nonverbal tasks (Kee et al, 1986). Kinsbourne and Cook (1971) examined the effects of balancing a dowel on the right versus left index finger combined with a concurrent speaking task. Balancing times were longer in the verbal condition when the left hand was used compared with the right hand. Hellige, Cox, and Litvac (1979) found that holding a verbal memory load affected perception of brief lateralized displays in a way that the authors interpreted as showing that "the left hemisphere functions as a typical limited-capacity information processing system that can be influenced somewhat separately from the right hemisphere system" (p. 251).

Tasks such as tapping, holding memory loads, producing memorized speech, and the like would not expected to produce bottleneck-type interference, because they do not require decision making and planning of independent actions. It is not surprising, therefore, that the magnitude of the interference found with these tasks is generally quite modest. Kee, Hellige, and Bathurst (1983) found that concurrent verbal tasks decreased tapping rate by roughly 2% to 6%. When one focuses instead on PRP-type interference, where selection and production of two independent responses is required, there is no evidence for independent hemispheric functioning; presenting stimuli to and obtaining responses from different hemispheres does not reduce the PRP effect even slightly (Pashler and O'Brien, 1993).

How should one reconcile the findings of hemispheric effects in the cases described above with the absence of hemispheric effects in the PRP task? It appears that the central bottleneck may be central not only in the sense in which that term is used in information-processing psychology (to mean, roughly, modality-independent), but also in a neural sense. Nonetheless, Kinsbourne's cortical distance proposal may be essentially correct with regard to a wide variety of mental operations that do not involve decision making and response choice. For example, maintaining information in STM and producing preplanned motor responses may not cause queuing of other operations, but they may still be associated with a very mild, graded form of interference whose magnitude scales inversely with anatomical proximity of the brain regions involved.[16] The cortical distance principle may apply to those tasks that are truly carried out simultaneously, whereas the principles governing queuing seem indifferent to neural overlap of any sort studied thus far.

Evidence for another potential source of dual-task interference appears to be associated with a particular neural structure: competition for machinery specialized for timing. Based largely on observations involving patients who suffered cerebellar damage, Ivry and colleagues (Ivry and Keele, 1989; Ivry and Hazeltine, 1995) maintained that the cerebellum may provide timing functions that are critical for both controlling movement and perceiving temporal intervals. According to their analysis, the cerebellum provides what amounts to a single programmable interval timer that can be recruited for a variety of perceptual and motor functions. Several kinds of dual-task evidence would seem to be consistent with such a proposal. For example, producing a rhythmic series of finger movements impairs production of other sequences with harmonically unrelated rhythms (Klapp, 1979), which one would expect if there is only a single timer. Furthermore, tapping a rhythm interferes with people's ability to judge the rhythm of a sequence of unrelated sounds (Klapp et al., 1985). Tasks that require accurate response timing but lack response uncertainty (e.g., finger tapping) do not seem to interfere substantially with tasks that require response selection; this suggests that the hypothesized interval timer is basically independent of the central response-selection bottleneck.

Continuous versus Discrete Performance
Near the beginning of this section it was pointed out that studies of continuous tasks, which commonly were assumed to support graded capacity sharing and, in some cases, automaticity, cannot provide critical tests of such models. The reason for this is that they provide little evidence about the time course of processing. It was also noted that smooth tradeoffs between tasks as revealed in AOC functions are consistent with time sharing, as a bottleneck model would imply, as well as with graded resource sharing. The primary motivation for focusing on punctate tasks and the PRP effect was because here one can analyze the temporal dimension of dual-task performance in some detail.

The extensive evidence for a central bottleneck in punctate dual-task performance is obviously consistent with the idea that dual-task performance in continuous tasks might often reflect central switching, but it falls well short of proving it. Apparently continuous[17] tasks might differ from punctate tasks in some fundamental way that makes it inappropriate to generalize from punctate to continuous tasks. It seems conceivable, for example, that performing a discrete task actually induces a different mode of interference from a task that is performed repeatedly in close temporal succession. One might imagine that punctate stimulation seizes resources to a more extreme degree than would be the case in a continuous task (Neumann, 1987). Evidence useful in assessing such possibilities is provided by intriguing work carried out in the 1960s by J. W. H. Kalsbeek and colleagues in the Netherlands, work that has been unfortunately neglected by recent investigators, including the present author. Schouten, Kalsbeek, and Leopold (1960) analyzed continuous tasks in a way that seems particularly revealing from the perspective of a bottleneck theory. They trained subjects on a primary task that involved pressing a left or right foot pedal depending on the pitch of a tone (2000 or 250 Hz). After each subject was familiar with the task, the researchers determined the maximum rate at which he or she could perform it with a fixed (very low) error rate. In dual-task experiments, this primary task was combined with an interesting array of secondary tasks, always with the instruction that the subject should maintain performance on the primary task while attempting to perform the secondary ones. During dual-task observation intervals, the rate at which stimuli for the primary task were presented was varied from 0% up to 100% of the subject's single-task maximum.

When the secondary task required sequential motor behaviors requiring relatively little responses choice (e.g., putting nuts and washers on screws), people were able to perform it at near its maximum rate (about 20% decrease). When the secondary task required responding vocally with the sum of two visually presented numbers, however (e.g., 4 + 7 = ?), performance was cut in half as the rate of the primary task was increased up to its maximum. The investigators also tried as the secondary task the Porteus maze test, a nonverbal test sometimes used to measure IQ. When the rate of the primary task was increased, numerous errors occurred in the test, including many that one would have to judge intellectual rather than motoric. Dual-task performance reduced one subject's mental age from the adult range to 8 years, as assessed by the Porteus test. Figure 6.9 shows a typical record obtained with another

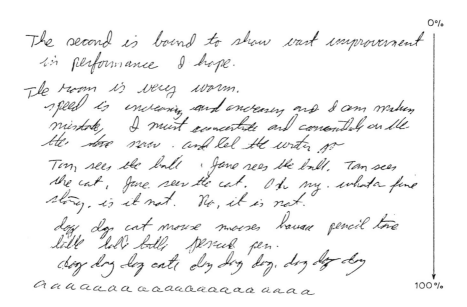

Figure 6.9
Step-by-step disintegration of writing provoked by increasing the rate of a con-current task, which required footpedal responses to high and low tones. The range from 0% to 100% (top to bottom) refers to the percent of the maximum number of tones per minute the subject was able to respond to without making more than two errors; at 50% rate, for example, tones would be presented at half the subject's maximum rate. Reprinted from Kalsbeek and Sykes (1967, figure 2), with permission.

secondary task, termed spontaneous handwriting; both content and writing style become more primitive as the primary task rate is increased. Substantial reductions in performance rate were also found when the primary task required making key press responses to lights and the tone-foot pedal task served as the secondary task (Kalsbeek and Sykes, 1967). As Kalsbeek and co-workers observed, these various results seem entirely consistent with the idea that the primary task occupies central decision-making machinery, and that residual performance reflects inter-digitated (and often inadequate) access to this machinery on the part of the secondary task.

Using a slightly different approach, Gladstones, Regan, and Lee (1989) examined the rate at which people could perform serial tasks paced by the experimenter (e.g., pressing a key in response to the position of a light, or saying a, b, or c in response to the color of a light). In some conditions, subjects performed just a single serial task, and in others they performed two concurrent serial tasks. The investigators determined the maximum rate at which subjects could perform these tasks at a fixed high level of accuracy. Using an information-theoretic measure of bits per second, they assessed the rate at which information was processed in the different task combinations. The basic finding was that the total rate at which information was processed was the same whether one task was performed or two. This finding held up over a considerable extent of training, and regardless of whether the tasks used the same or different input and output modalities. Fortunately, the interpretation of this result does not hinge on the (arguable) use of bits per second as a measure of processing rate.[18] Because subjects performed at similarly high levels of accuracy across conditions, the result amounts to the observation that total response rate was roughly the same in both dual- and single-task conditions: in one experiment, subjects produced roughly one response per 700 msec in the single-task condition, and two responses per 1400 msec in the dual-task condition.

This equivalence is roughly (although not exactly) predicted by a central bottleneck theory together with a further assumption that is discussed in the next section: that the central bottleneck prevents over-lapping selection of two successive responses in a single serial task. If this is correct, the maximum rate at which a serial task can be performed accurately will be achieved when each response selection commences just as selection of the preceding response is completed. To put it slightly differently, at the maximum rate of performance, selection of responses will be rate limiting, whereas other stages may sometimes overlap. When two serial tasks (call them A and B) are combined, according to the central bottleneck theory, selection of a response in either task will naturally have to wait whenever a response in one or the other task is being selected. Therefore, the rate at which responses will be produced will again be limited by the rate of response selections. When two serial tasks of comparable difficulty are combined, this should result in ap-proximately equal rates in both single- and dual-task conditions, as Gladstones observed.[19] Thus, the authors' contention that their findings provide support for a central bottleneck in continuously performed serial tasks can be confirmed without assuming that bits per second is a proper measure of human information processing. To put it crudely, a bottleneck in response selection predicts an upper limit on the rate at which responses can be selected (and hence produced) in one task or two, as Gladstones et al observed.

In another neglected contribution, Fisher (1975a, b) combined a serial task with an intermittent task involving simple mental arithmetic. In the serial task, subjects made compatible manual responses to visual stimuli; each response triggered a new stimulus almost instantaneously. The arithmetic task required adding seven to each intermittently presented spoken digit and saying the sum aloud. Almost unique among investigators of serial performance, Fisher analyzed the temporal relationship between responding in the two tasks. The speed of the a manual response was heavily dependent on its relationship to the digit responses, with marked slowing of the first manual response after each digit response. Fisher took this to be strong evidence for task switching.

In summary, scattered through the literature are some neglected experiments that involve continuous or relatively continuous performance and which suggest that the central bottleneck is not restricted to tasks involving pairs of isolated punctate stimuli. It is a reasonable working hypothesis that the same fundamental limitations in decision and response choice govern a wide range of human performance, including relatively continuous performance. Although these kinds of tasks are harder to analyze than punctate tasks, the results described here suggest that progress can be made.

Why a Central Bottleneck?

The conclusion that certain central mental operations are often forced to queue up is not particularly obvious or intuitive. Why should it be the case? Although it is not possible to answer the question definitively, several hypotheses deserve consideration. One natural suggestion is that the problem arises not because selecting two different responses at the same time is demanding, but rather because people have trouble maintaining the set to carry out the selection (this might be termed the *set-limitation hypothesis*). It was already stated that when people must prepare two tasks at the same time, responses to either task alone are slowed somewhat, but not to the same extent as when both tasks must be carried out on the same trial (see figure 6.3). The set-limitation hypothesis could potentially be reconciled with this, however: in the experiments shown in figure 6-3, people shift into the appropriate set fairly quickly; perhaps in the PRP experiments they cannot switch into one set while carrying out a task relying on the other set.

A better test of the set limitation hypothesis can be constructed, however. If the bottleneck occurs because of inability to keep two mappings prepared at the same time, response selection should no longer constitute a bottleneck when two or more tasks use the same mapping but different stimuli. One experimental paradigm in which the mapping remains constant while the stimuli change is the serial RT task just described. Here the subject responds to a whole run of stimuli, with the appearance of a stimulus triggered by a response. In one recent study, subjects carried out a self-paced serial task either with or without preview (Pashler, 1994b). In the no-preview condition, subjects did not see stimulus n+1 until they responded to stimulus n. In the preview condition, stimulus n+1 was made available even before the subjects responded to stimulus n. Potentially, then, people could begin processing stimulus n+1 while they were generating a response to stimulus n, as in the PRP task. The rate of responding was faster in the preview condition compared with the no-preview condition (first noted by Cattell, 1886). This implies that some overlap does indeed occur.

To determine which stages overlapped, several task difficulty manipulations were varied, selectively slowing perception, response selection, or response production. When response selection was made harder for the whole run of ten stimuli, the time between each response in the run was increased, and to the same extent with preview or without. On the other hand, making perceptual processing more difficult increased the time between the first stimulus and the first response, but did not thereafter affect the rate of responding. In short, preview swallowed up perceptual slowing in all responses beyond the first, just as the PRP task swallows up perceptual slowing in task 2, as described earlier. The results can be summarized by saying that response selection, but not perception, is rate limiting for serial performance even when stimuli are made available well before they are needed, indicating by reasoning identical to that described in principles 3 and 4 that only one response can be selected at a time. Figure 6.10 shows a model of the stages of processing occurring with

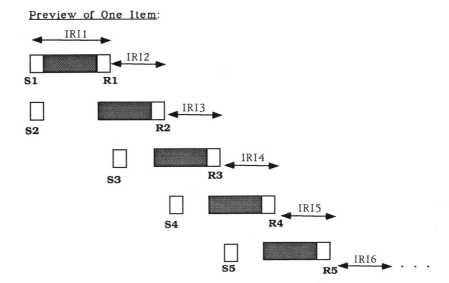

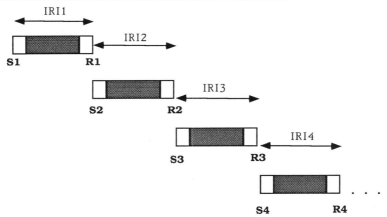

Figure 6.10
Proposed timing of mental operations in serial RT with and without preview. As in figure 6.4, bottleneck prevents shaded stages of response selection from overlapping, while unshaded stages are not so constrained. With preview of one (top panel), perceptual and response production stages overlap; consequently, inter-response intervals (IRI2, IRI3, etc.) have the same duration as response selection, and only shaded stages (plus perception of first stimulus) are rate-limiting. Without preview (bottom panel), each IRI is the sum of duration of all stages, and all stages are rate-limiting. Reprinted with permission from Pashler (1994d, figure 2).

and without preview that predicts these results very naturally; with preview, perceptual factors cease to be rate limiting, while response selection (shaded) remains so.

What can be concluded from this? Since the bottleneck in selecting responses is still present when stimulus-response mapping is fixed, it cannot result from an inability to keep two different mappings prepared at the same time. The set-limitation hypothesis is rejected. It appears, then, that the dual-task bottleneck results from inability actually to carry out the selection of two responses at the same time. Interesting early results of Jersild (1927) suggest, however, that in one situation people cannot keep two task mappings prepared at once: when the two mappings are in some sense contradictory. Consider a task in which a person must read aloud the first number on a list of numbers, add six to the second number and say that, then read aloud the third number, and so on, alternating between reading and adding. Jersild found that such an alternation requirement added hundreds of extra milliseconds to the time required to process each item on the list, compared with performing the same task over and over. The results were recently replicated and extended by Allport, Styles, and Hsieh (1994).

One way to understand these results is the following. Suppose people *can* keep two task mappings prepared in the ordinary PRP task as long as the combined mapping is a *function*, as mathematicians use that term (any single stimulus is mapped onto only a single response). When the combined mapping is not a function, however, a switch of set will be required. When a combined mapping is a function and therefore can be prepared, as in a dual-task experiment, the complexity of the combined mapping still carries a cost, resulting in additional slowing beyond that attributable to the central bottleneck (see figure 6.3). In the ordinary PRP situation, both tasks are probably affected. This preparatory cost also provides a plausible explanation for something that has puzzled PRP investigators for a long time: R2 is often slowed compared with a single-task control, even when S2 is presented after R1 has occurred. Welford (1952) explained this by supposing that the central bottleneck mechanism took time out to monitor feedback after the execution of the response. However, this seems unlikely with responses like key presses, given that adding more key presses in the first task response has so little effect on the second response time (Pashler and Christian, 1996). Dual-task performance is likely to be slower than single-task control performance simply because the situation requires preparing the mappings for both tasks.

Studies involving single-task performance disclose that preparation depends on the complexity of the mapping and suggest that preparatory state changes rather slowly. Dixon (1981) and Sudevan and Taylor (1987), for example, found that subjects took hundreds of milliseconds to use cues about upcoming stimulus-response alternatives. Logan and Zbrodoff (1982) cued subjects about the optimal strategy to use in a choice RT task, and found that it required 400 to 600 msec for maximum benefits of the cue to be achieved. Consistent with these findings is the fact that, in the PRP situation, a gradual decline in RT2 is often observed out to very long SOAs of more than 1 second, and, as noted above, asymptote is not usually reached even when S2 follows R1. This suggests that the state of preparation for the second task usually changes quite slowly.

In addition to dual-task and alternating-task experiments, this preparatory limitation is likely to show up in various single-task designs. Consider a choice RT task that maps a single stimulus onto a single response, for example. As the number of stimulus-response alternatives increases, so too does the RT (Hick, 1952). This increase depends on the number of alternatives that the subject must prepare for, rather than the number of different alternatives the person has been exposed to during the current block of trials (Dixon, 1981). It seems reasonable to suppose that when people must prepare a larger number of different stimulus-response links, they cannot prepare as fully, and performance is therefore slowed (Gottsdanker, 1980; Logan, 1979). This still leaves open the question of exactly how poor preparation affects execution of a task; that is, what stage(s) are affected and in what way (e.g., are they slowed, or is their onset delayed?). Experiments involving concurrent memory loads, discussed below, provide some clues.

The fact that some dual-task slowing can be attributed to limitations in preparing the tasks has important methodological implications. The first is that, for many purposes, single-task performance is an inappropriate baseline against which to compare dual-task interference. As McLeod (1977) first commented, it is often more useful to compare performance at short and long SOAs when the goal is to determine which mental events can operate at the same time. Another useful control is described in figure 6.3.

A second implication is that one must use caution in interpreting the effects of variables that change the amount of preparation a subject has to carry out. For example, increasing the number of alternatives in task 2 might affect RTs in task 1 by impairing preparation rather than, or in addition to, actual task performance. In that case, the factor should slow task 1 even when the SOA is long enough that the first task is finished before the second stimulus has even been presented. For this reason, variables that can be manipulated in mixed-list designs (e.g., intensity, compatibility) should generally be preferred to between-block manipulations.

Practice or Difficulty
Another fairly natural idea is that response selection might constitute a bottleneck because this stage has received less consistent practice than other stages. This is supported by the general assumption (quite unproved, it will be maintained in chapter 7) that consistent practice produces genuine automaticity, including elimination of capacity demands. In some tasks one might argue that response selection is the least practiced component of the task. For example, in tasks involving a button push response to the identity of a letter (Pashler and Johnston, 1989), people presumably have more experience reading the letter B or making a key press response with their index finger than they have recalling an association between the letter B and the idea of a left response. However, equally arbitrary and unpracticed visual operations like finding a color/form conjunction do not seem to be subject to the central bottleneck, either (Pashler, 1989). The intuitive concept of difficulty does not seem to help much, either. The central operations of response selection are so lacking in salience that most people can hardly be said to be aware of them,[20] much less aware of any difficulty associated with them; furthermore, few people would describe a two- or three-alternative forced-choice task as cognitively challenging.

If response choice is indeed subject to the stubborn processing bottleneck suggested by the studies described earlier, the question of why this should be the case is quite puzzling. As noted, it does not seem to be reducible either to limitations in task preparation or to commonsense concepts such as difficulty or (non)automaticity. At a psychological level, there may be no further explanation: the limitation may reflect neural structures or processes not reducible to any psychological principle. We recently observed that so-called split-brain patients (whose cerebral hemispheres were surgically disconnected) exhibit a normal PRP effect when carrying out two tasks whose input and output would seem to confine the tasks to separate hemispheres (Pashler et al., 1995). This implies that certain structures in the brain stem, which remain connected in these patients, may play a critical role in producing dual-task interference. These structures might conceivably carry out the mental functions that are subject to a bottleneck. More plausibly, they might implement a lockout process that temporarily suspends processing that may be distributed over various different brain regions. Such a lockout would not have to reflect the operation of an executive or controller; for this reason, the evidence that certain types of central mental operations cannot work at the same time need not contradict the contention of Allport (1980) that cognitive control is distributed (this problem is discussed further in chapter 8).

Whatever role subcortical structures play in the postponement of processing, the ultimate source of the inability to carry out memory retrievals and response choices in parallel may be in the neural underpinnings of these cognitive operations. One might speculate, for example, that the neural representation of something retrieved from memory (including a plan for an action) may not be activity in any handful of neurons, but rather a pattern of activity involving a great many widely distributed neurons. In that case, the inability to select two responses at once might stem from the fact that a given connected pool of neurons cannot settle simultaneously into two different patterns of activity. One behavioral observation that seems consistent with this account is that although use of two different stimuli to select two independent responses at the same time seems impossible, two stimuli do seem able to activate the same single response at the same time. Evidence for this can be seen in the speedup in choice reaction-time tasks produced by redundant stimulation, a phenomenon Miller (1982) aptly termed coactivation (e.g., when either a high tone or a letter A tells the subject to press the right key, responses are much faster when the high tone and the letter A are presented, compared with either one alone). The equivalent of coactivation is seen over much greater time scales in people's ability to use several cues to retrieve a desired item in permanent memory. An obvious example is solving crossword puzzles, but just about any difficult memory retrieval, and seemingly much of our higher mental processes, would be impossible without this capability.

If one thinks of information retrieval as it occurs in a digital computer or a file system, it seems paradoxical to suppose that two inputs can be used simultaneously to fetch one output, but not two different outputs (how do the fetching mechanisms know if the two fetches are going to end up with one file or two?). However, if outputs are really incompatible states of the same system, the paradox may be dissolved: if each input drives the system toward the same state, coactivation may occur; if each drives them toward different states, queuing will be necessary if both output are to be retrieved.

Selecting Multiple Responses

The discrete stimulus-response tasks described in this chapter are similar to activities that people undertake outside the laboratory, but at the same time they obviously differ in important ways from typical real-world performance. When one watches a musician, a tennis player, or a cook, for example, it is difficult to identify discrete stimuli and responses, if indeed there are any. The stimuli that trigger action in such cases may often consist of dynamic events rather than individual static visual or kinesthetic inputs. Furthermore, to the extent one can successfully break a task down into stimulus-response links, the response often appears to be a series of coordinated behaviors involving different effectors. For example, a volleyball player reaches for a ball with both hands at the same time, and a musician may simultaneously sing a note and use both hands to strum a chord. The obviously coordinated nature of these actions raises a challenge to the bottleneck analysis proposed here. What happens when several different motions are produced in response to a single stimulus? Does each motion require a distinct response selection operation? If so, should one expect to find bottleneck-type interference between the selection of each component? Clark Fagot and I (1992) investigated this issue in an admittedly austere context, using tasks in which a single visual stimulus triggered both a vocal and a manual choice response. In some of the experiments subjects would press one of several buttons depending on the color of a square while naming that color out loud. If the square was red, they might say "red" and press the middle response key; if it was green they might say "green" and press the right response key, and so on.

In this coupled dual-response task, we found little evidence of dual-task interference at all; subjects made each of the responses almost as quickly as in a single-task condition. They also showed an extremely high correlation across trials between RTs for the two responses. These two facts naturally suggest that the two responses were selected and produced as a unit. This interpretation was supported by the effects of manipulating the time required to choose each response. One manipulation slowed the manual response selection by making the position of the stimulus and the relative spatial position of the button incompatible (usually termed the Simon effect). The Simon effect does not ordinarily show up in vocal response latencies, but in the coupled dual-response task it slowed both the manual and the vocal response, and to almost exactly the same degree. In a similar way the Stroop effect, which ordinarily slows vocal responses much more than manual responses, delayed both manual and vocal responses in the coupled dual-response task. These results reveal that the manual and vocal responses were selected as a single response unit, even though the two actions were not likely to have been associated in any way prior to the experiment. This suggests a remarkable flexibility to response selection. It may correspond in certain ways to what computer scientists call a production system architecture (Anderson, 1976; Logan, 1980). That is, the individual may prepare relatively arbitrary condition-action linkages ("if these conditions arise, perform actions $A_1, \ldots,$ and A_n"), where the list of actions may encompass unrelated responses ("say 'red' and press middle key").

The ability to plan several different actions as a unit, even though they involve different effector systems, may help reconcile people's evident ability to produce several actions close together in time with the idea of a central bottleneck in response planning. Another element helps recon-cile these two ideas, however. As described earlier, even in a conventional PRP task, two responses that were selected asynchronously may overlap in their execution, particularly when the first-selected response takes a long time to complete. Thus, someone drinking coffee and having a conversation might plan to move the coffee cup up to their lips, then plan an utterance and even finish saying it before the coffee cup has reached the lips. Given these considerations, therefore, the existence of a bottle-neck in action planning should not lead one to expect that people would produce motions in a jerky, sequential fashion, like robots in early science fiction movies. There is obviously a great deal more to be learned, however, about the relationship between the fluent coordination of be-havioral streams one sees outside the laboratory and the interference in discrete choice responses that is revealed in the laboratory.

Central and Perceptual Capacity Limits

The central bottleneck analysis suggested by the PRP experiments claims that perceptual processing in task 2 will often occur in parallel with central processing in task 1 (as in figure 6.4). This claim of independence makes clear predictions for experiments in which accuracy rather than latency is used as the primary dependent measure. If people can perceive one stimulus while they are choosing a response to another, they should be able to do so even when the first stimulus appears briefly and disap-pears; perception should commence immediately. Figure 6.11 shows an experiment that tested this prediction. A display of characters was pre-sented briefly and replaced by a mask, abruptly terminating perceptual processing. Subjects made a speeded response to a tone and searched the visual display for a target; after the speeded response and at their leisure, they indicated whether or not they found a target (Pashler, 1989). As predicted, the accuracy of visual search was essentially the same whether the SOA was long (no overlap) or very short (requiring perceptual analy-sis of the display to overlap with response selection in the tone task). This result held even with what one would suppose to be especially difficult search tasks involving feature conjunction targets (see chapter 3) or requiring the subject to find the highest of an array of digits. The result

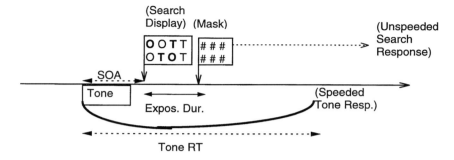

Figure 6.11
Method for testing independence of perceptual analysis (searching for green O in display of green Ts and red Os) and concurrent choice RT task involving a speeded response to a tone. At short stimulus-onset asynchronies (SOAs), the display and mask that follow it occur while the tone task is performed; at long SOAs, the tone task is usually complete before the display appears. Accuracy of the unspeeded response to visual display is nonetheless comparable in the two conditions (tone responses are sometimes faster at short SOAs).

was replicated in subsequent unpublished experiments. Subjects were required to search several successively exposed frames of characters rather than just a single frame followed by a mask, so the effects do not seem likely to reflect ineffectiveness of the mask in terminating perceptual processing.

These results seem to confirm the independence of perceptual processing and central processing reflected in the central bottleneck theory. One might object, however, that the tone task is easy. Intuitively speaking, this may be so, but recall that it is quite sufficient to postpone central processing in unrelated choice tasks. Indeed, this was demonstrated within the set of experiments just described by including a condition in which the display remained available and subjects were required to name the highest digit aloud as fast as possible. In this case, the timing of the tone and the digit display affected task 2 RTs as one might expect (PRP effect). In summary, when one combines speeded responses to tones with unspeeded responses to brief masked visual stimuli, accuracy measurements suggest that the perception of the visual stimuli is not delayed by the speeded task.

Intuition would suggest, however, that the independence of perception and central processing (more generally, seeing and thinking) cannot be as total as the experiments discussed thus far would suggest. For example, one would surely hesitate to advise a radar operator scanning for an incoming plane and a hunter staring at a distant hillside that they could safely do square roots in their head with no cost to their primary task. Although no one has examined these exact situations, several dual-task experiments provide a reasonably good analogue to them, combining relatively complex concurrent tasks that last many seconds with perceptual monitoring of some kind. Consider a study performed by Kahneman, Beatty, and Pollack (1967). In their perceptual task, subjects saw a sequence of letters presented at a rate of five letters per second and reported whether they thought a K was presented in the sequence. The concurrent task involved adding one to every digit of a spoken four-digit number (so 4236 would bring the response 5347). Subjects detected 88.5% of the Ks when they did nothing but monitor for Ks, but only 68.5% when performing the concurrent arithmetic (the arithmetic task suffered as well).

How can this dual-task interference be reconciled with the lack of interference between central and perceptual operations found in the punctate tasks described earlier? One factor that may be critical is preparation. Even easy perceptual tasks such as finding Ks must require mental preparation (after all, if one was not instructed to look for Ks, one would have no reason to spot them rather than any other letters). This state of preparedness may diminish over time if it is not actively maintained or refreshed. Even if a concurrent task involving thinking does not prevent a person from carrying out a perceptual task that has been prepared, it may still prevent preparation for a perceptual task from being refreshed and maintained. An experiment that Johnston and I carried out supports this conjecture (Pashler and Johnston, submitted). The two tasks were making a button push response to a tone and finding a digit target in a display of letters followed by a mask, tasks found to generate no mutual interference in the experiments described earlier. When subjects heard a single tone and then saw the display, accuracy in the digit task was essentially unaffected by temporal overlap; that is, subjects did just about as well when they were near simultaneously as when they were separated by a considerable lag, replicating earlier results (Pashler, 1989). When subjects had to respond to a whole series of tones, on the other hand, with each tone sounding shortly after the response to the previous one, accuracy in the digit task fell substantially. More interesting, though, was the fact that there was still no strong relationship between temporal overlap of the tasks and performance; thus, we found no evidence that the tone task delayed any stage of processing in the letter detection task.

A natural interpretation of these results is as follows. When the tone task must be done over and over, the state of preparation for the digit task dissipates, causing accuracy on that task to fall; however, when the time comes to carry out the digit task, it does not use the same machinery as the tone task, and performance remains independent. The following analogy, though admittedly contrived, may be somewhat helpful. Imagine two mousetraps that have a peculiar defect: after they are set, they slowly fall back into a relaxed state after, say, 30 seconds. If a person wanted to keep two such traps set in different parts of the house, it would be difficult to do so. However, by running back and forth fast enough, the person might manage to keep the traps at least partially set at the same time. In that case, the defect in the traps would not help two mice who happened to walk into the traps at the same time: each trap would fire off completely independent of the other trap and of the trap tender. Along the same lines, in the experiment of Kahneman et al, the arithmetic task may have prevented the subjects from periodically reminding themselves that they had to look for Ks; the actual performance of the arithmetic task may not have directly affected the perception of the letters, as Kahneman and colleagues assumed.[21]

So far we have discussed the question of whether response selection can overlap with perceptual activity of various sorts. This brings us back to the issue of perceptual capacity limits. As described in chapter 3, ample evidence shows that when two or more perceptual tasks are combined and they are difficult enough, capacity limits are often exceeded and performance suffers. For example, if a person must read two words that are flashed briefly and simultaneously, accuracy may suffer greatly (Kahneman and Treisman, 1984). Does this limitation reflect the same capacity limit as the central bottleneck that emerges in the dual-response tasks? If the preceding analysis is correct, one would suspect not. Many theorists have reasoned to the contrary, however. Posner (1982) proposed that a central executive might carry out all kinds of operations (central and perceptual) whenever these operations become difficult enough.

Several findings argue quite strongly against that account, however, and demonstrate that when perceptual limitations do emerge, their source is quite separate from the central bottleneck. Some of this evidence comes from experiments in which two tasks both involved fairly difficult visual discriminations (Pashler, 1989). First, perceptual interference remains constant whether the response in one task must be produced immediately or can be selected later. When the response is delayed, neither response selection nor response execution is forced to take place concurrently with the other task. If there were only one pool of limited capacity, postponing it should greatly alleviate the dual-task interference seen in accuracy measures, but it has no such effect. Second, when task 1 requires a speeded response, the speed with which R1 actually occurs is essentially uncorrelated with task 2 accuracy. That is, trial-to-trial variation in the speed of R1 does not predict task 2 accuracy. If perceptual analysis of stimulus 2 were delayed by processing in task 1, then slower task 1 responses should have been associated with poorer accuracy in task 2. Third, capacity limits involved whenever two perceptual detections occur at the same time (Duncan, 1980b) are circumvented when the detections pertain to two attributes of a single object (Duncan, 1984); on the other hand, the magnitude of bottleneck-based interference (PRP effect) seems unchanged (Fagot and Pashler, 1992). Speaking roughly, one might say that perceptual capacity limits involve competition between processing of different objects, whereas response-selection limitations depend on the number of responses to be chosen, irrespective of how many objects provide the input for these choices. All these results disclose that the central bottleneck implicated by the PRP studies must be altogether separate from the perceptual capacity limits discussed in chapters 3 and 5.

We can suggest some further conjectures, although these go well beyond what has so far been demonstrated. One is that the perceptual capacity limits might reflect graded sharing whereas the bottleneck mechanism generates only discrete queuing. As described earlier, most cognitive psychologists assumed that mental resources are all subject to graded sharing; although there is little evidence for this in the case of central limitations, it seems more plausible in the case of perceptual limitations. A second conjecture is that the allocation of perceptual capacity to stimuli may function on a catch-as-catch-can basis, with each stimulus grabbing what it can use; on the other hand, the order in which stimuli access the bottleneck may typically be prepared in advance (de Jong, 1995; Pashler, 1994d).

A final question to be discussed in this section concerns the relationship of the central bottleneck to the aspect of attention considered in chapter 2, the control of visual selective attention. Many theorists suggested that selecting a visual stimulus involves allocating general-purpose attentional resources to processing it; Kahneman (1973), for example, viewed perceptual attention and dual-task limitations as having a common source. From a very different perspective, some neuropsychologists proposed that attending to a position in (auditory or visual) space involves the machinery that plans actions relating to that location, such as manual reaching movements (e.g., Rizzolatti and Camarda, 1987). If action selection and stimulus selection depend on a single mechanism, tasks requiring response selection should delay shifts of visual attention in any concurrently performed task.

We examined this issue using hybrid tachistoscopic/speeded dual-task experiments that are again quite similar to the experiments shown in figure 6.11. The difference, however, was that the tachistoscopic task required a cued attention shift. As in the experiments described earlier, in each trial subjects made a speeded response to a tone and an unspeeded response to a visual display. The display contained a cue (e.g., an arrow) indicating the subject should shift attention to a particular element in the array and, at leisure, report this cued element. At short SOAs, the task had to be carried out concurrently with the tone task; at long SOAs, the tone task was usually finished before the display appeared. The effects of SOA were minimal, again indicating parallel processing (Pashler, 1991). This situation provided the opportunity to introduce a single-task control condition to test the assumption—critical to this experiment and also to the experiments shown in figure 6.11—that the masks abruptly terminate perception of the display (whether by interruption or integration). This assumption is required to conclude that attention shift takes place immediately. In the control condition, there was no tone task, and subjects had to identify the cued element in a display followed by a mask; however, the cue itself was delayed on some trials, thereby directly delaying the attention shift. Cue delay caused error rates to increase dramatically. This confirms that when an array is followed by a mask, a desired target item must be quickly read into short-term memory before the mask wipes it out. (The reader will note that the control condition essentially replicates the classic results of Averback and Coriell, 1961, and Sperling, 1960, using stimuli comparable to the other experiments in this series.)

The results discussed in this section strongly distinguish between two forms of attentional limitation: a central bottleneck that forces queuing of response selection and decision making, and perceptual capacity limits that arise with overloading in a given sensory modality. The results show that these limitations do not have a common origin, and they may differ in the other ways conjectured above. They also show that the allocation of visual selective attention, which determines which sensory information is most thoroughly analyzed, can be changed in response to cues without requiring the central bottleneck machinery.

Conclusions

Attentional limitations associated with planning of actions (and, it will emerge in the next chapter, a variety of cognitive operations) appear substantially less flexible than those involved in perceptual processing. The massive parallelism that characterizes at least the earliest aspects of perception and probably, although to a lesser extent, object recognition does not seem to extend to selection of responses. The findings described in this chapter provide further arguments for the inadequacy of the term attention as a theoretical construct. In ordinary talk we attribute limitations in perception, thought, and action to attention as if a common structure or process were responsible. When this assumption is tested, it seems to be false. For example, a person's attention for seeing can be available for new inputs while attention for action selection is completely occupied. This conclusion is consistent with suggestions of multiple resource theorists (e.g., Wickens, 1984) who proposed separate resource pools based on studies involving continuous rather than punctate tasks. However, the results involving punctate tasks (PRP effect) suggest that graded capacity allocation does not characterize the competition involving selection of actions and decision making. In the next chapter we extend these analyses to operations involved in memory storage and retrieval.

7

Attention and Memory

Structural Models of Memory: Empirical Evidence

Before examining the relationship between attention to memory, it will be helpful to review some basic facts about the structure of memory. Over the past thirty years or so, several different structural analyses of memory have been proposed and debated. These models were motivated by studies of normal individuals and also by observations involving people suffering from various kinds of brain damage and disease. The most famous structural theory is the "modal model," which grew out of the work of Waugh and Norman (1965) and Glanzer and Cunitz (1966); one well-known formulation of the modal model was proposed by Atkinson and Shiffrin (1968). The model distinguishes three types of memory systems: sensory, short-term, and long-term. This three-part scheme has been controversial since its inception, and this chapter starts off by examining the empirical evidence for and against it. The next structural theory discussed is a more recently proposed distinction between implicit or procedural memory and explicit or declarative memory. No attempt is made to cover the entire literature relevant to the merits of these structural theories. Instead, the goal is to assess their validity as a basis for examining how storage, encoding, and retrieval in memory depends on attentional control and attentional limitations (for more extensive discussions of structural theories of memory, see Baddeley, 1990; Pashler and Carrier, 1996).

Distinguishing Sensory Memory from Other Memory Systems

One key distinction proposed by the modal model is between sensory memory and other memory systems. Strong evidence exists for a boundary between visual sensory (iconic) memory, on the one hand, and short- and long-term memory, on the other. This evidence first emerged in the well-known partial-report studies of Sperling (1960) and Averbach and Coriell (1961), discussed in chapter 3. When people try to report as many letters or digits as possible from a brief display, they can rarely report more than four or five, whether the display is exposed for 1 msec or 1,000 msec. A partial-report probe reveals, however, that for several hundred milliseconds after the display offset, substantially more than four or five items are potentially available. The conventional account attributes this advantage of partial-report cueing to visual sensory memory, which is claimed to hold a great deal of information for a very short time. It has occasionally been argued that partial-report results can be accounted for without postulating a separate sensory memory system. As Coltheart (1975) pointed out, however, attempts to do this failed to offer any reasonable account of the basic observation that partial-report performance declines rapidly as the partial report probe is delayed.

Another source of evidence for the distinct status of iconic memory comes from the elegant studies of Phillips (1974, 1983) that assessed recognition memory for black and white matrix patterns that were designed to be difficult to represent verbally; subjects saw a pattern to memorize, and then, after some delay, a test pattern that might be identical or slightly altered. Phillips showed that people have excellent ability to detect changes in these patterns when the original and test patterns are separated by an extremely brief offset; this performance he attributed to iconic memory. When the test pattern is delayed by even several hundreds of milliseconds, however, performance becomes much more sensitive to the complexity of the pattern (reflecting capacity limitations), but also relatively less sensitive to interposition of a masking pattern during the retention interval, or spatial displacement of the test pattern relative to the original. Phillips explained this by proposing that visual short-term memory retains abstract pattern information over the longer offsets.

The experience of visible persistence may offer another argument for iconic memory. As Sperling and Helmholtz before him noted, when a person watches a brief display, he or she reports seeing a fading trace that lasts noticeably after the offset of a stimulus (e.g., Haber, 1969). By contrast, a short-term memory representation is not typically experienced as continued persistence of an actual percept. In sum, there is broad empirical support for a distinct visual sensory memory system, although, as pointed out in chapter 3, the functional significance of this system remains somewhat obscure.

The existence of an auditory sensory memory (frequently called echoic memory) that holds onto information for 1 or 2 seconds was first proposed by Broadbent (1958) and is generally accepted. However, the evidence for this structure is not quite as overwhelming as the evidence for iconic memory. The most frequently cited studies involved auditory partial report and were modeled after Sperling's experiment. In one study, words were spoken on three different channels created with dichotic inputs, one subjectively localized on the left, one in the middle, and one on the right (Darwin, Turvey, and Crowder, 1972). The results showed some partial-report advantage, but its magnitude was scarcely impressive: barely one extra item available in partial report compared with whole report. One might expect that speeding up the presentation might make the effect larger, but a similar study that used compressed speech found no partial-report advantage whatever (Holding, Foulke, and Heise, 1973). Another approach is to use nonspeech sounds, which may have the advantage of minimizing the role of verbal short-term memory. It should be noted, however, that there is evidence for short-term memory for nonspeech sounds (McFarland and Cacace, 1992). In any case, M. Treisman and Rostron (1972) performed a study using tones and found a partial-report advantage, but the effect was not particularly large in this case either.

Given these results, one is tempted to follow Massaro (1972) and question the existence of any high-capacity auditory sensory persistence lasting on the order of seconds. However, methods other than partial report do seem to support echoic persistence as usually conceived. The split-span results described in chapter 3 are one example. Another particularly clear example comes from Norman (1969), who interrupted people while they shadowed a message played to one ear, and found they had good access to the last few seconds' worth of material played to the other ear (this study is described in more detail below).

What is not clear, however, is why the partial-report technique produces small effects in the auditory domain. One possible explanation might be that the studies used messages spoken by the same voice, which undoubtedly impedes the initial storage and segregation of the information to some extent. In Norman's experiment, in contrast, one message was spoken by a man, the other by a woman. Another point to consider is that selection by position is not necessarily as effective in audition as it is in vision; as mentioned above, segregation by pitch may be more fundamental for auditory information than segregation by place of origin.

Distinguishing STM and LTM
According to the modal model, two types of memory systems hold information for much longer periods of time than do sensory memory systems: short-term memory and long-term memory (LTM). Original formulations of this model postulated a one-way flow of information from sensory to STM to LTM, and many envisioned a single STM that relied on verbal coding. Neither of these ideas remains viable, even though the fundamental distinction between short-term memory *systems* and long-term memory is eminently viable. We start by examining the evidence that favors a distinction between STM and LTM.

Anterograde Amnesia and Short-Term Memory Deficits   The strongest evidence for a distinguishing between STM and LTM comes from the phenomenon of anterograde amnesia. Patients with this disorder, often caused by illness damaging the medial temporal lobe and/or diencephalon, show a profound impairment in their ability to store new information and retrieve it after even a brief intervening distraction (Milner, 1958; see McCarthy and Warrington, 1990, for a review). However, their performance in digit and other span tasks is often normal, and in some cases truly exceptional (Wilson and Baddeley, 1988). Their short-term retention of visual and visuospatial information is typically normal as well (Haxby, Lundgren, and Morley, 1983). Many patients have no trouble having an intelligent conversation, which requires keeping various kinds of information active for short periods of time (e.g., the topic of the conversation, what has been said, etc.). Their difficulty apparently cannot stem from any loss of the machinery for retrieving information stored in long-term memory, because access to remote memories is often excellent. Rather, the problem seems confined to forming, storing, or consolidating new and enduring memory traces, with transfer into and out of STM being unimpaired. In normal individuals, diazepam (Valium) and other benzodiazepine drugs can produce what amounts to a mild version of this syndrome, reducing LTM storage while sparing performance in STM tasks (Mewaldt, Hinrichs, and Ghoneim, 1983).

Deficits involving a specific impairment in short-term memory storage for verbal information have also been reported (Vallar and Shallice, 1990). Shallice and Warrington (1970), for example, described a patient suffering from left hemisphere damage whose digit span was restricted to a few digits but who had no trouble with long-term retention of verbal materials. The fact that patients have so little difficulty in long-term tasks challenges the view of STM as a necessary way-station en route to LTM, suggesting that these two structures are better viewed as having a parallel rather than serial arrangement.[1]

Free Recall   Another well-known source of support for the STM/LTM distinction comes from what are usually called serial position functions in free recall experiments. Here, subjects hear a list of words, say, twenty or thirty items, and report as many as they can in any order they choose. Items near the beginning and end of the original list are recalled more accurately than others, resulting in what are called the *primacy* and *recency effects,* respectively. The recency effect, according to the conventional view, occurs because the last few items in the list are in STM at the time when recall begins (Glanzer and Cunitz, 1966). This interpretation is supported by the fact that when amnesic patients attempt a free recall task, they show excellent performance on the last few items, but very poor performance on the initial and middle items (figure 7.1; Baddeley and Warrington, 1970). When normals perform a counting task during the retention interval, this reduces recency but not primacy,

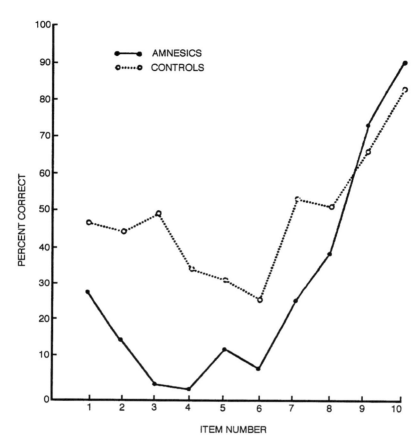

Figure 7.1
Mean percentage correct in an immediate free recall task for amnesic subjects (solid line) and normal controls (dotted line). Reprinted from Baddeley and Warrington (1970, figure 1, p. 179) with permission.

whereas speeding up the presentation rate of the list has just the opposite effect (Glanzer and Cunitz, 1966); both of these observations fit nicely with the conventional interpretation.

Critical Evaluation

In the past few years several authors strongly criticized the STM/LTM distinction (Crowder, 1993). Some of these criticisms fall short of being compelling. For example, some have pointed out that recency effects can be found not only in the standard free recall task, but also in recall tasks that use a retention interval much too long to have anything to do with STM (Bjork and Whitten, 1974; Baddeley and Hitch, 1977). The existence of such effects does not by itself disprove the STM explanation of the recency effect found in standard free recall, of course; last-presented items might enjoy various advantages in various tasks. Critics of the conventional two-store view suggest that acknowledging other types of recency not attributable to STM makes it unparsimonious to attribute the standard recency effect to STM (Crowder, 1993; Parkin, 1993).

One would have to give this argument some weight except for two key facts, which the critics have not dealt with. Brain-damaged patients with impaired memory span for verbal materials (attributable, in the standard view, to a deficit in verbal STM) also show a peculiarly shrunken recency effect in (standard) free recall, with enhanced recall of only the very last item on the list (Shallice and Warrington, 1970). This fits nicely with what one would expect on the traditional analysis, and seems hard to explain on any alternative theory. To make the case even stronger, when tested in experiments that show the long-term recency effects that are supposedly so troubling for the conventional theory, these patients behave just like normals—they show the expected long-term recency effect (Vallar, Papagno, and Baddeley, 1991). These two facts are readily understood by supposing that, first, recency in standard free recall does indeed depend on verbal STM, and second, long-term recency effects in other tasks must have some other source, presumably reflecting better storage in, or retrieval from LTM.

A more difficult challenge to the usual interpretation of recency in free recall was raised by Baddeley and Hitch (1977), who demonstrated that the effect is rather more robust than one might have expected.

Specifically, they observed that in conventional free recall task, recency persisted even when encoding was combined with other tasks that should, in their view, have eliminated recency if the traditional account is correct.[2] One task that failed to eliminate recency was concurrent articulation (saying "the the the . . . ") while a list of ten words was presented visually. If one assumes that articulation occupies the machinery required to get information into verbal STM, then there is clearly a problem here. Before accepting this argument, however, the reader is invited to try the following exercise: while saying "the the the . . . ", open a telephone book, read a telephone number to yourself silently, shut the book, stop articulating, and say the number. The fact that this is so easily accomplished with seven-digit numbers shows that concurrent articulation does not prevent verbal recoding. Also playing a role may be the fact that visual STM can be used to supplement verbal STM in span tasks, and therefore in recency as well. Baddeley and Hitch also reported a second, potentially more devastating result: people can, they claim, simultaneously store a digit load and store words for later free recall without eliminating recency in the recall task. If correct, this would certainly challenge the usual assumption that span and recency depend mostly on the same processes and structures. This result was obtained, however, in experiments where either the words or the digits were presented visually, which again raises the possibility that subjects were relying on visual STM for the last items in the word list or the span task. Further research on concurrent span and free recall tasks is in order.

As the evidence stands presently, a modified structural model of memory enjoys broad support from an impressive array of evidence. The most compelling data involve brain-damaged patients (amnesics and those with verbal STM defects), which is hardly surprising since in normal individuals, both short- and long-term memory would be expected to contribute in most situations. The claim of Glanzer and other researchers that even in normals examination of serial positions functions in tasks such as free recall can help isolate contributions of STM and LTM accounts for a wide range of observations and does not seem to be overturned by recent challenges.

In addition to disputing the interpretation of recency effects, some critics of the modal model have made a more abstract objection: that neuropsychological syndromes affecting short-term retention are typically associated with impairments in functions other than memory storage, such as receptive or productive language or visuospatial manipulation (Barnard, 1985). Therefore, it is proposed, one should not speak of dedicated short-term memory systems in the brain. This criticism relies on a rather weak kind of inference. As many neuropsychologists have observed, one cannot conclude very much from co-occurrence of symptoms, since functionally distinct systems may tend to be damaged at the same time simply because they are anatomically intertwined or share a mutual vulnerability to a particular sort of brain damage. Even if one accepts that the machinery for short-term retention always carries out other functions as well, the traditional analyses of memory systems would still not be overturned. These analyses define cognitive systems based on their role in memory storage; the value of such a description in no way hinges on the claim that this provides an exhaustive or exclusive picture of cognitive architecture.

The development on the STM/LTM distinction, especially in the writings of British psychologists, has been greatly enriched by evidence involving the effects of brain damage. Relatively neglected, however, are recent neurophysiological findings that also provide support. It has long been suggested that transient and permanent memories may be stored in the form of neural activity (cell firing) and changes in patterns of synaptic connectivity, respectively (Hebb, 1949). If this is correct, the STM/LTM distinction might have neurophysiological as well as psychological reality. Recent single-unit studies examine cell responses in awake animals performing tasks requiring short-term retention of visual patterns, usually, delayed matching to sample, where the animal picks the stimulus that matches a stored exemplar. A number of results seem consistent with the Hebbian hypothesis. For example, when monkeys perform delayed matching to sample, many cells in inferotemporal cortex continue firing, showing selectivity for properties of the stimulus that have to be retained (Desimone et al, 1995; Fuster, 1984, 1995). Fuster (1984) notes that "the discharge of such cells is usually altered only during presentation and retention of stimuli, and returns to the normal spontaneous rate as soon as the stimuli have been behaviorally utilized and their memorization is no longer necessary" (p. 282). John Maunsell (personal communication) observed that when a monkey retains a visual pattern over a delay period, a large portion of the cells showing continued firing in the absence of the stimulus maintain this firing even when a masking pattern is presented during the retention interval (as long as the monkey does not have to respond to this pattern). All of these findings are as one would expect if the neural substrate of what we have been calling visual STM for form is continuous firing of visually selective cells in the ventral stream of cortical visual processing. Short-term memory for location may involve similar activity in the dorsal stream (Gnadt and Andersen, 1992). On the other hand, the substrate of LTM presumably corresponds to synaptic changes. It remains to be seen whether this simple neural interpretation of the STM/LTM distinction will hold up in light of future research, but data thus far are encouraging.

These neurophysiological observations relate to another source of discomfort with the modal model: the fact that for stimulus to be identified, information in permanent memory has to be consulted, namely, the contents of what is usually called semantic memory. In older formulations of the modal model, identification of a stimulus is assumed to occur in the course of transferring or copying a trace from sensory to short-term memory. In more contemporary formulations, sensory memory no longer functions as a way station en route to STM, but identification still precedes STM. In either case, one must suppose that memory traces somehow contact LTM on their way to STM without leaving any residue there (cf. Norman, 1968 and Restle, 1974); these complications detract from the aesthetic appeal of the model. There are alternative ways of conceiving of this process, however. If a short-term memory trace is a pattern of continued activity in the neural machinery responsible for stimulus recognition or motor control, then patterns of firing may derive their content from the synaptic properties of the circuits in which this firing is embedded; these patterns of firing could arise and dissipate without those properties being modified in any way (i.e., no LTM storage would have taken place).

Distinguishing Separate Short-Term Memory Systems

As noted, early formulations of the modal model, and to this day, many textbooks, refer to short-term memory as if it were a single structure, but there is good evidence for the existence of several different forms of

STM. The evidence for a distinction between visual and verbal STM storage seems particularly clear. Certain kinds of left hemisphere damage produce a gross impairment in verbal STM tasks such as digit span, but leave relatively intact the ability to report briefly presented visual displays of characters (Warrington and Shallice, 1972). Basso et al. (1982) found that a patient with profound impairments in auditory verbal short-term memory was well above normal in retaining meaningless sequences of visual patterns over short intervals. The opposite pattern was observed in certain patients with right hemisphere damage: difficulties occurred in storing visuospatial material without impairment in storage of verbal materials (Hanley, Young, and Pearson 1991).

Equally compelling is the absence of interference when normal people concurrently store spoken digits, presumably in a speechlike format, and visually presented letters, presumably in a visual format, making a written report of the letters (Henderson, 1972; Scarborough, 1972; see also Frick, 1984; Margrain, 1967). Logically speaking, this kind of evidence—a demonstration that two different kinds of material can be stored simultaneously without displacing each other—provides about as compelling evidence for distinct storage capacity as one could conceivably find. It may not imply the existence of discrete storage systems, however; the capacity to store different items at the same time might be inversely related to their similarity, with auditory and visual inputs simply being low in similarity (cf Henderson, 1972; Sanders and Schroots, 1969).

Additional support for independent forms of STM storage comes from the observation that certain variables (e.g., irrelevant speech distraction, word length) affect the storage of one kind of material more than storage of another kind (Baddeley, 1986). Finally, brain imaging studies using positron emission tomography (PET) confirm that certain cortical areas are more strongly activated when people store one kind of material or another (compared with tasks with similar input requirements but no demand for memory storage; E. E. Smith and Jonides, 1995). Neither of these sources of evidence are quite as compelling as the double-dissociations or simultaneous storage of different kinds of material that were described above, but they do provide converging support. Putting it all together, the evidence against a unitary conception of short-term memory seems overwhelming.

One naturally wonders, therefore, whether there are other STM systems in addition to verbal and visual STM systems, or, if the continuum-of-similarity interpretation is correct, whether there are additional examples of materials so dissimilar that they can be independently stored. It appears that there are. First, studies involving simultaneous storage reveal that spatial information can be stored separately from letters and digits (Sanders and Schroots, 1969; Henderson, 1972). The differential effects of brain damage (Farah et al, 1988) and recent PET data show that distinct brain areas are activated during storage of spatial and visual material (Smith and Jonides, 1995). Several studies provide evidence of haptic short-term storage (Murray, Ward, and Hockley, 1975; Bowers et al, 1990). Although one would guess that these stimuli are stored separately from verbal, visual, or spatial materials, this has not so far been demonstrated.

Reisberg, Rappaport, and O'Shaughnessy (1984) showed that subjects could acquire a new form of short-term memory storage related to manual motor commands. When trained to encode a set of digits as a sequence of finger movements, their digit span performance was increased by almost 50%. This argues strongly for some additional mode of storage beyond ordinary verbal STM. In general, it seems that short-term storage capacity can be associated either with modality-specific imagery (at least visual and auditory) or with buffered storage of motor programs (Klapp, 1976). Monsell (1984) suggested that rehearsal in verbal STM may involve cycling material between articulatory (output) and phonological (input) domains, and Howard and Franklin (1993) presented neuropsychological evidence in support of this idea. What is particularly interesting about Monsell's proposal is that it may help explain an otherwise puzzling notion, namely, that information residing within a given processing module could be boosted by an outside controller. According to the alternative view that Monsell proposes, boosting is really a byproduct of transferring information from one processing module to another.

In summary, the broad three-part distinction postulated by the modal model has received an extraordinary amount of criticism over the years. The original, relatively primitive versions of the model (e.g., Atkinson and Shiffrin, 1968) require important modification, principally, abandoning the idea of serial information flow and the suggestion that short-term memory is unitary and exclusively verbal. Furthermore, the model must be read with the understanding that the proposed memory structures are not claimed to have, nor are they likely to have, the *exclusive* function of memory storage. Once modified and interpreted in this way, the model readily deflects most of the criticisms, and its core ideas enjoy broad and diverse empirical support. As a simple model of the vastly complex domain of human memory, it undoubtedly oversimplifies in important ways. Nevertheless, several decades of research suggests that it has important insights at its core and may represent one of the more significant accomplishments of contemporary experimental psychology.

Procedural/Declarative Distinction

Another influential distinction that has been the focus of a vast amount of research in recent years postulates two sorts of memory, one revealed by declarative, or explicit, tests such as recall and recognition, and another revealed by certain procedural, or implicit, tests in which memory is demonstrated indirectly without the subject consciously recollecting the original learning experience. Observations involving both brain-damaged (amnesic) and normal individuals have been taken as evidence for this distinction.

Evidence from Amnesia   Many researchers reported that despite having profound impairment in recall and recognition memory, patients suffering from anterograde amnesia sometimes perform normally in long-term memory tests that require no explicit reference to earlier events. Some of these tasks involve acquiring skills or procedures. Brooks and Baddeley (1976) found that amnesics showed essentially normal learning on a pursuit rotor task, a task that requires one to keep a stylus in contact with a moving target. Many examples of preserved implicit memory in amnesics involve various kinds of priming, changes in performance that are relatively stimulus-specific and that are presumed to reflect changes in preexisting memory representations (activation or tuning) rather than creation of new ones. Not all cases of preserved memory fall into this restricted category, however. Graf and Schacter (1985) measured priming in word fragment completion. Having seen the word BREAD, people are more likely to complete the fragment B_E_D as BREAD than they would if they had not seen the word. When people studied a pair of words, they were more likely to complete one member of the pair when tested in the context of the other member of the pair. This effect, which would seem to require forming an association between previously unassociated words, was observed for both amnesics and normal individuals. A fully satisfactory characterization of the kinds of memory spared in amnesia, presumably allowing one to infer the function of the damaged structures, continues to elude investigators.

Evidence from Normal Individuals   Two kinds of evidence involving normal individuals have been taken to support the structural distinction between implicit and explicit memory systems. First, implicit memory performance is sometimes unaffected by manipulations that improve recall and recognition, such as classifying words according to their meaning (Jacoby and Dallas, 1981). Second, subjects' success in explicitly recollecting an event often fails to predict their indirect memory for the same event; for example, words that are successfully recognized may not show any greater degree of priming than do unrecognized words (Graf and Schacter, 1985).

Critical Evaluation   What do these findings show? Those involving normal individuals clearly refute certain claims about memory that one might conceivably propose. For example, when a person studies a word, one could claim that the resulting memory representation consists of just a single trace, where the strength of this trace is the sole determinant of how well the person would perform on any memory task that refers back to the study of that word. If this view were correct, one should never find two study conditions (A and B) and two types of tests (1 and 2) where A causes better performance than B on test 1, and B causes better performance than A on test 2. Some of the results described above demonstrate just this sort of interaction, and thereby rule out the one-experience–one-trace account. However, this rejection does not lead inevitably to the idea of separate implicit and explicit memory *systems* (cf Roediger, 1990), because traces are not the same as systems. In fact, it is hard to see why any cognitive psychologist would be tempted to advocate a one-experience–one-trace model given the very critical role that the idea of separate stimulus codes plays throughout the field (see Posner, 1978, for a discussion). Even in the verbal learning tradition it was generally accepted that a single learning trial could result in the formation of various different associations (Jung, 1968), which is equivalent to multiple traces. Therefore, finding strong interactions between study task and memory test does not rule out any plausible memory theories, and does not require one to postulate different memory systems. What about the statistical independence between implicit and explicit memory test performance, which has sometimes been found? This too would reject the one-experience–one-trace view, since if there were only one trace, then trial-to-trial variability in the strength of that trace should produce a positive correlation in performance on any two tests.[3] Here again, it does not appear to rule out anything stronger or warrant postulating two or more distinct systems.

What would provide acceptable evidence for separate systems? If amnesics lose the ability to form explicit memories and retain the ability to form implicit or procedural memories, as many authors claim, this would provide such evidence. Before accepting that this has been shown, however, one must rule out the possibility that amnesics simply form *weaker* traces of all types, with this weakening having a bigger effect on some types of memory tests than on others. This is what is commonly termed a scaling problem (see Loftus, 1978, for a useful discussion). There is evidence that at least some implicit/explicit dissociations do indeed reflect scaling problems. For example, Jernigan and Ostergaard (1993) reported that what appeared to be spared priming in tachistoscopic word identification probably reflects differences in baseline word-identification performance between amnesics and normals. Indeed, one commonly finds that baseline performance of amnesics in most tasks used to assess priming or other implicit forms of implicit memory is not normal. However, there may be cases of preserved implicit memory that cannot be explained in this fashion. For example, in word fragment completion described earlier, amnesics' performance is sometimes completely indistinguishable from that of normal controls. To attribute the preserved performance of amnesics to a scaling problem, one would have to suppose that priming in word-fragment completion is indifferent to variations in trace strength (or, to put it differently, the effects of trace strength on priming would have to have reached saturation in normals). This possibility cannot be dismissed, since Musen (1991) found that increasing exposure duration of stimuli beyond 1 second produced no further increase in priming, though it did improve recognition memory. In the case of the pursuit rotor learning, on the other hand, densely amnesic subjects showed complete learning curves that were essentially indistinguishable from those of normals (Brooks and Baddeley, 1976), so preservation of at least this form of learning seems fairly clear.

In summary, strong evidence from diverse methodologies supports a distinction between sensory, short-term, and long-term memory systems. Despite the accumulation of this evidence, structural approaches seem to have fallen into a certain amount of disrepute, mostly based on criticisms that do not survive careful scrutiny, or so it is maintained here. By contrast, the distinction between implicit and explicit memory systems appears to have achieved wide acceptance even though the data taken to support it often seem well short of conclusive. This is not to say, of course, that the distinction or something like it will not ultimately prove valid.

Attentional Limitations in Memory Storage

The discussion in the first six chapters posited a fractionation of the concept of attention. The structural analyses of memory described in the preceding section suggest that memory, too, is fractionated. Given these conclusions, any analysis of the relationship between attention and memory is bound to be complex. The approach followed here is to consider each memory system in turn—sensory memory, STM, LTM, and, giving it the benefit of the doubt, implicit memory—and ask how storage or retrieval in that particular system is affected by each type or aspect of attention. The evidence is incomplete, but it does suggests some conclusions that will probably surprise many readers.

How should types or aspects of attention be subdivided for present purposes? One issue to be considered is what happens when voluntary attention is deployed to deliberately exclude an object as completely as possible. Chapters 2 and 5 suggested the existence of (imperfect) attentional filtering mechanisms that often succeed in preventing unattended materials from undergoing complete semantic analysis. It would seem unavoidable that when this kind of exclusion occurs, storage of information about an object in both short-term and long-term memory is greatly reduced. Indeed, we have already seen evidence for this, as in Moray's classic demonstration that words repeated thirty-five times in the unattended channel are not recognized reliably better than chance. The question of whether filtering prevents stimuli from being stored in sensory memory, on the other hand, is not so obvious, and the issue was addressed only obliquely in preceding discussions (of visual backward masking, for example). This issue will be considered explicitly in the next section. In addition to asking how deliberate attentional exclusion affects subsequent memory, we must consider how memory storage is affected by concurrent mental operations. Chapter 6 maintained that dual-task costs can arise as a consequence of two forms of competition: competition for central processing capacity, which often appears to be a discrete competition, resulting in queuing, and competition for perceptual capacity that is probably modality specific and allocated in a graded fashion. It is necessary, therefore, to consider separately how each of these different types of capacity limit affects memory. We start with sensory memory.

Sensory Memory Storage

The first question is whether items that are deliberately ignored are nonetheless stored in visual or auditory sensory memory. For auditory stimuli, the answer seems to be yes. In a study already mentioned, Norman (1969) had people shadow a message played in one ear while ignoring a series of two-digit numbers played in the other ear. At a certain point the shadowing was interrupted, and listeners were tested for their memory from the unattended ear.[4] Their performance suggested they could retain several seconds' worth reasonably well. Given the demanding nature of shadowing, we can be pretty confident that the message containing the numbers would be excluded to the maximum possible extent. This finding does not, however, rule out the possibility that sensory memory storage can be enhanced when one has the conscious goal of storing as much as possible. It would be interesting to know whether patterns of sounds that cannot easily be rehearsed are remembered better when they are attended rather than ignored; designs such as those used by Norman could be adapted for this purpose.[5]

What about storage of ignored stimuli stored in visual sensory (iconic) memory? Ideally, one would want to address this question by having an observer respond immediately and selectively to complex visual stimuli in a briefly flashed display (say, a centrally presented word) while ignoring an accompanying supraspan array such as a large number of characters; within a few hundred milliseconds a probe stimulus would tell the subject to report one of these characters. Unfortunately, such an experiment does not seem to have been carried out. One interesting study that approaches the same issue was conducted by Palmer (1991), who performed a partial-report experiment involving recognition judgments of line length (the dependent variable measured sensitivity to length differences between the original and the probe). When subjects were told to attend to one item preferentially, their accuracy when this item was probed did not decline with probe delay. In trials where another item was probed, cue delay had the usual deleterious effect. The results make sense if the probed item is stored in STM and the uncued items are stored in iconic memory.

Further evidence for this conclusion comes from a study by Shiffrin and Diller (1996), who had subjects monitor a sequence of geometric patterns rapidly presented in the center of the visual field. Letters or color patches sometimes appeared at the same time in more peripheral locations. Occasionally, the central monitoring task was interrupted and subjects were probed in various ways. Priming measures showed no evidence that the peripheral stimuli had been identified. However, subjects performed fairly well when a probe appearing immediately after offset of the peripheral stimulus required them to describe that stimulus. Evidently, the peripheral stimulus was stored in iconic memory even when further analysis of this object was blocked. Farther afield, several studies attempted to determine the role of central capacity in iconic memory. Unfortunately, they used concurrent memory loads rather than competing stimulus-response tasks (Doost and Turvey, 1971; Chow and Murdock, 1975); this methodology suffers from conceptual weakneses that will emerge shortly.

Short-Term Memory Encoding and Retention

STM Encoding   Based on results described, one can infer that when a person tries to exclude stimuli from processing, traces of these stimuli are not ordinarily stored in short-term memory. If they were, results such as those of Sperling (1960; described in chapter 3) would be incomprehensible; the partial-report procedure could not circumvent the capacity limits of short-term memory unless the probe determined which items were stored in STM and which were not. In preceding sections we saw that visual stimuli often seem to draw attention when they appear without warning in relevant locations, as reflected, for example, in search tasks (e.g., Remington, Johnston, and Yantis, 1992). It is an open question whether involuntary attention shifting is sufficient to cause short-term memory storage of irrelevant information, thereby displacing its contents. There are some hints that this does happen to some extent at least: irrelevant speech, even in a foreign language, but not noise that does not resemble speech, reduces short-term memory for visually presented stimuli (Colle and Welsh, 1976; Salame and Baddeley, 1987).

What kinds of resource competition impair voluntary transfer of information into short-term memory? Does an unrelated task requiring central processing prevent information from being stored in short-term memory at the same time? So much has been written to equate STM with central processing capacity that one might expect the answer to this question would of course be yes. In fact, the available evidence points to the opposite conclusion. Consider a study by Murdock (1965). He had people listen to a list of words that they subsequently tried to recall. In some conditions, the subjects sorted cards into piles while listening to the words. This reduced primacy and recall for items in the middle of the list (LTM, on the standard story) while leaving the recency effect (hence STM) intact. This result seems robust, having been confirmed by Bartz and Salehi (1970) and Baddeley et al. (1969). It was later extended by Anderson and Craik (1974) using a concurrent visual-manual choice reaction-time task (figure 7.2), and Silverstein and Glanzer (1971) using a concurrent arithmetic task. Evidently, then, central interference does not affect storage in verbal STM.

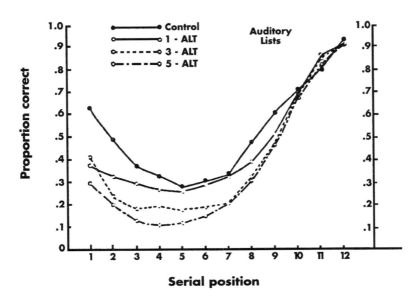

Figure 7.2
Effects of performing a concurrent choice task (of increasing difficulty: 1-ALT, 3-ALT, 5-ALT) on free recall for auditorily presented lists. Redrawn from Anderson and Craik (1974, figure 1, lefthand panel only, p. 110) with permission.

The same conclusion may apply to storage in visual short-term memory as well. Evidence for this comes from experiments requiring people to retain patterns of black and white squares (as used in Phillips' experiments described earlier). In several experiments (Pashler, 1993b), a grid was flashed briefly and followed by a mask (figure 7.3). The subject also performed a concurrent auditory-manual choice RT, with the interval between the auditory stimulus and the grid varying from trial to trial. After a 600-msec delay, a test grid appeared, and the subject said whether it was the same or different from the original grid. Recognition performance was comparable whether or not the choice task and the presentation of the original grid were overlapping in time. The results did not stem from STM being filled to capacity, because variation in the duration of the visual display had a big effect on performance.

These studies point to the same conclusion: information can be transferred into STM at what appears to be a normal rate while a person

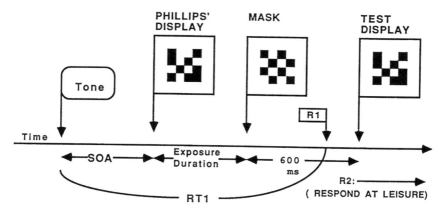

Figure 7.3
Procedure for experiments assessing whether storage in visual short-term memory (VSTM) can operate concurrently with central stages of a choice RT task. Subject stores a grid display (modeled after Phillips, 1974) in VSTM and makes a choice response to the tone; at short SOAs, the two tasks must be performed concurrently. This produced no reduction in accuracy, as assessed by subsequent same/different judgment. Reprinted from Pashler (1993b, figure 11.4, p. 256) with permission.

carries out unrelated central processing. This does not reflect the fact the unrelated central processing is easy: as we saw in chapter 6, it is sufficiently difficult to postpone other activities completely when these also involve mental events such as memory retrieval and response choice. The general claim that getting information into STM is free of capacity demands some qualifications and comments, however. One qualification is that this conclusion may apply only to what might be called modality-appropriate storage (e.g., storing speech in articulatory/verbal STM, storing visual patterns in visual STM). Not all storage in short-term memory is of this type: people can, when they choose, recode materials to be remembered in a different format (e.g., recode and store a visually presented character in verbal STM; see Broadbent, 1989, for a discussion). Recoding might place additional demands on central mechanisms beyond what is evident in the studies described. The second qualification is that although the existing evidence points to the independence of STM storage and central limitations, further tests of this hypothesis remain to be carried out. For example, one test would have people listen to a list of digits as long as their memory span (typically, seven or eight digits) while doing an unrelated centrally demanding task, and then immediately recall the digits. They should, according to the account suggested above, be able to recall the digits with little difficulty.

STM Retention   What about retaining information in STM after it has already been stored there? In many studies, subjects were required to hold onto a memory load for a short interval (usually several seconds) while they performed some task, as a means of determining whether particular mental operations require processing capacity. This approach is based on the assumption that filling up short-term memory depletes capacity. When it was applied with choice RT tasks, the results were fairly consistent. Retention of the memory load was hardly affected by the RT task, whereas the RT task was slowed, although usually only to a modest degree. Egeth, Pomerantz, and Schwartz (1977) and Logan (1978b) assessed the effects of memory load together with manipulations targeted to prolong different particular stages of the concurrent choice RT tasks. Both studies found that the slowing was additive, with factors affecting stages from perceptual analysis through response execution. If one assumes that tasks require a fixed amount of capacity, and that the memory load depletes this capacity, then one should have expected overadditive interactions: bigger factor effects with the memory load than without one. Therefore, the additivity of these factors with concurrent memory loads suggests that depletion of graded capacity may not be a correct analysis of how memory load affects performance.

How else might it affect performance? One plausible alternative is that holding onto the memory load neither uses up processing resources nor preempts access to machinery that carries out the concurrent task. Rather, as Logan (1978b) suggested, it may cause the person to be unable to prepare as effectively for the particular S-R mapping required by the choice RT task. For example, rehearsing the memory load before beginning the RT task might prevent the subject from rehearsing the S-R mapping; alternatively, the instructions for the speeded task and the memory load might compete for space in short-term memory.[6] In either case, the result would be that whichever processing stages depended most critically on preparation[7] operate more slowly, without any stages actually being *delayed* as they are in a true dual-task (PRP) situation. Logan (1979) did find that memory load interacted with one variable—the number of alternatives in choice RT tasks—which, as he observed, would be consistent with this kind of preparation-based account.

It seems likely that information in STM is lost fairly rapidly if it is not rehearsed, even without new information coming in to displace it (Shiffrin and Cook, 1978). Whereas passively maintaining the contents of STM may not generate central interference, *initiating* rehearsal of material shortly after it is first presented may do so (Naveh-Benjamin and Jonides, 1984). It is not clear whether central interference occurs again every time a new cycle of rehearsal begins. Even if it does, in light of the relatively slow decay of STM, subjects could probably schedule their rehearsals so as to avoid delaying the central processing on concurrent tasks. Therefore, it is not surprising that holding a memory load rarely produces much disruption of a concurrent task.

Short-Term Memory and Limited Capacity The results described above suggest that a concurrent centrally demanding task has little or no effect on the ability to store and maintain information in STM, except perhaps for those moments when active rehearsal is under way, which may occur only intermittently. These conclusions contradict the remarkably widespread assumption that short-term memory capacity can be equated with, or used as a measure of, central resources (e.g., Shiffrin, 1976). This assumption[8] underlies many studies in which people are required to hold on to a memory load to see what mental operations are affected by resource depletion, and, by elimination, which ones are automatic. This sort of logic has been applied in fields as diverse as psycholinguistics (Blackwell and Bates, 1995) and social cognition (Swann et al, 1990). Its prevalence is hard to understand, given that casual introspection would suggest that retaining a telephone number, for example, requires intermittent rather than continuous mental activity. Another telling fact is that holding a memory load barely affects cognitive operations such as making numerical comparisons, unless the task must be performed immediately after the memory load is presented (Klapp, Marshburn, and Lester, 1983).

Long-Term (Explicit) Memory

As noted above and in chapter 2, when people set out to ignore a stimulus they can rarely recall or recognize that stimulus later. How does performing a concurrent task affect deliberate storage in permanent memory of stimuli unrelated to that task? Many studies found substantial decrements. In fact, this is one of the more reliable findings in the human cognition literature. The first experiment on this issue was probably performed by W. G. Smith (1895), who had people remember sets of letters while doing sums or other tasks. A more recent example has already been mentioned: worse performance in a free recall task on items early in the list (primacy) when people perform a concurrent card-sorting task while the list is presented (Murdock, 1965). The dual-task decrement in long-term memory storage is found in both recall and recognition measures (Mandler and Worden, 1973), and it occurs for semantically categorized as well as uncategorized materials (Park et al, 1989). The material to be remembered does not have to be similar in any obvious way to the material the person must manipulate in the concurrent task. For example, Perkins and Cook (1990) had people play a computer game while they smelled some odors, and found that this impaired subsequent recognition of the odors. In those few studies in which researchers failed to find dual-task decrements in LTM encoding (e.g., Tun, Wingfield, and Stine, 1991) the secondary tasks seem to have been very undemanding, specifically, to have required central processing only rather infrequently.

It might be suggested that concurrent tasks do not really reduce memory storage, but merely make the context at encoding different from the context at test. Changes in context from study to test are known to impair retrieval (e.g., studying underwater and being tested above water; Godden and Baddeley, 1975). Context changes seems unlikely to be responsible for dual-task decrements, however, because carrying out a concurrent task during encoding harms later memory even when the same concurrent task is performed during retrieval (Baddeley et al, 1984; Craik et al, 1996). One particularly intriguing feature of the dual-task decrement in LTM storage is that it occurs even with incidental memory tasks, where subjects do not expect to be asked to remember anything. Of course, if there were no incentive to do anything at all with the materials later tested, many subjects would completely ignore them, in which case we would be back to the unattended stimuli category discussed above. In most incidental memory studies, the experimenter does not wish this to happen, and therefore requires subjects to perform some kind of orienting task. Mandler and Worden (1973) had subjects copy down visually presented words and classify each one as a noun or a verb while performing a concurrent task (adding spoken digits). The adding task caused a major decrement in memory for the words. Carrier and I also found a decrement when we had people semantically classify visually presented words and perform a secondary choice task involving keypress responses to tones.

Why would a secondary task impair memory if it does not actually stop people from carrying out the orienting task, as it does not in these studies, at least in the great majority of trials? What mental events are being prevented or altered? This answer is not obvious. If memory storage and competing tasks are subject to the central limitation and perhaps even discrete bottleneck, as proposed in the preceding chapter, selecting a response in a secondary choice RT task cannot occur simultaneously with the central processing in the orienting task in any case. Therefore, the secondary task can only be delaying, not preventing, processing of the stimuli for which memory is later tested. Why, then, should there be any decrement in memory? A similar question can be asked if one supposes that dual-task impairment of memory storage involves graded capacity sharing rather than a discrete bottleneck. That is, if the secondary task drains capacity but leaves enough capacity free to perform the orienting task, why should there be a decrement?

One natural way to explain why a dual-task decrement would arise in incidental memory experiments that have orienting tasks is as follows. Suppose in the single-task condition the subject often engages in certain additional processing of the stimulus information above and beyond what is required to perform the orienting task, and suppose this *extra* manipulation is prevented or impaired by the secondary task. According to a bottleneck analysis, one would have to assume that in the single-task condition, this additional processing is performed during blank time, whereas in the dual-task condition less blank time is available. In a graded competition framework, on the other hand, one would suppose that free capacity that would be allocated to the secondary task in the dual-task condition is instead allocated to extra processing of the material to be remembered in the single-task condition.

The suggestion that people would devote blank time or spare capacity to processing of stimuli that is unnecessary for the orienting task may seem gratuitous, but it can be tested directly. Carrier and I recently carried out some incidental memory experiments with no secondary tasks at all. Subjects were told to classify each word in a series; each response was followed by 0, 0.5, or 1 second of blank time, followed by presentation of the next word. The blank time enhanced memory, despite the fact subjects had no incentive to do anything but wait for the next stimulus. What extra processing do subjects carry out when they have blank time? One could of course propose that college students find a list of common words so interesting that they voluntarily ruminate on each one, but this is surely implausible. Perhaps these experiments reveal not conscious rumination, but rather an unconscious consolidation process that is subject to disruption by competing tasks. Whatever the nature of the mental/neural activity disrupted by concurrent (or perhaps more accurately, adjacent) tasks, people can use blank time to enhance memory. This makes it less puzzling that a secondary task impedes memory even when it does not prevent a person from carrying out an orienting task.

Implicit Memory

A number of researchers proposed that implicit memories can be formed not only in the absence of the hippocampal circuit that is damaged in amnesia, but also without attention. Various evidence has been cited to support this. For example, M. E. Smith and Oscar-Berman (1990) had subjects carry out a speeded lexical decision task, reporting whether a string of letters was a word or nonword.[9] In the dual-task condition, subjects concurrently monitored a sequence of characters exposed on the screen, watching for prespecified visual targets and keeping a running count of how many were presented. Implicit memory took the form of faster responses to words that were presented previously. Performing a concurrent task did not alter the repetition priming effect found with words, although priming for nonwords was reduced somewhat. A different and ingenious kind of implicit memory measure was used by Jacoby,

Woloshyn, and Kelley (1989), who asked subjects to read names aloud from a computer screen. A concurrent task required subjects to monitor a list of auditory digits for the occurrence of three successive odd digits, to which they responded by pressing a key. Performing the concurrent task reduced storage of the names as assessed by a recognition (explicit) memory test. However, when a more indirect measure of memory was used—subjects' tendency to classify erroneously as famous those non-famous names previously presented in the experiment—no decrement was observed. That is, the illusory fame effect was just as big for names studied with a concurrent task as for names studied without one.

One difficulty with these studies is that the concurrent tasks may have required central processing only infrequently. For example, Smith and Oscar-Berman's concurrent task involved counting stimuli that occurred no more than once every three-and-a-half seconds, and sometimes less frequently. Carrier, McFarland, and I (1996) used concurrent serial choice reaction-time tasks in which there was little or no time between when subjects responded to one stimulus and when they had to deal with the next, thereby requiring frequent response selection. Subjects had to perform an orienting task on a list of words, either with or without the concurrent task, and were then given an implicit memory test on the words. The concurrent task reduced implicit memory, as indicated by commonly used implicit measures including word-stem completion.

In light of these results, any global assertion that implicit memory storage occurs without attention cannot be sustained. However, the fact remains that in several of the studies a particular concurrent task affected explicit but not implicit memory performance. If all forms of memory tests depend on traces resulting from encoding that is subject to dual-task competition, why should this interaction occur? One possibility is that while a concurrent task may result in weaker memory traces—with both implicit and explicit memory tests depending on these same traces—the implicit memory measures may be relatively insensitive to variations in trace strength above some minimum level. This potential scaling problem was also noted in connection with apparent sparing of implicit memory in amnesia. If increases in trace strength beyond a certain level improve performance on explicit but not implicit memory tests,[10] then any variable, be it amnesia or a concurrent task, could affect explicit but not implicit memory tests. In light of this possibility, one cannot rule out the idea that the same attentional processes and brain structures are involved in forming both implicit and explicit memories. Until this can be ruled out, one cannot confidently make any distinction between the two in the first place. One hopes that future research will provide more clear-cut evidence on the validity of this possible distinction. The primary focus of this chapter—divided-attention studies—does not seem to provide support for it.

Attentional Limitations and Memory Retrieval

Does retrieval from long-term memory place significant demands on central processing resources? Introspection might suggest that it does, because memory retrieval often seems to require noticeable effort. However, the conscious experience of effort could be misleading. More relevant are the results of studies examining dual-task decrements in memory retrieval, of which there are a number. Rohrer et al. (1995) had subjects retrieve words from semantic memory while, in some trials, concurrently performing a serial choice reaction time task (pressing keys in response to colored asterisks). The retrieval task required the subject to produce instances of a small category (e.g., farm animals) as rapidly as possible. The rate at which they produced instances was substantially diminished by the concurrent task (figure 7.4), despite the lack of any obvious input or output conflict between these two activities. Park et al. (1989) and Trumbo and Milone (1971) found interference between various concurrent tasks and memory retrieval. The trend in these studies is for the effects to be asymmetric, with the probability of successful memory retrieval being relatively little affected (compared, for example, with the effects of concurrent tasks at encoding); the concurrent task seems to bear the brunt of the interference. This asymmetry seems rather stubborn, being little affected by instructions to vary the emphasis on memory retrieval and the concurrent task (Craik et al., 1996). The reason for this asymmetry is not clear; one explanation may be that memory retrieval is inherently an all-or-none process (see below). Alternatively, it may be that a concurrent task that forces a person repeatedly to attempt memory retrievals actually has some benefit for retrieval. In any case, the obser-

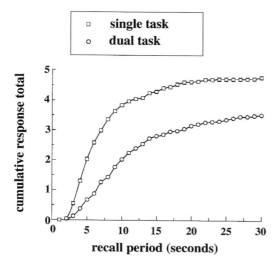

Figure 7.4
Cumulative recall from semantic memory as a function of dual-task versus single-task condition. Redrawn from Rohrer et al. (1995, figure 6, p. 1133).

vation of interference, whichever task it shows up with, implies that memory retrieval is subject to central capacity limitations of some form.

Before accepting this, however, we should consider a well-known study that drew a different conclusion. Baddeley et al. (1984) found that the difficulty of a concurrent sorting task had little effect on concurrent memory retrieval, and concluded that there was no central interference with retrieval per se. Rather, they suggested, interference may stem from the production of responses in the two tasks. As with some of the implicit memory studies described above, the concurrent task they used probably imposed only sporadic demands on response selection. Therefore, the lack of an effect is not strong evidence against central interference. In studies that found interference, it was not likely to reflect conflict in response production. In the study by Rohrer et al. (1995), for example, overt recall was brief and infrequent enough that simultaneous output in the two tasks would rarely occur even if the tasks were independent in the very strongest sense (e.g., if one person carried out one task and another person carried out the other).

Recent results strengthen the case for central interference even further, concluding that memory retrieval is subject to the same discrete processing bottleneck that prevents simultaneous response selection in two speeded choice tasks (the PRP effect described in chapter 6). In a PRP experiment, Carrier and I (1995) paired a first task requiring a manual response to a tone with a second, cued paired-associate memory retrieval task. In the retrieval task, the stimulus term was presented visually. The memory-retrieval task was much more time consuming than the choice RT task, often taking 1 or 2 seconds. Therefore, if the two tasks were carried out completely independently, responses would rarely occur at the same time, even when stimuli were nearly simultaneously. Nonetheless, there was substantial slowing of the paired-associate recall. Furthermore, manipulation of the difficulty of the memory retrieval produced the additive pattern of effects predicted if the memory retrieval stage itself was postponed by the concurrent task (following the logic described above). In essence, these results suggest that until people have finished deciding what button they will press in response to a tone, they cannot start remembering what word was associated with the cue.

The results suggest that memory retrieval is subject to the same bottleneck as action selection. The conclusion should be regarded as tentative, however, primarily because of the asymmetric pattern of interference observed in studies of continuous retrieval, noted earlier. Whereas the discrete retrieval situation (Carrier and Pashler, 1995) implies complete interference between retrieval and other central processing, the more modest decrements in memory when continuous retrieval tasks (e.g., free recall) are performed together with concurrent tasks (e.g., Craik et al, 1996) might suggest otherwise; possible explanations for this were alluded to earlier. If retrievals cannot be combined with other centrally demanding mental acts, period, then the conclusions reached in this and the preceding chapter might reflect the same basic underlying principle. This principle is as follows, roughly speaking: when a stimulus is used as a probe to recall associated information from memory, another recall process that would yield a different output cannot commence until the first one has finished. When the information to be retrieved consists of responses to be made in two choice tasks, this postponement is manifested in the response selection bottleneck and the PRP effect. When one task requires a speeded response and the other requires more difficult memory retrieval, one finds the kinds of dual-task interference observed by Carrier and Pashler (1995); selecting a choice response delays retrieval of a paired associate, for example. If this principle is correct, we would expect that people cannot carry out two distinct and simultaneous memory retrievals simultaneously (e.g., remembering a telephone number and recalling what one ate for breakfast). Oddly, this issue does not appear to have been studied systematically.

One phenomenon that would seem to challenge this idea is the so-called incubation effect. Having given up on a difficult memory retrieval or other mental problem of some kind, people often claim that the answer pops into their head unbidden. Undoubtedly, something like this occurs from time to time. One cannot be sure, however, that these instances necessarily reflect two streams of simultaneous cognitive work. Instead, what might be happening is the following. One attempts a memory search, fails, and gives up; a short time later, being somehow reminded of the unfinished goal, one tries again and achieves immediate success; the second effort, however, is not salient and not remembered. The immediate success may occur more often than might be expected because it is a fresh start, not handicapped by whatever temporary inhibition or ruts stopped the first search from succeeding (cf S. M. Smith, 1995). This is mere speculation, of course, and unfortunately it is rather difficult to distinguish empirically from retrieval that operates in the background.

The claim that only one retrieval can operate at any given time is more than a little vague, in the absence of a definition of what counts as one retrieval. To start with, the term "retrieval" is used here to refer to operations such as cued recall—bringing a new piece of information to mind on the basis of some cue—not merely relying on memory to obtain a fuller description of an object, as in pattern recognition. What is "one" retrieval? There can be no doubt that people can use several different cues in combination to search memory, resulting in retrieval of a single target. For example, in solving a crossword puzzle one often uses several unrelated pieces of information (e.g., that the second letter is an A, that the word has something to do with a river) and pulls from memory a single instance fitting both specifications. Searches of episodic memory in daily life often seem to rely on the same thing. This triangulation ability is at the core of what is often called the content-addressibility of human memory, which has proven difficult to implement in data-storage systems that use digital computers (e.g., Bruza and Huibers, 1996).

If the one-retrieval-at-a-time generalization is to stand, one must count the use of two or more cues to retrieve a single instance from memory as just one retrieval, since in none of these cases is it remotely plausible that different cues access memory sequentially. What counts as a single retrieval depends on the number of items retrieved, not the number of items used to trigger the retrieval. This fits well with conclusions drawn from studying mental events over much briefer time scales. As mentioned in chapter 6, J. O. Miller (1982) observed an effect he called coactivation, whereby two redundant stimuli both activate a single response simultaneously in speeded choice tasks.

The available evidence seems consistent, therefore, with a simple and ambitious generalization that might characterize mental events whose durations range all the way from a few hundred milliseconds to minutes. That is, two or more pieces of information cannot be retrieved from memory simultaneously, although two or more pieces of information can be used simultaneously as cues to retrieve a single piece of information.

Levels of Processing Theory and The Nature of Encoding

The word "encoding" is used in some very different ways in different areas of cognitive psychology (something that seems to bother alert undergraduates more than it does textbook writers). On the one hand, memory researchers use it to refer to creation of a memory trace (as in "encoding information into LTM"). On the other hand, students of perception and elementary information processing use the word to refer to the identification of a stimulus. Are these two senses of encoding synonymous? Is perceptual identification the same thing as forming a memory trace? If the conclusions about encoding that are widely held within the memory and attention fields are correct, the answer must be "no."

Consider the research taken to support the levels of processing theory (Craik and Lockhart, 1972). This theory proposed, among other things, that long-lasting memory storage is facilitated by semantic encoding (i.e., analyzing the meaning of a stimulus). (This generalization later proved too broad, but for reasons not relevant to the present point; Stein, Morris, and Bransford, 1978.) In various experiments, the stimulus was assumed to have been encoded only to the extent the experimenter explicitly demanded this (e.g., Hyde and Jenkins, 1973). For example, a subject told to classify a word on the basis of its sound would be assumed to have encoded the word at the phonological, but not semantic, level. By contrast, attention researchers generally assume that very extensive analysis of a stimulus, including identification at a semantic level, occurs rapidly and immediately after stimulus presentation (at least if it is attended to; some theorists claim that it occurs automatically, but as we saw in earlier chapters, evidence for this is weak). This general assumption (for lack of a better phrase, we might call it multiple analyses) has been accepted by attention theorists holding diametrically opposing views about other issues (e.g., Kahneman and Treisman, 1984; Shiffrin, 1976). One kind of evidence favoring multiple analyses comes from observations such as the Stroop effect and priming tasks, discussed in chapter 2: even when people try to ignore different dimensions, they are analyzed anyway. Another kind comes from experiments in which observers view rapid serial displays of pictures and appear capable of identifying objects at rates of 125 msec per item or better (e.g., Potter, 1983, 1993).

To give a concrete example, it is widely believed by attention theorists that when a person is instructed to classify a word on the basis of its sound, the semantics of the word are encoded along with the sound, whether or not this is related to any task the person is trying to carry out. In the parlance of memory theorists, however, only the sound is encoded. Is one or the other of these claims wrong? Or are there two senses of encoding: encoding for memory, which is controlled by conscious encoding strategies and which determines what is stored in permanent memory, and encoding for perception, whereby several descriptions of a stimulus are derived irrespective of conscious strategies?

To try to sort this out, it is useful to remind ourselves of the empirical observations that led to these hypotheses in the first place. On the one hand, long-term memory is heavily dependent on what kinds of decisions a person consciously attempts to carry out, On the other hand, in tasks involving target detection, priming, and similar kinds of indirect measures, one finds evidence that analysis proceeds along many different dimensions at once regardless of intention or task set. Furthermore, when people are given as little as 100 msec to look at a picture before it is replaced by a new picture, they seem to be able to identify a great deal of information, at least for the purpose of detecting some kind of target.

Findings about variables that enhance long-term memory are also pertinent here. Both recall and recognition of words are enhanced by increasing the number of decisions a subject makes about the words that have a *positive* outcome (e.g., judging whether cola is a consumable solid would count as one positive outcome; McClelland, Rawles, and Sinclair, 1981). Of interest, the number of positive decisions determines later memory much more than the total number of decisions made, and this holds for recognition as well as for recall (Hanley and Morris, 1987).

Putting these various clues together, along with a good bit of speculative license, we can try to reconcile the different senses of encoding as follows (these suggestions build on ideas proposed in chapter 5). Attending to an object (in the sense of chapter 5) results in the accumulation of activation in large numbers of detectors that represent different descriptions of the object, ranging from its elementary features to various high-level semantic descriptions (perhaps activating detectors for conceptually related items as well). This pattern of activation is what attention theorists mean by encoding, and it is sufficient to perform many of tasks they investigate, such as search and others discussed in chapter 3. It is also sufficient to produce effects that can be seen with the sensitive measures they favor, such as Stroop interference and others discussed under the label indirect measures in chapter 2. The resulting patterns of activation, representing many different interpretations of a stimulus, and sometimes representing more than one object at a time when perceptual attention is distributed broadly, may permit a person to detect a target on a very abstract basis (e.g., the animal, the highest digit in an array, perhaps even the object that does not make sense in the scene). With symbolic input such as a word in the context of a sentence, this may also involve activation of different meanings or interpretations, thereby allowing the appropriate one to be selected among various possibilities. Only the target interpretations (in a search, targets; in language comprehension, the appropriate meaning) actually end up being selected, however. What changes with selection? The target comes to be represented in the modality-appropriate short-term memory system (for a visual pattern, this would be visual short-term memory; for speech, phonological-articulatory short-term memory; Baddeley, 1990). Information in STM is preserved from masking (hence, it is reportable in experiments involving multiple frames or masks), and other contents of STM may be displaced. What is termed "detection," then, *is* storage in the appropriate form of short-term memory. As we have seen, however, this is transient and vulnerable to any subsequent selected information, so it can leave little or no long-term traces. For this reason it might best be termed stabilization rather than storage.

What is the role of perceptual attention in this process? The reader will have anticipated that perceptual filtering, whose reality was documented in chapter 2, can safely be assumed to preclude activation from arising in the first place, since unattended locations are readily excluded from detection. It is tempting, but still somewhat speculative, to suppose that stabilization always, as an obligatory rather than strategic matter, operates in conjunction with the narrowing of attention onto the object whose representations are stabilized. This brings us back to one of the core issues discussed in chapter 5: the maladaptive two-target effect, whereby detection of one target makes another less detectable, even when targets and distractors are sorted without mutual interference (Duncan, 1980b). All of the phenomena described in this paragraph and the preceding one are entirely independent of central interference, the bottleneck-type attentional limitation revealed by dual-task experiments described in chapter 6. This can be asserted with confidence simply because secondary tasks do not impair storage in STM or detection of targets, nor do they even cause shifts of visual attention to be delayed. To put it crudely, the entirety of what might be termed front-end processing (from a neurophysiologists' point of view, perhaps more aptly nicknamed back-end processing) are modality specific and operate independent of the sort of single-channel central processing that limits retrieval and the control of action. This includes not only perceptual analysis but also storage in STM and whatever processing may feed back to change the allocation of perceptual attention itself.

When we come to more or less permanent memory storage, however, the central mechanisms become highly relevant. Studies of maintenance rehearsal show that some degree of LTM storage takes place when something is stored in STM even without conscious elaboration. The registration in STM may represent a single, albeit modest, decision (a tiny bit of encoding in the sense of Craik and Lockhart), but further storage time merely maintains that stabilization, without enhancing permanent storage. As noted above, memory, at least for words, is enhanced when multiple decisions are made that result in positive judgments. One can speculate, then, that some modifications in permanent memory occur when a temporary representation is judged to be an instance of a well-learned category. This judging process does not consist merely of activation or even of stabilization. It must involve assessing and extracting information in a way that makes the results available to central mechanisms. Beyond this, the data provide little guidance. Indeed, it is possible that the reality we are awkwardly trying to capture in words may not be amenable to psychological analysis. Suppose, for example, that the theory mentioned earlier in this chapter turns out to be correct, and short-term memory is represented by patterns of neural firing whereas long-term memory consists of synaptic changes. In that case, the key question becomes why certain ways of using activation would result in synaptic changes. To tackle this question further would require detailed knowledge of the neural mechanisms of decision making and memory retrieval that are presently unavailable (for some clues see, e.g., Fuster, 1995).

The reader may notice that this proposed sketch shared some features with several earlier accounts. The notion that perception involves widespread and unselective activation has been widely suggested, although it happens to have been associated mostly with late selection theories (e.g., Posner, 1978; Shiffrin, 1976; Norman, 1968). Naturally, these theorists argued that perception was also unselective at the level of objects (i.e., unattended objects were fully analyzed) and typically, they equated short-term memory storage with central limitations or general capacity. The current suggestion is that although central limitations are demonstrably real and central in the sense of being modality independent (chapter 6), they should not be equated with or considered necessary for short-term storage. This formulation partially overlaps suggestions of Potter (1983), whose experiments with rapid presentations of pictures led her to postulate a rich but transient semantic activation, which she termed the conceptual very-short-term memory buffer. The term seems appropriate, but it should be kept in mind that the activation under discussion seems insufficient to support the knowledge or awareness that one might ordinarily assume that a structural concept like memory buffer would imply.

Conclusions

The first part of this chapter maintained that evidence for the tripartite distinction between sensory persistence, short-term memory, and long-term memory appears quite strong; an excellent convergence from behavioral studies, neuropsychological findings, and neurophysiological results was noted. In contrast, the evidence for a distinction between explicit and implicit memory systems appeared more tenuous.

The results described in the second part demonstrate strong interactions between attentional control and attentional limitations, on the one hand, and memory storage on the other hand. A voluntary decision to ignore a stimulus often prevents that stimulus from being registered in either short-term or long-term memory. It is widely assumed that attentional filtering does not prevent information being stored in sensory memory. Available evidence is scanty, but consistent with this assumption. The previous chapter described "single-channel" limitations in selection of actions and other decision-making operations. These limitations are indifferent to input modality and type of response, and they often cause processing bottlenecks to arise when people try to perform two tasks at the same time. Evidence described in this chapter suggested that both retrieval from and storage in long-term memory are subject to this same central bottleneck, or at least some milder form of interference associated with the same mental operations. Thus, if a person is required to carry out a task involving action planning, they are less able to store other information in long-term memory, even if this other information is completely unrelated to the task and not in any way confusable with it.

Dual-task interference with LTM storage is not intuitively surprising; what is more remarkable is the evidence suggesting that central interference does not affect storage of information in STM. A completely unrelated task (such as sorting cards or selecting a response to a tone) does not impede transfer of spoken or visually perceived information into articulatory or visual STM, respectively, as far as one can tell. Naturally, this holds only so long as modality-specific perceptual capacity limitations are not exceeded; thus, one would not expect that a person could read aloud sequentially exposed words while retaining other visual stimuli that are presented concurrently. The lack of interference with STM storage is striking, and it refutes very commonly held assumptions about the relationship STM and central processing limitations.

The results described in this chapter indicate that while STM storage is not subject to a central processing bottleneck, it is nonetheless closely tied to perceptual attention. For one thing, perceptual selection of a stimulus is a necessary condition for short-term storage to take place. The results described here suggest, though they do not prove, that STM storage and full perceptual analysis are both direct and unavoidable consequences of perceptual selection. If this is correct, people should be unable to fully analyze a stimulus without storing it in the modality-appropriate STM, thereby displacing any previous memory contents; this prediction is testable but the appropriate experiments have not yet been performed. The idea that perceptual analysis and STM storage would be tied in this way is congenial to the proposal, originally suggested by D. O. Hebb, that the neural basis of short-term storage is maintained firing in neurons specialized for stimulus analysis.

It was argued above that the traditional case for distinguishing between sensory, short-term, and other memory systems enjoys strong empirical support. To the extent this is true, box diagrams provide a reasonable if coarse way of representing memory systems, and computer-inspired terms like "transfer" are not seriously misleading. However, if STM and perceptual analysis are intertwined as suggested, then a term like "stabilization," proposed by Styles and Allport (1986), may be the most apt way to describe the registration of new inputs in STM. In that case, the word "transfer" should perhaps be reserved for recoding, as when a visually presented item is stored in speechlike format, an auditorily presented item is imaged, and so forth.

8

Automaticity, Effort, and Control

Automaticity: Theory and Phenomena

One encounters the idea of automaticity throughout contemporary psychology, not just in discussions of visual search and motor skill where its relevance seems rather obvious, but also in analyses of such phenomena as social interaction and psychopathology (e.g., Bargh, 1994; McNally, 1995). The idea that mental events operate automatically after a certain amount of practice is a well-entrenched doctrine of folk psychology, and it has a long history in academic psychology. James, for example, said "habit diminishes the conscious attention with which our acts are performed" (1890/1950, p. 114). In recent years, a number of investigators have tried to develop more specific and concrete descriptions of automaticity. According to them, mental operations that are practiced sufficiently not only come to be performed more quickly and accurately, but also undergo qualitative changes (e.g., Posner and Snyder, 1975a; Schneider and Shiffrin, 1977).

At least two changes are widely agreed upon and constitute the core of the concept of automaticity. The first is that practiced operations no longer impose capacity demands, so they can operate without experiencing interference from, or generating interference with, other ongoing mental activities. The second change is that practiced operations are not subject to voluntary control: if the appropriate inputs are present, processing commences and runs to completion whether or not the individual intends or desires this. In addition to these two core elements, many theorists propose that automatic processes have certain additional properties. One of these is functioning without the accompaniment of conscious awareness. Another is requiring little or no mental effort. In some accounts, the latter is directly tied to one of the first features: imposing no capacity demands.

Contemporary theorists differ in which features they ascribe to automatic processes beyond the core set of two as well as in other respects. Some propose that once automatic processing has developed, these operations function independent of and in parallel with nonautomatic processes that could potentially carry out the same job. In this view, the transition from nonautomatic (controlled) to automatic processing involves the emergence of a new kind of process that coexists with and supplements nonautomatic processing (Shiffrin, 1988). Other theorists envision processing undergoing a smooth transition from controlled to automatic (MacLeod and Dunbar, 1988). Another issue on which differences exist is whether the various features of automaticity all emerge at the same time. As Zbrodoff and Logan (1986) point out, automaticity might be a useful concept even if its different features are not acquired simultaneously.

These issues address the question of whether automaticity should be regarded as a discrete and unitary state. In the discussion that follows we first consider a more basic question: whether the core propositions that automaticity theories have in common (lack of interference with competing tasks, functioning without voluntary control) are empirically valid—whether practice, in fact, produces such changes. If these core propositions are not valid, then a theory of practice will require different conceptual foundations.

Empirical Evidence on Practice

Lack of Capacity Demands   When tasks have been sufficiently well practiced, do they cease to impose capacity demands or, as it is sometimes put, do they stop requiring attention? An adequate test of that proposition requires giving a person extensive practice with mental operations that demonstrably interfere with each other early in practice. The question, then, is whether practice eliminates or greatly diminishes the interference. As described in chapter 6, the most clear-cut interference effects are found with pairs of independent stimulus-response tasks that require response choice or certain other forms of decision making. Interference in this situation shows up as a slowing—the PRP effect. Does the PRP effect disappear with dual-task practice or practice of the component tasks by themselves? Although the question is straightforward enough, few studies have addressed it. Gottsdanker and Stelmach (1971) had subjects perform a PRP task for more than 100 sessions. The PRP effect (i.e., magnitude of task 2 slowing as a function of S1-S2 interval) was reduced but it still did not completely disappear. What can one conclude? On the one hand, suppose central operations such as response selection in the two tasks were subject to queuing both before and after practice. In that case, one would still expect that the critical stages in both tasks would be speeded up (in fact, practice in choice RT tasks seems to affect primarily response selection; Pashler and Baylis, 1991). As a consequence of this speed-up, the amount of second task slowing found at short versus long SOAs would inevitably be reduced. Thus, Gottsdanker and Stelmach's results are consistent with the persistence of bottleneck-type interference. On the other hand, the data do not definitely exclude the possibility that the response-selection bottleneck *was* eliminated with practice. The reason is that the study involved two manual responses, and a small amount of residual interference may reflect conflicts in manual response initiation that are normally masked when response selection in task 2 is time consuming, as it would be early in practice.[1]

Dutta and Walker (1995) examined more modest amounts of practice in the PRP situation and found direct evidence that central queuing persisted. They had subjects practice a PRP task for 2500 trials; there was no change in the pattern of RT effects indicating central queuing (additive effects of task 2 response-selection difficulty and interval between stimuli). In summary, existing data do not show that the PRP effect (or central interference at response selection and decision making) goes away with practice, and significant but not enormous amounts of practice may leave it intact. Of course, it is entirely possible that hundreds or thousands of hours of practice might accomplish what a few or a dozen hours cannot.

Outside the scope of discrete tasks and the psychological refractory period, a number of well-known studies evaluated the effects of extensive practice in continuous dual tasks, observing a reduction or elimination of interference. Spelke, Hirst, and Neisser (1976) examined a phenomenon first investigated around the turn of the last century under the title "automatic writing" (see Koutstaal, 1992, for an interesting review of this topic, which was the subject of widespread fascination about 100 years ago). They had two subjects practice reading short stories while writing down spoken words (taking dictation) as soon as the words were spoken; the experimenter read the next word aloud as soon as both subjects had written the current word. Subjects participated for about an hour a day for seventeen weeks. After about thirty sessions of training, they were reading approximately as fast while taking dictation as they were in the single-task condition. Taking dictation did not reduce subjects' understanding of the stories or memory of their contents, as indicated by subsequent comprehension tests. Remarkably, this performance was maintained even when the experimenters changed the instructions to require the subjects to write down the superordinate category to which the word belonged, rather than the word itself.

Another way to study highly skilled performance is to find individuals who have already practiced an activity for a long time outside the laboratory. This strategy has not been widely used, but it has yielded some evidence of elimination of dual-task interference with practice. In one well-known study, Shaffer (1975) found that a highly skilled typist could type at nearly normal speed and accuracy while carrying out any of several other activities, including reciting nursery rhymes and shadowing (repeating spoken input).

These results are often cited as demonstrating that after practice, central (and, indeed, all) mental operations in these various verbal tasks come to work simultaneously with and independent of other mental activities.[2] There can be no doubt of one thing: subjects in both studies were able to produce simultaneous streams of activity in two tasks, that is, they were undeniably talking and moving their hands at the same time. The question is whether this implies that the mental operations involved in each task came to function independently. In chapter 6 we saw examples of PRP studies in which the first task required a prolonged response sequence (e.g., three key presses) and the second involved a punctate vocal response. The second response often came out roughly in the middle of the first task response sequence, with no apparent interference between these response productions (Pashler and Christian, 1994; Van Galen and ten Hoopen, 1976). However, other results from these studies indicated that central processing in the two tasks was not independent at all—in fact, it was subject to queuing. One should expect from a central bottleneck model (e.g, figure 6.4) that responses selected sequentially may overlap in their execution, particularly if the first one to be selected takes longer to produce.

This observation has interesting implications for the interpretation of continuous-task results such as those of Spelke et al. and Shaffer (some of these implications were alluded to earlier). Most obviously, it demonstrates that simultaneous response streams in continuous tasks do not exclude the possibility that response selection and other central operations in the two tasks were performed at different times. Such a strategy (asynchronous planning and continuous production) was mentioned by Shaffer (1975), Welford (1980), and Broadbent (1982); it is referred to here as central switching. This switching is likely to be rather slow, with central processing on each task lasting for 100 msec or more. Suggestions of switching at rates of a few milliseconds or tens of milliseconds seem neurally implausible (cf Sejnowski, 1986).

Is central switching really a psychologically plausible account for findings such as those of Shaffer and of Spelke et al.? For switching to result in continuous output, certain conditions must be met. If the central processes in each task consumed more than half the total time during which that task was performed, it would not be possible to perform the tasks at full speed due to competition for central processing. Suppose the central processing in each task requires, say, 300 msec of every 2 seconds that the task is being performed. If responses for each task are held in a buffer and emitted at the appropriate time, it might not be terribly critical exactly when the 300 msec of central processing is carried out, since it would be well before the 2 seconds of response output. On assumptions like these, it should not be particularly difficult for the person to schedule mental events so that both tasks result in a continuous stream of output (figure 8.1), but it should be quite difficult for an experimenter to detect the fact that this is going on.

We have used the term switching to describe a conception about what might be going on in continuous tasks; what is the relationship between

Response Stream 1

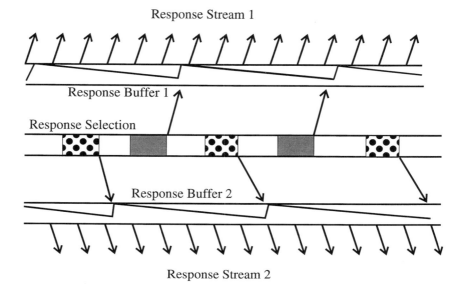

Figure 8.1
How central switching may produce two apparently continuous and independent response streams (stream 1 and stream 2). With time proceeding from left to right, response selection for the two tasks actually occurs asynchronously (alternating gray and polka-dot regions). Each response selection fills up a first-in-first-out response buffer for a given task; meanwhile, responses are rapidly and continuously emitted from each buffer.

switching and queuing? Both are ways of making the best of an inability to carry out central operations in two tasks simultaneously. In the PRP task, the subject has the goal of completing both tasks as quickly as possible. Given this constraint, queuing is the only reasonable strategy; failing to perform the central stages of task 2 as soon as the corresponding stages of task 1 are complete would only delay completion of the tasks. Because queuing involves one task waiting for another, it is readily detectable with the chronometric analyses described earlier. In continuous tasks such as those studied by Spelke et al. and Shaffer, on the other hand, the goal is to maintain a continuous output stream in each task. Given the assumptions in the preceding paragraph, central switching may result in two fluent streams of processing and may therefore be essentially undetectable (possible tests are suggested below, however).

Is it plausible that the preconditions for switching would hold in tasks such as typing, shadowing, and taking dictation? All of these tasks involve words and some involve sentences. If people planned individual actions corresponding to smaller units such as letters and phonemes, the hypothetical time estimates suggested earlier (300 msec selection for 2 seconds of action) would be far off the mark; each task would make incessant demands for central processing. The evidence that people use higher-level units in these tasks is very strong, however. For example, practice not only allows typists to type faster, it also causes their typing speed to depend more on the familiarity of the letter strings they type (Fendrick, 1937). This suggests that practice allows a transition from planning single key strokes to planning response units at the level of the word. Another piece of evidence is the fact that skilled typists also benefit more from "look-ahead" (sometimes referred to as preview), the opportunity to view characters to the right of the one currently being typed. There is also a significant eye-hand span in typing, in which the character being fixated is well to the right of the character being typed at the same instant (Salthouse and Saults, 1987). All of these observations suggest that practiced typists select key stroke sequences corresponding to units about the size of a word (Salthouse, 1984; Shaffer and Hardwick, 1970). Similar chunking may also occur in shadowing, reading aloud, and taking dictation, among other tasks.

In experiments like Shaffer's, then, one would expect that skilled typists would have acquired the ability to select response units that take some time to produce. In the experiment by Spelke et al., one would suspect that practice taking dictation would build on preexisting experience with auditory word recognition and writing. In addition, as Broadbent, 1982, points out, the absence of interference in Spelke et al.'s experiments should not be overstated. The subjects made substantially more errors taking dictation while reading than they did while taking dictation by itself. Therefore, one would not have to propose flawlessly executed central switching to reconcile their results with central switching.

In summary, the literature contains impressive examples of people performing two practiced continuous tasks at the same time with little apparent interference. This is a striking fact about human performance, but its implications for underlying mental operations are not clear.

Practiced continuous tasks are likely to impose only intermittent demands on central processing machinery, and for this reason covert switching of central processing will usually be undetectable.

The reader might wonder whether this discussion of central switching conjures up unobservable events to avoid reaching the obvious conclusions of these studies. Perhaps so, but the switching analysis is eminently testable. Suppose an activity such as typing (for a skilled typist) occupies central decision-making machinery only intermittently, as suggested above. Although there may be little or no interference when this task is combined with another task that also makes intermittent central demands, interference should arise as soon as such a task is combined with another task that imposes demands that are *not* intermittent. How does one construct a task that lasts for a significant period of time and makes continuous rather than intermittent central demands? The task must require nonstop decision making or response choice, and the performance measure must reveal any delays in central processing. The self-paced serial tasks with previewed stimuli and relatively quick responses provide one solution in that subjects choose one response after another. Because of preview, they have access to stimuli ahead of the one they are currently responding to, so central processing does not have to wait for stimulus processing. The responses are punctate so, unlike in an activity such as typing, central processing does not have to wait for execution of lengthy responses.

An example would be making quick vocal responses to tones, where the response to tone n triggers presentation of tone n+2. Other kinds of tasks that could be used for this purpose would be self-paced tasks in which each internally generated response is the stimulus for the next operation (e.g., counting backward by threes). Studies of self-paced tasks involving stimulus preview demonstrate that response selection does indeed become the rate-limiting factor, as one would expect from the preceding discussion (Pashler, 1994b). To return to the problem at hand, then, when a self-paced task of this type is combined with another continuous task such as skilled typing, any underlying switching in the continuous task will, in the view suggested here, have to result in significant dual-task interference. On the other hand, if typists can type and perform self-paced tasks with negligible interference in either task, the switching analysis will be rejected. Our preliminary results with five highly skilled typists seem to be in line with the switching account (Pashler and Fagot, unpublished observations).

As mentioned in chapter 6, Kalsbeek and Sykes (1967) examined the effects of five days of practice using a design fairly similar to the one suggested here. Subjects performed a primary task involving manual responses to lights and a secondary task involving foot responses to tones. After five days of practice, performing the first task at 70% of its maximum rate reduced performance on the second task to about 70% of its maximum rate; given the overlap one would expect in perception and response production, this seems roughly consistent with the idea that central stages in the two tasks were performed asynchronously.

So far we have discussed the question of whether practice eliminates the central interference in mental operations such as decision making and response selection. The core proposition of automaticity theory—that practice eliminates capacity demands—implies that limitations not only in central processing but also in perception and control over selective attention should go away with practice. Research described in chapter 3 revealed that perceptual capacity limitations arise with complex stimuli (e.g., identifying two simultaneously presented words). In chapter 6 it was argued that this form of capacity limitation is independent of the central processing bottleneck we have just been discussing. A natural question, therefore, is whether practice allows visual search to be carried out independent of visual attention, eliminating the interference effects described in chapter 3. To answer this question, Hoffman, Nelson, and Houck (1983) had people practice searching for particular targets for up to twenty sessions. Performance stabilized after about six sessions. When the search task was combined with another concurrent visual discrimination, interference between visual detections in the tasks remained. It seems, therefore, that automatization of search does not eliminate capacity demands on visual attention.

Search Tasks and Memory Loads as Evidence of Automaticity   Despite the limited amount of relevant data, the findings described in the previous section raise serious doubts about the idea that automaticity eliminates competition at the level of central processing stages. The data of Hoffman et al. demonstrate that it does not eliminate competition for visual attention. Why, then, is the concept of automaticity so widely accepted? The observations that may be cited most frequently to show that practice eliminates capacity demands do not involve stimulus-response tasks at all, but instead involve effects of load within visual search or memory search tasks, or a combination of the two. In two well-known papers, Schneider and Shiffrin (1977) described effects of practice on a combined memory/visual search task. Subjects tried to find a target (any item belonging to a target set) anywhere in a display composed of one or more characters. Two training conditions were compared. The first was termed consistent mapping (CM) practice. In the CM condition, targets and distractors were drawn from two nonoverlapping sets. The second condition was termed varied mapping (VM) search; here, targets and distractors varied from one trial to the next, and they were drawn from a common set. Thus, a target in one trial might be a distractor in the next. With CM practice, performance improved steadily, and the effects of display set size and memory set size on RTs diminished (in other experiments, the dependent variable was the exposure duration required to achieve a given level of accuracy). In some cases, practice reduced these set size effects to the point at which they were negligible. By contrast, VM search performance was poorer than CM from the beginning, with substantial effects of display and memory set size, and it remained poor even after a great deal of practice.

According to Schneider and Shiffrin's interpretation, CM practice resulted in the search for targets becoming automatic. As a consequence, each display element could be matched against different targets in STM at the same time; meanwhile other display elements would be matched against the memory set as well. In the view of Schneider and Shiffrin, this shift to parallel processing accounted for the flat slopes. On the other hand, VM search was said to depend on sequential comparison of display elements with memory set items stored in STM, which VM practice does not overcome. If this analysis is correct, the memory/visual search task would seem to be a positive instance of the general claim under discussion—that with sufficient practice, mental operations operate independent of limited-capacity mental resources or mechanisms.

However, subsequent research has revealed serious problems for this analysis. First, VM search may not be an appropriate baseline from which to assess unpracticed performance, since subjects not only lack consistent practice, they also experience negative transfer from preceding trials. A second and related problem is that the two tasks combined in visual/memory search, memory scanning and visual search, are not necessarily serial at the beginning of practice. Consider a pure CM memory-scanning task in which a single probe is compared against a memory set, with this set always drawn from a fixed pool. When the number of items in the memory set in any individual trial is varied, slopes usually start out low even at the beginning of practice, and do not fall much farther with continued practice (Logan and Stadler, 1991). This obviously challenges the view that unpracticed memory scanning is necessarily serial. It also raises the possibility that in the experiments of Schneider and Shiffrin and their collaborators, it was visual search rather than memory search that was most profoundly affected by practice.

Detailed analyses of VM memory scanning do not support the view that without consistent practice, memory scanning is obligatorily serial. Sternberg's (1966) original proposal of serial exhaustive memory scanning was based on his finding of a linear function relating RTs to memory set size with approximately the same slope for "no" and "yes" responses. For the most part, memory-scanning experiments using Sternberg's paradigm involved either a VM procedure or what was usually called a fixed-set procedure in which lists change between sessions (Sternberg, 1975). Recent studies using both paradigms make a strong case for limited-capacity parallel search rather than serial search (McElree and Dosher, 1989). One sort of evidence is the observation that "no" responses to probes that are not in the current memory set but were in previous memory sets are slowed compared with other "no" responses (Monsell, 1978). According to the serial exhaustive model, only the current memory set is searched, and when this search has been completed, the negative response is chosen; in that account, there is no mechanism for determining the relationship of the probe to previous memory sets, and therefore this factor should have no effect on negative response latencies. Detailed analyses of RT distributions also lend strong support to a parallel model; a full description of these findings would lead beyond the scope of this book (see Hockley and Corballis, 1982; McElree and Dosher, 1989).

Schneider and Shiffrin's analysis of the effects of CM practice can also be questioned. According to their view, the memory set is held in short-term memory and targets are compared with it; after CM practice, these comparisons operate in parallel rather than sequentially. By the very nature of CM search, the memory set in any given trial is drawn from what may be called a superset, that is, a fixed pool from which targets in any given trial are selected. Logan and Stadler (1991) showed that in CM memory scanning, subjects search not just the current memory set, but the entire superset, because they frequently make false alarms to probes from the superset that are not in the current target set. After practice, therefore, the task may involve access to LTM rather than STM.

Together, these observations demonstrate that the simple serial-to-parallel transition envisioned by Schneider and Shiffrin (1977) is questionable for several reasons. First, if memory scanning does not start off as a serial process, then improvement in this task cannot provide support for any proposed serial-to-parallel transition. Second, if practice changes the task so it involves access to long-term memory for the entire memory superset, practice altered the mental operations, not merely their temporal relationship. One might respond to this argument by saying that if the comparison process does not start out serial or end up relying on STM, it nonetheless does culminate in a parallel process, as automaticity theories maintain. The problem with this view is that access to long-term memory has never been supposed to be a bottleneck in human information processing. Our ability to read words, to solve crossword puzzles, to remember what we had for breakfast, all of these involve simultaneously matching a probe against a huge number of potentially relevant long-term memory traces. Whether or not serial search is necessary for item recognition in short-term memory, it cannot possibly account for search of long-term memory, given the vast number of memory traces to be searched (Juola et al., 1971).

So far we have focused on memory scanning. We suggested that practice in tasks such as Schneider and Shiffrin's may affect visual search more markedly than it affects memory scanning. This brings us to the interesting issue of how practice changes visual search. Performance in visual search with simple stimuli is above all a function of the difficulty of discriminating targets and distractors, as the research described in chapter 3 demonstrated. With sufficiently complex target/background discriminations, especially those relating to the spatial arrangements of features, serial search is likely to be required. Does this remain so with practice? In tasks involving search for letters, slopes relating RTs to display set size typically fall with practice (Rabbitt, 1978). However, with some tasks involving spatial arrangement of features, steep slopes may remain even after extensive practice (e.g., Logan, 1994).

When practice produces an improvement in visual search, one can examine the way this transfers or fails to transfer to different tasks to elucidate the effects of practice. When targets stay the same and new distractors are introduced, good transfer is often observed (Rabbitt, Cumming, and Vyas, 1979). In some cases, improvement is maintained when the distractors remain the same and the target changes (Dumais, 1980). There does not seem to be much in the way of transfer from search to other tasks, however. Treisman, Vieira, and Hayes (1992) gave subjects many sessions of practice searching for target characters, either sets of letters or figures created by arranging five line segments, and found that search became much more efficient. The improvement was specific to visual search, however, and targets did not come to function as elementary features for other purposes. For example, they did not permit easy texture segregation (e.g., in a grid of letters, a region made up of target characters did not stand out for the subjects). It appears, then, that one important consequence of visual search training may be a specific tendency for the target characters to draw visual attention and a specific tendency for distractor characters not to do so, both of which may be dependent on having a particular task set, however. This account would be consistent with the observation that practiced visual search still interferes with concurrent visual tasks (Hoffman, Nelson, and Houck, 1983). Whereas practice in search has not been found to facilitate other tasks, practice in categorizing stimuli outside the laboratory may well facilitate search. When targets and distractors belong to nonoverlapping, well-learned sets such as letters and digits, search can be remarkably efficient. With letter targets among digits (or vice versa), for example, search for a single prespecified character is often about as efficient as search for any (unspecified) member of the set[3] (Egeth, Jouides, and Wall, 1972; Sperling et al., 1971). These conclusions about visual search are not all inconsistent with Schneider and Shiffrin's interpretations; for example, they spoke of targets coming to attract automatic attention responses. However, the changes that occur in visual search are not illuminated in any detail by the concept of automatization.

So far we have discussed changes in slopes observed in memory scanning and visual search tasks. Although practice improves performance in various ways, we have encountered no strong evidence that it eliminates capacity demands in tasks where such demands are evident early in practice. Another methodology has been used to examine effects of practice on capacity demands: having subjects hold onto a memory load while doing some other task (described in chapter 7). The effects of a concurrent memory load do not usually disappear with practice, but they are often reduced (e.g., Brown and Carr, 1989). Logan (1979) looked at the effects of a memory load in a choice RT experiment that also varied the number of stimulus-response alternatives. Early in practice, memory load interacted with the number of stimulus-response alternatives; that is, the combined effect of adding a memory load and increasing the number of alternatives exceeded the sum of the two effects alone. After approximately a half-dozen hours of practice, however, the effect of a memory load shrank and the two manipulations began to combine in a roughly additive manner. By contrast, when a new mapping was used each day, the interaction of memory load and number of alternatives continued throughout training. Logan suggested that the elimination of these interactions might provide a better criterion for automaticity than the elimination of memory and display set size effects proposed by Schneider and Shiffrin.

If one could assume that memory loads depleted available capacity, then the elimination of interactions might indicate that certain stages were ceasing to require capacity. As Logan himself noted (1978b), however, there is little evidence that holding information in short-term memory requires continuous activity or siphons off mental fuel. It seems more likely that maintaining a memory load makes people perform other tasks more slowly because rehearsing the memory load prevents them from optimally preparing for the other task. There are several reasons why this might be the case. For one thing, it may not be possible to rehearse the memory load and prepare for the speeded task simultaneously. Alternatively, perhaps the memory load and the set for the speeded task are represented in a common short-term memory[4] (Gottsdanker, 1980). In either case, if memory loads impair preparation but do not draw continuously on mental capacity throughout the retention interval, then changes in the pattern of memory load effects do not provide strong evidence for automaticity. The natural alternative is that practice facilitates preparation and that memory loads have their primary effects on preparation. This is a testable proposition, since preparatory effects can be assessed by measuring costs of task uncertainty (e.g., figure 6.3).

We have reviewed the results most widely cited as showing that capacity demands can be eliminated with practice. These results demonstrate that practice improves the efficiency of various processes including categorization, visual search, and task preparation; as far as one can tell, the improvements are largely stimulus specific. What the results fail to document, however, is the general claim that, with practice, mental processes stop demanding limited resources or interfering with concurrent operations. In summary, we have no good evidence that practice causes a qualitative change in the demands on central or peripheral processing capacity imposed by a given task. There is, of course, no doubt that practice speeds performance, reduces error rates, and produces relatively permanent changes in memory that allow a person to prepare a task more quickly and carry it out more effectively. Depending on the methodology used to assess interference effects, these improvements may reduce dual-task interference.

Lack of Voluntary Control

The second of the two core propositions of automaticity theory asserts that highly practiced mental operations, ranging from perception to response execution, can be triggered by mere presentation of an appropriate input to the process regardless of a person's voluntary intentions. Taken literally, this claim seems inconsistent with casual observations of human behavior. Most of us have had a great deal of practice pressing a brake pedal in response to a stop sign or reading aloud a word like "the," for example. Nonetheless, we do not often find ourselves making braking motions with our foot when we are sitting in the passenger seat and see a stop sign, nor do we often read "the" aloud when we happen to look at a newspaper in a crowded train.[5]

To account for such commonplace observations, the involuntariness hypothesis can be modified (proponents may indeed have had some modifications in mind but not mentioned them). For example, one could claim that the initiation of an automatic action can be prevented voluntarily, or that it requires appropriate contextual cues or mental set, but once it is begun, it proceeds ballistically. The data do not seem to support even this modified view, however. Logan (1982) had skilled typists type words (and in other cases, sentences) presented on a computer screen. In some trials, a stop signal sounded without warning, indicating that the typists should immediately cease typing. The subjects were perfectly able to stop typing in the middle of a word, usually freezing one or two key strokes after the stop signal. In fact, Logan noted, stopping speed was comparable with that when stop signals were presented in relatively unpracticed choice reaction time tasks. There is no support for the idea that practiced action sequences become involuntary in the sense that they start even when the person wishes to suppress them, or once started, proceed in a ballistic fashion.

Several other kinds of evidence are commonly taken to show that practice results in mental operations becoming involuntary. The most cited of these is the Stroop effect and its various kin. In the classic Stroop task, a person tries to read aloud the color of the ink in which a word is printed; responses are slowed when the word is an incompatible color word (e.g., "red" printed in green ink versus "bat" printed in green ink). The effect is usually attributed to response competition; that is, the color word is thought to activate an inappropriate name, which in turn slows down selection of the correct response (e.g., Duncan-Johnson and Koppell, 1981; Glaser and Dolt, 1977). Thus, the Stroop effect demonstrates that even when it would be advantageous to turn off one's word reading machinery, one cannot do so. This is claimed to demonstrate the automatic nature of the overlearned operation of reading.

Does the Stroop effect show that the activation of an internal representation of a word takes place completely independent of a person's intentions? Not necessarily, for several reasons. First, the subject has a task set to make judgments that involve color and to utter color words. The inadvertent processing of color-related information may be contingent on this set (cf Treisman, 1964c). Second, although the Stroop effect surely implies that *some* lexical analysis has taken place, one cannot assume that this analysis is as complete or rapid as it would be if the individual had the goal of reading the word (cf Zbrodoff and Logan, 1986). Third, as noted in chapter 2, the Stroop effect is substantially larger when the color and the word are part of the same object rather than different objects, which demonstrates that the processing reflected in the effect can be affected by attentional factors (Kahneman and Treisman, 1984).

For these reasons, the Stroop effect should not be taken as compelling evidence that reading is completely involuntary. Furthermore, the role of practice is not as obvious as one might assume. It is true, of course, that subjects have had extensive practice reading color words, and that if they had had not had any practice at all they would not show a Stroop effect (Color words in Turkish would obviously produce no Stroop effect for nonreaders of Turkish). However, Strooplike interference effects can be induced by irrelevant stimuli that are linked to competing responses through a mapping that the subject has never experienced prior to the experiment (e.g., in the Eriksen flanker effect described in chapter 2). This does not show that practice is *irrelevant* to response competition effects, of course. In fact, practice does modulate the relative strength of Strooplike effects.

This was demonstrated by MacLeod and Dunbar (1988), who trained subjects to pronounce color words in response to arbitrary shapes. Early in training, subjects named the color of these shapes with little interference from the shape-color-word associations (analogous to the Turkish example); on the other hand, the irrelevant color interfered with pronouncing the color words to the shapes. After twenty practice sessions the asymmetry had reversed: associations between shapes and color-word names intruded on the color naming task, whereas the effect in the other direction virtually disappeared. This postpractice asymmetry corresponds to what is normally found in the conventional Stroop task. Thus, the relative "Stroop power" of the word-to-name and color-to-name mappings seems to reflect differences in the amount of practice people have had with the different mappings. One can conclude, therefore, that practice plays some role in modulating these indirect effects. However, in light of the fact that practice is not a necessary condition for obtaining response-competition effects with nominally irrelevant stimuli, together with the other points raised in preceding paragraphs, one cannot reasonably claim that the Stroop effect illustrates a general tendency for practiced operations to be executed regardless of people's intentions. A more justifiable conclusion would be that people are not able to inhibit completely the processing of irrelevant inputs along dimensions that are closely related to their current task goals, and that practice exacerbates this inability somewhat.

Zbrodoff and Logan (1986) provided an interesting demonstration of the fact that Strooplike effects need not imply truly involuntary or ballistic processing. Their task involved arithmatic calculation, and focused on one of the more esoteric Strooplike phenomena: a slowing in reporting the falsity of an equation like 4 + 3 = 12, an equation that would be true if a different arithmetic operator were substituted, in this case, multiplication for addition. This effect could be taken to show that people cannot prevent an unwanted calculation from being executed. Using what appears to be a more sensitive measure, however, Zbrodoff and Logan revealed that arithmetic calculation can be substantially inhibited voluntarily. When subjects heard a stop signal shortly after beginning an arithmetic task (e.g., stating the sum of 8 + 3 aloud) they succeeded in inhibiting their responses in a large fraction of trials. Furthermore, their ability to recognize the equations in a recognition-memory test declined the earlier the stop signals were presented in a given trial, suggesting that with early stop signals, subjects were able to inhibit the underlying calculation rather than merely block the overt response.

What can be concluded, then? The results described in this section seem to argue for modest limitations on the extent to which people can exert voluntary control over various kinds of processing, with practice playing some role but not necessarily a critical role in determining the extent of this control. When people have a set to process a stimulus in a certain way, irrelevant stimuli or irrelevant aspects of the relevant stimulus often undergo some of the same kind of processing as relevant stimuli. More heavily practiced routines will sometimes result in larger effects (e.g., Stroop or flanker), but completely unpracticed task sets may produce effects of these kinds as well. What the results do not demonstrate is that extensive practice renders any kind of processing wholly independent of task set.

Reassessing Automaticity

This review reveals that the empirical literature either refutes or remains silent on the core propositions of automaticity theory. The fact that many textbooks present automaticity as an established fact is therefore rather disconcerting. The theory has not escaped criticism, however; the empirical arguments raised here complement other recent critiques. Duncan (1986) concluded that the definition of consistent practice is inherently vague. Even in a VM search, he noted, there is a consistent relationship between stimuli and responses if one construes the memory set and the imperative stimulus to be part of the effective stimulus (i.e., even in VM search, whenever the memory set contains a K and the imperative stimulus is a K, the response is "yes"). This criticism points out that the distinction between CM and VM relies on an intuitive but ill-defined conception of what counts as a stimulus. Cheng (1985) offered another critique that focused on Schneider and Shiffrin's formulation. She suggested that the changes in practice are likely to involve what she termed "restructuring" of the task—coming to perform it in a different way. This conclusion is consistent with the suggestions raised above regarding how practice may affect visual/memory search.

Logan (1988) proposed a theory about practice effects that he referred to as a theory of automaticity. It attempts to account for the effects of practice by supposing that new traces (instances) are accumulated in memory as a result of particular experiences in carrying out the task. According to this proposal, relatively unpracticed performance usually involves some kind of algorithmic calculation, but with practice, people come to rely more and more on direct memory retrieval. The task that Logan explored most extensively in this connection is mental arithmetic, which obviously can be carried out either by rule-based calculation or by rote memory retrieval. Direct retrieval and algorithmic calculation are performed simultaneously and effectively race against each other;

whichever process finishes more quickly determines the response and its latency. Over the course of practice, the race has more and more participants, because a new trace is laid down after each trial capable of supporting direct memory retrieval in subsequent trials. A response is generated as soon as any retrieval process has been completed. It is a statistical fact that the more participants in a race, the faster the average time for the winner, even if all participants are drawn from the same distribution of speeds. This simple and rather elegant conception makes remarkably accurate predictions about how response times change with practice, without assuming strengthening of traces or tuning of weights. It not only predicts that the speedup in mean RTs should follow a power function, but it also makes accurate predictions about how practice should affect the shape of the entire RT distribution (Logan, 1992).

This theory does an impressive job of accounting for the speedup that occurs as a result of practice, but it does not directly predict either of the core propositions of automaticity theory—elimination of capacity limits and loss of voluntary control. Logan (1988) maintained, however, that it could easily be supplemented with further assumptions to make these predictions, something he regarded as a virtue. Based on the empirical findings described earlier, though, it may be a virtue of the theory that it does *not* predict these propositions, since they enjoy little empirical support. Logan's theory provides an interesting possible mechanism for the one consequence of practice whose occurrence cannot be denied: speedups in performance.

The theory has some limitations, however. As presently formulated, it proposes that latencies depend on the total number of times the subject has made the same response to the same stimulus, but not with the lag between the current trial and the last such instance encountered. In fact, lag has powerful effects: people respond more rapidly the more recently they have encountered the same stimulus (Kornblum, 1973; Pashler and Baylis, 1991). According to Logan (personal communication), simulations suggest that variability in trace strength leaves the successful predictions of the theory intact. A second debatable point is whether algorithmic retrieval operates in parallel with direct memory retrieval. Based on the evidence for central queuing described in chapter 6, it would seem surprising if these operations could always work in parallel, although they might sometimes.[6] Indeed, Rickard (in press) presented data that appears to argue that subjects may use only the algorithm or memory retrieval (but not both) in a given trial.

Speculations: Germs of Truth in Automaticity Theory

As noted, automaticity is a common feature of folk psychology, and in one form or another it was accepted by the pioneers of introspective attention theory including James (1890) and Külpe (1902). Surely, one might insist, one idea would not have found its way into so much everyday psychology and been endorsed by such insightful writers if it had no validity. Is it possible to reconcile the informal observations that lead people to assume automaticity with the negative findings described above? It is a speculative but perhaps instructive exercise to try, speculative partly because the negative findings themselves do not rest on terribly firm ground, as acknowledged earlier. Readers who see no value in such exercises may wish to skip this section.

No systematic method of surveying people's introspections enjoys any general acceptance at the present time; the best approach may be to consider some different propositions associated with automaticity theory—lack of attention demands, involuntary operation, and lack of awareness—and try to find paradigm cases of the everyday experiences that people regard as instances of these propositions. Why do people say that practiced tasks stop demanding attention? Most everyone would probably agree that when we first begin to acquire a skill such as driving an automobile, it requires "exclusive concentration." After sufficient practice, however, we seem able to combine it with other activities such as having a conversation or fiddling with the radio.[7] How should our apparent ability to perform concurrent tasks while driving be reconciled with the possibility that central interference in pairs of punctate tasks may persist after substantial amounts of practice?

In analyzing an activity such as driving, it may be helpful to make a distinction between what might be called self-paced and nonself-paced tasks. In nonself-paced tasks, which include most tasks performed in a laboratory, the subject's pace is determined by an external agents or events; the amount of work performed per unit of time is therefore independent of how quickly the subject works. In self-paced tasks (e.g., serial RT), when one piece of work is finished, it is time to start the next. Consider driving. The perceptual monitoring demands of this task are essentially continuous but usually somewhat forgiving of brief lapses. The components that are likely to be centrally demanding (e.g., planning steering maneuvers) arise intermittently as a function of events on the road. For all practical purposes, these aspects of driving constitute a nonself-paced task. This has important implications for changes in dual-task interference that occur when people acquire driving skills. Suppose that practice does not produce automaticity at all, but merely makes whatever operations impose central demands (e.g., planning a steering maneuver, initiating a motor program to change gears) comes to be performed more quickly. Because driving is nonself-paced, this speedup increases the proportion of driving time during which other centrally demanding mental activities can be carried out. Of course, one would still expect that immediate planning of responses would be required from time to time, thereby delaying concurrent activities, such as deciding what to say next in a conversation. Early in the learning process, driving might require almost continuous central processing, especially given the need to prepare as well as carry out maneuvers. With practice, however, these central operations may become quicker and more infrequent, consuming less and less of one's time. Of course, perceptual monitoring demands remain continuous, but these would not be expected to interfere with central operations, based on the findings described in chapter 6.

One might question whether this analysis is sufficient to account for our subjective experiences, which, according to some, suggest that after years of driving, there is no interference at all between conversing and driving. First of all, many people, especially urban drivers, might disagree with this claim. Even assuming that many people do have such introspections, however, they may simply be failing to notice small delays. As noted earlier, people seem to have little awareness of brief interruptions produced by competing tasks when these do not seriously disrupt performance. A delay of 500 msec in a conversation, caused by the need to plan a steering maneuver, may be indistinguishable from the pauses that occur in conversations for a variety of other reasons. Our STM capabilities are more than adequate to allow us to hold onto the context and resume the conversation without disruption. Of course, any interference that led to a breakdown in task set or confusions between the concurrent talk and the conversation would probably be salient, but these are rare, presumably because driving and conversing are so dissimilar. The point, then, is that what we casually regard as independent processing in situations such as driving might, when examined in fine-grained detail, turn out to involve the same brief processing bottlenecks found in laboratory tasks. In the absence of any reason to assume otherwise, this would seem to be a reasonable working hypothesis. It could be tested with experiments conducted in driving simulators.

What about involuntary action? The examples from everyday life that people seem to find most compelling are categorized by Reason (1990) under the heading of capture errors. These occur when a person under stress or subject to distraction carries out a habitual action (e.g., driving home) when he or she intended to do something different and nonhabitual (e.g., stopping to pick up some laundry). These effects, noted by James and other early writers on attention, are highly compelling to many. They can also be elicited experimentally (della Malva et al., 1993; Fischman and Lim, 1991). How should one reconcile such effects with the evidence that practice does not induce truly involuntary (uninhibitable) performance in laboratory tasks? What differentiates the driver who fails to pick up the laundry and the skilled typists studied by Logan (1982) who were perfectly capable of stopping on command? At one moment, the driver has a plan to stop and pick up the laundry; a few minutes later, he or she fails to put this plan into effect. A goal was violated. One does not have to run the experiment to be confident that if commanded by an experimenter sitting in the passenger seat to turn off toward the laundry at the appropriate time, the driver would in fact have done so (and been grateful for the reminder!).

The capture error is fundamentally failure to remember to adopt the proper task set at the proper time. It is not an instance of zombielike automatism or ballistic behavior, and therefore does not conflict with the observation that skilled performers are capable of inhibiting practiced behaviors. Here again, our ordinary intuitions classify behavior at a relatively molar level, not differentiating between goals and momentary intentions. This is not to deny that capture errors are interesting psychological phenomena. Active preparatory work seems to be necessary to adopt and maintain a task set, a point that is discussed further below; in the absence of such work, plans seem to drift toward highly practiced routines they may resemble. This is intriguing, but it constitutes involuntary action in only a very loose sense.

What about awareness? As pointed out earlier, talking about awareness of behavior is ambiguous. The phrase could refer to conscious access to different kinds of information, ranging from recognition of the existence of stimulation triggering a response all the way to awareness of kinesthetic and other feedback resulting from carrying out the action. Awareness of these different kinds of information may be independent of each other, and the ability to report one might even vary inversely with the ability to report another. The claim that automatic activities are carried out without awareness has to be sharpened.

What kinds of observations lead people to make such claims? A highly informal survey suggests that people are most struck by their inability to verbalize *how* they carry out a practiced action sequence such as dialing a telephone number, even when they might earlier have been able to describe it. For example, I have trouble writing down the numbers that I dial most often, even though, when placed in front of a telephone (or even when imagining one), I can easily dial them. Is it sensible to say that dialing has become automatic? As far as I can tell, having tried the experiment only informally, it does not satisfy other criteria of automaticity; I cannot, for example, dial one of these numbers while doing a self-paced task such as counting backward from 400 by threes. (This claim could be properly tested, of course.) Assuming this to be correct, what can be concluded? The concept of automaticity is simply not very illuminating here. Another common expression seems to come closer to the heart of the matter however; people say that memory is "in their fingers." This idea was alluded to by James (1890) and by Bahrick and Shelly (1958), who spoke of practiced manual tasks operating under proprioceptive control. What might this mean? The first representation one has of a telephone number is presumably stored in some form of speechlike code. With sufficient practice, programming the actions involved in dialing may come to rely on associative links between codes for finger movements and/or codes registering feedback from such movements; verbal mediation, and ultimately the verbal codes themselves, may drop out. What we call lack of awareness of the motor-based codes may simply reflect the elimination of verbal coding. Obviously, many cognitive routines are not easily verbalized. To label them unconscious for that reason presumes a very narrow conception of consciousness.

Another experience that people sometimes mention in connection with automatism and awareness is performing a highly routine task and then having scarcely any memory of having done it. This seems especially common when one follows a stream of thought unrelated to the task at hand. Does this imply that one is actually unconscious of the experiences and actions in the routine task at the moment they are taking place? Certainly, failure to remember a mental event is not tantamount to having been unaware of it when it happened. These experiences may occur under conditions in which people have engaged in little of what memory theorists call elaboration: retrieval of related information or recognition of connections between the events and any other stored information. In the absence of elaboration, extremely rapid forgetting takes in the laboratory as well (Muter, 1980) even in cases where there is no question that people have adequately processed the material initially.

The foregoing discussion is admittedly highly speculative, although surely no more so than the sweeping claims about automaticity that have been critiqued here. A number of these speculations could potentially be tested. It seems that psychologists beginning around the turn of the last century took the notion of automatism literally. It has not been demonstrated that practice makes mental operations involuntary or free of capacity demands, although, of course, subsequent research may demonstrate that these things do happen. In the absence of such demonstrations, one wonders why strong claims about automatization have attained the status of orthodoxy, at least judging from textbooks? Perhaps it is because these ideas resonate well with commonsense intuitions. To some writers, the phenomenology of automatization may be so compelling that experimental data scarcely seem necessary. If the speculations in the preceding section have any merit, however, observations about mental life that are valid over a relatively coarse temporal scale (seconds, minutes, hours) are mistakenly assumed to apply at the fine time scales over which more elementary cognitive operations take place. Such a mistake would be understandable given that we have no training in monitoring our own behavior over brief time scales, nor any good reason to learn to do so. If these suggestions are correct, a more accurate approach to automatism would take as its starting point the ideas of Oliver Munsell, who suggested in 1871 that "each physical act require[s] a separate act of attention but, with practice, the degree of attention required diminishe[s], until, at last, the act bec[omes] seemingly, but not really automatic" (p. 11).

Mental Effort

"Effort" is a common word in everyday language. Like "attention," ordinary talk about effort goes hand in hand with a number of widely shared and informal ideas about mental life. In this regard, the ordinary notion of effort is part of a folk psychological theory, just as attention is. One tenet is that effort is something we choose to apply or not to apply by a conscious act of will. Whereas we may or may not be able to achieve a desired level of performance by dint of mental effort, it would make little sense to say that we could not control how much effort we expend. In contrast, it clearly makes sense to say that a person's attention has been captured against his or her will. The second element of the folk theory is that performance on a task or activity is improved by effort, or at least that this is often the case for many tasks. A third idea is that devoting effort carries subjective costs and perhaps objective ones as well. The subjective costs include an immediate aversive state (a sense of being taxed or a desire to relax), and the objective costs are generally supposed to arise only after some protracted effort, causing decrements in performance (sometimes labeled fatigue).

As with the concept of attention, many psychologists have taken this informal theory of effort for granted and used it freely in interpreting experimental results. Sometimes these results do not have any demonstrable connection to the claims about effort just described. For example, a large literature describes research in which psychophysiologists examined the effects of varying task difficulty (e.g., short vs long memory loads, small vs large response ensembles) on cardiac, respiratory, pupillary, and skin responses. The results are often described as providing psychophysiological indexes of effort. However, they do not demonstrate that these manipulations and measures have any strong relationship to effort per se (e.g., to graded voluntary control or to subjective perception of effort). In the absence of such a demonstrated linkage, this research might better be described as revealing physiological concomitants of information-processing demands rather than effort.

In the first few chapters of this book we held the concept of attention at arm's length and examined different empirical propositions related to it. The concept of effort can be treated similarly. There are a number of interesting questions about how performance is affected by incentives or other factors that may affect how hard people try to perform a task well. These questions can be examined without assuming any mental commodity or resource corresponding to "effort." One natural place to start is whether people can actually control the efficiency of their cognitive or sensorimotor performance in a graded fashion. This leads naturally to how subjective sensations of effort relate to the processing demands of a task, and what kinds of short- or long-term costs (physiological, hedonic, or performance changes) are associated with demanding mental tasks.

To what extent can people improve the quality of their performance by "trying harder"? Kahneman (1973) suggested that control over sensorimotor performance is often limited to merely deciding whether or not to carry out a task in the first place. Once one decides to proceed, the amount of effort expended depends on the task. One cannot put as much effort into an easy task as into a difficult one. If one tries to add four plus five as if one's life depended on it, it is hard to do it any differently than if one merely thought it would be nice to know the answer. Although Kahneman highlighted the concept of effort (his book was titled *Attention and Effort*), he nonetheless rejected the lay view that effort can be allocated in a graded fashion, while proposing that tasks demand different amounts of effort.

An obvious way to examine the effects of varying levels of deliberate effort is by manipulating incentives or instructions. In the realm of choice RT tasks, the first study along these lines may have been performed by Collyer (1968). He found that incentives to perform especially well led subjects to improve both speed and accuracy. This suggests that Kahneman underestimated the extent to which people can control their performance. Of interest, the speedup was additive with variables affecting several different processing stages. This additivity is not easy to interpret; it is, however, reminiscent of Logan's (1978b) finding that slowing caused by memory loads is also additive with most factor manipulations in choice reaction time tasks.[8]

N. E. Johnson, Saccuzzo, and Larson (1995) manipulated incentives with payoffs in three fairly simple tasks: inspection time comparing the length of lines followed by masks, letter matching, and a counting task requiring subjects to keep a running total of several quantities in working memory. Whereas incentives led subjects to report having tried harder in all of the tasks, only on the counting task did objective performance improve. The authors suggested that the difference was one of complexity, with motivation having greater effects on the more cognitively complex activity. The speeded letter-matching task does not appear grossly different in complexity from Collyer's choice RT tasks, however, so the different outcomes of these studies could bear further investigation. At the very least, one can conclude that people are sometimes capable of exerting continuous control over levels of performance.

Focusing on studies of the effects of stressors on human performance, Sanders (1983) suggested effort may primarily function to correct suboptimal levels of arousal and activation. This idea was motivated by the observation that sleep-deprived individuals often perform simple information-processing tasks at a normal level for a short-time, especially when given incentives or knowledge of results. However, they usually find it very unpleasant to keep their performance level up, and they rarely maintain it for long in the laboratory. In Sanders' view, application of effort works to counteract low arousal, although it can do so only for short periods.

Even if people can control their performance to some extent by varying how hard they try, different tasks often seem to entail a minimum level of effort, as Kahneman suggested. This raises the question of what properties of a task determine effortfulness. Many different characteristics of a task might potentially affect the subjective effort required to carry it out. Tasks vary in the extent to which they require different information-processing operations. Some of these operations are describable in terms of processing stages in elementary tasks, for example, perceptual analysis, decision making, response execution, and timing. Tasks also vary in other respects as well; they make different demands on working memory, they require long-term memory retrieval to different extents, they differ in the number and salience of errors, and so on. The question about how these contribute to mental effort boils down to a question of classic psychophysics: what function relates subjective effortfulness to the processing requirements or other features of a task?

To analyze the psychophysics of effortfulness in a comprehensive way, one would have to collect effort ratings in a broad range of different tasks, preferably including pairs of fairly simple tasks that differ only in specified ways. Unfortunately, few comparisons of this kind have been made. Measures of subjective effort have largely been the province of applied psychologists interested in predicting usability of human/machine interfaces from workload ratings (questionnaires asking people about effortfulness and other stressful aspects of a task). The tasks examined in this literature are heterogeneous and mostly rather complicated. Within a given task, however, subjective judgments of workload turn out to be reasonably reliable (Tsang and Vidulich, 1994). Most variables that produce poorer performance in a task also increase ratings of effortfulness. Performing two tasks at the same time, for example, almost invariably has both of these effects (Yeh and Wickens, 1988). Some variables produce different patterns of effects, however. Increasing the rate at which events occur in experimenter-paced tasks often increases effort ratings without affecting performance (Vidulich and Wickens, 1986). This may not be so surprising, if people assess total effort by integrating over time rather than assessing maximum demand. Increasing incentives often raises workload ratings and performance at the same time (Vidulich and Wickens, 1986), which one might expect if it motivates a greater allocation of limited resources.

Studies of subjective workload with applied tasks produced a number of broad generalizations about what processing demands contribute most to ratings of effortfulness (Vidulich, 1988). First, increases in response execution difficulty do not seem to increase subjective workload very much. Second, working memory demands seem strongly related to subjective workload. For example, Derrick (1988) found that a relatively complex visual search task was rated substantially less effortful than a task requiring subjects to categorize tones into a handful of frequency categories (absolute judgment tasks are likely to place high demands on working memory). These generalizations are vague, of course; future research might provide better information by assessing the effects of precisely targeted task differences and looking specifically at ratings of mental effort rather than overall task workload.

What connections can one draw between effort and capacity limitations restricting our ability to perform more than one task at any given time? Many writers (e.g., Kahneman, 1973) equated subjective effort with processing capacity, and suggested that processing capacity can be allocated to more than one task in a graded fashion. By contrast, we saw in chapter 6 that, at a fine-grained level, interference in central mental processing is likely to reflect discrete interference (queuing) rather than graded sharing. Does this effectively sever any connection between effort and capacity limitations? At the very least, such a linkage becomes more elusive than in Kahneman's theory. One could entertain the hypothesis that the effortfulness of performing a task reflects the proportion of the time during which operations subject to a central bottleneck are occurring. The data described earlier are not grossly inconsistent with this, but it is my impression that some tasks that involve essentially continuous response selection (e.g., visual-manual serial RT with preview) would be described by most subjects as engrossing but not particularly effortful.

Subjective Effort: Causes and Consequences?

In trying to understand why certain mental processes should be accompanied by a stronger sense of effort than others, one is led to a basic question that has rarely been discussed in the literature: why people find mental activity taxing in the first place. Presumably the ultimate reason in the evolutionary sense that people experience aversive sensations when they exert themselves physically is because doing so uses energy, and energy is often in short supply; an organism wired up to spend energy for no gain will tend to lower its Darwinian fitness. Could energy conservation be the ultimate basis for our sensations of mental exertion as well? Brain function actually has a metabolic cost that is not trivial. Hoyer (1982) reviewed the literature on brain blood flow and oxidative metabolism, and concluded that in young adults the brain accounts for about 20% of cardiac output and between 20% and 25% of oxygen and glucose requirements.

The critical question, however, is whether the mental tasks that people find subjectively effortful actually increase consumption of metabolic energy more than subjectively easy tasks. Studies of blood flow and glucose uptake suggest that they do not. Overall, cerebral blood flow does not seem to differ as a function of whether the subject is thinking hard or passively sitting, for example (Sokoloff et al., 1955). Positron emission tomography reveals patterns of glucose uptake. For our purposes, these data have to be interpreted with caution, since they are usually normalized to facilitate comparing uptake across different regions, rather than across different tasks. Despite this limitation, results of PET studies do suggest that the brain's large visual areas, which can be heavily activated by passive viewing, usually take up far more glucose than the comparatively small frontal and prefrontal areas that would be expected to be critically involved in what people would likely judge "difficult thinking" tasks (A. Roskies, personal communication). Thus, what most people would call hard thinking may well consume no more total energy than watching television.

If physical and mental exertion draw on a single limited pool of energetic resources, which seems rather unlikely a priori, some relationship should exist between exertion in one domain and performance in the other. This topic was a subject of much interest around the end of the last century. Loeb (1887) found that mental exertion reduced the maximum amount of muscular force people generated when instructed to apply as much as possible. This finding was confirmed by Welch (1898), whose careful measurements using a wide variety of perceptual and cognitive tasks were published in the first volume of the *American Journal of Physiology*. Her subjects started a mental task, and while performing it, tried to impose as much force as they could on a dynamometer. Almost all mental tasks reduced maximum force, often by as much as 50%. This puzzling phenomenon remains unexplained.

It has also been found, however, that moderate amounts of physical exertion often *improve* mental performance, at least on simple tasks. Bills (1927), for example, had people learn nonsense syllables while resting or imposing a constant force on a dynamometer. Adding columns of digits benefited substantially from the simultaneous exertion. More recent studies confirmed this effect, but demonstrated that it typically exhibits an inverted-U shaped function. For example, Sjoberg (1975) found that people performed a serial choice-reaction task faster when pedaling a bicycle up to a certain level of exertion; beyond that, reaction times increased. Levitt and Gutin (1971) observed the same thing with subjects who walked or ran on a treadmill. The improvements in sensorimotor task performance with physical exertion are probably related to increases in arousal, and the inverted-U shaped function is well known in that domain (Sjoberg, 1975).

Despite the odd reduction in maximum physical output caused by mental activity, the idea of a single pool of limited energetic resources does not seem promising. A more plausible explanation for the experience of mental effort would be that repeated use of certain neural systems produces a transient reduction in their efficiency. A need to keep these systems in readiness could be the ultimate cause for the sensation of mental effort; effort, in this account, provides a beneficial disincentive to depleting cognitive reserves needlessly. This sounds plausible enough, but laboratory studies suggest that protracted cognitive activity during normal waking hours in people who are not sleep deprived does not actually impair performance. Several hours of performing continuous repetitive sensorimotor tasks such as serial reaction time seems to produce few reliable decrements (Bertelson and Joffe, 1963; Gaillard and Trumbo, 1976).[9] Unpublished data suggest that tasks that place heavy demands on working memory, which people seem to find especially effortful, do not do so, either.[10] In vigilance tasks that require observers to detect infrequent signals, on the other hand, a well-known decline emerges over the first ten minutes or so of performance (Parasuraman, 1984). This decline appears to be related to reduced activation or arousal, however, rather than fatigue or overuse of particular neural/mental structures. The relationship of vigilance decrement to physiological measures of arousal has nonetheless proved somewhat elusive (see Warm, 1977).

If the experience of mental effort is not an adaptation to conserve metabolic energy or to prevent processing machinery from being fatigued, what function does it serve? Perhaps the experience of effortfulness does not (or at least not exclusively) reflect consumption of any kind of limited resources, as writers on the topic have generally assumed. It might instead reflect internal recognition of a variety of different signs of impending cognitive failure or near-failure, akin to what engineers call exception signals. When heavy demands are imposed on working memory, for example, frequent exception signals may indicate the need for immediate rehearsal, and these may occur more often than they can be responded to. Inadequate levels of arousal (as in sleeplessness) may generate internal signals of cognitive difficulties; this would be consistent with Sanders' interpretation of effort. This account might seem to collapse the concepts of mental effort and stress. However, mental effort might differ from other sources of stress if effort reflected primarily internal indications of cognitive difficulty rather than anticipation of harmful events. These might be experimentally dissociable. In threshold-detection tasks, for example, people have a high error rate (and through feedback, may recognize this to be so) but if the problem is attributable to noise (unreliable association between internal state and what is being judged), there may be no exception signals. Biochemical comparisons of physical and mental effort reveal contrasting effects on urinary noradrenaline/adrenaline ratio and, possibly, salivary cortisol; the results are broadly consistent with the idea that effortful mental tasks have similar effects to noxious or threatening events (Fibiger and Singer, 1989).

The problem of mental effort should also be considered in the context of a other affective phenomena associated with cognitive activity, including positive as well as negative experiences (e.g., curiosity, engagement, fun). People do not always find solving difficult problems aversive and effortful, as the dozens of puzzle books found at any newsstand clearly attest. Although our understanding of mental effort is inadequate at present, many of these issues at the border of cognition and affect deserve further study and thought.

Control

In almost all of the experiments described in this book people carried out what are conventionally called tasks. Tasks generally involve a mapping between stimuli and responses; usually this mapping was completely arbitrary and unfamiliar to the subject. In some cases, it was described by a rule (press left for letters, right for digits), but it often consisted of nothing more than a list of S-R linkages. Rarely if ever did these mappings correspond to anything a subject would be inclined to do unless he or she had been instructed appropriately and wished to comply.

This strategy of analyzing cognitive processes by looking at discrete instructed tasks tends to focus research on mental events that one can trigger in response to imperative stimuli. This strategy has obvious advantages: it allows one to examine the behavior that occurs in situations where a particular cognitive operation of interest has occurred (at least in the great majority of the trials in which a correct response was produced); it also allows one to infer when this operation started. This makes it possible to analyze the time course of mental operations and their interactions with other processes.

This strategy is appealingly tidy, but it excludes important forms of mental activity. Even within the domain of laboratory tasks, it excludes preparatory processes that occur after the subject receives instructions but before the imperative stimuli are presented. The fact that subjects would not have performed the task unless instructed indicates that these events are important. Focusing on stimulus-response tasks also excludes a wide range of mental phenomena that cannot readily be triggered to occur over and over again in response to stimuli. For example, although the word "decision" has been used here to refer to certain central stages in stimulus-response tasks, there is a sense in which almost everything one would refer to in daily life as decision making (e.g., contemplating options, choosing a course of action) is beyond the scope of such tasks. Speeded laboratory tasks involve a highly prepared but unreflective and stimulus-controlled mode of behavior; early introspectionists sometimes described this as a prepared reflex to emphasize its distinctive character (cf Logan, 1978b).

The limitations of conventional methodologies are sometimes raised as a criticism of the value of information-processing psychology (Neisser, 1976); the point here is not to criticize, but to suggest the value of asking how these limitations might be circumvented. The following sections describe research that looks at preparatory events that occur before an imperative stimulus is presented in a laboratory task, and more generally, at the control of mental processes and its relation to attention theory.

Task Set in Laboratory Tasks

Cueing Task Set   An obvious way to examine changes in task set is to cue the subject to adopt one of several possible task sets. The subject receives instructions that specify several possible tasks that he or she might have to perform; a task cue presented before each imperative stimulus indicates which particular one should be performed on a given trial. Sudevan and Taylor (1987) had subjects perform one of two different incompatible tasks involving a digit, classifying the digit as odd versus even, or as low (less than 6) versus high (greater than 5). They presented a cue between 400 and 4000 msec before the digit, indicating which task should be performed. Both speed and accuracy improved as the lead time between the cue and the target was lengthened to about 2 or 3 seconds.

The asymptote of the cueing function indicates how much time people require to use the cue as fully as they can. It does not tell us, however, whether people can use the cue to prepare themselves to the same extent as if there were no task uncertainty and task variation within a given block of trials. Fagot (1994) replicated Sudevan and Taylor's basic experiment, but included pure-task blocks in which people performed either task alone. Responses were slower in variable-task blocks then in pure-task blocks, even when cues were presented 4 seconds in advance; at the 4-second cue interval, responses were still about 100 msec slower than in pure-task blocks. Fagot also varied the cue-digit interval and found found that the bulk of the benefit of cues appeared by the time the interval was lengthened to a few hundred milliseconds (shorter than the smallest interval examined by Sudevan and Taylor).

In Sudevan and Taylor's design, the subject must process the cue to perform the task correctly. Several studies evaluated task set cues that were helpful but not necessary. Logan and Zbrodoff (1982) had subjects respond to the identity of a word ("above" or "below") that might or might not match its position. Cueing subjects about the relationship between the identity and position facilitated performance, reaching an asymptote at around 400 to 600 msec. The cueing studies show first, that subjects can use arbitrary cues to reorganize their task set to some extent; second, that they often do so relatively quickly although perhaps the process sometimes takes several seconds; and third, that this reorganization may still not bring them to the same degree of preparation as a pure-task block of trials.

Task Switching: the Jersild Effect   Jersild (1927) and Spector and Biederman (1976) developed a different experimental approach to task set: comparing sequences of trials in which people must alternate between two different tasks (alternating-task blocks) with sequences in which the same task was performed on every trial (pure-task blocks). They measured the total time subjects required to work through lists of stimuli. In alternating-task blocks in which all stimuli were potentially appropriate inputs for either task, subjects took much longer than they did in pure blocks of either task alone. For example, when the stimuli were lists of two-digit numbers and the subject was to add three to the first number, subtract three from the second, add three to the third, and so on, the total time to complete the list was five to ten seconds greater than on corresponding pure-task blocks. The situation in which all stimuli are potential inputs for either task are referred to as a *bivalent stimulus* condition (following Fagot, 1994), and the extra time for alternating lists as *alternation cost*. Of interest, when each stimulus was a possible input only for the appropriate task (e.g., saying the antonym of an adjective in trial 1, subtracting three from a two-digit number in trial 2, etc.), they found no alternation cost; in fact, there was sometimes a slight alternation benefit. Sequences in which each stimulus would only be appropriate for the relevant task are referred to as a *univalent stimulus* condition. The alternation cost is not caused by occasional confusions resulting in very long RTs; Fagot (1994) examined the response time distributions for alternating and pure lists and found that the entire distribution was shifted rightward, with substantial cost even in the fifth percentile.

The simplest and most natural interpretation of these phenomena would hypothesize that a discrete switch of task sets takes place after every response in the alternating bivalent lists, but not with alternating univalent lists or pure lists. According to this analysis, before selecting a response to a bivalent stimulus, the subject must switch out the task set appropriate for the previous stimulus and switch in the task set appropriate for the current stimulus. With univalent lists, however, alternating lists do not require any such shift. because even if both task sets remain active, they will not yield incorrect responses.

Recent studies challenge the idea of a discrete task switch. If there were such a switch, providing a sufficiently long interval between the response to one stimulus and presentation of the next stimulus (*response-stimulus interval*, or *RSI*) should make the alternation cost disappear, because subjects would use the blank time to complete the shift. When subjects are allowed 0.5 second, the alternation cost is usually reduced by about one-third, but extending the interval does not seem to eliminate what remains of it (Fagot, 1994; Rogers and Monsell, 1995). This fits nicely with the observation by Fagot, described above, that even after a long cue-target interval, task cueing does not improve to the level of a pure-task block.

When people switch from task A to task B and then perform B for several successive trials, the initial response in task B seems to bear the brunt of the alternation cost; little or no further speedup occurs after the second repetition of task B (Rogers and Monsell, 1995). Even when the task is performed repeatedly the entire cost of alternation does not disappear, as seen in figure 8.2. Fagot (1994) compared three conditions: a pure list (A-A-A-A- . . .), and alternating list (A-B-A-B- . . .), and a pairwise alternating list (A-A-B-B- . . .). The second trial in a task in the pairwise alternating list (e.g., B-B-A-*A*) was faster than the first, but still substantially slower than a pure list (A-A-A-A).

The fact that performance speeds up with the second performance of a task suggests that carrying out the task somehow tunes the mental machinery, as Fagot put it. Evidently, this tuning is at the level of the task not the stimulus. There is, of course, a further benefit whenever a stimulus is repeated from one trial to the next in choice RT tasks (Kornblum, 1973; Pashler and Baylis, 1991). However, the task-repetition benefit found in the Jersild paradigm arises even in sequences that do not involve stimulus repetition (Fagot, 1994). These data raise another question: why, even after someone has performed the task, do they still respond slower

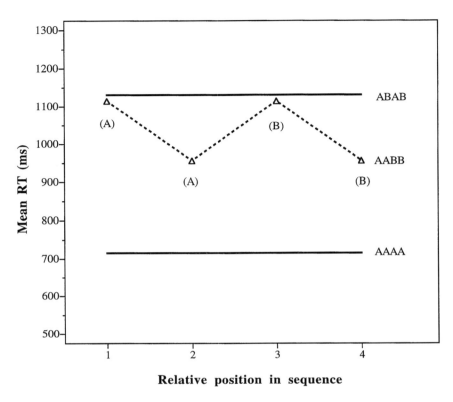

Figure 8.2
Mean latencies in experiment requiring switching between two tasks consisting
of incompatible responses to the same set of stimuli. Subjects alternated between
task A and B (A-B-A-B blocks), or performed the same task on each trial
(A-A-A-A blocks), or performed two repetitions of one task, followed by two of
the other, etc. (A-A-B-B blocks). Redrawn from Fagot (1994).

in blocks involving alternation than in pure-task blocks? One possible explanation is that in all blocks involving switching, subjects must prepare not only for the tasks themselves but also for the switches. One would expect that some slowing would be attributable to total preparatory load. (This simple generalization has cropped in a variety of contexts in this book; see, e.g., figure 6.3.)

The evidence described thus far suggests that task set shifts are not discrete in the sense that they do not completely eliminate the consequences of task alternation. A discrete conception of task set shift is further undermined by the fact that in alternating-task blocks, when a subject is maximally prepared to perform task B, effects of task A mapping can still be discerned. This is shown by a peculiar form of response competition: slowing of task B responses when the stimulus would have resulted in a different response on the task A mapping, or vice versa, compared with stimuli that would have elicited the same response (Fagot, 1994; Rogers and Monsell, 1995). For example, in Fagot's experiments, subjects made key press responses to color in task A and to form in task B. Consider a trial in an alternating-task block where the subject performs task B, selecting the left key press response to the letter A. The letter might be red, mapped onto the left button in task A, or it might be another color mapped into a different button in task A. Responses were slower in the latter condition than in the former, evidently reflecting competition from the response that would have been selected by the other mapping.

This form of response competition arose even when the RSI was long, allowing the person every opportunity to prepare for the appropriate task. In Fagot's experiments, the effect was larger in alternating blocks than in pure blocks, and in pure blocks that followed alternating blocks, it showed up only on the first run within the block. Both Rogers and Monsell and Fagot presented occasional univalent stimulus probes in the middle of an alternating bivalent stimulus sequence. In the example considered above, a purple letter A would be univalent because purple is not mapped onto any response in task A. Responses to these stimuli were faster than responses to either compatible or incompatible bivalent stimuli, but they were still slower than responses in pure block conditions.

This suggests that some of the slowing observed in alternating block lists cannot be attributed to response competition.

What can we conclude? Preparing to perform one task rather than another triggers an internal shift, but not a fully discrete shift. Previously active task mappings seem to be inhibited but not completely flushed or dissolved. The intention to switch task sets does not produce optimal performance on the task being shifted to; actually performing a task produces further improvement, but some costs remain in any block involving shifts among incompatible tasks (i.e., tasks involving bivalent stimuli).

Executive Control and Attention

A number of cognitive psychologists maintain that a general account of cognitive architecture has to include one or more structures responsible for what might be termed *executive control*. Baddeley (1990), for example, proposed what he called a central executive, primarily to account for the control of information flow in memory tasks. A related proposal was suggested by Norman and Shallice (1986) and subsequently modified and extended by Shallice (1988). According to their theory, selection of routine actions is normally triggered by appropriate environmental stimuli. Nonroutine control of behavior, on the other hand, requires the intervention of a structure they term the *supervisory attentional system* (*SAS*). The execution of a given activity or task (e.g., driving, shadowing) is governed by what they call schemas; individual schemas may call other schemas as subroutines. For example, the schema for driving might call subordinate schemas for braking, steering, and other driving functions. Schemas are ordinarily triggered by stimuli without the intervention of the SAS, and terminate when the goal state associated with the schema has been accomplished.

Several different schemas may be active at a given time, according to Norman and Shallice. Naturally, there may sometimes be a conflict between the behaviors that different schemas active at any time might generate. In this case, the action that ensues will depend on competition among these schemas, a process the authors termed contention scheduling. Whenever novel behaviors or changes in task set are required, or when routine responses to stimuli would be inappropriate, this sort of routine decentralized action planning is inadequate. In such cases, the SAS intervenes by inhibiting or priming one or another schema.

Contention scheduling, according to Shallice (1988), is distributed among many different brain areas; the SAS, on the other hand, is largely dependent on frontal lobe structures. Neurologists have long noted that patients with frontal lobe damage exhibit problems in planning and controlling behavior. These difficulties include problems in sequencing behaviors appropriately, impulsivity, difficulty shifting tasks, perseveration, and a tendency to forget goals (Lhermitte, 1973; McCarthy and Warrington, 1990). Of interest, patients with frontal lobe damage and planning deficits may still perform well on IQ tests. The diagnostic instrument most commonly used to assess behavioral flexibility and planning is the Wisconsin card sorting test (Grant and Berg, 1948). It requires a subject to sort cards according to rules that change from time to time (e.g., according to color or shape); subjects are usually told only whether or not they have sorted correctly. Patients with frontal damage often persist in following a rule after it has led to incorrect responses (Milner, 1964); this sometimes happens even after they have been instructed that a switch must be performed (Nelson, 1976). Although frontal patients usually show deficits in the Wisconsin card sorting test, some of them perform well but nonetheless have profound difficulty planning activities in ordinary life (Goldstein et al., 1993; Shallice and Burgess, 1991).

The idea of an SAS (or central executive) is consistent with findings involving task shift that were described in the preceding section. One could, for example, imagine that switching between different task sets in the alternating task conditions, to the degree this is possible, reflects inhibition or boosting of task schemas by the SAS. Rogers and Monsell (1995) suggest that the fact that optimal performance depends on actually performing at least one repetition of a task, not merely deciding to perform it, is congenial with the view that task set selection can be triggered by stimuli. However, the fit between the task switching results and Norman and Shallice's theory is general, and the data do not specifically support a distinct mechanism that controls shifts of task set. The possibility that the machinery involved in selecting actions may somehow reconfigure itself, for example, is not excluded.

The idea of a discrete controlling mechanism seems superficially congenial to the hypothesis of a central bottleneck in action planning, evidence for which was discussed in chapter 6. In reality, the two ideas have at most a fairly tenuous relationship. As pointed out earlier, the suggestion that while a memory retrieval or action selection is in progress other operations of the same type are inhibited, should not be taken to imply that a single neural structure is responsible for this function. Memory retrieval and action selection might take place in anatomically separate areas, but any one process of this type might trigger a mutual inhibition, similar to Norman and Shallice's contention scheduling, but affecting the selection, rather than just the execution of actions. This could result in queuing of response selection, memory retrieval, and other central mental operations. Queuing seems to occur even when seemingly routine action selection is called for, with no requirement for any change of task set (the core function of the proposed SAS). The notion of a central executive or controller may therefore have little or nothing to do with the idea of a central processing bottleneck. Similarly, the role that attentional mechanisms play in perceptual processing does not require a central controller. In chapter 5 it was suggested that attentional deployment ordinarily depends heavily on the interplay of two factors: a tendency for attention to shift toward channels that provide stimulation associated with previously activated concepts or representations, and a (perhaps suppressible) tendency to shift toward novel or unexpected stimulation. These inherent biases or mechanisms of attentional control do not require a central processor or controller; attentional control could emerge from activation in processing modules specialized for analysis of many different aspects of the stimulus environment (Duncan et al., 1995).

Conclusions

The preceding chapters suggested a number of broad conclusions about attentional mechanisms and processes. In this final section, I recap some of these conclusions and suggest a few implications for future research.

Selectivity and Capacity Limits in Perception

Research on selectivity and capacity limits in perception was for many years, and to some extent still is, driven by the debate between early- and late-selection theories. These theories addressed fundamental questions about the relation between attention and perception, and stimulated an enormous amount of debate and research. In the past ten years or so discussion of these theories appears to have diminished somewhat. While a few writers have contended that the questions were flawed to begin with, and others have proclaimed the unequivocal triumph of one theory or the other, many simply seem weary of the battle but uncertain of its resolution.

The first four chapters of this book argue for a resolution that boils down to three basic claims. First, that the questions these theories posed are not only sensible but also basic and inescapable. Second, that it is nonetheless a mistake to view these two theories as exhausting the set of possibilities or even anchoring the endpoints of a single continuum. Rather, each theory combines claims about several logically distinct issues, notably the existence of perceptual capacity limits and the existence of perceptual selectivity. Third, that thanks to several decades of ingenious experimentation, there is now enough evidence to reject both theories and sketch the outlines of an alternative.

Early-selection theory combined the claim that perceptual identification is invariably selective with the claim that capacity limits are severe to the point that object identification is invariably sequential. Late-selection theory combined the claim that perceptual capacity limits are nonexistent with the claim that perceptual selectivity is impossible. Neither combination of claims seems correct. Rather, the findings suggest that while perceptual selectivity exists, so does parallel processing as an optional strategy that can be adopted in many circumstances where it is useful; and furthermore, that perceptual capacity limits exist as well, but only above some threshold of processing demands. Thus, while to-be-ignored stimuli sometimes undergo some perceptual analysis, when conditions for selection are favorable, this analysis is substantially curtailed. On this point there is a pleasing convergence of behavioral, neurophysiological, and electrophysiological results. At the same time, there is strong evidence that parallel stimulus analysis is possible when tasks require processing multiple stimuli to detect one or more targets, even when targets are defined abstractly. While capacity limits exist, these limits are far less severe than early selection theorists envisioned. When total processing demands falls below a moderate threshold (reflecting both complexity of the required analysis and number of inputs to be processed), processing is parallel and capacity limitations are not in evidence; when demands exceed the threshold, processing becomes less efficient. There is little evidence that this normally causes sequential analysis of objects, however; more likely, processing is parallel but less efficient. Capacity limits also arise when two or more targets must be detected close together in time. The clearest evidence for parallel processing is found in experiments using one of several methodologies: comparing accuracy with simultaneous versus successive presentations, measuring search response times as a function of both display set size and stimulus quality, and analyzing effects of display set size on accuracy with reference to quantitative models.

The existence of both perceptual selectivity and parallel processing naturally suggests the simple and obvious account that was termed controlled parallel processing (CPP) in chapter 1. On this view, we may voluntarily choose to analyze a single stimulus (suppressing the perceptual analysis of other stimuli) or we may choose to analyze several stimuli in parallel, or even analyze a number of stimuli in parallel while suppressing analysis of others. The results support a modified CPP which stipulates that when the total complexity of perceptual processing is exceeded, capacity limitations emerge.

In addition to the core issues of selectivity and capacity limits, the first five chapters considered several other related issues that have loomed large in recent research. One is the effect of providing prior information about stimulus attributes, e.g., by holding a dimension fixed over a block of trials rather than having it vary from trial to trial, or by presenting pre-cues in advance of a stimulus. As we saw, interpreting the effects of prior information is a treacherous business. One reason is that, even for an "ideal observer" that analyzes each of multiple channels simultaneously just as accurately as it can analyze a single channel at a time, having to monitor more channels increases the likelihood *of* an error (and conversely, cues reducing the number of channels monitored reduce that chance). Therefore, error rates can be affected by cueing, uncertainty, or display set size even when capacity limitations play no role. This effect is termed decision noise, although benefits attributable to decision noise might reflect exclusion of irrelevant inputs (noise) at early stages of perceptual analysis.

Uncertainty effects are regularly observed in studies of visual and auditory stimuli presented at threshold without masks, and the magnitude of these effects is close to the quantitative predictions derived from models that assume decision noise but no capacity limitations. This is to be expected if the relatively impoverished displays used in these studies do not exceed the threshold for perceptual capacity limits, as one would expect from the conclusions described in the previous paragraphs. On the other hand, cueing effects (differences between valid and invalid cueing conditions) have sometimes been observed in speed and accuracy of responses to isolated stimuli presented well above threshold, where uncued locations would not be expected to introduce decision noise. It was argued in chapter 4 that these effects probably reflect a combination of several factors, including changes in criteria (especially in simple RT tasks), speed-accuracy tradeoff, and costs produced by invalid cues. This conclusion is admittedly open to debate, however.

The controlled parallel processing framework, supplemented with the idea of capacity limitations above a threshold, departs from commonly considered theories, but it also seems rather commonsensical. Essentially, it proposes that limited perceptual resources are used in a fairly optimal fashion and that mechanisms for suppression exist. The suggestion that, when it is useful, our perceptual machinery can process inputs in unexpected locations without sacrifice also seems rather reasonable. What may be more surprising, however, are the conclusions reached about effects of advance information about the identity of a stimulus. Knowing what stimulus is likely to appear does not generally produce improvements in the efficiency of immediate perceptual analysis as one might expect it to if it permitted different sorts of hypothesis-testing to take place. Instead, it seems to produce a bias toward interpreting evidence in line with what is probable.

Some of the most important conclusions described in the first half of the book pertain to differences in the role played by different kinds of stimulus attributes—essentially, the question of what constitutes a channel in the strictest sense. While visual selectivity is enormously flexible (one can, in the crudest sense, attend based on location, color, form, semantic category, etc.), selection by any criterion seems to be ultimately mediated by location selection. This is seen, for example, in the occurrence of location confusions in tasks that require selection by criteria other than location. A number of experimental results have recently been seen as arguing for object-based selection rather than location-based selection. Opposing these ideas seems conceptually untenable because spatiotemporal continuity is part of our very concept of what an object is. The results in question can probably be best understood by assuming that grouping processes whose function is to segregate features belonging to different objects have a guiding effect on location-based selection. It remains to be determined whether, in modalities other than vision, certain dimensions are privileged in the way that location seems privileged in visual selection.

A further fleshing out of the CPP account was proposed in chapter 5. The simplest viable conception of perceptual attention postulates separate and relatively early gating mechanisms within individual sensory modalities (vision, audition, and presumably other modalities as well). Stimuli that are not excluded compete with each other for processing resources that are largely if not completely modality specific. The intriguing interference that arises when two targets are detected close together in time is, on this account, attributed to a tendency for detection to cause exclusion of competing stimuli even when their exclusion does not facilitate performance.

On this analysis, one should probably use the terms "visual attention" and "auditory attention" to refer to the gating process itself. Attending, then, is failing to exclude, which is a necessary condition for a stimulus accessing limited processing resources or controlling a response. Limited resources should not themselves be equated with attention, however tempting that may be. Any such equation leaves one unable to explain, for example, how selective attention could facilitate performance in cases where capacity limits are not exceeded (as seen in the benefit observed when one cues the location of a low-contrast grating or the frequency of a faint tone presented against a background of noise).

Assuming these conclusions are roughly correct, many basic questions still remain to be resolved. One question is the nature and source of the capacity limitations that arise with perceptual overload. There is presently little evidence about what causes these limitations. Another important issue is the nature of the internal perceptual representation that is created when we attend to a complex scene. One might assume, given that parallel processing takes place in search tasks, that our perceptual machinery simultaneously builds a representation of the location and properties of multiple objects. If this were the case, people ought to have certain abilities that they in fact lack (e.g., the ability to detect changes in scenes introduced during very brief offsets, the ability to identify a cued object in a previewed display without reanalyzing this scene from scratch). The fact that we cannot do these things challenges our naive assumptions about perceptual experience and raises interesting questions at the border of experimental psychology and the philosophy of mind.

Perceptual and Central Attentional Limitations

The second half of the book moved beyond issues of perceptual processing to consider limitations arising at more central stages of mental processing. These central limits are attentional in the sense that they affect processes that are subject to voluntary control, but they do not seem to reflect the same attentional mechanisms as those discussed earlier in this concluding section. Central processing limitations are revealed most plainly when people try concurrently to select and produce two independent speeded responses, as in the PRP paradigm. Planning one response delays planning of another, even when the person attempts to produce both as fast as possible. This queuing, sometimes called a single-channel bottleneck, arises even when the tasks involves different input modalities and different types of responses. While there may be circumstances under which people can plan two independent responses simultaneously (e.g., after extensive practice), this has not yet been demonstrated. The single-channel limitation is not restricted to planning of actions; it also seems to apply to perceptual comparisons and manipulations of certain types (e.g., comparison of line lengths, mental rotation) and to memory retrieval more generally. It seems probable, therefore, that many operations that comprise thinking are limited to taking place one at a time.

An obvious and key question is how this single-channel limitation relates to the perceptual capacity limitations described earlier. Various lines of evidence suggest the two are quite distinct. For one thing, certain variables that mitigate perceptual overload do not affect central interference. For example, presenting stimuli through different input modalities attenuates perceptual overload, but it does not reduce central interference. Requiring judgments about two aspects of the same object (e.g., color and shape) also minimizes perceptual but not central interference; thus, people seem unable to plan independent responses to color and form simultaneously. Even more compelling is the fact that in tasks requiring difficult perceptual judgments, the amount of perceptual interference is unaffected when one of the responses must be produced immediately; if perceptual and response-selection limitations had the same source, this could only exacerbate the interference. These dissociations, and others described in chapter 6, all suggest that attentional limitations come in two quite different forms. On the one hand, there is obligatory queuing of cognitive operations such as response selection and associative retrieval that is independent of sensory modality. On the other hand, perceptual overload depends only on modality-specific perceptual demands and does not generally result in queuing. Perceptual analysis, whether overloaded or not, typically occurs without interference from ongoing central operations.

While this functional characterization of central processing limitations seems well supported, we have little understanding as yet about the causes of these limitations. The most obvious explanation of why certain mental operations would be carried out one at a time is because there is only a single neural structure capable of performing them. However reasonable this sounds, it may not be right. For one thing, dual-task interference has been observed in split-brain patients even when inputs and outputs for each task are lateralized to a different hemispheres, presumably allowing each to be carried out by different neural machinery. It is possible, then, that even mental operations carried out by different neural structures may queue up as a result of scheduling or inhibition organized by subcortical brain structures. Of course, this is only a conjecture. The detailed evidence for queuing that has emerged from recent dual-task studies harks back to some of the earliest theorizing about human performance, notably that of Craik and Walford. It is also reminiscent of the early infatuation of cognitive psychology with analogies between the mind and the digital computer. The results do suggest that such analogies may be illuminating in some respects. On the other hand, studies of elementary mental processing also point up important differences between human information processing at fine-grained levels and corresponding functions in digital computers. Recall that when two simultaneous stimuli redundantly call for the same response, each stimulus seems to activate this response concurrently; similarly, solving crossword puzzles obviously requires using different retrieval cues to triangulate in on particular items in memory. Thus, the inability to retrieve two memories or plan two actions concurrently does not reflect any inability to probe memory with more than one cue at a time, as the digital computer metaphor might suggest. Instead, it seems that while many inputs can simultaneously activate a given output, they cannot generally activate different outputs, or if they can, the process of utilizing one output somehow flushes or degrades activation of the other. One suspects that these slightly paradoxical properties of human information processing may ultimately be illuminated by a better understanding of memory retrieval at the level of neural circuitry.

Attention and Memory

The concept of short-term memory has long played a central role in cognitive psychology. Recently, however, some writers have expressed skepticism about the value of the concept. Chapter 7 argued that the distinction between sensory, short-term, and long-term memory is alive and well, and in fact greatly strengthened by recent behavioral, neuro-psychological, and neurophysiological data. However, the idea that there is just one short-term memory system that relies on articulatory coding can clearly be rejected; there appear to be several, perhaps many, distinct STM systems associated with different input systems and motor buffers, each capable of holding onto information without displacing the contents of other STM systems.

Attention theorists have almost unanimously agreed that short-term memory and attention are deeply interconnected. Some writers have equated attentional resources with STM storage capacity. This assumption underlies experiments in which subjects are required to retain concurrent memory loads while carrying out additional tasks with the goal of assessing the effects of depleted attentional resources on performance. Chapters 7 and 8 argued that attention and STM are indeed closely linked, but that the nature of the linkage is quite different than what such formulations suggest. Perceptual gating is a necessary condition for storage of information in STM, and may in some cases be sufficient. On the other hand, the central mental operations that are associated with the single-channel limitation described earlier (e.g., response selection) seem quite able to take place in parallel with storing of unrelated information in STM. To put it simply and concretely, a person can select a response to a tone while storing a visual pattern in visual STM, but they seem unable to select a response to the tone while planning an action in response to the visual pattern. Nevertheless, central operations almost invariably impair storage of information in long-term memory. Whether storage is postponed (i.e., a bottleneck) or merely slowed by concurrent tasks has yet to be determined. In any case, the dissociation between the effects of a concurrent task on short term and long-term storage provides still further support for the distinction between STM and LTM. By contrast, the presently popular distinction between explicit and implicit, or procedural, memory and the claim that implicit memory storage takes place "without attention," rely on comparatively weak evidence that may be vitiated by scaling and other methodological problems.

Automaticity

Practice powerfully affects performance. In both simple and complex tasks, it speeds up processing and generally improves accuracy as well. The speedup is often quite specific to the materials encountered during practice, resulting in very limited transfer to new stimuli or different tasks. Attentional theorists have long been inclined to follow common sense and suppose that after practice, mental operations come to function automatically, i.e., without regard to voluntary control and independently of limited-capacity mechanisms. Evidence for this claim is rather unconvincing, or so it was argued in the present chapter. It is certainly true that by most measures, practicing a task results in less interference when the task is combined with a concurrent task. However, such a reduction would be expected if the practiced task simply took less time as a result of practice, but remained dependent on limited-capacity mechanisms for whatever time it was being executed. Appropriate tests of whether practice eliminates bottleneck-type interference are feasible but have not yet been reported. It has been found, however, that extensive practice with visual search does not eliminate the tendency for target detection to impair concurrent visual tasks, which by itself refutes the strongest automaticity claims. As for inhibition, while certain mental operations may become slightly more difficult to inhibit with practice, in general people seem quite capable of inhibiting responses in highly practiced tasks such as typing. It was suggested that our intuitions about automaticity are likely to reflect the very coarse level at which we are capable of introspecting on our own mental processes.

Concluding Comment

Some of the general conclusions described here will probably turn out to be mistaken, and most or even all will undoubtedly prove to be oversimplifications. Characterizing a system as complex as the brain in information processing terms is by its very nature a great simplification. The functional systems and processes described at this level of analysis are highly abstract depictions of an underlying biological reality that may be anything but discrete and compartmentalized. Nonetheless, a reasonable functional analysis of attentional mechanisms and limitations now seems to be within reach, if still not quite at hand. A solid functional understanding of attention is likely to be a necessary condition for making satisfactory sense of neural mechanisms and processes of attention, just as the circuitry of color vision and the biochemical processes of digestion tend to be incomprehensible except in light of their overall organization and purpose. At the same time, better understanding of the biological reality underlying attention will undoubtedly illuminate and explain puzzling phenomena that arise in the course of the information processing analysis, several of which were noted earlier in this concluding section. It is hoped that the progress described in this book is sufficient to convince the reader that the analysis of attention by means of careful analysis of human performance in simple tasks is worthwhile. This enterprise, begun by Broadbent, Welford, and other pioneers only a small number of decades ago, seems to be producing genuine and sometimes quite surprising insights into the architecture of human mental machinery.

Notes

Chapter 1 Introduction

1. In a fascinating essay on theorizing about attention, Hatfield (in press) offers many examples of insightful observations by writers before the nineteenth century, including Aristotle, Lucretius, Descartes, Christian Wolff, and Charles Bonnet.

2. As McNamara (1992) put it, "Crucial experiments may be possible occasionally, but theory testing is usually a war of attrition: A theory is deemed successful if it accounts for most of the data most of the time, with a minimum number of unprincipled modifications" (p. 658).

3. The term *frame* refers to a set of stimuli presented at a single moment in time; thus, a display consisting of a set of six characters replaced by another six in the same positions would be a two-frame display.

Chapter 2 Selective Attention

1. Kahneman and Treisman (1984, p. 30) stated that this occurred on only 6% of trials in the 1960 study, but the original report seems to make it clear that it is 30%.

2. One might worry that this could generate a demand effect favoring divided attention, but this does not seem to have happened.

3. In almost all of these studies, the term color is used in the broadest sense, since differences in hue were probably accompanied by differences in luminance.

4. In a personal communication, J. O. Miller pointed out that further analyses would be worth while, since with small numbers of trials, empirical cumulative distribution functions (CDFs) are subject to bias effects in such situations (see Miller and Lopes, 1988).

5. However, Singer et al. (1975) observed smaller effects with color/word fragments compared with the full color words.

6. The strictest definition of exogenous would imply no effects of psychological variables on the component, but by such a rigorous definition, it would of course be impossible to find effects of attentional manipulations on an exogenous component. In practice, what are called exogenous components are roughly those that can be elicited under passive viewing conditions.

7. Hoffman and Subramaniam's effects were measured with masked stimuli presented near threshold; reduced sensitivity in that situation might correspond to relatively modest effects in detection of suprathreshold stimuli, of course.

8. Graham (1989) also summarizes evidence that when people detect a grating at threshold, they can accurately report the location to which the channels they report from are sensitive. Atkinson and Braddick (1989) found some evidence that location was reported more accurately than identity for horizontal or vertical line segments against a background of oblique segments. One explanation of the result might be that both horizontal and verticals exemplify some common feature (Johnston and Pashler, 1991).

9. Suppose someone has to decide whether target A or B is present in a display (2-AFC). If target A is easier to detect than target B and the observer becomes aware of this, when the observer fails to detect either target on a trial, this constitutes good reason to guess that target B rather than A was present. This will, however, give the observer no basis for guessing anything about location. By presenting blank trials, Johnston and Pashler measured the extent to which individual subjects used this guessing strategy and found no evidence for knowledge of identity without location beyond what could be attributed to this strategy.

10. The implications of this conclusion are questioned to some degree by data of Monheit and Johnston (1994), who demonstrated dependencies even for reports of different dimensions at the same location.

Chapter 3   Divided Attention

1. According to Sperling, this whole report limit was first observed by Schumann (1904).

2. The only serious challenge to this account was offered by Townsend (1981), who analyzed the statistical relationship between accuracy in different positions in the whole-report task. His results showed almost complete independence among the different positions. However, subjects only saw five letters (barely more than span), and, perhaps due to acuity limitations, were able to whole-report only about four. Sperling's account would most clearly predict dependencies under slightly different conditions, for example, with displays of ten clearly legible letters.

3. This should not be taken to mean that masking SOAs offer a pure measure of perception time. As Styles and Allport (1986) put it, "masking SOA cannot be interpreted as simply revealing the time-course of perceptual processing of the target display alone, but rather the processing of the target display *in the presence of interference* resulting from the mask" (p. 198).

4. A slightly more extended defense of the traditional analysis of iconic memory and partial report is presented by Pashler and Carrier (1996).

5. If illumination is turned on only while an observer is actually making a saccade, the observer does see a great smear (Campbell and Wurtz, 1978).

6. This may or may not be intuitively obvious; if it is not, the following question, which embodies the same principle taken to extremes, may tug one's intuitions in the right direction. Who is likely to be taller: the tallest person in Kansas, or the tallest person in a tiny town of thirty people in Nebraska, assuming, of course, that the distributions of heights in the two states is identical?

7. Of course, if there is *any* decay one might expect that discriminations performed later would be less effective, thereby producing a capacity limitation; given the assumption-laden nature of the analyses used to assess capacity limitations, however, this inference probably rests on less than secure ground.

8. Note that the masks used by Shiffrin and Gardner as place holders did not introduce abrupt onsets at the same time as the arrival of the characters.

9. Shiffrin and Gardner observed that lateral masking could produce the appearance of capacity limitations. However, it occurs at relatively close separations, at least when retinal eccentricity is not too great (see Wolford and Chambers, 1983), so one can increase display loads substantially without encountering that form of nonattentional limitation.

10. Fisher had subjects report the location of the target digit; using this as an index of detection assumes that genuine detections will be accompanied by accurate location information. Given the facts reviewed earlier in the chapter, it is very likely that location reports would be a reasonable proxy for detections.

11. Oddly, Duncan (1980, p. 281) stated that he had run a character search experiment with a similarly constructed target/distractor set and found only a very minimal advantage for successive displays. It is not clear how to interpret these findings.

12. In the case of successively presented words, it made little difference whether the words appeared in the same or different positions or whether the target word was presented first or second, indicating that eye movements, positional biases, and memory decay are not likely to have affected the results much.

13. To avoid having color enter into the same/different judgments, the color in any given position in the two displays was always the same.

14. Logically speaking, slopes are usually shallow, say, under 10 msec per item, rather than flat. Although one could potentially attribute such slopes to serial search proceeding at rates greater than 100 items per msec, most investigators doubted the existence of such superfast scanning. Sejnowski (1986) described some neurobiological considerations that would justify this skepticism.

15. As Treisman concluded, reading out the total activity in a set of detectors would not suffice to determine the location of a target, and indeed, she and Gelade (1980) claimed that presence could be detected without location. As described, in Chapter 2, however, this conclusion is questionable. Treisman's interpretation of search asymmetries could still apply even if detection of activity

in a feature map conveyed reliable information regarding the location of that signal (Johnston and Pashler, 1991).

16. The findings with search RTs might partly reflect a difficult-to-suppress tendency for subjects to make eye movements toward words in displays, which typically stayed up until response (eccentricity reduces readability of words noticeably). However, eye movements are not a factor in the accuracy experiments, which yielded essentially the same conclusions.

17. This is also supported by a result of Shiffrin, Pisoni, and Castaneda-Mendez (1974, experiment 2) who compared performance on simultaneously and successively presented speechlike sounds. In each trial, one target was presented, namely, a stop consonant (BA, PA, DA, or GA). In the simultaneous condition, the consonant was sounded to one ear and a distractor syllable (WU) was sounded to the other. In the successive condition, two observation intervals were separated by 700 msec. The consonant was either sounded to the right ear in the first observation interval, or to the left ear in the second observation interval, with WU played in every other observation interval/ear combination. There was no benefit in the successive condition compared with the simultaneous condition.

18. It is possible to demonstrate both backward and forward masking effects, but they do not seem to reflect the sort of interruption shown by Turvey (1973; see Kallman, Hirtle, and Davidson, 1986).

19. This conjecture is supported by some recent unpublished studies of my own in which a difficult tone discrimination was combined with a masked letter discrimination. Simultaneous and successive presentations showed comparable performance, but pure single-task blocks showed slightly better performance. The results suggest no competition in the discrimination itself, but some minor costs of preparing both tasks at once.

20. It would be a mistake, however, to say that tasks limited by contrast or exposure duration are data limited, as if this excluded their being resource limited as a matter of logic. This line of thought was encouraged by a well-known paper of Norman and Bobrow (1975), which introduced a distinction between resource-limited and data-limited processes. What the paper overlooked is that performance in a task can depend both on (perhaps multiple) resources and on stimulus parameters. It is an empirical proposition, not a conceptual truth, therefore, that reducing stimulus contrast so that people have trouble seeing it does not result in its interfering with other visual discriminations.

Chapter 4   Attentional Set

1. The application of signal detection theory in this situation is far from straightforward, however (Muller, 1994).

2. To see why, suppose the cue was 99.99% valid; in that case, the optimal decision would of course depend almost entirely on the strength of the signal from the cued location, giving negligible weight to the other locations.

3. Hawkins et al (1990) partially acknowledged this point, suggesting that one account of their results would be that "attentional cueing governs the order, or schedule, by which information is read out of an early processing stage where representations are subject to rapid decay and masking" (p. 808). The readout process envisioned here *is* what is termed the decision process in the present discussion, with cueing affecting decision weights rather than order. This possibility is completely consistent with Mulligan and Shaw's (1981) account as well.

4. Some of these studies have other problematic features. For example, many of them involved detecting a target in a cluttered visual display composed of many small boxes and the like, so they have limited relevance to the claim that cueing enhances perception of an item against a blank field. When extraneous stimuli are potentially confusable with the target to some degree, spatial cueing may again produce benefits due to exclusion of accumulated decision noise.

5. The authors of these studies emphasized that their results argued against a *motor* locus for the cueing effect, and suggested that the results were consistent with a perceptual-enhancement account. They might be consistent with such an idea, but they are also consistent with a criterion-adjustment explanation.

6. This is not logically impossible; perhaps only a single location can enjoy enhancement when its location is known in advance, and this enhancement precludes any processing of other locations. In that case, it would be counter to subject's interests to engage in such enhancement in the SUCC/SIM paradigm.

7. It seems plausible that the analyzers monitored in threshold spatial vision tasks are sets of cortical neurons in the visual cortex (e.g., V1 or V2). Given the anatomy of these areas, the types of monitoring discussed thus far may all involve checking the outputs of anatomically contiguous regions of cortex (Graham, 1988).

8. For example, perhaps an effect would occur with (a) exposure durations closer to the recognition threshold (our exposures were long enough to make recognition easy), (b) overt recognition judgment made before the judgment of contrast on each trial, or (c) variation in background luminance to remove the confound of stimulus contrast and target luminance.

Chapter 5   Capacity and Selection

1. The word probably is inserted here because of the uncertainties described in chapter 3.

2. One wonders, however, if observers in the Miller and Bonnel task made the length comparisons during the initial very brief exposure. Perhaps they simply stored a visual image of the lines, and made the comparison later, in which case the authors' conclusions would apply to the storage, not to the comparison.

3. In an elegant study, Gardner (1973) manipulated target-distractor similarity in each of two concurrent search tasks, and found that doing so reduced accuracy only for that particular search, not for the one performed concurrently. As he

supposed, performance in this task ensemble was probably limited by decision noise not capacity limitations, so his result cannot answer the question presently on the table. A similar study performed with words might be very informative, however.

4. Duncan (1984) suggests that this view should be seen as an object-based view; given the conceptual linkage of objects and locations noted earlier, there is probably no reason to quibble about this.

5. Johnston, Hawley, and Farnham (1993) claimed to have observed what they called novel pop-out in what was basically a short-term memory task. They presented displays composed of four words, some used only once and others used repeatedly in the course of the experiment, and found better memory for novel words in some cases. This conclusion has been criticized partly because of the memorial demands of the task, and requires further investigation (Christie and Klein, 1996; but see Johnston and Schwarting, 1996).

6. One hint that this may be so comes from a study by Dark and Scheerhorn (1994), who found that a prime biased people toward reporting only the semantically related word in a subsequent, brief, masked two-word display.

7. Mewhort et al found different effects, when they took the display away before the probe appeared. However, accuracy in this condition was poor: the number available was similar to the capacity of whole report (4–5). It is not surprising that the kind of short-term memory storage underlying whole report does not maintain items in a raw, unprocessed form. Even if the format were a schematic visual representation, one would expect that the degradation would be cleaned up at that point.

8. Jeremy Wolfe (personal communication) carried out intriguing studies involving visual search that add further support to this conclusion. He had subjects repeatedly search the same display, looking for different targets each time; display-set-size slopes did not flatten out, suggesting, as he puts it, that the postattentive representation contains more information about the display than did the preattentive representation.

9. Wolfe's research, described in note 8, might argue against this account. However, he informed his subjects what target they should search for by presenting it visually in the center of the screen; perhaps shifting attention to the center destroyed whatever representations had been built up while visual attention was devoted to the entire scene.

10. The effect has also been observed with cues consisting of stimulus offsets (Hikosaka, Miyauchi, and Shimojo, 1993); this does not necessarily eliminate the possibility that cues and stimuli are confused or amalgamated, however.

11. One way to do this would be to have subjects adjust the asynchrony of the stimuli until they perceive them to be simultaneous, as Stelmach and Herdman (1991) did in their experiment 5.

12. Libet et al. (1979) described experiments involving brain stimulation during surgery that provide some empirical evidence for the idea that this form of neural back-dating actually takes place.

Chapter 6 Central Processing Limitations in Sensorimotor Tasks

1. As Gordon Logan has pointed out to me, common usage may be agnostic about whether sharing attention involves resource sharing or time sharing (allocating exclusive access to a mechanism or mechanisms).

2. I am grateful to Torsten Schubert for assistance in translating the Bornemann article.

3. We do not use the word "trial" here because that suggests brief punctate events on the order of a second; performance here usually involves many individual stimuli and movements.

4. Davis (1962) observed some slowing of the response to the second stimulus in a choice RT task in which the first stimulus did not require any response. However, the effect was small, and may partly reflect the fact that the two stimuli were highly confusable.

5. This must be distinguished from the suggestion of a minimum interval between the times when two central processing operations can be *initiated*; this would predict the PRP effect, but it can be rejected on the basis of other observations.

6. Looking back into the history of PRP research, many early investigators seem to have doubted Welford's proposal because they observed slopes relating mean RT2 to SOA that fell short of −1. Assuming that Welford is correct, the slope should reach −1 over the range between SOA = a and SOA = b (b>a), only if (b + task 2 perception > task 1 perception + task 1 response selection) in essentially all trials. Given that b is often 200 msec or longer in these studies, and especially given the variability in stage durations, finding slopes less steep than −1 hardly rejects Welford's analysis. In any case, the effects of factor manipulations are more revealing than slopes unless one could reliably estimate actual stage durations, which we usually cannot.

7. Grouping (first distinguished by Borger, 1963) does not imply that the central processing in the two tasks is combined; rather, it seems that the central processing is serial but the first-selected response is saved until the other has been selected, and both are then emitted close together in time (Pashler and Johnston, 1989, experiment 2).

8. Varying the number of alternatives is likely to increase preparatory demands, and is therefore not an altogether ideal variable to use in such studies.

9. Probability is likely to affect both identification and response selection (Sternberg, 1969).

10. In the difficult task 2 mapping, three digits were mapped onto each of two buttons, compared with one in the easy condition. The effect was not reduced at short SOAs in the first experiment, but the second experiment showed some reduction after practice (one stimulus auditory and the other visual). With practice, subjects may come to categorize the stimuli in two groups, with the result that this factor affects a categorization stage, rather than response selection.

11. A somewhat different strategy to analyze the role of response production in the PRP effect often occurs to people using a go–no-go task as task 1. The general finding here is that go trials cause more slowing of task 2 than no-go trials (M. C. Smith, 1967b; Bertelson and Tisseyre, 1969). One might conclude from this that response production in task 1 does delay task 2. The problem is that no-go trials probably differ from go trials in various ways aside from not including a response; they may not include response selection either on some trials (Pashler, 1994a) or they may include additional inhibitory processes (for electrophysiological evidence, see Watanabe, 1986).

12. This result may be limited to situations in which rapid responding is required; informal observations suggest that slow, continuous hand movements may be affected quite differently.

13. To put it slightly more precisely, what is suggested is that central operations in one task cannot overlap central operations in another. Nor can the much more rapid process of initiating manual responses overlap between two tasks, although central processes in one task can overlap with manual response initiation in another.

14. The purpose of including a range of SOAs was to discourage grouping, which was partly successful; explicitly discouraging grouping would have undermined the purpose of the experiment.

15. In the human factors literature, some results described as demonstrating the harmful effects of similarity in continuous tasks relate to the use of manual responses in both tasks. This form of similarity may impair performance because of the specific conflicts in bimanual responding noted earlier.

16. Tresch, Sinnamon, and Seamon (1993) found that retention of spatial and visual object information in short-term memory was subject to particularly strong interference from concurrent tasks involving motion and color processing, respectively. This suggests that the same principle may apply not only to entire hemispheres and to the brain's motor areas, but also to the two main streams of visual cortical processing.

17. If Craik was right, even such paradigmatically continuous tasks as tracking are not really continuous in the strong sense. This section considers a number of cases that involve at least a train of stimuli.

18. For a discussion of some of the problems with information theory measures of mental processes, see Laming (1973).

19. These predictions are only approximate for two reasons. First, one might expect processing to be slightly slower in the dual-task condition due to preparatory limitations. Second, it appears that Gladstones et al did not always allow a response to be made after the stimulus for the following response had been presented, which would mean the two tasks were not compressed to allow response selection to be solely rate limiting. However, the rough equivalence they observed, and its independence of stimulus and response modality, are still generally in line with predictions of a central bottleneck theory.

20. One reflection of this fact is that researchers investigating choice RT in the 1950s and 1960s often insisted on partitioning effects of factors such as stimulus probability or repetition into only two categories (perception vs response); in many cases, it turns out these factors primarily affect the stage that links the two, response selection.

21. de Jong and Sweet (1994) reported more modest but still significant effects of temporal overlap on perceptual accuracy. Given the timing of stimuli in these experiments, the results may reflect preparatory changes occurring during individual trials.

Chapter 7   Attention and Memory

1. Some versions of the serial account might be defended in light of the fact that these patients can typically recall at least one item. It should also be noted that acquisition of foreign language vocabulary is not normal in these patients (Baddeley, Papagno, and Vallar, 1988), suggesting that forming new representations of articulatory or phonological patterns depends on short-term storage. The rejection of serial information flow advocated here pertains only to storing episodic information about familiar items such as words.

2. Baddeley and Hitch did not view these results as rejecting the concept of short-term memory; rather, they contended that the recency effect was misconstrued in the traditional account.

3. Even verifying stochastic independence may not even rule out this strong (and implausible) theory, since any observed dependence would be weakened to the extent that subjects' responses on individual trials are mediated by variables other than strength of memory (Ostergaard, 1992).

4. The reader will note that, logically speaking, this experiment might create incentives favoring divided attention; in fact, shadowing severely impairs detection of words in another channel (Rollins and Hendricks, 1980), and subjectively at least, seems to force listeners to ignore the other channel to the best of their ability.

5. Murray and Hitchcock (1969) demonstrated that memory for dichotically presented digit pairs was enhanced for digits presented in whichever ear the subject was required to process (repeating or mouthing the digits aloud); for such speech sounds, however, the enhancement might simply reflect the contribution of verbal STM.

6. This seems slightly implausible given that patients with verbal-STM impairment discussed earlier do not have profound problems with planning or controlling action, unlike those with frontal lobe damage (see also Shallice, 1988).

7. From the perspective of the additive factors methodology (Sternberg, 1969), poor preparation must affect *some* stage(s) and might reasonably be expected to affect several; this makes it mysterious that memory loads did not interact with a number of factors. It should be kept in mind that interactions reflecting a

common stage locus may be relatively small and hard to detect; there is no reason to expect the massive interactions caused by postponement of processing stages.

8. Along similar lines, Allport (1980) suggested that cognitive psychology has suffered from the importation of concepts from computer technology, of which "a classic example is the enduring belief in a system called STM (short-term memory) as responsible not only for the repetition span for lists of spoken words but also—quite gratuitously—as the 'central processor' through which all inputs and outputs to and from an individual's knowledge base . . . must pass" (p. 27).

9. Smith and Oscar-Berman did not make any global claims about attention not being involved in forming the traces that are accessed by implicit memory tests.

10. The fame-judgment task might fail to show a monotonic dependence on trace strength for a more insidious reason: stronger traces would lead to more complete recollection of the episode, raising subjects' awareness that they encountered the name only in the experimental context. Thus, whereas the fame-judgment task would seem at first glance to offer an ingenious measure of implicit memory, it is not well suited to *validating* that concept: On the alternative theory that implicit memory is in no way a separate system, fame judgment would be quite likely to depend on trace strength in a nonmonotonic fashion.

Chapter 8   Automaticity, Effort, and Control

1. As noted in chapter 6, interference in producing two manual responses is especially likely to show up when task 2 is easy, as when it involves simple RT (de Jong, 1993).

2. It should be noted that neither Spelke et al nor Shaffer interpreted their results in terms of automaticity (Shaffer wrote disparagingly of the concept). Others have drawn such a connection, however, and the data are obviously relevant to the issue.

3. This category effect, which has been replicated several times, should not be confused with the oh-zero effect—the purported fact that search for a *single* character "O" works better when it is described to the subject as a member of a different category than the distractors; this effect seems to be unreplicable (Duncan, 1983; Krueger, 1984). There is reason to suspect that physical differences between letters and digits contribute to between-category search, but the semantic significance of letters versus digits may contribute as well. To resolve the relative contribution of these factors one would have to train people to use artificial alphabets of letters and numbers whose visual properties were carefully selected. This experiment has not been performed to my knowledge, and would obviously be very time consuming.

4. Neuropsychological evidence would not seem to favor the second option; severe impairments in verbal short-term memory are not necessarily associated with impaired ability to prepare tasks or make plans (Shallice, 1988).

5. William James (1890/1950, p. 120) cites an anecdote from Thomas Huxley that, if true, might dispute this. A practical joker was said to have caused a heavily

drilled military veteran to drop a plate of food by shouting "Attention!" Of course, we do not know what would have happened if he had simply shouted "boo!"

6. As described in chapter 6, multiple inputs can simultaneously help retrieve the same target in memory at a given time, but since algorithmic retrieval often involves intermediate steps, one would not expect that it could operate in parallel with the direct memory retrieval. I am grateful to T. Rickard for pointing this out.

7. One of the few objective demonstrations of this intuitively compelling phenomenon was reported by Wierda and Brookhuis (1991), who found that, compared with cyclists with little experience, cyclists with more experience were better able to perform a concurrent detection task while cycling; they had to press a button on the handlebars when a buzzer went off from time to time.

8. As described in chapter 7, such a pattern may suggest that these effects have their locus in preparatory processes; by itself, however, this would not necessarily predict precise additivity. Since most reports of additivity demonstrate only approximate additivity, this may not be a problem.

9. Bills (1931) made the interesting observation that in a variety of different kinds of serial reaction time tasks with preview (his experiments involved printed lists of stimuli), people show periodic blocking: in intermittent trials response latencies are greatly elevated. Bills found that blocking, the causes of which are unknown, becomes worse with protracted performance.

10. Observed independently by R. de Jong (personal communication) and N. Christenfeld (personal communication).

References

Alfonso, A. (1992). Selective attention to visual and auditory stimuli. Unpublished honors thesis (May, 1992). Department of Psychology, University of California, San Diego.

Allport, D. A. (1971). Parallel encoding within and between elementary stimulus dimensions. *Perceptions and Psychophysics, 10,* 104–108.

Allport, D. A. (1980). Patterns and actions: Cognitive mechanisms are content-specific. In G. Claxton (Ed.), *Cognitive Psychology: New Directions.* London: Routledge and Kegan Paul, pp. 26–64.

Allport, D. A. (1989). Visual attention. In M. I. Posner (Ed.), *Foundations of Cognitive Science.* Cambridge, MA: MIT Press, pp. 631–682.

Allport, D. A., Antonis, B., and Reynolds, P. (1972). On the division of attention: A disproof of the single-channel hypothesis. *Quarterly Journal of Experimental Psychology, 24,* 225–235.

Allport, D. A, Styles, E. A., and Hsieh, S. (1994). Shifting intentional set: Exploring the dynamic control of tasks. In C. Umilta and M. Moscovitch (Eds.), *Attention and Performance 15: Conscious and Nonconscious Information Processing.*

Anderson, C. M. B., and Craik, F. I. (1974). The effect of a concurrent task on recall from primary memory. *Journal of Verbal Learning and Verbal Behavior, 13,* 107–113.

Anderson, J. R. (1976). *Language, Memory and Thought.* Hillsdale, NJ: Erlbaum.

Anderson, J. R. (1987). Methodologies for studying human knowledge. *Behavioral and Brain Sciences, 10,* 467–505.

Antes, J. R. (1974). The time course of picture viewing. *Journal of Experimental Psychology, 103,* 62–70.

Antes, J. R., Singsaas, P. A., and Metzger, R. L. (1978). Components of pictorial informativeness. *Perceptual and Motor Skills, 47,* 459–464.

Atkinson, J., and Braddick, O. J. (1989). "Where" and "what" in visual search. *Perception 18,* 181–189.

Atkinson, R., and Shiffrin, R. M. (1968). Human memory: A proposed system and its control processes. In K. W. Spence (Ed.), *The Psychology of Learning and Motivation: Advances in Research and Theory Vol. 2.* New York: Academic Press, pp. 89–185.

Atkinson, R. C., Holmgren, J. E., and Juola, J. F. (1969). Processing time as influenced by the number of elements in a visual display. *Perception and Psychophysics, 6,* 321–326.

Averbach, E., and Coriell, A. S. (1961). Short-term memory in vision. *Bell System Technical Journal, 40,* 309–328.

Backus, B. T., and Sternberg, S. (1988, November). Attentional tradeoffs across space early in visual processing: New evidence. Paper presented at the 29th annual meeting of the Psychonomic Society, Chicago.

Bacon, F. (1620/1960). *The New Organon, and Related Writings.* Edited with an introduction by Fulton H. Anderson. New York: Liberal Arts Press.

Bacon, W., Johnston, J. C., and Remington, R. W. (1995, November). Spatial attention enhances perceptual processing of single-element displays. Paper presented to the 35th annual meeting of the Psychonomic Society, St. Louis, MO.

Baddeley, A. D. (1966). Short-term memory for word sequences as a function of acoustic, semantic and format similarity. *Quarterly Journal of Experimental Psychology, 18,* 362–365.

Baddeley, A. D. (1986). *Working Memory.* Oxford: Oxford University Press.

Baddeley, A. D. (1990). *Human Memory: Theory and Practice.* Boston: Allyn & Bacon.

Baddeley, A. D., and Hitch, G. (1977). Recency reexamined. In S. Dornic (Ed.), *Attention and Performance VI.* Hillsdale, NJ: Erlbaum, pp. 647–667.

Baddeley, A. D., and Warrington, E. K. (1970). Amnesia and the distinction between long-term and short-term memory. *Journal of Verbal Learning and Verbal Behavior, 9,* 176–189.

Baddeley, A. D., Lewis, V., Eldridge, M., and Thomson, N. (1984). Attention and retrieval from long-term memory. *Journal of Experimental Psychology: General, 113,* 518–540.

Baddeley, A. D., Papagno, C., and Vallar, G. 1988). When long-term learning depends on short-term storage. *Journal of Memory and Language, 27,* 586–595.

Baddeley, A. D., Scott, D., Drynan, R., and Smith, J. C. (1969). Short-term memory and the limited capacity hypothesis. *British Journal of Psychology, 60,* 51–55.

Badgio, P. C. (1987). Mechanisms of visual attention. Ph.D. Dissertation, University of Pennsylvania. Abstracted in *Dissertation Abstracts International, 47,* (no. 10-B), 4326.

Bahrick, H. P., and Shelly, C. (1958). Time sharing as an index of automatization. *Journal of Experimental Psychology, 56,* 288–293.

Bargh, J. A. (1994). The four horsemen of automaticity: Awareness, intention, efficiency, and control in social cognition. In R. S. Wyer, Jr., and Thomas K. Srull (Eds.), *Handbook of Social Cognition, Vol. 1: Basic Processes*, pp. 1–40.

Barlow, H. (1980). [Title]. in D. McFadden (Ed.), *Neural Mechanisms of Behavior: A Texas Symposium*. New York: Springer-Verlag.

Barnard, P. (1985). Interacting cognitive subsystems: A psycholinguistic approach to short-term memory. In A. Ellis (Ed.), *Progress in the Psychology of Language Vol. 2*. Hillsdale, NJ: Erlbaum, pp. 197–258.

Bartz, W. H., and Salehi, M. (1970). Interference in short- and long-term memory. *Journal of Experimental Psychology, 84*, 380–382.

Bartz, W. H., Satz, P., and Fennell, E. (1967). Grouping strategies in dichotic listening: The effects of instructions, rate, and ear asymmetry. *Journal of Experimental Psychology, 74*, 132–136.

Bashinski, H. S., and Bacharach, V. R. (1980). Enhancement of perceptual sensitivity as the result of selectively attending to spatial locations. *Perception and Psychophysics, 28*, 241–248.

Basso, A., Spinnler, H., Vallar, G., and Zanobio, M. E. (1982). Left hemisphere damage and selective impairment of auditory verbal short-term memory: A case study. *Neuropsychologia, 20*, 263–274.

Bauer, B., Jolicoeur, P., and Cowan, W. B. (1996). Visual search for colour targets that are or are not linearly separable from distractors. *Vision Research, 36*, 1439–1466.

Baxt, N. (1871). Über die Zeit welche nötig ist damit ein Geschichtseindruck zum Bewustsein kommt und über die Grösse der bewussten Wahrnehmung bei einem Geschichtseindruck von gegebener Daner. *Pflager's Archiv Physiologie, 4*, 325–326.

Baylis, G. C., and Driver, J. (1992). Visual parsing and response competition: The effect of grouping factors. *Perception and Psychophysics, 51*, 145–162.

Becker, C. A. (1976). Allocation of attention during visual word recognition. *Journal of Experimental Psychology: Human Perception and Performance, 2*, 556–566.

Becker, C. A., and Killion, T. H. (1977). Interaction of visual and cognitive effects in word recognition. *Journal of Experimental Psychology: Human Perception and Performance, 3*, 389–401.

Benson, D. A. and Hienz, R. D. (1978). Single-unit activity in the auditory cortex of monkeys selectively attending left vs. right ear stimuli. *Brain Research, 159*, 307–320.

Berlyne, D. E. (1957). Attention to change, conditioned inhibition, and stimulus satiation. *British Journal of Psychology, 48*, 138–140.

Berry, G., and Klein, R. (1993). Does motion-induced grouping modulate the flanker compatibility effect? A failure to replicate Driver and Baylis. *Canadian Journal of Experimental Psychology, 47*, 714–729.

Bertelson, P. (1966). Central intermittency twenty years later. *Quarterly Journal of Experimental Psychology, 18,* 153–163.

Bertelson, P. (1967). The refractory period of choice reactions with regular and irregular interstimuli intervals. *Acta Psychologica, 27,* 45–56.

Bertelson, P., and Tisseyre, F. (1969). Refractory period of c-reactions. *Journal of Experimental Psychology, 79,* 122–128.

Best, J. B. (1986). *Cognitive Psychology.* St. Paul, MN: West Publishing.

Biederman, I., and Checkosky, S. F. (1970). Processing redundant information. *Journal of Experimental Psychology, 83,* 486–490.

Biederman, I., and Ju, G. (1988). Surface vs. edge-based determinants of visual recognition. *Cognitive Psychology, 20,* 38–64.

Biederman, I., Mezzanotte, R. J., and Rabinowitz, J. C. (1982). Scene perception: Detecting and judging objects undergoing relational violations. *Cognitive Psychology, 14,* 143–177.

Biederman, I., Teitelbaum, R. C., and Mezzanotte, R. J. (1983). Scene perception: A failure to find a benefit from prior expectancy or familiarity. *Journal of Experimental Psychology: Learning, Memory, and Cognition, 9,* 411–429.

Bills, A. G. (1927). The influence of muscular tension on the efficiency of mental work. *American Journal of Psychology, 38,* 227–251.

Bills, A. G. (1931). Blocking: A new principle of mental fatigue. *American Journal of Psychology, 43,* 230–245.

Bjork, R. A., and Whitten, W. B. (1974). Recency-sensitive retrieval processes in long-term free recall. *Cognitive Psychology, 6,* 173–189.

Blackwell, A., and Bates, E. (1995). Inducing agrammatic profiles in normals— Evidence for the selective vulnerability of morphology under cognitive resource limitation. *Journal of Cognitive Neuroscience, 7,* 228–257.

Blanchard, H. E., McConkie, G. W., Zola, D., and Wolverton, G. S. (1984). Time course of visual information utilization during fixations in reading. *Journal of Experimental Psychology: Human Perception and Performance, 10,* 75–89.

Borger, R. (1963). The refractory period and serial choice-reactions. *Quarterly Journal of Experimental Psychology, 15,* 1–12.

Boring, E. G. (1942). *Sensation and Perception in the History of Experimental Psychology.* New York: Appleton-Century Crofts.

Boring, E. G. (1957). *History of Experimental Psychology,* 2nd edition. New York: Appleton-Century Crofts.

Bornemann, E. (1942). Untersuchungen über den Grad der geistigen Beanspruchung. *Zeitschrift für Arbeitsphysiologie,* 142–172.

Bowers, R. L., Mollenhauer, M. S., and Luxford, J. (1990). Short-term memory for tactile and temporal stimuli in a shared-attention recall task. *Perceptual and Motor Skills, 70,* 903–913.

Braun, J., and Sagi, D. (1990). Vision outside the focus of attention. *Perception and Psychophysics, 52*, 277–294.

Braun, J., and Sagi, D. (1991). Texture-based tasks are little affected by second tasks requiring peripheral or central attentive fixation. *Perception, 20*, 483–500.

Brebner, J. (1977). The search for exceptions to the psychological refractory period. In S. Dornic (Ed.), *Attention and Performance VI*. Hillsdale, NJ: Erlbaum, pp. 63–78.

Brewer, W. F. (1974). There is no convincing evidence for operant or classical conditioning in adult humans. In W. B. Weimar, and D. S. Palermo (Eds.), *Cognition and the Symbolic Processes*. Hillsdale, NJ: Erlbaum.

Brindley, G. S. (1970). *Physiology of the Retina and Visual Pathway*, 2nd edition. London: Edward Arnold.

Broadbent, D. E. (1954). The role of auditory localization in attention and memory span. *Journal of Experimental Psychology, 47*, 191–196.

Broadbent, D. E. (1956). Successive responses to simultaneous stimuli. *Quarterly Journal of Experimental Psychology, 8*, 145–152.

Broadbent, D. E. (1957). Immediate memory and simultaneous stimuli. *Quarterly Journal of Experimental Psychology, 9*, 1–11.

Broadbent, D. E. (1958). *Perception and Communication*. London: Pergamon Press.

Broadbent, D. E. (1982). Task combination and the selective intake of information. *Acta Psychologica, 50*, 253–290.

Broadbent, D. E. (1989). Lasting representations and temporary processes. In H. Roediger and F. I. Craik (Eds.), *Varieties of Memory and Consciousness*. Hillsdale, NJ: Erlbaum, pp. 211–228.

Broadbent, D. E. and Broadbent, M. (1987). From detection to identification: Response to multiple targets in rapid serial visual presentation. *Perception and Psychophysics, 42*, 105–113.

Broadbent, D. E., and Broadbent, M. (1988). Anxiety and attentional bias: State and trait. *Cognition and Emotion, 2*, 165–183.

Broadbent, D. E., and Gathercole, S. E. (1990). The processing of non-target words: Semantic or not? *Quarterly Journal of Experimental Psychology: Human Experimental Psychology, 42*, 3–37.

Broadbent, D. E., and Gregory, M. (1967). Psychological refractory period and the length of time required to make a decision. *Proceedings of the Royal Society of London B, 168*, 181–193.

Brooks, B. A., Impelman, D. M., and Lum, J. T. (1981). Backward and forward masking associated with saccadic eye movement. *Perception and Psychophysics, 30*, 62–70.

Brooks, D. N., and Baddeley, A. D. (1976). What can amnesic patients learn? *Neuropsychologia, 14*, 111–122.

Brooks, L. R. (1968). Spatial and verbal components of the act of recall. *Canadian Journal of Psychology, 22,* 349–368.

Brooks, L. R. (1970). An extension of the conflict between visualization and reading. *Quarterly Journal of Experimental Psychology, 22,* 91–96.

Brown, T. L., and Carr, T. H. (1989). Automaticity in skill acquisition: Mechanisms for reducing interference in concurrent performance. *Journal of Experimental Psychology: Human Perception and Performance, 15,* 686–700.

Bruza, P. D., and Huibers, T. W. C. (1996). A study of aboutness in information retrieval. *Artificial Intelligence Review, 10,* 381–407.

Buchtel, H. A. and Butter, C. M. (1988). Spatial attentional shifts: Implications for the role of polysensory mechanisms. *Neuropsychologia, 26,* 499–509.

Burns, D. (1979). A dual-task analysis of detection accuracy for the case of high target-distractor similarity: Further evidence for independent processing. *Perception and Psychophysics, 25,* 185–196.

Bushnell, M. C., Duncan, G. H., Dubner, R., Jones, R. L., and Maixner, W. (1985). Attentional influences on noxious and innocuous cutaneous heat detection in humans and monkeys. *Journal of Neuroscience, 5,* 1103–1110.

Butter, C. M., Buchtel, H. A., and Santucci, R. (1989). Spatial attentional shifts: Further evidence for the role of polysensory mechanisms using visual and tactile stimuli. *Neuropsychologia, 27,* 1231–1240.

Cairney, P. T. (1975a). Bisensory order judgement and the prior entry hypothesis. *Acta Psychologica, 39,* 329–340.

Cairney, P. T. (1975b). The complication experiment uncomplicated. *Perception, 4,* 255–265.

Campbell, F. W. and Wurtz, R. H. (1978) Saccadic omission: Why we do not see a grey-out during a saccadic eye movement. *Vision Research, 18,* 1297–1303

Carlson-Radvansky, L. A., and Irwin, D. E. (1995). Memory for structural information across eye movements. *Journal of Experimental Psychology: Learning, Memory and Cognition, 21,* 1441–1458.

Carrier, M., and Pashler, H. (1996). The attention demands of memory retrieval. *Journal of Experimental Psychology: Learning, Memory and Cognition, 21,* 1339–1348.

Carrier, M., McFarland, K., and Pashler, H. (1996). Is implicit memory automatically encoded? Manuscript under review.

Cattell, J. M. (1886). The time it takes to see and name objects. *Mind, 11,* 63–65.

Cattell, J. M. (1893/1947). Attention and reaction. Reprinted in *James McKeen Cattell, 1860–1944, Man of Science.* Lancaster, PA.: Science Press.

Cavanagh, P. (1987). Reconstructing the third dimension: Interactions between color, texture, motion, binocular disparity and shape. *Computer Vision, Graphics, and Image Processing, 37,* 171–195.

Cavanagh, P., and Chase, W. G. (1971). The equivalence of target and nontarget processing in visual search. *Perception and Psychophysics, 9,* 493–495.

Cavanagh, P., and Parkman, J. M. (1972). Search processes for detecting repeated items in a visual display. *Perception and Psychophysics, 11,* 43–45.

Cavanagh, P., Arguin, M., and Treisman, A. (1990). Effect of surface medium on visual search for orientation and size features. *Journal of Experimental Psychology: Human Perception and Performance, 16,* 479–492.

Cave, K. R., and Pashler, H. (1995). Visual selection mediated by location: Selecting successive visual objects. *Perception and Psychophysics, 57,* 421–432.

Chamberlin, T. C. (1897). The method of multiple working hypotheses. *Journal of Geology, 5,* 837–848.

Chan, T-C., and Chan, K-I. (1995). Effect of frequency ratio and environmental information on spatial coupling: A study of attention. *Ecological Psychology, 7,* 125–144.

Chaudhuri, A. (1990). Modulation of the motion aftereffect by selective attention. *Nature, 344,* 60–62.

Cheng, P. W. (1985). Restructuring versus automaticity: Alternative accounts of skill acquisition. *Psychological Review, 92,* 414–423.

Cherry, E. C. (1953). Some experiments on the recognition of speech, with one and with two ears. *Journal of the Acoustical Society of America, 25,* 975–979.

Chow, S. L., and Murdock, B. B. (1975). The effect of a subsidiary task on iconic memory. *Memory and Cognition, 3,* 678–688.

Christie, J., and Klein, R. (1996). Assessing the evidence for novel popout. *Journal of Experimental Psychology: General, 125,* 201–207.

Chun, M. M., and Potter, M. C. (1995). A two-stage model for multiple target detection in rapid serial visual presentation. *Journal of Experimental Psychology: Human Perception and Performance, 21,* 109–127.

Cohn, T. E., and Lasley, D. J. (1974). Detectability of a luminance increment: Effect of spatial uncertainty. *Journal of the Optical Society of America, 64,* 1715–1719.

Colegate, R. L., Hoffman, J. E., and Eriksen, C. W. (1973). Selective encoding from multielement visual displays. *Perception and Psychophysics, 14,* 217–224.

Colle, H. A. and Welsh, A. (1976). Acoustic masking in primary memory. *Journal of Verbal Learning and Verbal Behavior, 15,* 17–32.

Collewijn, H., Curio, G., and Grusser, O.-J. (1982). Spatially selective visual attention and generation of eye pursuit movements. *Human Neurobiology, 1,* 129–139.

Collyer, S. C. (1968). Incentive motivation and choice reaction time performance. Unpublished dissertation, Johns Hopkins University, Baltimore, MD. Abstracted in *Dissertation Abstracts, 29* (n5-B), 1855.

Coltheart, M. (1972). Visual information processing. In P. C. Dodwell, (Ed.), *New Horizons in Psychology.* Harmondsworth, England: Penguin Books.

Coltheart, M. (1975). Iconic memory: A reply to Professor Holding. *Memory and Cognition, 3,* 42–48.

Coltheart, M. (1977). Contemporary models of the cognitive processes. I: Information input and storage. In V. Hamilton and M. D. Vernon (Eds.), *The development of cognitive processes.* London: Academic Press, pp. xx–yy.

Coltheart, M. (1980). Iconic memory and visible persistence. *Perception and Psychophysics, 27,* 183–228.

Coltheart, M., and Coltheart, V. (1972). On Rumelhart's model of visual information-processing. *Canadian Journal of Psychology, 26,* 292–295.

Comstock, E. M. (1973). Processing capacity in a letter-matching task. *Journal of Experimental Psychology, 100,* 63–72.

Cooper, L. A., and Shepard, R. N. (1973). The time required to prepare for a rotated stimulus. *Memory and Cognition, 1,* 246–250.

Corballis, M. C. (1988). Recognition of disoriented shapes. *Psychological Review, 95,* 115–123.

Corteen, R. S., and Wood, B. (1972). Autonomic responses to shock-associated words in an unattended channel. *Journal of Experimental Psychology, 94,* 308–313.

Cowan, N. (1988). Evolving conceptions of memory storage, selective attention, and their mutual constraints within the human information-processing system. *Psychological Bulletin, 104,* 163–191.

Craik, F. I. M., and Lockhart, R. S. (1972). Levels of processing: A framework for memory research. *Journal of Verbal Learning and Verbal Behavior, 11,* 671–684.

Craik, F. I. M., Giovoni, R., Naveh-Benjamin, M., and Anderson, N. D. (1996). The effects of divided attention on encoding and retrieval processes in human memory. *Journal of Experimental Psychology: General, 125,* 159–180.

Craik, K. W. J. (1947). Theory of the human operator in control systems. I. The operator as an engineering system. *British Journal of Psychology, 38,* 56–61.

Creamer, L. R. (1963). Event uncertainty, psychological refractory period, and human data processing. *Journal of Experimental Psychology, 66,* 187–194.

Crowder, R. G. (1993). Short-term memory: Where do we stand? *Memory and Cognition, 21,* 142–145.

Currie, C., McConkie, G. W., Carlson-Radavanski, L. A., and Irwin, D. E. (1995). Maintaining visual stability across saccades: Role of the saccade target object. Human Perception and Performance Technical Report UIUC-BI-HPP-95-01, University of Illinois.

Dai, H., Scharf, B., and Buus, S. (1991). Effective attenuation of signals in noise under focused attention. *Journal of the Acoustical Society of America, 89,* 2837–2842.

Dalgleish, T. (1995). Performance on the emotional Stroop task in groups of anxious, expert, and control subjects: A comparison of computer and card presentation formats. *Cognition and Emotion, 9,* 341–362.

Dallas, M., and Merikle, P. M. (1976). Semantic processing of non-attended visual information. *Canadian Journal of Psychology, 30,* 15–21.

Dalrymple-Alford, E. C., and Budayr, B. (1966). Examination of some aspects of the Stroop color-word test. *Perceptual and Motor Skills, 23,* 1211–1214.

Dark, V. J., and Scheerhorn, P. A. (1994, November). Semantic relatedness and spatial location: Two facets of the split personality of attention. Presented at the 35th meeting of the Psychonomic Society, St. Louis, MO.

Darwin, C. J., Turvey, M. T., and Crowder, R. G. (1972). An auditory analogue of the Sperling partial report procedure: Evidence for brief auditory storage. *Cognitive Psychology, 3,* 255–267.

Davidson, M. I., Fox, M. J., and Dick, A. O. (1973). Effect of eye movements on backward masking and perceived location. *Perception and Psychophysics, 14,* 110–116.

Davis, E. T. (1981). Allocation of attention: Uncertainty effects when monitoring one or two visual gratings of noncontiguous spatial frequencies. *Perception and Psychophysics, 29,* 618–622.

Davis, E. T., Kramer, P., and Graham, N. (1983). Uncertainty about spatial frequency, spatial position, or contrast of visual patterns. *Perception and Psychophysics, 33,* 20–28.

Davis, R. (1959). The role of "attention" in the psychological refractory period. *Quarterly Journal of Experimental Psychology, 11,* 211–220.

Davis, R. (1962). Choice reaction times and the theory of intermittency in human performance. *Quarterly Journal of Experimental Psychology, 14,* 157–166.

Dawson, M. E., and Schell, A. M. (1982). Electrodermal responses to attended and nonattended significant stimuli during dichotic listening. *Journal of Experimental Psychology: Human Perception and Performance, 8,* 315–324.

de Jong, R. (1993). Multiple bottlenecks in overlapping task performance. *Journal of Experimental Psychology: Human Perception and Performance, 19,* 965–980.

de Jong, R. (1995). The role of preparation in overlapping-task performance. *Quarterly Journal of Experimental Psychology: Human Experimental Psychology, 48A,* 2–25.

de Jong, R., and Sweet, J. B. (1994). Preparatory strategies in overlapping-task performance. *Perception and Psychophysics, 55,* 142–151.

della Malva, C. L., Stuss, D. T., D'Alton, J. D., and Willmer, J. (1993). Capture errors and sequencing after frontal brain lesions. *Neuropsychologia, 31,* 363–372.

de Renzi, E., Gentilini, M., and Pattacini, F. (1984). Auditory extinction following hemisphere damage. *Neuropsychologia, 22,* 733–744.

De Ruiter, C., and Brosschot, J. F. (1994). The emotional Stroop interference effect in anxiety: Attentional bias or cognitive avoidance. *Behavioral Research and Therapy, 32,* 315–319.

Dennett, D. (1991). *Consciousness Explained.* Boston: Little, Brown.

Derrick, W. L. (1988). Dimensions of operator workload. *Human Factors, 30,* 95–110.

Desimone, R., and Duncan, J. (1995). Neural mechanisms of selective visual attention. *Annual Review of Neuroscience, 18,* 193–222

Desimone, R., Miller, E. K., Chelazzi, L., and Lueschow, A. (1995). Multiple memory systems in the visual cortex. In M. S. Gazzaniga (Ed.), *The Cognitive Neurosciences.* Cambridge, MA: MIT Press, pp. 475–486.

Desimone, R., Schein, S. J., Moran, J., and Ungerleider, L. G. (1985). Contour, color and shape analysis beyond the striate cortex. *Vision Research, 25,* 441–452.

Deubel, H., and Schneider, W. X. (1996). Saccade target selection and object recognition—Evidence for a common attentional mechanism. *Vision Research, 36,* 1827–1837.

Deutsch, D. (1986). Auditory pattern recognition. In K. Boff, L. Kaufman, and J. Thomas (Eds.), *Handbook of Perception and Performance,* Vol. II. New York: Wiley, pp. 32-1–32-49.

Deutsch, J. A., and Deutsch, D. (1963). Attention: Some theoretical considerations. *Psychological Review, 70,* 80–90.

Dixon, P. (1981). Algorithms and selective attention. *Memory and Cognition, 9,* 177–184.

Donnelly, N., Humphreys, G. W., and Riddoch, M. J. (1991). Parallel computation of primitive shape descriptions. *Journal of Experimental Psychology: Human Perception and Performance, 17,* 561–570.

Doost, R., and Turvey, M. T. (1971). Iconic memory and central processing capacity. *Perception and Psychophysics, 9,* 269–274.

Downing, B. D., and Gossman, J. R. (1970). Parallel processing of multidimensional stimuli. *Perception and Psychophysics, 8,* 57–60.

Downing, C. J. (1988). Expectancy and visual-spatial attention: Effects on perceptual quality. *Journal of Experimental Psychology: Human Perception and Performance, 14,* 188–202.

Driver, J., and Baylis, G. C. (1989). Movement and visual attention: The spotlight metaphor breaks down. *Journal of Experimental Psychology: Human Perception and Performance, 15,* 448–456.

Driver, J. and Spence, C. J. (1994). Spatial synergies between auditory and visual attention. In C. Umilta and M. Moscovitch, (Eds.), *Attention and Performance 15: Conscious and Nonconscious Information Processing.* Cambridge, MA: MIT Press, pp. 311–331.

Driver, J., and Tipper, S. P. (1989). On the nonselectivity of "selective seeing": Contrast between interference and priming in selective attention. *Journal of Experimental Psychology: Human Perception and Performance, 15,* 304–314.

Dumais, S. T. (1980). Perceptual learning in automatic detection: Processes and mechanisms. *Dissertation Abstracts International, 40,* n10-B, 5048–5049.

Duncan, J. (1979). Divided attention: The whole is more than the sum of its parts. *Journal of Experimental Psychology: Human Perception and Performance, 5,* 216–228.

Duncan, J. (1980a). The demonstration of capacity limitation. *Cognitive Psychology, 12,* 75–96.

Duncan, J. (1980b). The locus of interference in the perception of simultaneous stimuli. *Psychological Review, 87,* 272–300.

Duncan, J. (1981). Directing attention in the visual field. *Perception and Psychophysics, 30,* 90–93.

Duncan, J. (1983). Category effects in visual search: A failure to replicate the "oh-zero" phenomenon. *Perception and Psychophysics, 34,* 221–232.

Duncan, J. (1984) Selective attention and the organization of visual information. *Journal of Experimental Psychology: General, 113,* 501–517.

Duncan, J. (1985). Visual search and visual attention. In M. I. Posner and O. S. M. Marin (Eds.), *Attention and Performance X.* Hillsdale, NJ: Erlbaum, pp. 85–105.

Duncan, J. (1986). Consistent and varied training in the theory of automatic and controlled information processing. *Cognition, 23,* 279–284.

Duncan, J. (1987). Attention and reading: Wholes and parts in shape recognition—A tutorial review. In M. Coltheart (Ed.), *Attention and Performance XII: The Psychology of Reading.* Hillsdale, NJ: Erlbaum, pp. 39–61.

Duncan, J. (1990). Similarity between concurrent visual discriminations—Dimensions and objects. *Perception and Psychophysics, 54,* 425–430.

Duncan, J., and Humphreys, G. W. (1989). Visual search and stimulus similarity. *Psychological Review, 96,* 433–458.

Duncan, J., Burgess, P., and Emslie, H. (1995). Fluid intelligence after frontal lobe lesions. *Neuropsychologia, 33,* 261–268.

Duncan, J., Ward, R., and Shapiro, K. (1994). Direct measurement of attentional dwell time in human vision. *Nature, 369,* 313–315.

Duncan-Johnson, C. C., and Kopell, B. W. (1981). The Stroop effect: Brain potentials localize the source of interference. *Science, 214,* 938–940.

Dutta, A., and Walker, B. N. (1995, November). Persistence of the PRP effect: Evaluating the response-selection bottleneck. Presented at the 36th annual meeting of the Psychonomics Society, Los Angeles, California.

Duysens, J., Orban, G. A., Cremieux, J., and Maes, H. (1985). Visual cortical correlates of visible persistence. *Vision Research, 25,* 171–178.

D'Zmura, M. (1991). Color in visual search. *Vision Research, 31,* 951–966.

Egan, J. P., Carterette, E. C., and Thwing, E. J. (1954). Some factors affecting multichannel listening. *Journal of the Acoustical Society of America, 26,* 774–782.

Egeth, H. E. (1966). Parallel versus serial processes in multidimensional stimulus discrimination. *Perception and Psychophysics, 1,* 245–252.

Egeth, H. (1967). Selective attention. *Psychological Bulletin, 67,* 41–57.

Egeth, H. (1977). Attention and preattention. In G. H. Bower (Ed.), *The Psychology of Learning and Motivation,* Vol. 11. New York: Academic Press, pp. 277–320.

Egeth, H., and Dagenbach, D. (1991). Parallel versus serial processing in visual search: Further evidence from subadditive effects of visual quality. *Journal of Experimental Psychology: Human Perception and Performance, 17,* 551–560.

Egeth. H., and Smith, E. (1967). Perceptual selectivity in a visual recognition task. *Journal of Experimental Psychology, 74,* 543–549.

Egeth, H., Jonides, J., and Wall, S. (1972). Parallel processing of multielement displays. *Cognitive Psychology, 3,* 674–698.

Egeth, H., Pomerantz, J. R., and Schwartz, S. P. (1977, November). Is encoding really effortless? Paper presented at the 18th annual meeting of the Psychonomic Society, Washington, DC.

Egeth, H. E., Virzi, R. A., and Garbart, H. (1984). Searching for conjunctively defined targets. *Journal of Experimental Psychology: Human Perception and Performance, 10,* 32–39.

Eijkman, E., and Vendrik, A. J. H. (1965). Can a sensory system be specified by its internal noise? *Journal of the Acoustical Society of America, 37,* 1102–1109.

Enns, J. T., and Rensink, R. A. (1991). Scene based properties influence visual search. *Science, 247,* 721–723.

Ericsson, K. A., and Simon, H. A. (1980). Verbal reports as data. *Psychological Review, 87,* 215–251.

Eriksen, B. A., and Eriksen, C. W. (1974). Effects of noise letters upon the identification of a target letter in a nonsearch task. *Perception and Psychophysics, 16,* 143–149.

Eriksen, B. A., Eriksen, C. W., and Hoffman, J. E. (1986). Recognition memory and attentional selection: Serial scanning is not enough. *Journal of Experimental Psychology: Human Perception and Performance, 12,* 476–483.

Eriksen, C. W., and Collins, J. F. (1969). Temporal course of selective attention. *Journal of Experimental Psychology, 80,* 254–261.

Eriksen, C. W., and Hoffman, J. E. (1972a). Some characteristics of selective attention in visual perception determined by vocal reaction time. *Perception and Psychophysics, 11,* 169–171.

Eriksen, C. W., and Hoffman, J. E. (1972b). Temporal and spatial characteristics of selective encoding from visual displays. *Perception and Psychophysics, 12,* 201–204.

Eriksen, C. W., and Hoffman, J. E. (1973). The extent of processing of noise elements during selective encoding from visual displays. *Perception and Psychophysics, 14,* 155–160.

Eriksen, C. W., and Rohrbaugh, J. W. (1970). Some factors determining efficiency of selective attention. *American Journal of Psychology, 83,* 330–342.

Eriksen, C. W., and Spencer, T. (1969). Rate of information processing in visual perception: Some results and methodological considerations. *Journal of Experimental Psychology Monograph, 79* (Part 2), 1–16.

Eriksen, C. W., and St. James, J. D. (1986). Visual attention within and around the field of focal attention: A zoom lens model. *Perception and Psychophysics, 40,* 225–240.

Erkelens, C. J., and Collewijn, H. (1991). Control of vergence: Gating among disparity inputs by voluntary target selection. *Experimental Brain Research, 87,* 671–678.

Estes, W. K., and Taylor, H. A. (1964). A detection method and probabilistic models for assessing information processing from brief visual displays. *Proceedings of the National Academy of Science, 52,* 446–454.

Estes, W. K., and Taylor, H. A. (1965). Visual detection in relation to display size and redundancy of critical elements. *Perception & Psychophysics, 1,* 9–15.

Eysenck, M. (1992). *Anxiety: The Cognitive Perspective.* Hillsdale, NJ: Erlbaum.

Fagot, C., and Pashler, H. (1992). Making two responses to a single object: Exploring the central bottleneck. *Journal of Experimental Psychology: Human Perception and Performance, 18,* 1058–1079 (see errata, same journal, *19,* 443).

Fagot, C. (1994). Chronometric investigations of task switching. Ph.D. dissertation, University of California, San Diego.

Farah, M. J. (1990). *Visual Agnosia: Disorders of Object Recognition and What They Tell Us About Normal Vision.* Cambridge, MA: MIT Press.

Farah, M. J., Wong, A. B., Monheit, M. A., and Morrow, L. A. (1989). Parietal lobe mechanisms of spatial attention: Modality-specific or supramodal? *Neuropsychologia, 27,* 461–470.

Farell, B., and Pelli, D. G. (1993). Can we attend to large and small at the same time? *Vision Research, 33,* 2757–2772.

Fendrick, P. (1937). Hierarchical skills in typewriting. *Journal of Educational Psychology, 28,* 609–620.

Fera, P., Jolicoeur, P., and Besner, D. (1994). Evidence against early selection: Stimulus quality effects in previewed displays. *Journal of Experimental Psychology: Human Perception and Performance, 20,* 259–275.

Feynman, R. P. (1985). *Surely you're joking, Mr. Feynman!: Adventures of a curious character.* New York: Bantam Books.

Fibiger, W., and Singer, G. (1989). Biochemical assessment and differentiation of mental and physical effort. *Work and Stress, 3,* 237–247.

Fischman, M. G. and Lim, C. (1991). Influence of extended practice on programming time, movement time, and transfer in simple target-striking responses. *Journal of Motor Behavior, 23,* 39–50.

Fisher, D. L. (1982). Limited-channel models of automatic detection: Capacity and scanning in visual search. *Psychological Review, 89,* 662–692.

Fisher, D. L. (1984). Central capacity limits in consistent mapping, visual search tasks: Four channels or more? *Cognitive Psychology, 16,* 449–484.

Fisher, S. (1975a). The microstructure of dual-task interaction: 1. The patterning of main-task responses within secondary-task intervals. *Perception, 4,* 267–290.

Fisher, S. (1975b). The microstructure of dual-task interaction: 2. The effect of task instructions on attentional allocation and a model of attention-switching. *Perception, 4,* 459–474.

Flowers, J. H., and Lohr, D. J. (1985). How does familiarity affect visual search for letter strings? *Perception and Psychophysics, 37,* 557–567.

Flowers, J. H., Warner, J. L., and Polansky, M. C. (1979). Response and encoding factors in "ignoring" irrelevant information. *Memory and Cognition, 7,* 86–94.

Fodor, J. A. (1983). *The Modularity of Mind: An Essay on Faculty Psychology.* Cambridge, MA: MIT Press.

Folk, C. L., and Annett, S. (1994). Do locally defined feature discontinuities capture attention? *Perception and Psychophysics, 56,* 277–288.

Folk, C., and Egeth, H. (1985, March). Size invariance in perception? Paper presented at the Eastern Psychological Association, Boston.

Folk, C. L., Remington, R. W., and Johnston, J. C. (1992). Involuntary covert orienting is contingent on attentional control settings. *Journal of Experimental Psychology: Human Perception and Performance, 18,* 1030–1044.

Franz, E. A., Zelaznik, H. N., and McCabe, G. (1991). Spatial topological constraints in a bimanual task. *Acta Psychologica, 77,* 137–151.

Frick, R. W. (1984). Using both an auditory and a visual short-term store to increase digit span. *Memory and Cognition, 12,* 507–514.

Friedman, A. and Polson, M. C. (1981). Hemispheres as independent resource systems: limited-capacity processing and cerebral specialization. *Journal of Experimental Psychology: Human Perception and Performance, 7,* 1031–1058.

Fuster, J. (1984). The cortical substrate of memory. In L. R. Squire and N. Butters (Eds.), *Neuropsychology of Memory.* New York: Guilford Press.

Fuster, J. M. (1995). *Memory in the Cerebral Cortex: An Empirical Approach to Neural Networks in the Human and Nonhuman Primate.* Cambridge, MA: MIT Press.

Gaillard, A. W., and Trumbo, D. A. (1976). Drug effects on heart rate and heart rate variability during a prolonged reaction task. *Ergonomics, 19,* 611–622.

Gardner, G. T. (1973). Evidence for independent parallel channels in tachistoscopic perception. *Cognitive Psychology, 4,* 130–155.

Gardner, G. T., and Joseph, D. J. (1975). Parallel perceptual channels at "deep" processing levels. *Bulletin of the Psychonomic Society, 6,* 658–660.

Garner, W. R., Hake, H. W., and Eriksen, C. W. (1956). Operationism and the concept of perception. *Psychological Review, 63,* 149–159.

Gatti, S. W., and Egeth, H. (1978). Failure of spatial selectivity in vision. *Bulletin of the Psychonomic Society, 11,* 181–184.

Gerver, D. (1974). Simultaneous listening and speaking and retention of prose. *Quarterly Journal of Experimental Psychology, 26,* 337–341.

Gescheider, G. A., Sager, L. C., and Ruffolo, L. J. (1975). Simultaneous auditory and tactile information processing. *Perception and Psychophysics, 18,* 209–216.

Gibson, J. J. (1941). A critical review of the concept of set in contemporary experimental psychology. *Psychological Bulletin, 38,* 781–817.

Gillie, T., and Broadbent, D. E. (1989). What makes interruptions disruptive? A study of length, similarity, and complexity. *Psychological Research, 50,* 243–250.

Gilliom, J. D., and Mills, W. M. (1976). Information extraction from contralateral cues in the detection of signals of uncertain frequency. *Journal of the Acoustical Society of America, 59,* 1428–1433.

Gilliom, J. D., and Sorkin, R. D. (1974). Sequential vs simultaneous two-channel signal detection: More evidence for a high-level interrupt theory. *Journal of the Acoustical Society of America, 56,* 157–164.

Gladstones, W. H., Regan, M. A., and Lee, R. B. (1989). Division of attention: The single-channel hypothesis revisited. *Quarterly Journal of Experimental Psychology: Human Experimental Psychology, 41(A),* 1–17.

Glanzer, M., and Cunitz, A. R. (1966). Two storage mechanisms in free recall. *Journal of Verbal Learning and Verbal Behavior, 5,* 351–360.

Glaser, W. R., and Dolt, M. O. (1977). A functional model to localize the conflict underlying the Stroop phenomenon. *Psychological Research, 39,* 287–310.

Gnadt, J. W., and Andersen, R. A. (1992). Memory related motor planning activity in posterior parietal cortex of macaque. In S. Kosslyn and R. A. Andersen (Eds.), *Frontiers in Cognitive Neuroscience.* Cambridge, MA: MIT Press, pp. 468–472.

Godden, D. R., and Baddeley, A. D. (1975). Context-dependent memory in two natural environments: On land and underwater. *British Journal of Psychology, 66,* 325–331.

Goldstein L. H., Bernard, S., Fenwick P. B., Burgess P. W., and McNeil J. (1993). Unilateral frontal lobectomy can produce strategy application disorder. *Journal of Neurology, Neurosurgery and Psychiatry, 56,* 274–276.

Goodale, M. A., and Milner, A. D. (1992). Separate visual pathways for perception and action. *Trends in Neurosciences, 15,* 20–25.

Goodrich, S., Henderson, L., Allchin, N., and Jeevaratnam, A. (1990). On the peculiarity of simple reaction time. *Quarterly Journal of Experimental Psychology, 42(A),* 763–775.

Gopher, D., and Navon, D. (1980). How is performance limited: Testing the notion of central capacity. *Acta Psychologica, 46,* 161–180.

Gopher, D., Brickner, M., and Navon, D. (1982). Different difficulty manipulations interact differently with task emphasis: Evidence for multiple resources. *Journal of Experimental Psychology: Human Perception and Performance, 8,* 146–157.

Gottsdanker, R. (1980). The ubiquitous role of preparation. In G. E. Stelmach and J. Requin (Eds.), *Tutorials in Motor Behavior.* Amsterdam: North-Holland Press, pp. 355–371.

Gottsdanker, R. and Stelmach, G. E. (1971). The persistence of psychological refractoriness. *Journal of Motor Behavior, 3,* 301–312.

Graf, P., and Schacter, D. L. (1985). Implicit and explicit memory for new associations in normal and amnesic patients. *Journal of Experimental Psychology: Learning, memory and cognition, 13,* 45–55.

Graham, N. (1985). Detection and identification of near-threshold visual patterns. *Journal of the Optical Society of America A, 2,* 1468–1482.

Graham, N. (1989). *Visual Pattern Analyzers.* Oxford: Oxford University Press.

Grant, D. A., and Berg, E. A. (1948). A behavioural analysis of degree of reinforcement and ease of shifting to new responses in a Weigl-type card-sorting problem. *Journal of Experimental Psychology, 38,* 404–411.

Gray, C. M., Engel, A. K., Konig, P., and Singer, W. (1992). Synchronization of oscillatory neuronal responses in cat striate cortex. *Visual Neuroscience, 8,* 337–347.

Gray, J. A., and Wedderburn, A. A. I. (1960). Grouping strategies with simultaneous stimuli. *Quarterly Journal of Experimental Psychology, 12,* 180–184.

Green, D. M. (1961). Detection of auditory sinusoids of uncertain frequency. *Journal of the Acoustical Society of America, 33,* 897–303.

Green, M. (1991). Visual search, visual streams, and visual architectures. *Perception and Psychophysics, 50,* 388–403.

Green M. (1992). Visual search: detection, identification, and localization. *Perception, 21,* 765–77.

Greenberg, G. Z., and Larkin, W. D. (1968). Frequency-response characteristic of auditory observers detecting signals of a single frequency in noise: The probe-signal method. *Journal of the Acoustical Society of America, 44,* 1513–1523.

Greenwald, A. G. (1970). Selective attention as a function of signal rate. *Journal of Experimental Psychology, 86,* 48–52.

Greenwald, A. G., and Shulman, H. G. (1973). On doing two things at once: II. Elimination of the psychological refractory period effect. *Journal of Experimental Psychology, 101,* 70–76.

Grindley, G. C., and Townsend, V. (1968). Voluntary attention in peripheral vision and its effects on acuity and differential thresholds. *Quarterly Journal of Experimental Psychology, 20,* 11–19.

Gross, C. G. (1971). Visual functions of inferotemporal cortex. In R. Jung (Ed.), *Handbook of Sensory Physiology*, Vol. 7, Part 3B. Berlin: Springer-Verlag, pp. 451–482.

Guttman, N., and Julesz, B. (1963). Lower limit of auditory periodicity analysis. *Journal of the Acoustical Society of America, 36*, 757–765.

Haber, R. N. (1969). Direct measures of visual short-term storage. *Quarterly Journal of Experimental Psychology, 21*, 43–54.

Haber, R. N. (1985). An icon can have no worth in the real world: Comments on Loftus, Johnson, and Shimamura's "How much is an icon worth?" *Journal of Experimental Psychology: Human Perception and Performance, 11*, 374–378.

Hafter, E. R., and Buell, T. N. (1985). The importance of transients for maintaining the separation of signals in auditory space. In M. I. Posner and O. S. M. Marin (Eds.), *Attention and Performance X*. Hillsdale, NJ: Erlbaum, pp. 337–354.

Hall, G. (1991). *Perceptual and associative learning*. Oxford: Oxford University Press.

Hamlin, A. J. (1895). On the least observable interval between stimuli addressed to disparate senses and to different organs of the same sense. *American Journal of Psychology, 6*, 564–573.

Hanley, J. R., and Morris, P. (1987). The effects of amount of processing on recall and recognition. *Quarterly Journal of Experimental Psychology, 39A*, 431–449.

Hanley, J. R., Young, A. W., and Pearson, N. A. (1991). Impairment of the visuo-spatial sketch pad. *Quarterly Journal of Experimental Psychology, 43A*, 101–125.

Hansen, J. C., and Hillyard, S. A. (1980). Endogeneous brain potentials associated with selective auditory attention. *Electroencephalography and Clinical Neurophysiology, 49*, 277–290.

Harris, C. S., and Haber, R. N. (1963). Selective attention and coding in visual perception. *Journal of Experimental Psychology, 65*, 328–333.

Hatfield, G. (in press). Attention in early scientific psychology. To appear in R. D. Wright (Ed.), *Visual Attention*. New York: Oxford Univ. Press.

Hawkins, H. L., Church, M., and de Lemos, S. (1978). Time-sharing is not a unitary ability. University of Oregon Technical Report (No. 2), prepared for the Office of Naval Research.

Hawkins, H. L., Hillyard, S. A., Luck, S. J., Mouloua, M., Downing, C. J., and Woodward, D. P. (1990). Visual attention modulates signal detectability. *Journal of Experimental Psychology: Human Perception and Performance, 16*, 802–811.

Hawkins, H. L., Shafto, M. G., and Richardson, K. (1988). Effects of target luminance and cue validity on the latency of visual detection. *Perception and Psychophysics, 44*, 484–492.

Haxby, J. V., Lundgren, S. L., and Morley, G. K. (1983). Short-term retention of verbal, visual shape and visuospatial location information in normal and amnesic subjects. *Neuropsychologia, 21*, 25–33.

Heathcote, A., and Mewhort, D. J. K. (1993). Representation and selection of relative position. *Journal of Experimental Psychology: Human Perception and Performance, 19,* 488–516.

Hebb, D. O. (1949). *The Organization of Behavior: A Neuropsychological Theory.* New York: Wiley.

Heffner, R. S., and Heffner, H. E. (1992). Evolution of sound localization in mammals. In D. B. Webster, R. R. Fay, and A. N. Popper (Eds.), *The Evolutionary Biology of Hearing.* New York: Springer-Verlag, pp. 691–715.

Heilman, K. M., Watson, R. T., and Valenstein, E. (1993). Neglect and related disorders. In K. Heilman and E. Valenstein (Eds.), *Clinical Neuropsychology,* 3rd edition. New York: Oxford University Press, pp. 279–336.

Hellige, J. B., Cox, P. J., and Litvac, L. (1979). Information processing in the cerebral hemispheres: Selective hemispheric activation and capacity limitations. *Journal of Experimental Psychology: General, 108,* 251–279.

Helmholtz, H. (1924). *Helmholtz's Treatise on Physiological Optics,* translated from the 3d German edition. Edited by James P. C. Southall. Rochester, NY: The Optical Society of America.

Helmholtz, H. (1968). R. M. Warren and R. P. Warren (Eds.), *Helmholtz on Perception, Its Physiology, and Development.* New York: Wiley.

Henderson, J. M. (1991). Stimulus discrimination following covert attentional orienting to an exogenous cue. *Journal of Experimental Psychology: Human Perception and Performance, 17,* 91–106.

Henderson, J. M. (1996). Spatial precues affect target discrimination in the absence of visual noise. *Journal of Experimental Psychology: Human Perception and Performance, 22,* 780–787.

Henderson, L. (1972). Spatial and verbal codes and the capacity of STM. *Quarterly Journal of Experimental Psychology, 24,* 485–495.

Heuer, H. (1985). Intermanual interactions during simultaneous execution and programming of finger movements. *Journal of Motor Behavior, 17,* 335–354.

Hick W. E. (1952). On the rate of gain of information. *Quarterly Journal of Experimental Psychology, 4,* 11–26.

Hikosaka, O., Miyauchi, S., and Shimojo, S. (1993). Focal visual attention produces illusory temporal order and motion sensation. *Vision Research, 33,* 1219–1240.

Hillstrom, A. P., and Yantis, S. (1994). Visual motion and attentional capture. *Perception and Psychophysics, 55,* 399–411.

Hillyard, S. A., and Münte, T. F. (1984). Selective attention to color and locational cues: An analysis with event-related brain potentials. *Perception and Psychophysics, 36,* 185–198.

Hillyard, S. A., and Picton, T. W. (1987). Electrophysiology of cognition. In F. Plum (Ed.), *Handbook of Physiology Section 1: The Nervous System,* Vol. 5. *Higher Functions of the Brain, Part 2.* Bethesda, MD: American Physiological Society, pp. 519–584.

Hillyard, S. A., Hink, R. F., Schwent, V. L., and Picton, T. W. (1973). Electrical signs of selective attention in the human brain. *Science, 182,* 177–179.

Hinde, R. A. (1966). *Animal Behavior.* New York: McGraw-Hill.

Hinton, G. E. (1981, August). A parallel computation that assigns canonical object-based frames of reference. In *Proceedings of the Seventh international Joint Conference on Artificial Intelligence, Vol. 2.* Vancouver, BC, Canada.

Hinton, G. E. (1989). Connectionist learning procedures. *Artificial Intelligence, 40,* 185–234.

Hirst, W., and Kalmar, D. (1987). Characterizing attentional resources. *Journal of Experimental Psychology: General, 116,* 68–81.

Hiscock, M. (1982). Verbal-manual time sharing in children as a function of task priority. *Brain and Cognition, 1,* 119–131.

Hochberg, J. (1978). *Perception,* 2nd edition. Englewood Cliffs, NJ: Prentice-Hall.

Hockley, W. E., and Corballis, M. C. (1982). Tests of serial scanning in item recognition. *Canadian Journal of Psychology, 36,* 189–212.

Hoffding, H. (1896). *Outlines of Psychology.* London: Macmillan.

Hoffman, J. E. (1979). A two-stage model of visual search. *Perception and Psychophysics, 25,* 319–327.

Hoffman, J. E. (1986). Spatial attention in vision: Evidence for early selection. Special Issue: Visual selective attention. *Psychological Research, 48,* 221–229.

Hoffman, J. E., and MacMillan, F. W. (1985). Is semantic priming automatic? In M. I. Posner and O. S. M. Marin (Eds.), *Attention and Performance XI.* Hillsdale, NJ: Erlbaum, pp. 585–600.

Hoffman, J. E., and Subramaniam, B. (1995). Saccadic eye movement and visual selective attention. *Perception and Psychophysics, 57,* 787–795.

Hoffman, J. E., Nelson, B., and Houck, M. R. (1983). The role of attentional resources in automatic detection. *Cognitive Psychology, 51,* 379–410.

Holding, D. H., Foulke, E., and Heise, R. L. (1973). Brief storage of compressed digits. *Journal of Experimental Psychology, 101,* 30–34.

Holmgren, J. E. (1974). The effect of a visual indicator on rate of visual search: Evidence for processing control. *Perception and Psychophysics, 15,* 544–550.

Horlitz, K., Johnston, J. C., and Remington, R. (1992, November). What makes it difficult to process multiple targets in rapid serial visual presentations (RSVP)? Paper presented at the Psychonomics Society Meeting, St. Louis, MO.

Houck, M. R., and Hoffman, J. E. (1986). Conjunction of color and form without attention: Evidence from an orientation-contingent color aftereffect. *Journal of Experimental Psychology: Human Perception and Performance, 12,* 186–199.

Howard, D., and Franklin, S. (1993). Dissociations between component mechanisms in short-term memory: Evidence from brain-damaged patients. In D. Meyer and S. Kornblum (Eds.), *Attention and Performance XIV.* Cambridge, MA: MIT Press, pp. 425–450.

Howson, C., and Urbach, P. (1989). *Scientific Reasoning: The Bayesian Approach.* Lasalle, IL: Open Court Press.

Hoyer, S. (1982). The young-adult and normally aged brain. Its blood flow and oxidative metabolism. A review—Part I. *Archives of Gerontology and Geriatrics, 1,* 101–116.

Hubel, D., and Wiesel, T. (1962). Receptive fields, binocular interaction, and functional architecture in the cat's visual cortex. *Journal of Physiology, 160,* 106–154.

Humphreys, G. W., Quinlan, P. T., and Riddoch, M. J. (1989). Grouping processes in visual search: Effects with single- and combined-feature targets. *Journal of Experimental Psychology: General, 118,* 258–279.

Hyde, T. S., and Jenkins, J. J. (1973). Recall for words as a function of semantic, graphic, and syntactic orienting tasks. *Journal of Verbal Learning and Verbal Behavior, 12,* 471–480.

Inhoff, A. W., and Brihl, D. (1991). Semantic processing of unattended text during selective reading: How the eyes see it. *Perception and Psychophysics, 49,* 289–294.

Ivry, R. B., and Hazeltine, R. E. (1995). Perception and production of temporal intervals across a range of durations: Evidence for a common timing mechanism. *Journal of Experimental Psychology: Human Perception and Performance, 21,* 3–18.

Ivry, R. B., and Keele, S. W. (1989). Timing functions of the cerebellum. *Journal of Cognitive Neuroscience, 1,* 136–152.

Iwasaki, S. (1993). Spatial attention and two modes of visual consciousness. *Cognition, 49,* 211–233.

Jacoby, L. L., and Dallas, M. (1981). On the relationship between autobiographical memory and perceptual learning. *Journal of Experimental Psychology: General, 110,* 306–340.

Jacoby, L. L., Woloshyn, V., and Kelley, C. (1989). Becoming famous without being recognized: Unconscious influences of memory produced by dividing attention. *Journal of Experimental Psychology: General, 118,* 115–125.

James, W. (1890/1950). *The Principles of Psychology,* Vol 1. New York: Dover.

Jaskowski, P. (1993). Selective attention and temporal order judgment. *Perception, 22,* 681–689.

Jeannerod, M. (Ed.) (1987), *Neurophysiological and Neuropsychological Aspects of Spatial Neglect. Advances in Psychology,* No. 45. Amsterdam: Elsevier Science.

Jefferys, W. H., and Berger, J. O. (1992). Ockham's razor and Bayesian analysis. *American Scientist, 80,* 64–72.

Jernigan, T. L., and Ostergaard, A. L. (1993). Word priming and recognition memory are both affected by mesial temporal lobe damage. *Neuropsychology, 7,* 14–26.

Jersild, A. T. (1927). Mental set and shift. *Archives of Psychology,* whole number 89.

Johnson, D. M., and Hafter, E. R. (1980). Uncertain-frequency detection: Cuing and condition of observation. *Perception and Psychophysics, 28,* 143–149.

Johnson, N. E., Saccuzzo, D. P., and Larson, G. E. (1995). Self-reported effort versus actual performance in information processing paradigms. *Journal of General Psychology, 122,* 195–210.

Johnson, P. J. Forester, J. A., Calderwood, R., and Weisgerber, S. A. (1983). Resource allocation and the attentional demands of letter encoding. *Journal of Experimental Psychology: General, 112,* 616–638.

Johnston, A., Hill, H., and Carman, N. (1992). Recognising faces: Effects of lighting direction, inversion, and brightness reversal. *Perception, 21,* 365–375.

Johnston, J. C. (1981). Effects of advance precuing of alternatives on the perception of letters alone and in words. *Journal of Experimental Psychology: Human Perception and Performance, 7,* 560–572.

Johnston, J. C., and Hale, B. L. (1984). The influence of prior context on word identification: Bias and sensitivity effects. *Attention and Performance X,* 243–255.

Johnston, J. C., and McClelland, J. L. (1973). Visual factors in word perception. *Perception and Psychophysics, 14,* 365–370.

Johnston, J. C., and Pashler, H. E. (1991). Close binding of identity and location in visual feature perception. *Journal of Experimental Psychology: Human Perception and Performance, 16,* 843–856.

Johnston, J. C., McCann, R., and Remington, R. (1996). Selective attention operates at two processing loci. In A. Kramer and G. Logan (Eds.), *Essays in Honor of Charles Eriksen.* Washington, DC: American Psychological Association, pp. 439–458.

Johnston, J. C., van Santen, J. P. H., and Hale, B. L. (1985). Repetition effects in word and pseudoword identification: Comment on Salasoo, Shiffrin, and Feustel. *Journal of Experimental Psychology: General, 114,* 498–508.

Johnston, W. A., and Dark, V. J. (1982). In defense of intraperceptual theories of attention. *Journal of Experimental Psychology: Human Perception and Performance, 8,* 407–421.

Johnston, W. A., and Dark, V. J. (1985). Dissociable domains of semantic processing. In M. I. Posner and O. S. M. Marin (Eds.), *Attention and Performance X.* Hillsdale, NJ: Erlbaum, pp. 567–584.

Johnston, W. A., and Heinz, S. P. (1979). Depth of nontarget processing in an attention task. *Journal of Experimental Psychology: Human Perception and Performance, 5,* 168–175.

Johnston, W. A., and Schwarting, I. S. (1996). Reassessing the evidence for novel popout. *Journal of Experimental Psychology: General, 125,* 208–212.

Johnston, W. A., and Wilson, J. (1980). Perceptual processing of nontargets in an attention task. *Memory and Cognition, 8,* 372–377.

Johnston, W. A., Hawley, K. J., and Farnham, J. M. (1993). Novel popout: Empirical boundaries and tentative theory. *Journal of Experimental Psychology: Human Perception and Performance, 19,* 140–153.

Jolicoeur, P., and Landau, M. J. (1984). Effects of orientation on the identification of simple visual patterns. *Canadian Journal of Psychology, 38,* 80–93.

Jonides, J., and Mack, R. (1984). On the cost and benefit of cost and benefit. *Psychological Bulletin, 96,* 29–44.

Julesz, B. (1971). *Foundations of Cyclopean Perception.* Chicago: University of Chicago Press.

Jung, J. (1968). *Verbal Learning.* New York: Holt, Rhinehart and Winston.

Juola, J. F., Fischler, I., Wood, C. T., and Atkinson, R. C. (1971). Recognition time for information stored in long-term memory. *Perception and Psychophysics, 10,* 8–14.

Kahneman, D. (1973). *Attention and Effort.* New York: Prentice-Hall.

Kahneman, D., and Chajczyk, D. (1983). Tests of the automaticity of reading: Dilution of Stroop effects by color-irrelevant stimuli. *Journal of Experimental Psychology: Human Perception and Performance, 9,* 497–509.

Kahneman, D., and Henik, A. (1981). Perceptual organization and attention. In M. Kubovy, and J. R. Pomerantz (Eds.), *Perceptual Organization.* Hillsdale, NJ: Erlbaum.

Kahneman, D., and Treisman, A. (1984). Changing views of attention and automaticity. In R. Parasuraman and D. R. Davies (Eds.), *Varieties of Attention.* New York: Academic Press, pp. 29–62.

Kahneman, D., Beatty, J., and Pollack, I. (1967). Perceptual deficit during a mental task. *Science, 157,* 218–219.

Kallman, H. J., Hirtle, S. C., and Davidson, D. (1986). Recognition masking of auditory duration. *Perception and Psychophysics, 40,* 45–52.

Kalsbeek, J. W. H., and Sykes, R. N. (1967). Objective measurement of mental load. *Acta Psychologica, 27,* 253–261.

Karlin, L. (1959). Reaction time as a function of foreperiod duration and variability. *Journal of Experimental Psychology, 58,* 185–191.

Karlin, L., and Kestenbaum, R. (1968). Effects of number of alternatives on the psychological refractory period. *Quarterly Journal of Experimental Psychology, 20,* 167–178.

Karlin, M. B., and Bower, G. H. (1976). Semantic category effects in visual word search. *Perception and Psychophysics, 19,* 417–424.

Kee, D. W., Hellige, J. B., and Bathurst, K. (1983). Lateralized interference of repetitive finger tapping: Influence of family handedness, cognitive load, and verbal production. *Neuropsychologia, 21,* 617–625.

Kee, D. W., Morris, K., Bathurst, K., and Hellige, J. B. (1986). Lateralized interference in finger tapping: Comparisons of rate and variability measures under speed and consistency tapping instructions. *Brain and Cognition, 5,* 268–279.

Keele, S. W. (1973). *Attention and Human Performance.* Pacific Palisades, CA: Goodyear.

Kelly, J. B., and Potash, M. (1986). Directional responses to sounds in young gerbils (*Meriones unguiculatus*). *Journal of Comparative Psychology, 100,* 37–45.

Kingstone, A. (1992). Combining expectancies. *Quarterly Journal of Experimental Psychology, 44,* 69–104.

Kinsbourne, M. (1981). Single channel theory. In D. Holding (Ed.), *Human Skills* Chichester, England: Wiley, pp. 65–89.

Kinsbourne, M. (1987). Mechanisms of unilateral neglect. In M. Jeannerod (Ed.), *Neurophysiological and Neuropsychological Aspects of Spatial Neglect. Advances in Psychology,* No. 45. Amsterdam: Elsevier Science, pp. 69–86.

Kinsbourne, M., and Cook, J. (1971). Generalized and lateralized effects of concurrent verbalization on a unimanual skill. *Quarterly Journal of Experimental Psychology, 23,* 341–345.

Kinsbourne, M., and Hicks, R. E. (1978). Functional cerebral space: A model for overflow, transfer, and interference effects in human performance. In J. Requin (Ed.), *Attention and Performance VII* Hillsdale, NJ: Erlbaum, pp. 345–362.

Klapp, S. T. (1976). Short-term memory as a response preparation state. *Memory and Cognition, 4,* 721–729.

Klapp, S. T. (1979). Doing two things at once: The role of temporal compatibility. *Memory and Cognition, 7,* 375–381.

Klapp, S. T., Hill, M. D., Tyler, J. G., Martin, Z. E., Jagacinski, R. J., and Jones, M. R. (1985). On marching to two different drummers: Perceptual aspects of the difficulties. *Journal of Experimental Psychology: Human Perception and Performance, 11,* 814–827.

Klapp, S. T., Marshburn, E. A., and Lester, P. T. (1983). Short-term memory does not involve the "working memory" of information processing: The demise of a common assumption. *Journal of Experimental Psychology: General, 112,* 240–264.

Klein, R. (1980). Does oculomotor readiness mediate cognitive control of visual attention? In R. S. Nickerson (Ed.), *Attention and Performance VIII.* Hillsdale, NJ: Erlbaum, pp. 259–276.

Klein, R., and Farrell, M. (1989). Search performance without eye movements. *Perception and Psychophysics, 46,* 476–482.

Kleiss, J. A., and Lane, D. M. (1986). Locus and persistence of capacity limitations in visual information processing. *Journal of Experimental Psychology: Human Perception and Performance, 12,* 200–210.

Klemmer, E. T. (1957). Simple reaction time as a function of time uncertainty. *Journal of Experimental Psychology, 54,* 195–200.

Koch, R. (1994). Paper presented at the Royal Dutch Academy of Sciences Symposium on Discrete versus Continuous Processing of Information, Amsterdam, The Netherlands, 28 Nov.–2 Dec., 1994.

Kolers, P. (1972). *Aspects of Motion Perception.* New York: Pergamon Press.

Koriat, A., and Norman, J. (1984). What is rotated in mental rotation? *Journal of Experimental Psychology: Learning, Memory, and Cognition, 10,* 421–434.

Kornblum, S. (1973). Sequential effects in choice reaction time: A tutorial review. In S. Kornblum (Ed.) *Attention and Performance IV.* New York: Academic Press, pp. 259–288.

Koster, W. G., and van Schuur, R. (1973). The influence of the intensity of tone bursts on the psychological refractory period. In S. Kornblum (Ed.), *Attention and Performance IV.* New York: Academic Press, pp. 55–69.

Koutstaal, W. (1992). Skirting the abyss: A history of experimental explorations of automatic writing in psychology. *Journal of the History of the Behavioral Sciences, 28,* 5–27.

Kowler, E. (1989). Cognitive expectations, not habits, control anticipatory smooth oculomotor pursuit. *Vision Research, 29,* 1049–1057.

Kowler, E., and Steinman, R. M. (1979). The effect of expectations on slow oculomotor control-I. Periodic target steps. *Vision Research, 19,* 633–646.

Kowler, E., and Zingale, C. (1985). Smooth eye movements as indicators of selective attention. In Posner, M. I., and Marin, O. S. M. (Eds.), *Attention and Performance XI: Mechanisms of Attention.* Hillsdale, NJ: Erlbaum, pp. 285–300.

Kowler, E., Anderson, E., Dosher, B., and Blaser, E. (1995). The role of attention in the programming of saccades. *Vision Research, 35,* 1897–1916.

Kowler, E., van der Steen, J., Tamminga, E. P., and Collewijn, H. (1984). Voluntary selection of the target for smooth eye movement in the presence of superimposed, full-field stationary and moving stimuli. *Vision Research, 24,* 1789–1798.

Kramer, A. F., and Hahn, S. (1995). Splitting the beam: Distribution of attention over noncontiguous regions of the visual field. *Psychological Science, 6,* 381–386.

Kramer, A. F., and Jacobson, A. (1991). Perceptual organization and focused attention: The role of objects and proximity in visual processing. *Perception and Psychophysics, 50,* 267–284.

Kramer, A., and Spinks, J. (1991). Capacity views of human information processing. In J. R. Jennings and M. G. H. Coles (Eds.), *Handbook of Cognitive Psychophysiology: Central and Autonomic Nervous System Approaches.* New York: Wiley, pp. 179–249.

Kramer, A. F., Tham, M., and Yeh, Y. (1991). Movement and focused attention: A failure to replicate. *Perception and Psychophysics, 50,* 537–546.

Kraut, R. E., and Lewis, S. H. (1982). Person perception and self-awareness: Knowledge of influences on one's own judgments. *Journal of Personality and Social Psychology, 42,* 448–460.

Krueger, L. E. (1984). The category effect in visual search depends on physical rather than conceptual differences. *Perception and Psychophysics, 35,* 558–564.

Külpe, O. (1902). Attention. *Monist, 13.*

Külpe, O. (1904). Versuche uber Abstraktion. *Berlin Internationaler Kongress für Experimentalpsychologie, 58–68.*

LaBerge, D. (1983). Spatial extent of attention to letters and words. *Journal of Experimental Psychology: Human Perception and Performance, 9,* 371–379.

LaBerge, D., and Brown, V. (1989). Theory of attentional operations in shape identification. *Psychological Review, 96,* 101–124.

LaBerge D., and Samuels, S. J. (1974). Toward a theory of automatic information processing in reading. *Cognitive Psychology, 6,* 292–323.

Lakatos, I. (1978). *The Methodology of Scientific Research Programmes.* Cambridge: Cambridge University Press.

Lambert, A. J., Beard, C. T., and Thompson, R. J. (1988). Selective attention, visual laterality, awareness, and perceiving the meaning of parafoveally presented words. *Quarterly Journal of Experimental Psychology: Human Experimental Psychology, 40,* 615–652.

Laming, D. R. J. (1973). *Mathematical Psychology.* New York: Academic Press.

Lang, P. J., Greenwald, M. K., Bradley, M. M., and Hamm, A. O. (1993). Looking at pictures: Affective, facial, visceral, and behavioral reactions. *Psychophysiology, 30,* 61–273.

Lankheet, M. J. M., and Verstraten, F. A. J. (1995). Attentional modulation of adaptation to two-component transparent motion. *Vision Research, 35,* 1401–1412.

Lasley, D. J., and Cohn, T. (1981). Detection of a luminance increment: Effect of temporal uncertainty. *Journal of the Optical Society of America, 71,* 845–850.

Lawrence, D. H. (1971). Two studies of visual search for word targets with controlled rates of presentation. *Perception and Psychophysics, 10,* 85–89.

Lawrence, D. H., and Coles, G. R. (1954). Accuracy of recognition with alternatives before and after the stimulus. *Journal of Experimental Psychology, 47,* 208–214.

Lawrence, D. H, and LaBerge, D. L. (1956). Relationship between recognition accuracy and order of reporting stimulus dimensions. *Journal of Experimental Psychology, 51,* 12–18.

Leatherman, C. D. (1940). The limits of toleration for simultaneity in the complication experiment. *American Journal of Psychology, 53,* 21–45.

Levin, H. (1979). *The Eye-Voice Span.* Cambridge, MA: MIT Press.

Levitt S., and Gutin, B. (1971). Multiple choice reaction time and movement time during physical exertion. *The Research Quarterly, 42,* 405–410.

Levy, J., and Pashler, H. (1995). Does perceptual analysis continue during selection and production of a speeded response? *Acta Psychologica, 90,* 245–260.

Lewis, J. L. (1970). Semantic processing of unattended messages using dichotic listening. *Journal of Experimental Psychology, 85,* 225–228.

Lhermitte, F. (1983). "Utilization behavior" and its relation to lesions of the frontal lobes. *Brain, 106,* 237–255.

Libet, B., Wright, E. W. Feinstein, B., and Pearl, D. K. (1979). Subjective referral of the timing for a conscious sensory experience. *Brain, 102* 193–224.

Lindsay, P. H., Taylor, M. M., and Forbes, S. M. (1968). Attention and multidimensional discrimination. *Perception and Psychophysics, 4,* 113–117.

Liss, P. (1968). Does backward masking by visual noise stop stimulus processing? *Perception and Psychophysics, 4,* 328–330.

Loeb. Muskelthätigkeit als Maass psychischer Thätigkeit. *Archiv für die Gesellschaft Physiologie, xxxix,* 592 (cited by Welch, 1898).

Loftus, E. F. (1974). On reading fine print. *Quarterly Journal of Experimental Psychology, 26,* 324.

Loftus, G. R. (1978). On the interpretation of interactions. *Memory and Cognition, 6,* 312–319.

Loftus, G. R., and Mackworth, N. H. (1978). Cognitive determinants of fixation location during picture viewing. *Journal of Experimental Psychology: Human Perception and Performance, 4,* 565–572.

Logan, G. D. (1978a). Attention demands of visual search. *Memory and Cognition, 6,* 446–453.

Logan, G. D. (1978b). Attention in character classification tasks: Evidence for the automaticity of component stages. *Journal of Experimental Psychology: General, 107,* 32–63.

Logan, G. D. (1979). On the use of a concurrent memory load to measure attention and automaticity. *Journal of Experimental Psychology: Human Perception and Performance, 5,* 189–207.

Logan, G. D. (1980). Short-term memory demands of reaction-time tasks that differ in complexity. *Journal of Experimental Psychology: Human Perception and Performance, 6,* 375–389.

Logan, G. D. (1982). On the ability to inhibit complex movements: A stop-signal study of typewriting. *Journal of Experimental Psychology: Human Perception and Performance, 8,* 778–792.

Logan, G. D. (1988). Toward an instance theory of automatization. *Psychological Review, 95,* 492–527.

Logan, G. D. (1992). Shapes of reaction-time distributions and shapes of learning curves: A test of the instance theory of automaticity. *Journal of Experimental Psychology: Learning, Memory, and Cognition, 18,* 883–914.

Logan, G. D. (1994). Spatial attention and the apprehension of spatial relations. *Journal of Experimental Psychology: Human Perception and Performance, 20,* 1015–1036.

Logan, G. D., and Stadler, M. A. (1991). Mechanisms of performance improvement in consistent mapping memory search: Automaticity or strategy shift? *Journal of Experimental Psychology: Learning, Memory, and Cognition, 17,* 478–496.

Logan, G. D., and Zbrodoff, N. J. (1982). Constraints on strategy construction in a speeded discrimination task. *Journal of Experimental Psychology: Human Perception and Performance, 8,* 502–520.

Long, E. R., Henneman, R. H., and Garvey, W. D. (1960). An experimental analysis of set: The role of sense-modality. *American Journal of Psychology, 73,* 563–567.

Long, E. R., Reid, L. S., and Henneman, R. H. (1960). An experimental analysis of set: Variables influencing the identification of ambiguous, visual stimulus-objects. *American Journal of Psychology, 73,* 553–562.

Long, J. (1976). Division of attention between non-verbal signals: All-or-none or shared processing? *Quarterly Journal of Experimental Psychology, 28,* 47–69.

Lorch, E. P., Anderson, D. R., and Well, A. D. (1984). Effects of irrelevant information on speeded classification tasks: Interference is reduced by habituation. *Journal of Experimental Psychology: Human Perception and Performance, 10,* 850–864.

Lovie, A. D. (1983). Attention and behaviourism—fact and fiction. *British Journal of Psychology, 74,* 301–310.

Lowe, D. G. (1979). Strategies, context, and the mechanism of response inhibition. *Memory and Cognition, 7,* 382–389.

Lowe, G. (1967). Interval of time uncertainty in visual detection. *Perception and Psychophysics, 2,* 278–280.

Lowe, G. (1968). Auditory detection and recognition in a two-alternative, directional uncertainty situation. *Perception and Psychophysics, 4,* 180–182.

Luck, S. J., Hillyard, S. A., Mangun, G. R., and Gazzaniga, M. S. (1994). Independent attentional scanning in the separated hemispheres of split-brain patients. *Journal of Cognitive Neuroscience, 6,* 84–91

Luck, S. J., Hillyard, S. A., Mouloua, M., and Hawkins, H. L. (1996). Mechanisms of visual-spatial attention— Resource allocation or uncertainty reduction? *Journal of Experimental Psychology: Human Perception and Performance, 22,* 725–737.

Lyon, D., and Slovic, P. (1976). Dominance of accuracy information and neglect of base rates in probability estimation. *Acta Psychologica, 40,* 286–298.

MacKay, D. M. (1973). Visual stability and voluntary eye movements. In R. Jung (Ed.), *Handbook of Sensory Physiology:* Vol. 8/3. Berlin: Springer-Verlag, pp. 307–331.

Mackintosh, N. J. (Ed.) (1994). *Animal Learning and Cognition.* San Diego: Academic Press.

Mackworth, J. F. (1963). The duration of the visual image. *Canadian Journal of Psychology, 17,* 62–81.

MacLeod, C. M. (1991). Half a century of research on the Stroop effect: An integrative review. *Psychological Bulletin, 109,* 163–203.

MacLeod, C. M., and Dunbar, K. (1988). Training and Stroop-like interference: Evidence for a continuum of automaticity. *Journal of Experimental Psychology: Learning, Memory, and Cognition, 14,* 126–135.

MacLeod, C., Mathews, A., and Tata, P. (1986). Attentional bias in emotional disorders. *Journal of Abnormal Psychology, 95,* 15–20.

MacMillan, N. A., and Schwartz, M. (1975). A probe-signal investigation of uncertain-frequency detection. *Journal of the Optical Society of America, 58,* 1051–1058.

Mandler, G., and Worden, P. E. (1973). Semantic processing without permanent storage. *Journal of Experimental Psychology, 100,* 277–283.

Mangun, G. R., Hillyard, S. A., and Luck, S. J. (1993). Electrocortical substrates of visual selective attention. In D. E. Meyer and S. Kornblum (Eds.), *Attention and Performance 14: Synergies in Experimental Psychology, Artificial Intelligence, and Cognitive Neuroscience.* Cambridge, MA: MIT Press, pp. 219–243.

Margrain, S. A. (1967). Short-term memory as a function of input modality. *Quarterly Journal of Experimental Psychology, 19,* 109–114.

Marr, D. (1982). *Vision.* San Francisco: Freeman.

Martin, M., Williams, R. M., and Clark, D. M. (1991). Does anxiety lead to selective processing of threat-related information? *Behaviour Research and Therapy, 29,* 147–160.

Massaro, D. W. (1972). Preperceptual images, processing time, and perceptual units in auditory perception. *Psychological Review, 79,* 124–145.

Massaro, D. W. (1976). Perceptual processing in dichotic listening. *Journal of Experimental Psychology: Human Learning and Memory, 2,* 331–339.

Massaro, D. W., and Warner, D. S. (1977). Dividing attention between auditory and visual perception. *Perception and Psychophysics, 21,* 569–574.

Mathews, A., and MacLeod, C. (1985). Selective processing of threat cues in panic disorder. *Behaviour Research and Therapy, 23,* 563–569.

Maunsell, J. H. R. and Gibson, J. R. (1992). Visual response latencies in striate cortex of the macaque monkey. *Journal of Neurophysiology, 68,* 1332–1344.

McCann, R. S., and Johnston, J. C. (1992). Locus of the single-channel bottleneck in dual-task interference. *Journal of Experimental Psychology: Human Perception and Performance, 18,* 471–484.

McCann, R. S., Folk, C. L., and Johnston, J. C. (1992). The role of spatial attention in visual word processing. *Journal of Experimental Psychology: Human Perception and Performance, 18,* 1015–1029.'

McCarthy, R. A., and Warrington, E. K. (1990). *Cognitive Neuropsychology: A Clinical Introduction.* San Diego: Academic Press.

McClelland, A. G. R., Rawles, R. E., and Sinclair, F. E. (1981). The effects of search criteria and retrieval cue availability on memory for words. *Memory and Cognition, 9,* 164–168.

McElree, B., and Dosher, B. A. (1989). Serial position and set size in short-term memory: The time course of recognition. *Journal of Experimental Psychology: General, 118,* 346–373.

McFarland, D. J., and Cacace, A. T. (1992). Aspects of short-term acoustic recognition memory: Modality and serial position effects. *Audiology, 31,* 342–352.

McLeod, P. (1977). Parallel processing and the psychological refractory period. *Acta Psychologica, 41,* 381–391.

McLeod, P. (1980). What can probe RT tell us about the attentional demands of movement? In G. E. Stelmach and J. Requin (Eds.), *Tutorials in Motor Behavior.* Amsterdam: North-Holland Press.

McLeod, P., and Mierop, J. (1979). How to reduce manual response interference in the multiple task environment. *Ergonomics, 22,* 469–475.

McLeod, P., and Posner, M. I. (1984). Privileged loops from percept to act. In H. Bouma and D. G. Bouwhuis (Eds.), *Attention and Performance X.* London: Erlbaum, pp. 55–66.

McNally, R. J. (1995). Automaticity and the anxiety disorders. *Behaviour Research and Therapy, 33,* 747–754.

McNamara, T. P. (1992). Priming and constraints it places on theories of memory and retrieval. *Psychological Review, 99,* 650–662.

Merikle, P. M. (1980). Selection from visual persistence by perceptual groups and category membership. *Journal of Experimental Psychology: General, 109,* 279–295.

Mewaldt, S. P., Hinrichs, J. V., and Ghoneim, M. M. (1983). Diazepam and memory: Support for a duplex model of memory. *Memory and Cognition, 11,* 557–564.

Mewhort, D. J. K., Johns, E. E., and Coble, S. (1991). Early and late selection in partial report—Evidence from degraded displays. *Perception and Psychophysics, 50,* 258–266.

Meyer, D. E., Osman, A. M., Irwin, D. E., and Yantis, S. (1988). Modern mental chronometry. *Biological Psychology, 26,* 3–67.

Meyer, D. E., Schvaneveldt, R. W., and Ruddy, M. G. (1974). Functions of graphemic and phonemic codes in visual word-recognition. *Memory and Cognition, 2,* 309–321.

Meyer, V., Gross, C. G., and Teuber, H-L. (1963). Effect of knowledge of site of stimulation on the threshold for pressure sensitivity. *Perceptual and Motor Skills, 16,* 637–640.

Miller, J. O. (1979). Cognitive influences on perceptual processing. *Journal of Experimental Psychology: Human Perception and Performance, 5,* 546–562.

Miller, J. O. (1982). Divided attention: Evidence for coactivation with redundant signals. *Cognitive Psychology, 14,* 247–279.

Miller, J. O. (1987). Priming is not necessary for selective-attention failures: Semantic effects of unattended, unprimed letters. *Perception and Psychophysics, 41,* 419–434.

Miller, J. O. (1991). The flanker compatibility effect as a function of visual angle, attention focus, visual transients, and perceptual load: A search for boundary conditions. *Perception and Psychophysics, 49,* 270–288.

Miller, J. O., and Anbar, R. (1981). Expectancy and frequency effects on perceptual and motor systems in choice reaction time. *Memory and Cognition, 9,* 631–641.

Miller, J. O., and Bonnel, A-M. (1994). Switching or sharing in dual-task line-length discrimination? *Perception and Psychophysics, 56,* 431–446.

Miller, J. O., and Lopes, A. (1988). Testing race models by estimating the smaller of two true mean or true median reaction times: An analysis of estimation bias. *Perception and Psychophysics, 44,* 513–524.

Milner, B. (1958). The memory defect in bilateral hippocampal lesions. *Psychiatry Research Reports, 11,* 43–58.

Milner, B. (1964). Some effects of frontal lobectomy in man. In J. M. Warren and K. Akert (Eds.), *The Frontal Granular Cortex and Behavior.* New York: McGraw-Hill.

Minsky, M. (1968). *Semantic Information Processing.* Cambridge, MA: MIT Press.

Miron, D., Duncan, G., and Bushnell, M. C. (1989). Effects of attention on the intensity and unpleasantness of thermal pain. *Pain, 39,* 345–352.

Mishkin, M., Ungerleider, L. G., and Macko, K. A. (1983). Object vision and spatial vision: Two cortical pathways. *Trends in Neurosciences, 6,* 414–417.

Monheit, M. A., and Johnston, J. C. (1994). Spatial attention to arrays of multidimensional objects. *Journal of Experimental Psychology: Human Perception and Performance, 20,* 691–708.

Monsell, S. (1978). Components of working memory underlying verbal skills: A "distributed capacities" view. In H. Bouma and D. G. Bouwhuis (Eds.), *Attention and Performance X.* London: Lawrence Erlbaum.

Monsell, S. (1987). Recency, immediate recognition memory, and reaction time. *Cognitive Psychology, 10,* 465–501.

Moore, C. M., and Osman, A. M. (1993). Looking for two targets at the same time: One search or two? *Perception and Psychophysics, 53,* 381–390.

Moore, J. J., and Massaro, D. W. (1973). Attention and processing capacity in auditory recognition. *Journal of Experimental Psychology, 99,* 49–54.

Moraglia, G., Maloney, K. P., Fekete, E. M., and Al-Basi, K. (1989). Visual search along the colour dimension. *Canadian Journal of Psychology, 43,* 1–12.

Moran, J., and Desimone, R. (1985). Selective attention gates visual processing in the extrastriate cortex. *Science, 229,* 782–784.

Moray, N. (1959). Attention in dichotic listening: Affective cues and the influence of instructions. *Quarterly Journal of Experimental Psychology, 11,* 56–60.

Moray, N. (1970). Introductory experiments in auditory time sharing: Detection of intensity and frequency increments. *Journal of the Acoustical Society of America, 47,* 1071–1073.

Moray, N. (1975). A data base for theories of selective listening. *Attention and Performance V* Hillsdale, NJ: Erlbaum, pp. 119–135.

Morton, J. (1969). Interaction of information in word recognition. *Psychological Review, 76,* 165–178.

Mozer, M. C. (1991). *The Perception of Multiple Objects: A Connectionist Approach.* Cambridge, MA: MIT Press.

Muller, H. J. (1994). Qualitative differences in response bias from spatial cueing. Special Issue: Shifts of visual attention. *Canadian Journal of Experimental Psychology, 48,* 218–241.

Muller, H. J., and Humphreys, G. W. (1991). Luminance-increment detection: Capacity-limited or not? *Journal of Experimental Psychology: Human Perception and Performance, 17,* 107–124.

Mulligan, R., and Shaw, M. L. (1981). Attending to simple auditory and visual signals. *Perception and Psychophysics, 30,* 447–454.

Munsell, O. S. (1873). *Psychology: The Science of the Mind.* New York: D. Appleton.

Munsterberg, H. (1894). The intensifying effect of attention. *Psychological Review, 1,* 39–44.

Murdock, B. B. (1965). Effects of a subsidiary task on short-term memory. *British Journal of Psychology, 56,* 413–419.

Murray, D. J., and Hitchcock, C. H. (1969). Attention and storage in dichotic listening. *Journal of Experimental Psychology, 81,* 164–169.

Murray, D. J., Ward, R., and Hockley, W. E. (1975). Tactile short-term memory in relation to the two-point threshold. *Quarterly Journal of Experimental Psychology, 27,* 303–312.

Musen, G. (1991). Effects of verbal labeling and exposure duration on implicit memory for visual patterns. *Journal of Experimental Psychology: Learning, Memory, and Cognition, 17,* 954–962.

Muter, P. (1980). Very rapid forgetting. *Memory and Cognition, 8,* 174–179.

Naatanen, R. (1992). *Attention and Brain Function.* Hillsdale, NJ: Erlbaum.

Nachmias, J., and Weber, A. (1975). Discrimination of simple and complex gratings. *Vision Research, 15,* 217–223.

Nakayama, K. (1990). The iconic bottleneck and the tenuous link between early visual processing and perception. In C. Blakemore (Ed.), *Vision: Coding and Efficiency*. Cambridge: Cambridge University Press, pp. 411–422.

Naveh-Benjamin, M., and Jonides, J. (1984). Maintenance rehearsal: A two-component analysis. *Journal of Experimental Psychology: Learning, Memory, and Cognition, 10,* 369–385.

Navon, D., and Gopher, D. (1979). On the economy of the human-processing system. *Psychological Review, 86,* 214–255.

Navon, D., and Miller, J. (1987). Role of outcome conflict in dual-task interference. *Journal of Experimental Psychology: Human Perception and Performance, 13,* 435–448.

Nazir, T. (1992). Effects of lateral masking and spatial precueing on gap-resolution in central and peripheral vision. *Vision Research, 32,* 771–777.

Neely, J. M. (1977). Semantic priming and retrieval from lexical memory: Role of inhibitionless spreading activation and limited capacity attention. *Journal of Experimental Psychology: General, 7,* 480–494.

Neisser, U. (1976). *Cognition and Reality.* San Francisco: Freeman.

Neisser, U., and Becklen, R. (1975). Selective looking: Attending to visually specified events. *Cognitive Psychology, 7,* 480–494.

Nelson, H. E. (1976). A modified card sorting test sensitive to frontal lobe defects. *Cortex, 12,* 313–324.

Netick, A., and Klapp, S. T. (1994). Hesitations in manual tracking: A single-channel limit in response programming. *Journal of Experimental Psychology: Human Perception and Performance, 20,* 766–782.

Neumann, E., and Deschepper, B. G. (1992). An inhibition-based fan effect: Evidence for an active suppression mechanism in selective attention. *Canadian Journal of Psychology, 46,* 1–40.

Neumann, O. (1987). Beyond capacity: A functional view of attention. In H. Heuer and A. Sanders (Eds.), *Perspectives on Perception and Action.* Hillsdale, NJ: Erlbaum, pp. 361–394.

Neumann, O., Esselmann, U., and Klotz, W. (1993). Differential effects of visual-spatial attention on response latency and temporal-order judgment. *Psychological Research, 56,* 26–34.

Newell, A. (1973). You can't play twenty questions with nature and win: Projective comments on the papers of this symposium. In W. G. Chase (Ed.), *Visual Information Processing.* New York: Academic Press, pp. 283–308.

Newhall, S. M. (1921). The modification of the intensity of sensation by attention. *Journal of Experimental Psychology, 4,* 222–243.

Newstead, S. E., and Dennis, I. (1979). Lexical and grammatical processing of unshadowed messages: A re-examination of the Mackay effect. *Quarterly Journal of Experimental Psychology, 31,* 477–488.

Ninio, A., and Kahneman, D. (1974). Reaction time in focused and in divided attention. *Journal of Experimental Psychology, 103,* 394–399.

Nisbett, R. E., and Wilson, T. D. Telling more than we know: Verbal reports on mental processes. *Psychological Review, 84,* 231–279.

Nissen, M. J. (1985). Accessing features and objects: Is location special? In M. Posner and O. S. M. Marin (Eds.), *Attention and Performance XI.* Hillsdale, NJ: Erlbaum, pp. 205–220.

Nolte, L. W., and Jaarsma, D. (1967). More on the detection of one of m orthogonal signals. *Journal of the Acoustical Society of America, 41,* 497–505.

Norman, D. A. (1968). Toward a theory of memory and attention. *Psychological Review, 75,* 522–536.

Norman, D. A. (1969). Memory while shadowing. *Quarterly Journal of Experimental Psychology, 21,* 85–93.

Norman, D. A., and Bobrow, D. G. (1975). On data-limited and resource-limited processes. *Cognitive Psychology, 7,* 44–64.

Norman, D. A., and Shallice, T. (1986). Attention to action: Willed and automatic control of behavior. In R. J. Davidson, G. E. Schwartz and D. Shapiro (Eds.), *Consciousness and Self-Regulation,* Vol 4. New York: Plenum.

Nothdurft, H-C. (1993). Faces and facial expressions do not pop out. *Perception, 22,* 1287–1298.

Osman, A., and Moore, C. (1993). The locus of dual-task interference: Psychological refractory effects on movement-related brain potentials. *Journal of Experimental Psychology: Human Perception and Performance, 19,* 1292–1312.

Ostergaard, A. L. (1992). A method for judging measures of stochastic dependence: Further comments on the current controversy. *Journal of Experimental Psychology: Learning, Memory and Cognition, 18,* 413–420.

Ostry, D., Moray, N., and Marks, G. (1976). Attention, practice, and semantic targets *Journal of Experimental Psychology: Human Perception and Performance, 2,* 326–336.

Oswald, I., Taylor, A. M. and Treisman, M. (1960). Discriminative responses to stimulation during human sleep. *Brain, 83,* 440–453.

Pachella, R. G. (1974). The interpretation of reaction time in information-processing research. In B. Kantowitz (Ed.), *Human Information Processing: Tutorials in Performance and Cognition.* Hillsdale, NJ: Erlbaum.

Pachella, R. G. (1975). The effect of set on the tachistoscopic recognition of pictures. In P. M. A. Rabbitt and S. Dornic (Eds.), *Attention and Performance V.* Hillsdale: Erlbaum, pp. 136–156.

Palmer, J. (1988). Very short-term visual memory for size and shape. *Perception and Psychophysics, 43,* 278–286.

Palmer, J. (1991). Isolating the components of very short-term visual memory. *Bulletin of the Psychonomic Society, 29,* 399–402.

Palmer, J. (1994). Set-size effects in visual search: The effect of attention is independent of the stimulus for simple tasks. *Vision Research, 34,* 1703–1721.

Palmer, J., Ames, C. T. and Lindsey, D. T. (1993). Measuring the effect of attention on simple visual search. *Journal of Experimental Psychology: Human Perception and Performance, 19,* 108–130.

Palmer, S., and Rock, I. (1994). Rethinking perceptual organization—the role of uniform connectedness. *Psychonomic Bulletin and Review, 1,* 29–55.

Parasuraman, R. (1984). Sustained attention. In R. Parasuraman and D. R. Davies (Eds.), *Varieties of Attention.* New York: Academic Press; pp. 243–271.

Park, D. C., Smith, A. D., Dudley, W. N., and Lafronza, V. N. (1989). Effects of age and a divided attention task presented during encoding and retrieval on memory. *Journal of Experimental Psychology: Learning, Memory, and Cognition, 15,* 1185–1191.

Parkin, A. J. (1993). *Memory: Phenomena, Experiment and Theory.* Oxford: Blackwell.

Paschal, F. C. (1941). The trend in theories of attention. *Psychological Review, 48,* 383–403.

Pashler, H. (1984a). Evidence against late selection: Stimulus quality effects in previewed displays. *Journal of Experimental Psychology: Human Perception and Performance, 10,* 429–448.

Pashler, H. (1984b). Processing stages in overlapping tasks: Evidence for a central bottleneck. *Journal of Experimental Psychology: Human Perception and Performance, 10,* 358–377.

Pashler, H. (1987). Detecting conjunctions of color and form: Reassessing the serial search hypothesis. *Perception and Psychophysics, 41,* 191–201.

Pashler, H. (1988). Familiarity and visual change detection. *Perception and Psychophysics, 44,* 369–378.

Pashler, H. (1989). Dissociations and dependencies between speed and accuracy: Evidence for a two-component theory of divided attention in simple tasks. *Cognitive Psychology, 21,* 469–514.

Pashler, H. (1990). Coordinate frame for symmetry detection and object recognition. *Journal of Experimental Psychology: Human Perception and Performance, 16,* 150–163.

Pashler, H. (1991). Shifting visual attention and selecting motor responses: Distinct attentional mechanisms. *Journal of Experimental Psychology: Human Perception and Performance, 17,* 1023–1040.

Pashler, H. (1993). Dual task interference and elementary mental mechanisms. In D. Meyer and S. Kornblum (Eds.), *Attention and Performance XIV* Cambridge, MA: MIT Press, pp. 245–264.

Pashler, H. (1994a). Divided attention: Storing and classifying briefly presented objects. *Psychonomic Bulletin and Review, 1,* 115–118.

Pashler, H. (1994b). Overlapping mental operations in serial performance with preview. *Quarterly Journal of Experimental Psychology, 47,* 161–191.

Pashler, H. (1994c). Overlapping mental operations in serial performance with preview-typing-comment. *Quarterly Journal of Experimental Psychology, 47,* 201–205.

Pashler, H. (1994d). Graded capacity-sharing in dual-task interference? *Journal of Experimental Psychology: Human Perception and Performance, 20,* 330–342.

Pashler, H. (1994e). Dual-Task interference in simple tasks: Data and theory. *Psychological Bulletin, 16,* 220–244.

Pashler, H. (1996). Structures, processes and the flow of information. In E. Bjork and R. Bjork (Eds.), *Handbook of Learning and Memory.* San Diego: Academic Press, pp. 3–29.

Pashler, H., and Badgio, P. C. (1985). Visual attention and stimulus identification. *Journal of Experimental Psychology: Human Perception and Performance, 11,* 105–121.

Pashler, H., and Baylis, G. C. (1991). Procedural learning: II. Intertrial repetition effects in speeded-choice tasks. *Journal of Experimental Psychology: Learning, Memory, and Cognition, 17,* 33–48.

Pashler, H., and Carrier, M. (1996). Structures, processes and flow of control. In Bjork, E. L., and Bjork, R. A. (Eds.), *Memory: Handbook of Perception and Cognition,* 2nd edition. San Diego: Academic Press, pp. 3–29.

Pashler, H., and Christian, C. (1996). Bottlenecks in planning and producing manual, vocal and foot responses. Unpublished manuscript.

Pashler, H., and Johnston, J. C. (1989). Interference between temporally overlapping tasks: Chronometric evidence for central postponement with or without response grouping. *Quarterly Journal of Experimental Psychology, 41A,* 19–45.

Pashler, H., and Johnston, J. C. (submitted). Continuous task performance and dual-task interference: Chronometric studies. Manuscript submitted for publication.

Pashler, H., and O'Brien, S. (1993). Dual-task interference and the cerebral hemispheres. *Journal of Experimental Psychology: Human Perception and Performance, 19,* 315–330.

Pashler, H., Carrier, M., and Hoffman, J. (1993). Saccadic eye movements and dual-task interference. *Quarterly Journal of Experimental Psychology, 46A,* 51–82.

Pashler, H., Luck, S., O'Brien, S., Mangun, R., and Gazzaniga, M. (1995). Sequential operation of disconnected cerebral hemispheres in "split-brain" patients. *Neuroreport, 5,* 2381–2384.

Pelli, D. G. (1981). The effect of uncertainty: Detecting a signal at one of ten-thousand possible times and places. *Association for Research in Vision and Ophthalmology Abstracts, 20,* 178.

Perkins, J., and Cook, N. M. (1990). Recognition and recall of odours: The effects of suppressing visual and verbal encoding processes. *British Journal of Psychology, 81,* 221–226.

Peterson, L. R. (1969). Concurrent verbal activity. *Psychological Review, 76,* 376–386.

Pew, R. W. (1974). Human perceptual-motor performance. In B. Kantowitz (Ed.), *Human Information Processing: Tutorials in Performance and Cognition.* Hillsdale, NJ: Erlbaum.

Phillips, W. A. (1974). On the distinction between sensory storage and short-term visual memory. *Perception and Psychophysics, 16,* 283–290.

Phillips, W. A. (1983). Short-term visual memory. *Philosophical Transactions of the Royal Society, London B, U302,* 295–309.

Phillips, W. A., and Christie, F. M. (1977). Interference with visualization. *Quarterly Journal of Experimental Psychology, 29,* 637–650.

Pillsbury, W. B. (1908). *Attention.* London: S. Sonnenschein and New York: Macmillan.

Platt, J. R. (1964). Strong inference. *Science, 146,* 347–353.

Pohlmann, L. D., and Sorkin, R. D. (1976). Simultaneous three-channel signal detection: Performance and criterion as a function of order of report. *Perception and Psychophysics, 20,* 179–186.

Popper, K. (1959). *The Logic of Scientific Discovery.* London: Hutchinson.

Porter, N. (1868). *The Human Intellect, with an Introduction upon Psychology and the Soul.* New York: Scribner.

Posner, M. I. (1978). *Chronometric Explorations of Mind.* Hillsdale, NJ: Erlbaum.

Posner, M. I. (1982). Cumulative development of attentional theory. *American Psychologist, 37,* 168–179.

Posner, M. I., and Boies, S. J. (1971). Components of attention. *Psychological Review, 78,* 391–408.

Posner, M. I., and Snyder, C. R. R. (1975) Attention and cognitive control. In R. L. Solso (Ed.), *Information Processing and Cognition: The Loyola Symposium.* Hillsdale, NJ: Erlbaum.

Posner, M. I., Snyder, C. R. R., and Davidson, B. J. (1980). Attention and the detection of signals. *Journal of Experimental Psychology: General, 109,* 160–174.

Potter, M. C. (1976). Short-term conceptual memory for pictures. *Journal of Experimental Psychology: Human Learning and Memory, 2,* 509–522.

Potter, M. C. (1983). Representational buffers: The eye-mind hypothesis in picture perception, reading and visual search. In *Eye Movements in Reading: Perceptual And Language Processing*. New York: Academic Press, pp. 413–437.

Potter, M. C. (1993). Very short-term conceptual memory. *Memory and Cognition, 21,* 156–161.

Prinzmetal, W., Amiri, H., Allen, K., and Edwards, T. (submitted). The phenomenology of attention. Manuscript submitted for publication.

Puleo, J. S., and Pastore, R. E. Critical-band effects in two-channel auditory signal detection. *Journal of Experimental Psychology: Human Perception and Performance, 4,* 153–163.

Purcell, D. G., and Stewart, A. L. (1970). U-shaped backward masking functions with nonmetacontrast paradigms. *Psychonomic Science, 26,* 361–363.

Pylyshyn, Z., and Storm, R. W. (1988). Tracking multiple independent targets: Evidence for a parallel tracking mechanism. *Spatial Vision, 3,* 179–197.

Rabbitt, P. M. S., and Vyas, S. (1978). Processing a display even after you make a response to it: How perceptual errors can be corrected. *Quarterly Journal of Experimental Psychology: Human Experimental Psychology, 33,* 223–239.

Rabbitt, P. M. S. (1978). Sorting, categorization and visual search. In E. Carterette and M. P. Friedman (Eds.), *Handbook of Perception, Vol. IX.* New York: Academic Press, pp. 85–134.

Rabbitt, P. M. S. (1979). How old and young subjects monitor and control responses for accuracy and speed. *British Journal of Psychology, 70,* 305–311.

Rabbitt, P. M. S., Cumming, G., and Vyas, S. (1979) Improvement, learning and retention of skill at visual search. *Quarterly Journal of Experimental Psychology, 31,* 441–459.

Ramachandran, V. S., Pashler, H., and Plummer, D. (1990, May). Visual pop-out and a 3-D vs. 2-D image features. Paper presented to the Association for Research in Vision and Ophthalmology, Sarasota, FL.

Ratcliff, R., McKoon, G., and Verwoerd, M. (1989). A bias interpretation of facilitation in perceptual identification. *Journal of Experimental Psychology: Learning, Memory and Cognition, 15,* 378–387.

Raymond, J. E., Shapiro, K. L., and Arnell, K. M. (1992). Temporary suppression of visual processing in an RSVP task: An attentional blink? *Journal of Experimental Psychology: Human Perception and Performance, 18,* 849–860.

Reason, J. (1990). *Human Error.* New York: Cambridge University Press.

Reisberg, D., Rappaport, I., O'Shaughnessy, M. (1984). Limits of working memory: The digit digit-span. *Journal of Experimental Psychology: Learning, Memory, and Cognition, 10,* 203–221.

Reisberg, D., Scheiber, R., and Potemken, L. (1981). Eye position and the control of auditory attention. *Journal of Experimental Psychology: Human Perception and Performance, 7,* 318–323.

Remington, R. W. (1980). Attention and saccadic eye movements. *Journal of Experimental Psychology: Human Perception and Performance, 6,* 726–744.

Remington, R. W., Johnston, J. C., and Yantis, S. (1992). Involuntary attentional capture by abrupt onsets. *Perception and Psychophysics, 51,* 279–290.

Restle, F. (1974). Critique of pure memory. In R. L. Solso (Ed.), *Theories in Cognitive Psychology: The Loyola Symposium.* Potomac, MD: Erlbaum.

Rhodes, G. (1987). Auditory attention and the representation of spatial information. *Perception and Psychophysics, 42,* 1–14.

Richmond, B. J., Optican, L. M., Podell, M., and Spitzer, H. (1987). Temporal encoding of two-dimensional patterns by single units in primate inferior temporal cortex. I. Response characteristics. *Journal of Neurophysiology, 57,* 132–146.

Rickard, T. (in press). Bending the power law: A model of strategy shifts and the automatization of cognitive skills. *Journal of Experimental Psychology: General.*

Rizzolatti, G., and Camarda, R. (1987). Neural circuits for spatial attention and unilateral neglect. In M. Jeannerod (Ed.), *Neurophysiological and Neuropsychological Aspects of Spatial Neglect.* Paris: Elsevier, pp. 289–313.

Roberts, S., and Pashler, H. (1996). Data fitting is not theory testing. Univ. of California, Berkeley. Submitted for publication.

Rock, I. (1973). *Orientation and Form.* New York: Academic Press.

Rock, I. (1983). *The Logic of Perception.* Cambridge, MA: MIT Press.

Rock, I., and Guttman, D. (1981). The effect of inattention on form perception. *Journal of Experimental Psychology: Human Perception and Performance, 7,* 275–285.

Roediger, H. L. (1990). Implicit memory: Retention without remembering. *American Psychologist, 45,* 1043–1056.

Rogers, R. D., and Monsell, S. (1995). Costs of a predictable switch between simple cognitive tasks. *Journal of Experimental Psychology: General, 124,* 207–231.

Rohrbaugh, J. W. (1984). The orienting reflex. In R. Parasuraman and D. R. Davies (Eds.), *Varieties of Attention.* New York: Academic Press, pp. 323–373.

Rohrer, D., Wixted, J. T., Salmon, D. P., and Butters, N. (1995). Retrieval from semantic memory and its implications for Alzheimer's disease. *Journal of Experimental Psychology: Learning, Memory and Cognition, 21,* 1127–1139.

Rollins, H. A., and Hendricks, R. (1980). Processing of words presented simultaneously to eye and ear. *Journal of Experimental Psychology: Human Perception and Performance, 6,* 99–109.

Ruthruff, E., and Miller, J. (1995). Negative priming depends on each of selection. *Perception and Psychophysics, 57,* 715–723.

Ruthruff, E., and Pashler, H. (1996). Processing bottlenecks in dual-task performance: Structural limitation or strategic postponement? Submitted for publication.

Ruthruff, E., Miller, J., and Lackmann, T. (1995). Does mental rotation require central mechanisms? *Journal of Experimental Psychology: Human Perception and Performance, 21,* 552–570.

Saariluoma, P. (1992). Visuospatial and articulatory interference in chess players' information intake. *Applied Cognitive Psychology, 6,* 77–89.

Salame, P., and Baddeley, A. (1982). Disruption of short-term memory by unattended speech: Implications for the structure of working memory. *Journal of Verbal Learning and Verbal Behavior, 21,* 150–164.

Salame, P., and Baddeley, A. (1987). Noise, unattended speech and short-term memory. *Ergonomics, 30,* 1185–1193.

Salthouse, T. A. (1984). The skill of typing. *Scientific American, 250,* 128–135.

Salthouse, T. A., and Saults, J. S. (1987). Multiple spans in transcription typing. *Journal of Applied Psychology, 72,* 187–196.

Salzman, C. D., Murasugi, C. M., Britten, K. H., and Newxome, W. T. (1992). Microstimulation in visual area MT: Effects on direction discrimination performance. *Journal of Neuroscience, 12,* 2331–2355.

Sanders, A. F. (1983). Toward a model of stress and human performance. *Acta Psychologica, 53,* 61–97.

Sanders, A. F., and Schroots, J. J. (1969). Cognitive categories and memory span: III. Effects of similarity on recall. *Quarterly Journal of Experimental Psychology, 21,* 21–28.

Saraga, E., and Shallice, T. (1973). Parallel processing of the attributes of single stimuli. *Perception and Psychophysics, 13,* 261–270.

Sathian, K., and Burton, H. (1991). The role of spatially selective attention in the tactile perception of texture. *Perception and Psychophysics, 50,* 237–248.

Scarborough, D. L. (1972). Memory for brief visual displays of symbols. *Cognitive Psychology, 3,* 408–429.

Scharf, B., and Buus, S. (1986). Audition I: Stimulus, physiology, thresholds. In K. Boff, L., Kaufman, and J. Thomas (Eds.), *Handbook of Perception and Performance.* Vol. I, New York: Wiley, pp. 14-1–14-71.

Scharf, B., and Houtsma, A. J. M. (1986). Audition II: Loudness, pitch, localization, aural distortion pathology. In Boff, K., Kaufman, L., and Thomas, J. (Eds.), *Handbook of Perception and Performance,* Vol. I. New York: Wiley, 1986, pp. 15-1–15-60.

Scharf, B., Canevet, G., Possamai, C., and Bonnel. A. (1986). Some effects of attention in hearing. Presented to the 18th International Congress of Audiology, Prague.

Scharf, B., Quigley, S., Aoki, C., Peachey, N., and Reeves, A. (1987). Focused auditory attention and frequency selectivity. *Perception and Psychophysics, 42,* 215–223.

Schneider, W., and Shiffrin, R. M. (1977). Controlled and automatic human information processing: I. Detection, search and attention. *Psychological Review, 84,* 1–66.

Schouten, J. F., Kalsbeek, J. W. H., and Leopold, F. F. (1960). On the evaluation of perceptual and mental load. *Ergonomics, 5,* 251–260.

Schultz, D. W., and Eriksen, B. A. (1977). Do noise masks terminate target processing? *Memory and Cognition, 5,* 90–96.

Schumann, F. (1904). Die erkennung von Buchstaben und Worten bei momentaner Beleuchtigung. In *Bericht über den erse Kongress für experimentelle Psychologie.* Leipzig: Barth, pp. 34–40.

Schvaneveldt, R. W., and McDonald, J. E. (1981). Semantic context and the encoding of words: Evidence for two modes of stimulus analysis. *Journal of Experimental Psychology: Human Perception and Performance, 7,* 673–687.

Schweickert, R. (1978). A critical path generalization of the additive factor method: Analysis of a Stroop task. *Journal of Mathematical Psychology, 18,* 105–139.

Schweickert, R., and Townsend, J. T. (1989). A trichotomy: Interactions of factors prolonging sequential and concurrent mental processes in stochastic discrete mental (PERT) networks. *Journal of Mathematical Psychology, 33,* 328–347.

See, J. E., Howe, S. R., Warm, J. S., and Dember, W. N. (1995). Meta-analysis of the sensitivity decrement in vigilance. *Psychological Bulletin, 117,* 230–249.

Sejnowski, T. (1986). Open questions about cerebral cortex. In D. E. Rumelhart, J. L. McClelland, and the PDP Research Group (Eds.), *Parallel Distributed Processing: Explorations in the Microstructure of Cognition.* Cambridge, MA: MIT Press.

Sekuler, R., and Ball, K. (1977). Mental set alters visibility of moving targets. *Science, 198,* 60–62.

Shaffer, L. H. (1975). Multiple attention in continuous verbal tasks. In P. M. A. Rabbitt and S. Dornic (Eds.), *Attention and Performance V.* New York: Academic Press, pp. 157–167.

Shaffer, L. H., and Hardwick, J. (1969). Monitoring simultaneous auditory messages. *Perception and Psychophysics, 6,* 401–404.

Shaffer, L. H., and Hardwick, J. (1970). The basis of transcription skill. *Journal of Experimental Psychology, 84,* 424–440.

Shaffer, W. O., and LaBerge, D. (1979). Automatic semantic processing of unattended words. *Journal of Verbal Learning and Verbal Behavior, 18,* 413–426.

Shallice, T. (1988). *From Neuropsychology to Mental Structure.* New York: Cambridge University Press.

Shallice, T., and Burgess, P. W. (1991). Deficits in strategy application following frontal lobe damage in man. *Brain, 114,* 727–741.

Shallice, T., and Warrington, E. K. (1970). Independent functioning of verbal memory stores: A neuropsychological study. *Quarterly Journal of Experimental Psychology, 22,* 261–273.

Shallice, T., McLeod, P., and Lewis, K. (1985). Isolating cognitive modules with the dual-task paradigm: Are speech perception and production separate processes? *Quarterly Journal of Experimental Psychology: Human Experimental Psychology, 37A,* 507–532.

Shapiro, K. L., Raymond, J. E., and Arnell, K. M. (1994). Attention to visual pattern information produces the attentional blink in rapid serial visual presentation. *Journal of Experimental Psychology: Human Perception and Performance, 20,* 357–371.

Shaw, M. L. (1984). Division of attention among spatial locations: A fundamental difference between detection of letters and detection of luminance increments. In H. Bouma and D. G. Bouwhuis (Eds.), *Attention and Performance X.* Hillsdale, NJ: Erlbaum, pp. 109–121.

Shaw, M., and Shaw, P. (1977). Optimal allocation of cognitive resources to spatial locations. *Journal of Experimental Psychology: Human Perception and Performance, 3,* 201–211.

Shepherd, M., Findlay, J. M., and Hockey, R. J. (1986). The relationship between eye movements and spatial attention. *Quarterly Journal of Experimental Psychology, 38A,* 475–491.

Shiffrin, R. M. (1976). Capacity limitations in information processing, attention and memory. In W. K. Estes (Ed.), *Handbook of learning and cognitive processes: Attention and Memory,* Vol. 4. Hillsdale, NJ: Erlbaum, pp. 177–236.

Shiffrin, R. M. (1988). Attention. In R. C. Atkinson, R. J. Herrnstein, G. Lindzey, and R. D. Luce, (Eds.), *Stevens' Handbook of Experimental Psychology, Vol. 1: Perception and Motivation.* New York: Wiley, pp. 739–811.

Shiffrin, R. M., and Cook, J. R. (1978). Short-term forgetting of item and order information. *Journal of Verbal Learning and Verbal Behavior, 17,* 189–218.

Shiffrin, R. M., and Diller, D. E. (1996, Oct. 31–Nov. 3). Do we process anything from unattended visual locations? Presented at the 37th annual meeting of the Psychonomic Society, Chicago.

Shiffrin, R. M., and Gardner, G. T. (1972). Visual processing capacity and attentional control. *Journal of Experimental Psychology, 93,* 78–82.

Shiffrin, R. M., and Grantham, D. W. (1974). Can attention be allocated to sensory modalities? *Perception and Psychophysics, 15,* 460–474.

Shiffrin, R. M., and Schneider, W. (1977). Controlled and automatic human information processing: II. Perceptual learning, automatic attending and a general theory. *Psychological Review, 84,* 127–190.

Shiffrin, R. M., Pisoni, D. B., and Castaneda-Mendez, K. (1974). Is attention shared between the ears? *Cognitive Psychology, 6,* 190–215.

Shiu, L-P., and Pashler, H. (1993, Nov. 5–7) Spatial precuing in single-element displays: Noise reduction or signal enhancement? Presented at the 34th annual meeting of the Psychonomic Society, Washington, DC.

Shiu, L-P. and Pashler, H. (1994). Negligible effect of spatial precuing on identification of single digits. *Journal of Experimental Psychology: Human Perception and Performance, 20,* 1037–1054.

Shiu, L-P. and Pashler, H. (1995). Spatial attention and vernier acuity. *Vision Research, 35,* 337–343.

Shor, R. E. (1971). Symbol processing speed differences and symbol interference effects in a variety of concept domains. *Journal of General Psychology, 85,* 187–205.

Shulman, G. L. (1990). Relating attention to visual mechanisms. *Perception and Psychophysics, 47,* 199–203.

Shulman, G. L. (1991). Attentional modulation of mechanisms that analyze rotation in depth. *Journal of Experimental Psychology: Human Perception and Performance, 17,* 726–737.

Shulman, G. L. (1992a). Attentional modulation of a figural aftereffect. *Perception, 21,* 7–19.

Shulman, G. L. (1992b). Attentional modulation of size contrast. *Quarterly Journal of Experimental Psychology, 45,* 529–546.

Shulman, G. L. (1993). Attentional effects on Necker cube adaptation. *Canadian Journal of Experimental Psychology, 47,* 540–547.

Shulman, G. L., and Posner, M. I. (1988). Relating sensitivity and criterion effects to the internal mechanisms of visual spatial attention. ONR Technical Report #88-2, Washington University School of Medicine Dept. of Neurology, April 30, 1988.

Siegel, R. A., and Colburn, H. S. (1989). Binaural processing of noisy stimuli: Internal/external noise ratios for diotic and dichotic stimuli. *Journal of the Acoustical Society of America, 86,* 2122–2128.

Silverstein, C., and Glanzer, M. (1971). Concurrent task in free recall: Differential effects of LTS and STS. *Psychonomic Science, 22,* 367–368.

Simons, D. J. (1996). In sight, out of mind—when object representations fail. *Psychological Science, 7,* 301–305.

Singer, M. H., Lappin, J. S., and Moore, L. P. (1975). The interference of various word parts on color naming in the Stroop test. *Perception and Psychophysics, 18,* 191–193.

Sjoberg, H. (1975). Relations between heart rate, reaction speed, and subjective effort at different work loads on a bicycle ergometer. *Journal of Human Stress, 1,* 21–27.

Smallman, H., and Boynton, R. M. (1990). Segregation of basic colors in an information display. *Journal of the Optical Society of America A, &,* 1985–1994.

Smith, E. E., and Jonides, J. (1995). Working memory in humans: Neuropsychological evidence. In M. S. Gazzaniga, (Ed.), *The Cognitive Neurosciences.* Cambridge, MA: MIT Press, pp. 1009–1020.

Smith, M. C. (1967a). Theories of the psychological refractory period. *Psychological Bulletin, 67,* 202–213.

Smith, M. C. (1967b). The psychological refractory period as a function of performance of a first response. *Quarterly Journal of Experimental Psychology, 19,* 350–352.

Smith, M. C. (1969). The effect of varying information on the psychological refractory period. *Acta Psychologica, 30,* 220–231

Smith, M. C., and Fabri, P. (1975). Post-cueing after erasure of the icon: Is there a set effect? *Quarterly Journal of Experimental Psychology, 27,* 63–72.

Smith, M. E., and Oscar-Berman, M. (1990). Repetition priming of words and pseudowords in divided attention and in amnesia. *Journal of Experimental Psychology: Learning, Memory, and Cognition, 16,* 1033–1042.

Smith, M. O. (1969). History of the motor theories of attention. *The Journal of General Psychology, 80,* 243–257.

Smith, S. L. (1962). Color coding and visual search. *Journal of Experimental Psychology, 64,* 434–440.

Smith, S. M. (1995). Getting into and out of mental ruts: A theory of fixation, incubation, and insight. In R. J. Sternberg and J. E. Davidson (Eds.), *The Nature of Insight.* Cambridge, MA: MIT Press, pp. 229–251.

Smith, W. G. (1895). The relation of attention to memory. *Mind, 4,* 47–73.

Snyder, C. R. R. (1972). Selection, inspection and naming in visual search. *Journal of Experimental Psychology, 92,* 428–431.

Sokoloff, L., Mangold, R., Wechsler, R. L., Kennedy, C., and Kety, S. S. (1955). The effect of mental arithmetic on cerebral circulation and metabolism. *Journal of Clinical Investigation, 34,* 1101–1108.

Sokolov, E. N. (1963). *Perception and the conditioned reflex.* New York: Pergamon Press.

Sorkin, R. D., Pastore, R. E., and Pohlmann, L. D. (1972). Simultaneous two-channel signal detection. II. Correlated and uncorrelated signals. *Journal of the Acoustical Society of America, 51,* 1960–1965.

Sorkin, R. D., Pohlmann, L. D., and Gilliom, J. D. (1973). Simultaneous two-channel signal detection. III. 630- and 1400-Hz signals. *Journal of the Acoustical Society of America, 53,* 1045–1050.

Spector, A., and Biederman, I. (1976). Mental set and mental shift revisited. *American Journal of Psychology, 89,* 669–679.

Spelke, E., Hirst, W., and Neisser, U. (1976). Skills of divided attention. *Cognition, 4,* 215–230.

Spence, C. J., and Driver, J. (1994). Covert spatial orienting in audition: Exogenous and endogenous mechanisms. *Journal of Experimental Psychology: Human Perception and Performance, 20,* 555–574.

Spence, C. J., and Driver, J. (1996). Audiovisual links in endogenous covert spatial attention. *Journal of Experimental Psychology: Human Perception and Performance, 22,* 1005–1030.

Sperling, G. (1960). The information available in brief visual presentations. *Psychological Monographs: General and Applied,* Vol. 74, whole number 498, 1–29.

Sperling, G. (1963). A model for visual memory tasks. *Human Factors, 5,* 19–31.

Sperling. G., and Dosher, B. A. (1986). Strategy and optimization in human information processing. In Boff, K., Kaufman, L., and Thomas, J. (Eds.), *Handbook of Perception and Performance,* Vol. I. New York: Wiley.

Sperling, G., and Melchner, M. J. (1978). Visual search, visual attention, and the attention operating characteristic. In J. Requin (Ed.), *Attention and Performance VII.* Hillsdale, NJ: Erlbaum, pp. 675–686.

Sperling, G., and Reeves, A. (1980). Measuring the reaction time of an unobservable response: A shift of visual attention. In R. S. Nickerson (Ed.), *Attention and Performance VIII.* New York: Academic Press., pp. 347–360.

Sperling, G., Budiansky, J., Spivak, J. G., and Johnson, M. C. (1971). Extremely rapid visual search: The maximum rate of scanning letters for the presence of a numeral. *Science, 174,* 307–311.

Stein, B. W., Morris, C. D., and Bransford, J. D. (1978). Constraints on effective elaboration. *Journal of Verbal Learning and Verbal Behavior, 17,* 707–714.

Steinman, R. M., Kowler, E., and Collewijn, H. (1990). New directions for oculomotor research. *Vision Research, 30,* 1845–1864.

Stelmach, L. B., and Herdman, C. M. (1991). Directed attention and perception of temporal order. *Journal of Experimental Psychology: Human Perception and Performance, 17,* 539–550.

Sternberg, S. (1966). High speed scanning in human memory. *Science, 153,* 652–654.

Sternberg, S. (1969). The discovery of processing stages: Extensions of Donders' method. In W. G. Koster (Ed.), *Attention and Performance II* Amsterdam: North Holland, pp. 276–315.

Sternberg, S., Knoll, R. L., and Gates, B. A. (1971, November). Prior entry reexamined: Effect of attentional bias on order perception. Presented at the annual meeting of the Psychonomic Society, St. Louis, MO.

Stewart, D. (1792/1971). *Elements of the Philosophy of the Human Mind.* New York: Garland.

Stone, S. A. (1926). Prior entry in the auditory-tactual complication. *American Journal of Psychology, 37,* 284–291.

Stormark, K. M., Nordby, H., and Hugdahl, K. (1995). Attentional shifts to emotionally charged cues: Behavioural and ERP data. *Cognition and Emotion, 9,* 507–523.

Stroop, J. R. (1935). Studies of interference in serial verbal reactions. *Journal of Experimental Psychology, 18,* 643–662.

Styles, E. A. and Allport, D. A. (1986). Perceptual integration of identity, location and colour. *Psychological Research, 48,* 189–200.

Sudevan, P., and Taylor, D. A. (1987). The cueing and priming of cognitive operations. *Journal of Experimental Psychology: Human Perception and Performance, 13,* 89–103.

Swann, W. B., Hixon, J. G., Stein-Seroussi, A., and Gilbert, D. T. (1990). The fleeting gleam of praise: Cognitive processes underlying behavioral reactions to self-relevant feedback. *Journal of Personality and Social Psychology, 59,* 17–26.

Swets, J. A. (Ed.) (1964). *Signal Detection and Recognition by Human Observers; Contemporary Readings.* New York: Wiley.

Swift, E. J. (1892). Disturbance of the attention during simple mental processes. *The American Journal of Psychology, 5,* 1–19.

Tanner, W. P., Jr. (1961). Physiological implications of psychophysical data. *Annals of the New York Academy of Science, 89,* 752–765.

Teder, W., Alho, K., Reinikainen, K., and Naatanen, R. (1993). Interstimulus interval and the selective-attention effect on auditory ERPs "N1 enhancement" versus processing negativity. *Psychophysiology, 30,* 71–81.

Telford, C. W. (1931). The refractory phase of voluntary and associative responses. *Journal of Experimental Psychology, 14,* 1–36.

Thomas, J. P. (1985). Detection and identification: how are they related? *Journal of the Optical Society of America A, 2,* 1475–1467.

Thompson, L. A. (1987). Central resource involvement during the visual search for single features and conjunctions of features. *Acta Psychologica, 66,* 189–200.

Tipper, S. P., and Cranston, M. (1985). Selective attention and priming: Inhibitory and facilitatory effects of ignored primes. *Quarterly Journal of Experimental Psychology, 37A,* 591–611.

Tipper, S. P., and Driver, J. (1988). Negative priming between response modalities: Evidence for the central locus of inhibition. *Perception and Psychophysics, 43,* 45–52.

Tipper, S. P., MacQueen, G. M., and Brehaut, J. C. (1989). Negative priming between response modalities: Evidence for the central locus of in selective attention. *Perception and Psychophysics, 43,* 45–52.

Tipper, S. P., Weaver, B., Cameron, S., Brehaut, J., and Bastedo, J. (1991). Inhibitory mechanisms of attention in identification and localization tasks—time course and disruption. *Journal of Experimental Psychology: Learning, Memory and Cognition, 17,* 681–692.

Titchener, E. B. (1908). *Lectures on the Elementary Psychology of Feeling and Attention.* New York: Macmillan.

Todd, S., and Kramer, A. F. (1994). Attentional misguidance in visual search. *Perception and Psychophysics, 56* 198–210.

Townsend, J. T. (1974). Issues and models concerning the processing of a finite number of inputs. In B. H. Kantowitz (Ed.), *Human Information Processing: Tutorials in Performance and Cognition.* Hillsdale, NJ: Erlbaum, pp. 133–168.

Townsend, J. T. (1981). Some characteristics of visual whole report behavior. *Acta Psychologica, 47,* 149–173.

Townsend, J. T., and Ashby, F. G. (1983). *The Stochastic Modeling of Elementary Psychological Processes.* New York: Cambridge University Press.

Travers, J. R. (1974). Word recognition with forced serial processing: Effects of segment size and temporal order variation. *Perception and Psychophysics, 16,* 35–42.

Treisman, A. (1960). Contextual cues in selective listening. *Quarterly Journal of Experimental Psychology, 12,* 242–248.

Treisman, A. (1964a). The effect of irrelevant material on the efficiency of selective listening. *American Journal of Psychology, 77,* 533–546.

Treisman, A. (1964b). Verbal cues, language and meaning in selective attention. *American Journal of Psychology, 77,* 206–219.

Treisman, A. (1964c). Monitoring and storage of irrelevant messages in selective attention. *Journal of Verbal Learning and Verbal Behavior, 3,* 49–459.

Treisman, A. (1982). Perceptual grouping and attention in visual search for features and for objects. *Journal of Experimental Psychology: Human Perception & Performance, 8,* 194–214.

Treisman, A. (1991). Search, similarity, and integration of features between and within dimensions. *Journal of Experimental Psychology: Human Perception & Performance, 17,* 652–676.

Treisman, A., and Davies, A. (1973). Dividing attention to ear and eye. In S. Kornblum (Ed.), *Attention and Performance IV.* NY; Academic Press, pp. 101–117.

Treisman, A., and Gelade, G. (1980). A feature integration theory of attention. *Cognitive Psychology, 12,* 97–136.

Treisman, A., and Gormican, S. (1988). Feature analysis in early vision: Evidence from search asymmetries. *Psychological Review, 95,* 15–48.

Treisman, A., and Riley, J. G. A. (1969). Is selective attention selective perception or selective response? A further test. *Journal of Experimental Psychology, 79,* 27–34.

Treisman, A., and Souther, J. (1985). Search asymmetry: A diagnostic for preattentive processing of separable features. *Journal of Experimental Psychology: General, 114,* 285–310.

Treisman, A., Squire, R., and Green, J. (1974). Semantic processing in dichotic listening? A replication. *Memory and Cognition, 2,* 641–646.

Treisman, A., Vieira, A., and Hayes, A. (1992). Automaticity and preattentive processing. *American Journal of Psychology, 105,* 341–362.

Treisman, M., and Rostron, A. B. (1972). Brief auditory storage: A modification of Sperling's paradigm applied to audition. *Acta Psychologica, 36,* 161–170.

Tresch, M. C., Sinnamon, H. M., and Seamon, J. G. (1993). Double dissociation of spatial and object visual memory: Evidence from selective interference in intact human subjects. *Neuropsychologica, 31,* 211–219.

Trevarthen, C. B. (1968). Two mechanisms of vision in primates. *Psychologische Forschung, 31,* 299–337.

Trumbo, D., and Milone, F. (1971). Primary task performance as a function of encoding, retention, and recall in a secondary task. *Journal of Experimental Psychology, 91,* 273–279.

Tsal, Y., and Lavie, N. (1988). Attending to color and shape: The special role of location in selective visual processing. *Perception and Psychophysics, 44,* 15–21.

Tsang, P. S., and Vidulich, M. A. (1994). The roles of immediacy and redundancy in relative subjective workload assessment. *Human Factors, 36,* 503–513.

Tulving, E., and Lindsay, P. H. (1967). Identification of simultaneously presented simple visual and auditory stimuli. In A. F. Sanders (Ed.), *Attention and Performance I.* Amsterdam: North-Holland, pp. 101–109.

Tun, P. A., Wingfield, A., and Stine, E. A. L. (1991). Speech-processing capacity in young and older adults: A dual-task study. *Psychology and Aging, 6,* 3–9.

Turvey, M. T. (1973). On peripheral and central processes in vision. *Psychological Review, 80,* 1–52.

Tweedy, J. R., and Lapinski, R. H. (1981). Facilitating word recognition: Evidence for strategic and automatic factors. *Quarterly Journal of Experimental Psychology: Human Experimental Psychology, 33A,* 51–59.

Tweedy, J. R., Lapinski, R. H. and Schvaneveldt, R. W. (1977). Semantic-context effects on word recognition: Influence of varying the proportion of items presented in an appropriate context. *Memory and Cognition, 5,* 84–89.

Ullman, S. (1984). Visual routines. *Cognition, 18,* 97–159.

Underwood, G., and Moray, N. (1971). Shadowing and monitoring for selective attention. *Quarterly Journal of Experimental Psychology, 23,* 284–295.

Vallar, G., and Shallice, T. (1990). *Neuropsychological Impairments of Short-Term Memory.* Cambridge: Cambridge University Press.

Vallar, G., Papagno, C., and Baddeley, A. D. (1991). Long-term recency effects and phonological short-term memory. A neuropsychological case study. *Cortex, 27,* 323–326.

van der Haeghen, V., and Bertelson, P. (1974). The limits of prior entry: Non-sensitivity of temporal order judgments to selective preparation affecting choice reaction time. *Bulletin of the Psychonomic Society, 4,* 569–572.

van der Heijden, A. H. C. (1975). Some evidence for a limited capacity parallel selfterminating process in simple visual search tasks. *Acta Psychologica, 39,* 21–41.

van der Heijden, A. H. C. (1992). *Selective Attention in Vision.* London: Routledge, Chapman and Hall.

Van Essen, D. C., Anderson, C. H., and Felleman, D. J. (1992). Information processing in the primate visual system—An integrated systems perspective. *Science, 24,* 419–423.

Van Galen, G. P., and ten Hoopen, G. (1976). Speech control and single channelness. *Acta Psychologica, 40,* 245–255.

Vaughan, H. G., Costa, L. D., and Gilden, L. (1966). The functional relation of visual evoked response and reaction time to stimulus intensity. *Vision Research, 6,* 645–656.

Vecera, S. and Farah, M. J. (1994). Does visual attention select objects or locations. *Journal of Experimental Psychology: General, 123,* 146–160.

Veniar, F. A. (1958). Signal detection as a function of frequency ensemble. I. *Journal of the Acoustical Society of America, 30,* 1020–1024.

Verghese, P. and Pelli, D. G. (1992). The information capacity of visual attention. *Vision Research, 32,* 983–995.

Vidulich, M. A. (1988). The cognitive psychology of subjective mental workload. In P. A. Hancock and N. Meshkati (Eds.), *Human Mental Workload.* New York: Elsevier, pp. 219–229.

Vidulich, M. A., and Wickens, C. D. (1986). Causes of dissociation between subjective workload measures and performance: Caveats for the use of subjective assessments. *Applied Ergonomics, 17,* 291–296.

Vince, M. (1949). Rapid response sequences and the psychological refractory period. *British Journal of Psychology, 40,* 23–40.

von Wright, J. M. (1970). On selection in visual immediate memory. *Acta Psychologica, 33,* 280–292.

von Wright, J. M., Anderson, K., and Stenman, U. (1975). Generalization of conditioned GSRs in dichotic listening. *Attention and Performance V,* 194–204.

Ward, L. M. (1985). Covert focussing of the attentional gaze. *Canadian Journal of Psychology, 39,* 546–563.

Ward, R., and McClelland, J. L. (1989). Conjunctive search for one and two identical targets. *Journal of Experimental Psychology: Human Perception and Performance, 15,* 664–672.

Wardlaw, K. A., and Kroll, N. E. A. (1976). Autonomic responses to shock-associated words in a non-attended message: A failure to replicate. *Journal of Experimental Psychology: Human Perception and Performance, 3,* 357–360.

Warm, J. S. (1977). Psychological processes in sustained attention. in R. R. Mackie (Ed.), *Vigilance: Theory, Experimental Performance, and Physiological Correlates.* New York: Plenum, pp. 623–644.

Warner, C. B., Juola, J. F., and Koshino, H. (1990). Voluntary allocation versus automatic capture of visual attention. *Perception and Psychophysics, 48,* 243–251.

Warren, R. M. (1982). *Auditory Perception: A New Synthesis.* New York: Pergamon Press.

Warren, R. M., and Bashford, J. A. (1981). Perception of acoustic iterance: Pitch and infrapitch. *Perception and Psychophysics, 29,* 395–402.

Warrington, E. K., and Shallice T. (1972). Neuropsychological evidence of visual storage in short-term memory tasks. *Quarterly Journal of Experimental Psychology, 24,* 30–40.

Warrington, E., and Shallice, T. (1969). The selective impairment of auditory verbal short-term memory. *Brain, 92,* 885–896.

Watanabe, M. (1986). Prefrontal unit activity during delayed conditional Go/No-go discrimination in the monkey: II. Relation to Go and No-go responses. *Brain Research, 382,* 15–27.

Waters, W. F., McDonald, D. G., and Koresko, R. L. (1977). Habituation of the orienting response: A gating mechanism subserving selective attention. *Psychophysiology, 14,* 228–236.

Watson, A. B., and Robson, J. G. (1981). Discrimination at threshold: Labelled detectors in human vision. *Vision Research, 21,* 1115–1122.

Waugh, N., and Norman, D. A. (1965). Primary memory. *Psychological Review, 72,* 89–104.

Welch, J. C. (1898). On the measurement of mental activity through muscular activity and the determination of a constant of attention. *American Journal of Physiology, 1,* 283–306.

Welford, A. T. (1952). The "psychological refractory period" and the timing of high speed performance—A review and a theory. *British Journal of Psychology, 43,* 2–19.

Welford, A. T. (1967). Single-channel operation in the brain. *Acta Psychologica, 27,* 5–22.

Welford, A. T. (1980). The single-channel hypothesis. In A. T. Welford (Ed.), *Reaction Time.* New York: Academic Press, pp. 215–252.

Wenderoth, P., Bray, R., Johnstone, S. (1988). Psychophysical evidence for an extrastriate contribution to a pattern-selective motion aftereffect. *Perception, 17,* 81–91.

Whang, K. C., Burton, H., and Shulman, G. L. (1980). Selective attention in vibrotactile tasks: Detecting the presence and absence of amplitude change. *Perception and Psychophysics, 50,* 157–165.

Wickelgren, W. (1977). Speed-accuracy tradeoff and information processing dynamics. *Acta Psychologica, 41,* 67–85.

Wickens, C. D. (1984). Processing resources in attention, dual task performance, and workload assessment. In R. Parasuraman and R. Davies (Eds.), *Varieties of Attention.* New York: Academic Press, pp. 63–102.

Wickens, C. D., Sandry, D., and Vidulich, M. (1983). Compatibility and resource competition between modalities of unput, central processing, and output: Testing a model of complex performance. *Human Factors, 25,* 227–248.

Wierda, M., and Brookhuis, K. A. (1991). Analysis of cycling skill: A cognitive approach. *Applied Cognitive Psychology, 5,* 113–122.

Wilson, B., and Baddeley, A. (1988). Semantic, episodic, and autobiographical memory in a postmeningitic amnesic patient. *Brain and Cognition, 8,* 31–46.

Wing, A., and Allport, D. A. (1972). Multidimensional encoding of visual form. *Perception & Psychophysics, 12,* 474–476.

Witkin, A. P., and Tenenbaum, J. M. (1983). On the role of structure in vision. In Beck, J., Hope, B., and Rosenfeld, A. (Eds.), *Human and Machine Vision.* New York: Academic Press, pp. 481–544.

Wohlgemuth, A. (1911). [Title to be provided]. *British Journal of Psychology, 1,* 1–117.

Woldorff, M. G., and Hillyard, S. A. (1991). Modulation of early auditory processing during selective listening to rapidly presented tones. *Electroencephalography and Clinical Neurophysiology, 79,* 170–191.

Wolfe, J. (in press). Visual search. In H. Pashler (Ed.), *Attention.* London: University College London Press.

Wolfe, J. M. (1994). Guided search 2.0: A revised model of visual search. *Psychonomic Bulletin and Review, 1,* 202–238.

Wolfe, J. M., Cave, K. R., and Franzel, S. L. (1989). Guided search: An alternative to the feature integration model for visual search. *Journal of Experimental Psychology: Human Perception and Performance, 15,* 419–433.

Wolfe, J. M., Friedman-Hill, S. R., Stewart, M. I., and O'Connell, K. M. (1992). The role of categorization in visual search for orientation. *Journal of Experimental Psychology: Human Perception and Performance, 18,* 34–49.

Wolford, G., and Chambers, L. (1983). Lateral masking as a function of spacing. *Perception and Psychophysics, 33,* 129–138.

Wolters, N. C. W. and Schiano, D. J. (1989). *On listening where we look: The fragility of a phenomenon. Perception and Psychophysics, 45,* 184–186.

Woods, D. L. (1990). The physiological basis of selective attention: Implications of event-related potential studies. In J. W. Rohrbaugh, R., Parasuraman, and R. Johnson, Jr., (Eds.), *Event-Related Brain Potentials: Basic Issues and Applications.* New York: Oxford University Press, pp. 178–209.

Yager, D., Kramer, P., Shaw, M. and Graham, N. (1984). Detection and identification of spatial frequency: Models and data. *Vision Research, 24,* 1021–1035.

Yantis, S. (1988). On analog movements of visual attention. *Perception and Psychophysics, 43,* 203–206.

Yantis, S. (1992). Multielement visual tracking: Attention and perceptual organization. *Cognitive Psychology, 24,* 295–340.

Yantis, S. (1993). Stimulus-driven attentional capture and attentional control settings. *Journal of Experimental Psychology: Human Perception and Performance, 19,* 676–681.

Yantis, S. (1994). Stimulus-driven attentional capture. *Current Directions in Psychological Science, 2,* 156–161.

Yantis, S. and Gibson, B. S. (1994). Object continuity in apparent motion and attention. Special Issue: Shifts of visual attention. *Canadian Journal of Experimental Psychology, 48,* 182–204.

Yantis. S., and Hillstrom, A. P. (1994). Stimulus-driven attentional capture: Evidence from equiluminant visual objects. *Journal of Experimental Psychology: Human Perception and Performance, 20,* 95–107.

Yantis, S., and Johnson, D. N. (1990). Mechanisms of attentional priority. *Journal of Experimental Psychology: Human Perception and Performance, 16,* 812–825.

Yantis, S., and Johnston, J. C. (1990). On the locus of visual selection: Evidence from focused attention tasks. *Journal of Experimental Psychology: Human Perception and Performance, 16,* 135–149.

Yantis, S., and Jonides, S. (1990). Abrupt visual onsets and selective attention: Evidence from visual search. *Journal of Experimental Psychology: Human Perception and Performance, 16,* 121–134.

Yeh, Y., and Wickens, C. D. (1988). Dissociation of performance and subjective measures of workload. *Human Factors, 30,* 111–120.

Zbrodoff, N. J., and Logan, G. D. (1986). On the autonomy of mental processes: A case study of arithmetic. *Journal of Experimental Psychology: General, 115,* 118–130.

Zurek, P. M. (1980). The precedence effect and its possible role in the avoidance of interaural ambiguities. *Journal of the Acoustical Society of America, 67,* 952–964.

Name Index

Subject Index